NOSTRADAMUS

NOSTRADAMUS
The Evidence

Ian Wilson

ORION

First published in Great Britain in 2002 by
Orion Books Ltd.
Orion House, 5 Upper St Martin's Lane,
London WC2H 9EA

A CIP catalogue record for this book is
available from the British Library

ISBN 0 75285 2639

Typeset by Selwood Systems,
Midsomer Norton

Printed and bound by
Butler & Tanner Ltd, Frome and London

CONTENTS

PICTURE CREDITS

AUTHOR'S PREFACE

Books about Nostradamus are mostly written by so-called 'Nostradamians' convinced that the sixteenth century Frenchman Michel de Nostredame had a genuine prophetic gift. Or by born-again sceptics like James Randi utterly determined to rubbish that idea. I belong to neither camp.

While I am no stranger to topics touching on the paranormal, I freely admit that until September 2001 Nostradamus had figured nowhere amongst my otherwise far-ranging list of interests. All that was changed by a message from my London publisher Trevor Dolby. Sent just six days after the horrifying destruction of New York's World Trade Center. Trevor e-mailed to my home in Australia: 'I don't know of a book on Nostradamus which looks objectively at the man, his times, his books, his prophecies and the psychology of why his prophecies are still rolled out (witness the last few days...). Is this something that might attract you?'

As my wife Judith vividly recalls, my first reaction was a very firm 'No'! To me all the speculation surrounding Nostradamus' prophecies represented crank territory, which I had no taste to explore, either as 'true believer' or sceptic. But Trevor had thoughtfully used the word 'objectively'. And one of many advantages of the time differences between Queensland and London is that it gives you time to reflect, even to do a little research. Not possessing a single book on Nostradamus I consulted the Internet to find out what might be stocked on the subject by the 32 interlinked public libraries scattered throughout the Brisbane City Council's region. The computer screen offered me 34 different titles, many possessing that so unpalatable flavour of the bizarre. But the surprise was that in every library virtually every copy was shown as 'checked out' or 'in transit'. So what was going on out there? Given that Nostradamus' lifetime was during the 16th century, a favourite historical period for me, and that he lived in Provence, where my wife and I had spent many happy camping vacations with our sons during their childhood, was it possible that there was a genuine need for a suitably serious Nostradamus biography?

Two weeks later, having forsaken Queensland's springtime sunshine for that of Provence's autumn, Judith and I stepped out onto the tarmac at Marseilles airport, Trevor having set me a daunting deadline of April 30, 2002 to provide him with a complete 100,000 word biographical study. A highly intensive period of getting to know Nostradamus began.

In the event, eschewing as I did virtually every English-language book written on the subject, essentially all the documentation on which this book is based, much of it never before translated into English, is owed to two Frenchmen, and to one French-speaking Canadian. First, to the late Dr Edgar Leroy, a physician of Nostradamus' birthplace St Rémy-de-Provence, who died in 1965. Leroy made exhaustive historical researches on Nostradamus, culminating in what for his time was by far the most authoritative French-language biography *Nostradamus, Ses Origines, Sa Vie, Son Oeuvre* posthumously published in 1972. Second, much is owed to Jean Dupèbe, a scholar of the University of Paris, who patiently edited a Latin manuscript containing 51 letters to and from Nostradamus which in 1983 became published as *Nostradamus – Lettres Inédites*. Third, I am particularly deeply indebted to the late Pierre Brind'Amour, Professor of Ancient Studies at the University of Ottawa, Canada, who sadly died in only his mid-fifties in 1995, but whose superbly-researched *Nostradamus Astrophile*, published in 1993 with innumerable historical quotations, has also provided much source material for this present work.

Since I do not profess any gifts as a linguist, one of the obstacles to be overcome has been a necessarily grappling not only with modern French, but also with documents in sixteenth century French and Latin, many of the latter never before translated into English. Conversely, in the case of Nostradamus' famous prophetic verses, the available English language translations are mostly so bad that I have preferred to avoid them and devise my own version, providing in a footnote the original text to enable those with specialist expertise to check my translation. Since this book is directed to the general reader with very likely little or no familiarity with French, I have in the text almost invariably translated French book titles into English, and supplied the original French wording via a footnote. Important to note, however, is that where in the original printing a 'u' may have been used where we would expected a 'v', and an 'f' (without crossbar) where we would expect an 's' I have automatically made the substitution without noting it.

Frustratingly, it has not been possible to consult the full texts of all the materials that I would have wished, access to Nostradamus' Almanacs presenting a particular difficulty. Not only have far from all of these survived, even as a single copy, some of those that have are in very reclusive private hands, their owners being rather more concerned with their value as a financial asset than with the historical value of their contents. A number of quoted extracts from these therefore derive from secondary sources.

Some very special thanks are due to Jacqueline Allemand, Directrice of the Maison de Nostradamus in Salon de Provence, who kindly allowed me a full morning studying the Nostradamus materials in her collection, including her facsimile edition of César de Nostredame's *Histoire et Chronique de Provence*. I am most grateful also to Mme Marielle Mouranche, chief conservator at the Mediathèque, Albi for granting my wife and I access to the rare first edition of Nostradamus' *Propheties* in her care. Also to Professor Gian Maria Zaccone of Turin for obtaining an important article on the Nostradamus inscription in Turin. To Kristina Eriksson of the Royal Library, Stockholm, Sweden for arranging a microfilm of the horoscope that Nostradamus cast for Prince Rudolf of Austria. To Dr Elmar Gruber for information on otherwise unknown French language versions of this same manuscript. Also to my wife's cousin Sheelagh Barry of Canada for tracing and obtaining a copy of Professor Brind'Amour's book.

As always the staff of the University of Queensland's libraries have been immensely helpful, obtaining books from even as far afield as the USA where these have not been available within Australia. Without the far-sightedness and initiative of Trevor Dolby of my publishers Orion, also the ever-enthusiastic encouragement of my editor Pandora White, this book would never have come into being. I am also particularly grateful for the assiduousness of copy-editor Elisabeth Ingles, who – working right up to within hours of her getting married – went way beyond the call of duty to check my translations from French and Latin, thereby saving me from a number of elementary errors. Because my grasp of German is very limited, for the translation of Nostradamus' Prince Rudolf horoscope I sought the help of German-speaking residents of Bellbowrie, the pleasant outer suburb of Brisbane where my wife and I have spent seven very happy years until a house move almost immediately following this book's completion. I am very grateful to Vroni and Erwin Kern, to Andrea Schaffer, also to the friends and relatives whom they in their turn consulted, for all their efforts to decipher this document's so elusive 16th century handwriting.

Finally, and far from least, I am as always immensely indebted to my wife Judith, who made herself photographer-in-chief during our October 2001 Nostradamus research travels around France, checked my every chapter at the manuscript stage, and unstintingly helped in innumerable other ways.

Ian Wilson
Bribie Island, Queensland, Australia
June 2002

INTRODUCTION

December 14, 2003 will mark the five hundredth anniversary of the birth of Michel de Nostredame, better known as Nostradamus. And there can surely have been no greater sign of the still highly active grip of this long-dead prophet upon the public imagination than the aftermath to the horrifying events of September 11, 2001. The dust cloud had scarcely settled from the collapse of the New York World Trade Center towers before Britain's *Daily Mail* was on the news-stands with a story headlined 'Did Nostradamus Predict it All?'[1] The French seer was quoted as predicting:

> *Earthshaking fire from the world's centre*
> *Will cause tremors around the New City.*[2]

Give or take some liberality in the translation from the original sixteenth-century French, Nostradamus had undeniably made some prediction along these lines in his pioneering little book *Les Prophéties* (henceforth to be known as the *Prophecies*), published in Lyons in the south of France in 1555.[3] Even more uncannily, particularly given the 45-degree angle at which the second suicide plane had plunged into the second tower, he had warned in another prophetic verse:

> *The sky will burn at 45 degrees*
> *Fire approaches the great New City*
> *Immediately a huge scattered flame leaps up.*[4]

The *Daily Mail* could hardly have been quicker off the mark in associating the New York attacks with such Nostradamus prophecies. Nonetheless, equally swift were some unknown disinformation merchants. The translations of Nostradamus' prophetic verses that were used by the *Daily Mail*'s columnist at least bore some passing resemblance to the French originals. This was not the case, however, with some considerably more variant and sinister 'Nostradamus' quotations that began circulating like wildfire amongst the United States media and, via the Internet, throughout the entire world. One version ran:

> *In the City of God there will be a great thunder*
> *Two Brothers torn apart by Chaos,*
> *While the fortress endures, the great leader will succumb.*
> *The third big war will begin when the big city is burning.*

Another threatened:

> *Two steel birds will fall from the sky on the Metropolis*
> *The sky will burn at 45 degrees latitude*
> *Fire approaches the great New City.*
> *Immediately a huge, scattered flame leaps up.*
> *Within months rivers will flow with blood*
> *The undead will roam earth for a little time.*

To anyone conversant with Nostradamus' true writings such quotations could readily be recognised as crude fakes. Odd lines had been taken from genuine verses, then combined with freely invented phrases such as 'two steel birds'. One such verse was found to have been concocted several years back by Neil Marshall, then a student at Brock University, Canada, purely as a demonstration of how Nostradamus had composed deliberately vague images that the credulous then perceived as 'fitting' real-life events.

But just who was it in the year 2001 who had taken and manipulated these particular verses? And how was it that they had been so quick to apply them to the September 11 tragedy? That whoever created the hoaxed predictions fully intended to spread the maximum terror is all too evident from the fact that the invented lines included the mega-horror phrases 'third big war', 'rivers will flow with blood', and 'the undead will roam the earth'. So could the hoaxer have been part of an al-Qaeda cell? Or just another brand of the sick-minded individuals who quite incomprehensibly gain satisfaction by their attempts to spread viruses over the Internet?

Whoever was responsible, what is certain is that they recognised, and utilised to the full, the astonishing power of the name 'Nostradamus', even after more than four centuries, to evoke a deeply superstitious awe amongst millions throughout the world. Accredited with predicting everything from the Great Fire of London to the invention of electricity, there is simply not another individual, alive or dead, whose prophetic reputation carries, even remotely, any equivalent kind of mass reverence, whether this be justified or otherwise. And regardless of whether the unknown hoaxers intended it, the huge resurgence of interest in Nostradamus that they thereby sparked off in the wake of September 11 was positively breathtaking.

Thus only four days after the New York attack, and with much of the world's book-buying business otherwise in freefall, the Nostradamus writer Erika Cheetham's *Nostradamus: The Complete Prophecies* – comprising a far from accurate translation of *Les Prophéties* plus interpretations of the verses – shot from nowhere to take the number one spot on the Amazon best-seller list.[5] Other Nostradamus books that happened to be in print leapt to fifth, sixth, eleventh, twelfth and twenty-fifth places in the same listing. Almost overnight every lending library throughout the English-speaking world found virtually its entire stock of Nostradamus books cleared from the shelves, as was certainly the case even in my own quiet corner of Queensland, Australia.

In the USA the leading Nostradamian expert Victor Baines of the Nostradamus Society of America stoically accepted being woken at all hours for interviews with TV and radio chat-show hosts, not only across the States, but as far afield as the UK, Australia, New Zealand and Canada.[6] On the Internet sites that are normally visited solely by Nostradamus aficionados began receiving so many general public hits that several temporarily shut down the majority of their pages in order to avoid being charged exorbitant operating costs by their server. It was an extraordinary set of circumstances – yet, as we will see in the course of this book, merely a twenty-first-century variant of other, earlier, equally intense waves of Nostradamus fever, often again accompanied by equally intense disinformation activities, that have recurred time and again whenever one or other European country has undergone a major crisis during the past four centuries.

This said, it is important to note one significant peculiarity that stands out from amidst all the present-day round of Nostradamus hype. This is that the English-language authors who currently claim to be experts on Nostradamus base their reputations almost solely upon their translations of the seer's published verses, their matching of these with historical happenings that occurred during and since Nostradamus' time, and their general astrological know-how. As to exactly who the historical Nostradamus was, and how he could have built up such a remarkable prophetic reputation for himself, all too few English-language Nostradamians have taken more than the sketchiest of interest. Indeed, there is simply no English-language biographical study of Nostradamus currently in print with even the remotest claim to being definitive or up-to-date. Symptomatic of this, even the brief biographical entry in the latest edition of *Encyclopaedia Britannica* contains a number of elementary factual errors.[7]

This glaring deficiency is all the more odd, and even unpardonable, as an impressive amount of new historical documentation concerning Nostradamus has come to light during only the last twenty years. In 1983 the assiduous French scholar Jean Dupèbe published a transcription and partial translation from Latin into French of a cache of some fifty-one letters that had passed between Nostradamus and a number of his astrological clients during the years 1556 to 1565.[8] Though the originals of these letters no longer exist they were gathered together by Nostradamus' eldest son César, and translated into Latin, apparently with the intention to publish them during the early seventeenth century. Despite César's intention never being realised, his Latin fair-copy manuscript found its way into France's National Library, the Bibliothèque Nationale in Paris,[9] where it eventually came to the attention of Dupèbe who thereupon made it accessible to the world at large. Since, aside from his published writings, the letters represent by far our closest insights into Nostradamus' mind, their interest value to the serious researcher has to be enormous, particularly given that the number of other extant items of Nostradamus correspondence can be counted on one hand.

Yet the extraordinary fact is that virtually the only English-language author who has given this correspondence even moderate attention has been the American former stage magician James Randi, an arch-debunker and avowed sceptic of all things Nostradamian. To his considerable credit in *The Mask of Nostradamus*,[10] published in 1990, Randi went to the trouble of providing translated extracts from several of Dupèbe's summaries of the letters' contents. However, in his over-anxiety to discredit Nostradamus' powers as a prophet Randi made a number of factual errors on matters of history and linguistics. But at least he blazed the right trail.

By contrast, and to their considerable shame, ostensibly top-flight Nostradamian authors who have relatively recently published supposedly authoritative books have effectively pretended that the Dupèbe Latin letter cache does not exist. The modern languages expert Peter Lemesurier is widely regarded as Britain's leading authority on Nostradamus. His *Nostradamus Encyclopaedia*,[11] published in 1997, represents itself as the 'definitive reference guide to the work and world of Nostradamus'. Yet with the exception of the briefest bibliographic listing of Dupèbe's book, he has otherwise ignored it and (more inexcusably) its entire contents.

Unlike Lemesurier and the generality of most other writers on

Nostradamus I have absolutely no enthusiasm for the astrology that our subject practised and held so dear. But neither have I any inclination to write merely a James Randi-style debunking of the seer. One of the undeniable historical facts about him is that he flourished throughout the first half of the sixteenth century, during the Renaissance, and is therefore a product of a particularly exciting and colourful period of Europe's history. From France's deepest south, where he lived for the greater part of his sixty-two years, Nostradamus annually issued sometimes dire forecasts of the events that he expected for the year to come. Whether they were believed or not they attracted much discussion amongst his contemporaries. Deservedly or otherwise, Nostradamus achieved surprising fame even in his lifetime. Kings, queens, cardinals, bishops, courtiers, lawyers, even mining magnates all sought him out. His name became a household word not only in his native France, but also in Italy, Austria, Germany, Spain and England. Even more remarkably, his reputation grew rather than waned in the wake of his death.

These were, and continue to be, no mean achievements. Accordingly it is my belief that, to mark the 500th anniversary of his birth, Nostradamus is long overdue a really in-depth, independent-minded study of his life, his times and his continued astonishing influence. This is my aim, and this is what I will now attempt to provide.

NOTES

1 *Daily Mail*, London, September 12, 2001
2 In Nostradamus' notation, Century I, quatrain 87
3 *Les Propheties de M. Michel Nostradamus*, Lyons, Macé Bonhomme, 1555
4 From C.VI, q.97
5 Erika Cheetham, *The Prophecies of Nostradamus*, Spearman, 1975, and subsequently repeatedly reissued, mostly by Corgi and Perigree
6 Victor Baines lists his interviews on the Nostradamus Society of America website www.nostradamususa.com
7 *The Encyclopaedia Britannica* entry contains basic errors in almost every line. (1) According to *Britannica* Nostradamus began his medical practice at Agen in 1529. Wrong: he enrolled as a medical student at Montpellier only in that year. (2) According to *Britannica* Nostradamus moved to Salon in 1544. Wrong: his residence there did not begin until 1547, and then it was only temporary. His permanent residency began around 1550. (3) According to *Britannica* Nostradamus' book of prophecies was called *Centuries*. Wrong: it was called *Les Prophéties*. (4) According to *Britannica* Nostradamus' fame during his lifetime was based on this book of prophecies. Wrong: it was principally based on his published almanacs. (5) According to *Britannica* Nostradamus was appointed physician-in-ordinary to King Charles IX in 1560. Wrong: this appointment was made late in 1564. (6)

According to *Britannica* Nostradamus' prophecies were condemned in 1781 by the Roman Catholic Church's Congregation of the Index. Wrong: the Vatican, as the Roman Catholic Church's supreme authority, has never condemned Nostradamus' works. The only list in which his books have been prohibited was issued in Spain between 1570 and 1790.

8 Jean Dupèbe, *Nostradamus Lettres Inédites*, Geneva, Librairie Droz, 1983
9 BN ms Lat. 8592
10 James Randi, *The Mask of Nostradamus*, New York, Charles Scribner, 1990
11 Peter Lemesurier, *The Nostradamus Encyclopaedia: The definitive reference guide to the work and world of Nostradamus*, New York, St Martin's Press, 1997

CHAPTER 1

Jewish Forebears

For anyone with the tendency to let the mind wander across centuries, even millennia, Nostradamus' corner of the Rhône delta in sunlit southern Provence was a singularly appropriate place to be born. Six hundred years before the birth of Jesus it was already settled by Gauls, a Celtic people proficient in metalwork and chariotry thought to have originated from Turkey. In the wake of Alexander the Great's empire-building, Hellenistic Greeks arrived in the second century BC in their sleek, sail-assisted galleys. On exploring the environs of the craggy, pine-clad hills a few miles inland from the flat delta terrain they discovered a huge resource of excellent building stone. This they quarried to construct a most attractive small town, the remains of which, a mere five-minute stroll from Nostradamus' birthplace, are now recognised as France's oldest-known civilised buildings.

The Romans in their turn further developed what the Greeks had begun, renaming the town Glanum. After their departure the now Christianised and ever independent-minded Provençals opted to build their own separate township, St-Rémy-de-Provence. Their perennial usage of Glanum's dressed stone, their repeated discoveries of buried Roman artefacts, and the survival above ground of some of the larger Roman monuments ensured that the region's ancient past was not forgotten. By the turn of the Christian era's sixteenth century St-Rémy had grown into a stout-walled little town of perhaps a couple of thousand inhabitants. And according to the local folklore, it was in a modest-looking house on the western side of its narrow Rue de Viguier (today renamed Rue Hoche) that the infant Michel de Nostredame, later to style himself 'Nostradamus', was born on December 14, 1503.[1]

What the St-Rémy Tourist Office insists is that same house, no. 6, still stands to this day, marked by a rather dingy post-Second World War marble plaque set above the doorway. Peter Lemesurier has sharply criticised his fellow Nostradamian John Hogue for illustrating the right street but the wrong house on the title-page of his lavishly illustrated *Nostradamus: The New Revelations*.[2] However, since my wife and I managed to miss the plaque during our first stroll down the street, our sympathies lie somewhat with Hogue. Undeniably no. 6, which is not open to the public, today has a distinctly uninviting and unprepossessing appearance. However, as pointed out by St-Rémy's early twentieth-century local historian Henri Rolland, structural alterations carried out since Nostradamus' time have caused the edifice to lose 'all of its character and distinctiveness, its chimney, its sculptures and the tower which once topped it'.[3]

As a year in which to be born, 1503 had a certain charm. Around the very same month that the infant Michel first sucked at his mother's breast the fifty-seven-year-old Christopher Columbus was crossing the Atlantic on his fourth and last voyage opening up the New World. The fifty-one-year-old Leonardo da Vinci was in Florence putting the finishing touches to his portrait of *Mona Lisa*. The twenty-eight-year-old Michelangelo was in the same city chipping away at his sculpture of David. The crusty, newly elected Pope Julius II, who would commission Michelangelo's Sistine Chapel ceiling, was just finding his way around the Vatican in Rome. And at the University of Erfurt in Germany a self-opinionated twenty-year-old student called Martin Luther was studying for his law examinations.

On Nostradamus' parents and their ancestry, the world of Nostradamian studies stands deeply indebted to a dedicated St-Rémy physician, Dr Edgar Leroy, who died in 1965, for some exhaustive researches[4] that have corrected many of the myths and misinformation promulgated by earlier Nostradamian 'authorities'. Ironically, not the least of this misinformation, sadly still peddled by many authors, was derived from members of the de Nostredame family themselves, whose penchant for social respectability could and sometimes did outweigh their concern for the truth.

The certain family facts are that Nostradamus' father was one Jaume (alternatively Jacques or James) de Nostredame, who made his living as a merchant, trading particularly in grain. Jaume seems to have enjoyed a comfortable enough living, no doubt because Frenchmen and women of the sixteenth century had every bit as much of a fondness for *baguettes* and other grain products as their modern-day descendants. Nostradamus' mother was named Reynière (or, in modern styling, Renée) de St-Rémy.

In English 'de Nostredame' means, of course, 'of Our Lady', the 'Lady' in question being the Virgin Mary. It is not exactly a typical French surname, and therefore of itself it provides an important clue

Top: A view of St-Rémy-de-Provence as it would have looked in Nostradamus' time. From a 17th century engraving.

Left: Number 6, Rue Hoche, St-Rémy-de-Provence, the house in which Nostradamus was born, seen to the left of the street.

Above: The notice that appears above the doorway of the Nostradamus birthplace house.

to the family's chequered past. Quite definitely Jaume's and possibly even Reynière's parents ascended from Jewish forebears. In the sixteenth century these were disparagingly known as *marrans* or (in Spanish) *marranos*, from their having been forced to convert to Christianity at a time when western Europe's Jews were about as popular as their descendants became in Germany during Hitler's Third Reich.

Long before Michel de Nostredame's birth, anti-Semitism had become deeply entrenched throughout much of Europe. When the devastating plague known as the Black Death broke out in the mid-fourteenth century, France's Jewish population were accused by none other than the court poet Guillaume de Machaut of having caused the epidemic by poisoning the wells.[5] Sometimes positively incited by their clergy, Christians committed terrible atrocities against Jews, among other things setting alight wooden houses in which they had trapped whole populations of men, women and children. Officially, Jews were banned altogether from France after 1394. Likewise in the Spanish kingdoms of Aragon and Castile life was made as intolerable as possible for them. Just nine years before Nostradamus' birth Columbus' patrons Ferdinand and Isabella, under whom the kingdoms of Aragon and Castile became united, expelled them from their entire territory.

Thankfully for Nostradamus' immediate forebears, before 1480 Provence's inhabitants belonged neither to French nor to Spanish jurisdiction. Instead, from 1433 their ruler had been the humane and enlightened René of Anjou, an independent and popular monarch with a passion for painting, music, poetry and theatrical entertainment, who also encouraged commerce to flourish. Mindful, no doubt, that Jewish communities tended to be very good at oiling the wheels of commerce, in 1454 'good King René' issued an edict specifically allowing Provençal Jews to practise their religion free of all duress. This inevitably attracted otherwise displaced Jews into the region, with Avignon, the former papal seat just to the north of St-Rémy, receiving a particularly sizeable cluster.

All went well for these new communities up to King René's death, at the age of seventy-two in 1480. Then, by simple, peaceful inheritance, Provence passed into French crown tutelage; whereupon, within eight years, the French King Charles VIII (ironically known as the Affable) began insisting that all Jews, and particularly the large number that had taken up residence in Provence, should choose between converting to Christianity or having everything that they owned forcibly confiscated. Charles' successor Louis XII followed this up with a similar demand in 1501.

One of the Jewish families thus affected was that of the Gassonets

The castle of Tarascon, seat of King René of Anjou, under whom Nostradamus' Jewish ancestors received toleration.

of Avignon, whose head, Guy de Gassonet, saw no alternative other than opting for conversion. His wife Astrugue, however, proved more intransigent, and so the couple went their separate ways. Guy thereupon re-married, this time to a Christian, Blanche de Sainte-Marie. The union appears to have inspired him to signify his acceptance of Christianity more publicly by changing his surname to de Nostredame and his forename to Peyrot, that is, Pierre or Peter. 'Peyrot' and Blanche duly went on to have six children, one of whom was Jaume. So when Jaume expanded upon his father's business by setting up shop and home in nearby St-Rémy, he did so under the name of Jaume de Nostredame. This was how, by succession (and some adroit Latinisation), the world subsequently acquired its prophet named 'Nostradamus'.

In the case of Michel de Nostredame's mother Reynière she, unlike her Avignon husband, actually hailed from St-Rémy, evident not least from her surname. One of her forebears was particularly fondly remembered by her son later in life, his maternal great-grandfather Jean de Saint-Rémy, whose house in the rue du Viguier Jaume appears to have received as dowry, along with various other lands, vineyards and a tile-works.[6] The elderly Jean would seem to have ceded the house to his grandson-in-law Jaume on the understanding that he would be allowed to live out his days there.

For visitors to Provence's Nostradamus Museum in Salon-de-Provence – the town south-east of St-Rémy where Nostradamus would spend the latter part of his life – the first scene in an attractively presented introductory sound-and-light show consists of a waxwork. The young Michel is represented as listening with rapt attention to words of wisdom being imparted to him by Jean de Saint-Rémy.

Behind the pair is painted an attractive diorama of St-Rémy's surrounding countryside, dotted with its still extant Roman landmarks

Concerning Jean, certain fictions would later be generated by
Michel's brother Jéhan, author of a *Lives of the Most Ancient
Provençal Poets* (1575)[7] upon which Nostradamus' son César later
drew heavily for his *History and Chronicle of Provence*.[8] These were
corroborated by others of the time who might be expected to be
knowledgeable. Incorrectly, he was supposed to have been a great
nobleman of the court of King René, none other than the official court
physician, and one of the popular monarch's chief officers. As Dr
Leroy has exhaustively determined, the hard historical facts are rather
different. Jean may well have been a physician. And as St-Rémy's
clavaire, or Treasurer, for which there is also documentary evidence,[9]
he may even have attended King René when the latter made one of his
periodic visits to St-Rémy, along with other towns in his realm. But as
to Jean's having had any noble status, or any long-term attachment to
the royal court, both may be firmly ruled out

This said, there is much to suggest, as the Nostradamus Museum's
colourful waxwork so strongly implies, that Jean de Saint-Rémy

The young Nostradamus receiving instruction from his maternal grandfather Jean
de Saint-Rémy. From a waxwork in the Maison Nostradamus, Salon-de-Provence.

played an important if not pivotal role in directing his young great-grandson's education. It is virtually certain that he was well versed in the astrology that Nostradamus would later pursue with such enthusiasm. In the fifteenth century Jean would almost automatically have been taught this as part of his medical training, and as such he may well have been the first to cast his great-grandson's horoscope.

For those with an interest in such matters, Nostradamus has been calculated by modern-day astrologers, using sixteenth-century methodology, to have been born with the Sun in Capricorn, and the three superior planets, Mars, Jupiter and Saturn, all on the opposite side of the zodiac, in Cancer.[10] Some corroboration of the accuracy of this derives from a later description by Nostradamus of the imprint that he had engraved on his signet ring: 'The Sun is represented at the top, and three planets at the bottom.'[11] Amongst those with astrological knowledge this powerful conjunction of planets, together with other facets of the same horoscope, is said to indicate Nostradamus' star-driven inclination towards occultism and like interests. Recognising this, Jean may well have deliberately fostered this tendency in the boy, teaching him the art of creating a horoscope himself, at the same time encouraging a familiarity with the Bible and with the works of classical writers. Jean may also have ensured that Michel would receive the necessary grounding in the Latin language, and may overall have been responsible for much that would later become the quintessential Nostradamus.

Prime corroborative evidence for this is to be found in a letter which Nostradamus would write in 1561, when he was fifty-eight. In this he specifically told a correspondent that he could possibly improve on a particular horoscope by 'using a planisphere with another instrument which came to me from my maternal great-grandfather Jean de Saint-Rémy'.[12] A planisphere is an instrument that, when set with a particular date and time, seemingly magically presents a two-dimensional map of the positions of the stars as these would have looked above the horizon at that moment. Though the ancient Greeks and Romans had planispheres, and the medieval Arabs and Persians followed them in this, such gadgetry was hardly one of the accoutrements to be expected in a normal sixteenth-century household. So Jean de Saint-Rémy's possession of both a planisphere and what was almost certainly an astrolabe (the 'other instrument' referred to by Nostradamus, basically a more advanced version of the planisphere), unmistakably indicates his serious interest in the stars, at a time, well over a century before the invention of the telescope, when astrology and astronomy were scarcely differentiated.

Additionally, the details of the sixteenth-century appearance of

Jean's Rue Viguier house, given in Jaume de Nostredame's dowry document, specifically describe it as having one floor open to the sky.[13] The topmost floor may well therefore have taken the form of the tower which can be seen in some early depictions of the house, but which, as pointed out by Henri Rolland, has long since disappeared. In an era centuries before street-lighting, such a top-floor 'observatory' would have provided Jean with an ideal vantage-point for his star-gazing. We may well imagine that it was he who introduced such delights to the young Michel, duly going on to bequeath him his treasured planisphere and his astrolabe on recognising his natural interest in these matters. Further corroboration of this derives from a brief biography that was compiled after Nostradamus' death by the secretary whom he had employed during his later years, Jean Aimé de Chavigny.[14] Though Chavigny's information cannot always be considered reliable, in his *Brief Discourse* he specifically described Nostradamus' maternal great-grandfather[15] as having given the youngster his 'first taste of the Celestial Sciences'.[16]

Again as suggested by Salon-de-Provence's Nostradamus Museum diorama, Jean de Saint-Rémy may also have been responsible for introducing his great-grandson to a quite different type of inspiration, the region's historic remains from the Roman era, some of which had never ceased to be visible. As earlier remarked, the former Roman town of Glanum lay less than a mile to the south of St-Rémy, and from this there had survived to Nostradamus' time, and still to this day, an imposing pair of Roman monuments known as 'Les Antiques'.

The first of these, long known locally as the 'Arc', is a Roman triumphal arch in the manner of London's Marble Arch, covered with relief sculptures that depict Julius Caesar's conquest of the former Greek colony of Gaul in 49 BC. The other monument, the 'Mausole', which stands only a few feet away and soars to over 19 metres high, consists of a two-storeyed mausoleum set on a square pedestal, its lower storey decorated with relief sculptures of scenes from the Trojan War, its upper storey replete with images of gods and sea-monsters.

If Nostradamus had strolled even a brief distance from St-Rémy with his great-grandfather he could hardly have missed these monuments, still evident to anyone approaching the town by road from Marseilles to this day. A positive confirmation that they were of considerably more than passing interest to young Michel is his clear reference to them amongst his later writings, dating from long after he had left St-Rémy.

Thus in a popular treatise that was published in 1555,[17] when he had long become settled in Salon-de-Provence, Nostradamus pointedly spoke of the town of his childhood as 'Saint-Rémy-de-Provence, "called *Sextrophea*"'.[18] This refers unmistakably to the fact that the

The Roman monuments known as 'Les Antiques', still extant just outside St-Rémy-de-Provence. Nostradamus' later writings show that he was clearly familiar with these during his childhood.

'Mausole', which in French is also called a *trophée*, bore a badly effaced Latin inscription of which the most legible letters are 'SEXT...', leading to the local belief that it had once belonged to a Roman called Sextus.[19]

Nostradamus also unmistakably referred to the same monument again in his *Prophecies*, published in stages between 1555 and his death:

> *Between two rocks the booty will be taken*
> *Of SEXT. the 'mansol' will lose its renown.*[20]

There is general recognition that 'mansol' is a misprint for 'mausol[e]' – misprints being not uncommon amongst early printed editions of Nostradamus' writings – as also in another verse:

> *Salon, Mansol, Tarascon of SEX. the arch,*
> *Where still stands the pyramid.*[21]

Salon and Tarascon are readily identifiable as towns in the same Nostradamian region where, in St-Rémy's environs, the 'SEX'-inscribed Mausole and arch are to be found. Salon is some seventeen miles south-east of St-Rémy, and, as pointed out earlier, is where Nostradamus spent much of the latter part of his life. Tarascon is six miles to St-Rémy's west and is where King René of Anjou had a particularly magnificent castle that still stands overlooking the mighty river Rhône.

And in this same context the 'pyramid' comprises another time-honoured landmark in the same locality, even if its shape is not what might normally be embraced by the word 'pyramid'. Less than a mile from St-Rémy, and only a few hundred yards from the Arch and the Mausole, there is still to be found the ancient quarry from which the Greeks and Romans constructed Glanum. The chisel-marks of the old stonemasons continue to be readily visible on its cavernous walls and ceilings. Privately owned, this quarry is commercially operated as a tourist attraction, offering visitors a self-guided tour of a motley collection of Roman and later antiquities, amongst which there stands a strangely isolated and crudely hewn pillar of stone traditionally known locally as the *Pyramide*. A number of authors have struggled to find the reason for this appellation,[22] the simple explanation being that in Nostradamus' sixteenth century, in both English and French, 'pyramid' was a term commonly used to describe the ancient Egyptian pillars we today call obelisks. For instance, in Shakespeare's Sonnet 123 the line 'pyramids built up with newer might' refers to four Egyptian-style obelisks crafted for the tomb of the second Earl of Southampton.[23]

Unmistakably, therefore, Nostradamus during his childhood in St-Rémy had wandered amongst these ancient remains. Arguably encouraged by his great-grandfather, he became fascinated by them. His Latin education, the acquisition of which is quite definite from his later writings, would have further fuelled this fascination. It would have enabled him to read the inscriptions on these ancient monuments and to relate them to the accounts of the past by Roman historians that, thanks to the printing press and the stimulation of interest by the Renaissance, were becoming increasingly accessible to those literate in Latin. And of course a mind that could become so absorbed by wandering thousands of years back into the past might well in time find a similar fascination for the future.

Evident from surviving documentation in Provençal archives is apparent that during Michel Nostradamus' childhood his father Jaume became sufficiently well-trusted in St-Rémy to become a notary for the town. That he took on this responsibility without giving up his occupation as a merchant is also apparent from a document of July 8, 1510 specifically recording him as a 'notary and merchant of the town of Saint-Rémy'.[24] When France's King Louis XII, hard-pressed for

The 'Pyramide', another monument local to St-Rémy with which Nostradamus showed familiarity.

cash because of the expenses of the wars he was waging in Italy, imposed a new 'ancestry' tax upon 'new Christians descended from true Judaic and Hebrew stock and race',[25] Jaume is listed along with two others from St-Rémy as dutifully paying 25 livres on 21st December 1512.[26] In further documents from 1513 to 1517 Jaume can be seen to have acted in the capacities of notary, scribe and official clerk, positions that he could not have held without considerable local respect together with the appropriate requirement of literacy and numeracy.

Adding to the impression of Jaume's prosperity – also the de Nostredames' general good health – is the fact that, as the first-born son, the young Michel, grew up, a sizeable number of further offspring were added to the family. The documentation is somewhat patchy. Nonetheless Michel appears to have been followed first by a sister, Delphine, of whom little is known. Then in 1507 Reynière produced Jéhan, clearly named after his maternal great-grandfather Jean. Some four years junior to Michel, young Jéhan probably sat side by side with his elder brother while the veteran Jean regaled them with stories from history, the apparent fruit of this in Jéhan's case being the history of Provence's poets that he wrote later in life. Jéhan went on to become well-respected and rewarded as lawyer and *procureur* to the Parlement, Provence's local government body, based at Aix. And since we will later hear of Michel visiting Jéhan, and the pair exchanging information, all the indications are that throughout the brothers' lives there was a close bond between them, something particularly fostered in Jewish families.

Peyrot and Reynière further produced Pierre and Hector, their birth-dates unknown; also Louis, born in 1522, by which time Michel was nineteen. There was also a Bertrand, and possibly a second Jean. Finally, in 1523 Reynière gave birth to Antoine, who, even though his mother had by now been child-bearing for some twenty years, seems to have been healthy enough, since he grew up to become St-Rémy's Consul, the equivalent of mayor, and to have ten children of his own.

All the indications, therefore, are that the de Nostredames were a healthy, well-educated, well-adjusted and financially comfortable family, and that despite their Jewish roots they achieved essentially complete acceptance as upright Christian citizens of St-Rémy and its surrounds. They may well have attended St-Rémy's main church, Saint Martin, dating, in its foundation at least from a thousand years before their time. Sadly, today all too little remains of this ancient edifice. On the night of August 29, 1818 the church collapsed into rubble and was rebuilt in more modern style. Today the fourteenth-century bell-tower is the only feature that the de Nostredames would still recognise. Alternatively, however, perhaps attracted by the name, it is possible that the family attended the Chapelle Notre-Dame de Pitié that still stands on the town's southern outskirts.

It is a matter of public record that by 1540 the brothers Jaume and Pierre de Nostredame, young Michel's father and uncle respectively, had won sufficient acceptance amongst both the Provençal and the wider community to become officially naturalised as Frenchmen. This was necessary not only because of their Jewish parentage, but also because their native Avignon, which had become a 'Vatican City' within France in the period of the Avignon Popes, had been papal property since 1348, and would remain so until the French Revolution. On October 22, 1540, far to the north at Nayssons-sur-Seine, King François I signed the formal document recognising Jaume's and Pierre's full French nationality. The preamble to this clearly sets out Jaume's known family background:

> We have received the humble supplication of our well-beloved Jacques de Nostredame, inhabitant of our town of Saint-Rémy in our said country of Provence, containing [the information] that he was born in the town of Avignon, a subordinate member of our said country of Provence, and that for the last forty years... he has lived in our country of Provence and in the said town of Saint-Rémy in which he has wife and children.[27]

While the date of Jaume's death is not known exactly, it must have been towards the end of 1546 or early in 1547, by which time he would have been well into his seventies at least. He certainly seems to have been dead some time before February 6, 1547, since a document issued in St-Rémy on that date speaks of Michel's brothers Jéhan, Bertrand, Hector and Antoine as being his children and co-heirs.

Long before this, however, the moment had inevitably come for Michel to carve out a career path for himself. And as we are about to discover, it was a path that would not be without its pitfalls and painful adversities.

NOTES

1 It is not to any surviving parish record, but to a monumental early seventeenth-century history of Provence written by Nostradamus' son César that we owe the information that his father was born 'in the year 1503, the 14th December, almost the year's last extremity' (César de Nostredame, *L'Histoire et Chronique de Provence de Caesar de Nostradamus Gentilhomme Provençal*, Lyons, Simon Rigaud, 1614, p.726E). Since César, who inherited his father's enthusiasm for astrology, found dates to be of absorbing interest there are reasonable grounds for trusting this particular piece of information, though, as we will discover, in other matters César sometimes needs to be treated with caution.

2 John Hogue, *Nostradamus: The New Revelations*, Element, 1994. Peter Lemesurier makes his criticism in *The Essential Nostradamus*, London, Piatkus, 1999, p.69

3 Henri Rolland, *Saint-Rémy-de-Provence*, Bergerac, 1934, p.163

4 Edgar Leroy, *Nostradamus, Ses Origines, Sa Vie, Son Oeuvre*, Bergerac, 1972, reprinted by Lafitte Reprints, 1993

5 Barbara W. Tuchman, *A Distant Mirror, The Calamitous 14th Century*, Harmondsworth, Penguin, 1979, p.109

6 The salient details of this dowry are given in Edgar Leroy, *Nostradamus, Ses Origines...*, op. cit., pp.26–7. A complementary note in the Lafitte Reprint edition identifies the document, drawn up by a notary, as AD84, 3E8/491, folio 361 recto.

7 Jéhan de Nostredame, *Les Vies de plus celebres & anciens poetes provensaux, qui ont floury du temps des comtes de Provence...par Jéhan de nostre Dame, Procureur en la Cour de Parlement de Provence*, Lyons, Alexandre Marsilii, 1575

8 César de Nostredame, *L'Histoire et Chronique de Provence...*, op. cit.

9 Arch. Dep. Des Bouches-du-Rhône, B. 2.607, '*Lous contes de my johan de Sant Romiech, clavaire de la cort realla de la villa de Sant Romiech, de l'an mille V^c, estant notari, mestre Antoni Almerani*', quoted in Leroy, *Nostradamus, Ses Origines...*, op. cit. p.30, n.2

10 David Ovason, *The Nostradamus Code*, London, Arrow, 1998, p.486. This was first published as *The Secrets of Nostradamus*, Century, 1997

11 Letter from Nostradamus to Lorenz Tubbe, October 15, 1561, Dupèbe, *Lettres Inédites*, op. cit., Letter XXXI

12 '*planisphaerium cum instrumento abavi mei materni Magistri Io. Sanremiglii ad harmoniam Astronomicam coniunxi...*' Letter from Nostradamus to Hans Rosenberger, October 15, 1651, Dupèbe, *Lettres Inédites*, op. cit., p.96

13 *'avec ciel ouvert, hospicium cum celesti'*, quoted in Leroy, *Nostradamus, Ses Origines...*, op. cit., p.26

14 Jean Aimé de Chavigny, *Brief Discours sur la Vie de M. Michel de Nostredame...*, published in Paris in 1596, and made available in a facsimile reprint by Éric Visier, *Nostradamus au XVIe Siecle, 10 Facsimilés*, available from the Nostradamus Museum, Salon-de-Provence

15 *'bisayeul maternel'*

16 *'un premier goust des celestes sciences'*

17 Nostradamus, *Traité des fardemens et confitures*, Lyons, Antoine Volant, 1555, Proeme

18 *'dite Sextrophea'*

19 The actual original inscription, according to Henri Rolland's best reconstruction of it, would seem to have read 'Sextius, Lucius and Marcus Julius, sons of Caius, have dedicated this monument to their parents'

20 *'Entre deux rocs sera prins le butin De SEXT. mansol faillit la renommee.'* From *Les Prophéties* C.V, q.57

21 *'Salon, Mansol, Tarascon de SEX. l'arc, Ou est debout encor la piramide...'* [C.IV, q.27]

22 Randi thought the side of the quarry resembled a pyramid. See his book *The Mask of Nostradamus* op. cit.

23 See Ian Wilson, *Shakespeare: The Evidence*, London, Headline, 1993, pp.167–8. Shakespeare's contemporary George Puttenham, in *The Art of English Poesie*, has a section 'Of the Spire or Taper called Pyramis' specifically describing obelisk shapes as pyramids

24 On July 8, 1510 Pierre Blancard de Saint-Rémy acknowledged receiving from Jacques de Notredame, 'notaire et marchand de la ville de Saint-Rémy', nineteen gold écus, forty florins and two gros for the sale of 120 hundredweight of wool'. Quoted in Leroy, *Nostradamus, Ses Origines...*, op. cit., p.27

25 *'nouveaux chrétiens descendus de vraye tige et race judaïque et hébraïque'*

26 Quoted in Leroy, *Nostradamus, Ses Origines ...*, op. cit., p.28, after Arch. Dep. des Bouches-du-Rhône, *Néophytes ou chrétiens de Provence*, Fonds Nicolai, carton 102, document 2, pp.5 and 19

27 Quoted in the original French in Leroy, *Nostradamus, Ses Origines...*, op. cit., p.29. A copy of this official naturalisation document is preserved in Marseilles, Arch. Dép. Des Bouches-du-Rhône, série B, reg. 36 (de Luna), covering the period from 1473 to 1542

CHAPTER 2

Fellow-Student of Rabelais

The phrase 'wandering Jew' may have only curiosity value for us living in the twenty-first century. For the sixteenth century it was a living reality. As we learned earlier, the era was one in which many Jews had been persecuted and pushed from pillar to post. So a not uncommon sight – later to be immortalised in literature and art – was that of a bearded Jewish pedlar moving from town to town like a gypsy or a Breton onion-seller, his back bowed under the weight of his travel pack. In this pack would be his stock of ingredients for the patent preparations which he sold to make a living – an exotic and (to the uninitiated) bewildering pharmacopoeia of herbs and potions with which he might claim to reverse ageing, relieve constipation, disperse gallstones, cure hair-loss, improve sexual potency, and much else. And partly because of the mystique of the dark ancestral 'magic' with which popular superstition associated Jews (much like that which would become associated with gypsies in our own time), every town would have a clientèle ready to part with cash in the belief that such remedies might actually do for them what was claimed.

Most biographers, contemporary and modern, have shied from portraying the young Nostradamus' early ventures in money-making as having been anything like so tawdry or humble. According to his later secretary, Chavigny, after he had had his 'first taste of the celestial sciences' from his maternal great-grandfather:

> He was sent to Avignon to study the Humanities. From there he happily mastered Philosophy and the theory of Medicine at the University of Montpellier until a plague which broke out in the country. He then took the road to Narbonne, Toulouse [and] Bordeaux, all of which towns and cities provided him with his first opportunities to try out the fruits of his studies up to his reaching twenty-two years of age. After spending four years in these parts practising medicine he returned to Montpellier to receive and pass

his doctorate, which he took in a short time, and not without approval, praise and admiration from all the College.[1]

That the late teenage or post-teenage Nostradamus spent some time in Avignon is perfectly feasible, since, as we have already seen, it was his father's home town and he had relatives still living there. Also quite definite is that around 1520, when he was still only seventeen, a virulent plague began raging in Provence, a bout that was so severe and so prolonged that the 'local' universities of Avignon and Montpellier felt obliged to shut down and to send their students home. At the age at which Nostradamus would most have expected to go on to higher education, therefore, circumstances beyond his control denied him this opportunity.

But a plain fact also to be faced is that until 1529, at which point the documentary evidence suggests that he began university education for the first time, the combing of Provençal academic records by numerous scholars has revealed absolutely no independent indication that Nostradamus even began formally to study medicine or any other discipline. As for his own writings, his only clear reference to this early part of his life[2] occurs in his Preface to a booklet of patent recipes for making cosmetics and jams, which he published in 1555. In this he remarked:

> After my having spent the greater part of my youthful years ... in pharmacy, and in the knowledge and understanding of medicinal herbs, I moved through a number of lands and countries from 1521 to 1529, constantly in search of the understanding and knowledge of the sources and origins of plants and other medicinal herbs – [exploring] medicine's very frontiers.[3]

It is important to note here that to the French sixteenth-century mind the social status of the pharmacist and/or herbalist was very considerably inferior to that of the physician. As in the case of mid-wives and barber-surgeons, similarly lowly regarded, these required no Latin to practise their trade, Latin being the recognised mark of 'true' education. So pharmacists and wandering Jew-type pedlars of pills and potions were considered much of a second-rate muchness. Among those holding a low opinion of such individuals were members of the medical establishment, as Nostradamus quickly found out when he at last enrolled at the University of Montpellier Medical School, fifty miles (80 km) from his home town of St-Rémy, in 1529.

For the first record of the twenty-six-year-old Nostradamus' arrival at Montpellier is the entry of his name as 'Michelet[4] de Nostre-Dame' on the Medical School's *Liber Scholasticorum* register for October 3, 1529. And the immediately arresting feature is that this can clearly be seen to have been struck out again, and an explanatory note in Latin added in the margin by the faculty tutor, Guillaume Rondelet:

Doctor and pharmacist of Nostradamus' time. From a woodcut of 1534.

> Note, reader, that he whom you see here struck out has been an apothecary or pharmacist. And this we have been assured by Chante, an apothecary of this town, and by students who heard him speak badly of doctors. This is why, by decree, and according to regulations, I am required to strike him from the book of students. Guillaume Rondelet, Proctor.[5]

On the strength of later instances in which Nostradamus was accused of making some undiplomatic or facetious comment, thereby getting himself into trouble with authority, the face-value interpretation of this passage is that much the same happened in this case. By all appearances the Montpellier medical establishment were stung by remarks that he had made. They accordingly invoked some statute by which they were entitled to bar any pedlar of pills and potions from joining their midst. Had they continued to uphold this, then of course Michel de Nostredame would never have become a physician and the world might never have had its Nostradamus.

In fact we will see later that there is another interpretation of this 'striking out', whereby the whole thing might have been a mere student prank. It is impossible to be sure which interpretation is the more likely, but certainly if Nostradamus had genuinely ruffled Montpellier's academic feathers, then somehow he managed to smooth them again. For the Medical School's still extant Register of its Matriculations, or Student Enrolments, has for October 23, 1529, just twenty days after the 'striking off', the following entry:

I ~~Pet~~ Michelet de Nostredame, of the district of Provence, of the

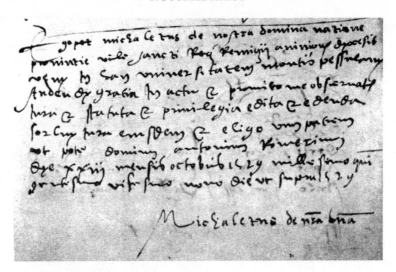

Nostradamus' registration for training as a doctor at the
Montpellier Medical School, 1529. From the original register as
preserved at the Faculty of Medicine, Montpellier.

town of Saint-Rémy, of the diocese of Avignon, am come to study
at the University of Montpellier, and I swear to observe the
statutes, rights and privileges, present and future. I have paid the
registration fee and choose Antoine Romier as patron, October 23,
1529.[6]

Not only does this confirm that Nostradamus *did* join Montpellier as
a medical student: not the least of this register entry's features of interest is that it is in his own handwriting. Later in his life several of his
astrological clients complained of his execrable hand. This was partly
why he eventually resorted to employing a secretary, Chavigny. In this
instance, however, his writing can be seen to be at least reasonably
legible.

Another curious aspect of the entry is that after the Latin word
'Ego' (for 'I'), Nostradamus began to write 'Pet' (as if for 'Petrus' or
Peter), only to scratch this out and substitute his Christian name
'Michelet'. Some researchers have been so puzzled by this that they
have tried to build elaborate explanatory theories. However, the sim-
plest and therefore likeliest reason for the erasure is that Nostradamus
had before him a specimen registration entry which had been made
out for one 'Petrus'. Slavishly copying from this, in his eagerness he
momentarily forgot to substitute his own name, a lapse in concentra-
tion all too easily committed by the more absent-minded among us. In
Nostradamus' case, however, it survived to perplex posterity.

Since popular belief has it that sixteenth-century medical knowledge was very primitive by twenty-first-century standards, it is important to set in proper perspective the sort of medical education that Nostradamus would have expected to receive at Montpellier. Even as far back as the ancient Egyptians, more than 3,000 years before Nostradamus, it had been known how to set broken bones, how to extract teeth and how to perform a number of other surgical operations. This knowledge had then been passed on to the ancient Greeks, whose medical texts were preserved by the Arabs during the Dark Ages. It then gradually percolated back to the West. Among the treatments described by Paul of Aegina, a Greek medical encyclopaedist of the seventh century AD whom Nostradamus specifically referred to with approval,[7] were such state-of-the-art procedures as breast amputation, the surgical removal of bladder stones and tonsils, the puncturing of body cavities in order to drain harmful fluids, and trepanation-type surgery on the skull to relieve inflammation of the brain.

Another important point to be noted is that Montpellier was by no means a run-of-the-mill medical teaching establishment which just happened to be geographically most convenient for Nostradamus' home town. Convenient it certainly was, since via horse or mule, the standard sixteenth-century means of travel for the able-bodied and well-to-do, Montpellier could be reached from St-Rémy by a straightforward fifty-mile (80 km) ride across the flat terrain of the Rhône delta, reasonably achievable in a day. But run-of-the-mill it certainly was not. In Nostradamus' time Montpellier had a long-established reputation for being not only France's finest medical school outside Paris, but also one of the best in all Europe, rivalled only by Leyden and Padua.

And it was in fact Montpellier's geographical location in the far south, as a seaport on the shores of the Mediterranean looking towards North Africa, that had helped bring this about. Throughout much of the Dark Ages Arab and Jewish traders from the North African littoral imported spices and other exotic products, the medicinal properties of which were always an important selling point. As far back as AD 1000, therefore, a medical school of sorts had been founded at Montpellier as a centre for collecting, evaluating and passing on the medical knowledge thereby gained, and by the thirteenth century this had become formalised into a proper medical university.

Despite the medieval Catholic Church's abhorrence of and prohibition of any dissection of human bodies for medical science purposes (hence the fact that physicians were commonly the less constrained Arabs and Jews), the Montpellier Medical School's *savants* pioneered some significant overriding of such restrictions. In 1340 they obtained approval from the town's burghers for the holding of an anatomy

class every two years. And in 1376 the then Duke of Anjou, a predecessor of 'good King René', actually authorised them to claim the
body of one executed criminal for dissection in their anatomy classes.
Such classes would last several days at a time, and consisted of a
barber-surgeon performing the actual cutting open of the body, while
a doctor of medicine expounded upon the anatomical details being
revealed.

During the early fourteenth century Montpellier also became associated with St Roch (1295–1327), who, according to his fifteenth-
century Venetian biographer Francis Diedo, had been born in the
town. Although little is known of Roch's life, he reputedly cured many
who had been stricken during a plague outbreak at the north Italian
town of Aquapendente, then went on to do much the same at Cesena,
Mantua, Modena, Parma and other north Italian cities. After ultimately falling victim to the disease himself he managed to get back to
Montpellier where he died.[8]

By Nostradamus' time the bulk of medical teaching at Montpellier
had come to consist of reading in Latin translation the medical books
of the great Greek and Arab authorities, Hippocrates, Galen,
Avicenna and others. Botanical studies were also popular, so that
despite the prevailing medical snobbery towards herbalists, the plant
and herbal lore that Nostradamus had gained during his 'wandering
Jew' years would not have gone to waste. Experiments were commonly carried out on 'dry anatomies', that is, on fleshless skeletons,
these no doubt being all that remained of the unfortunates who had
been victims of earlier dissections. The number of dissections performed on complete cadavers had also been stepped up, medical
school records showing that two were performed in 1530 and three in
1531.[9] During these, four so-called regenting doctors gave out
anatomy instruction from the Feast of St Luke (October 18) to Palm
Sunday. Lectures by professors were few in the second part of the
scholastic year. Medical textbooks were expounded by newly qualified
Bachelors of Medicine to display their learning.[10]

Less than a year after Nostradamus' successful enrolment at
Montpellier, another familiar name would be written into the Medical
School's still extant register. This was François Rabelais, shortly to
become famous for his satirical and very bawdy stories *Gargantua*
(published 1532) and *Pantagruel* (published 1534), who joined the
school on September 17, 1530.[11] At least nine years older than
Nostradamus,[12] Rabelais arrived similarly as a mature student, though
with a rather better-documented career behind him. A lawyer's son
from Chinon, near Tours in western France, Rabelais had first taken
holy orders as a Franciscan friar, using the opportunity to become

fluent in Greek as well as Latin. He then switched to the Benedictine order as a monk, and shortly before arriving at Montpellier had studied medicine at the school of the Italian-born Julius Caesar Scaliger at Agen near Bordeaux. One of Scaliger's earlier pupils, who had gone on to Montpellier to become professor there during Nostradamus' time, was Jean Schyron, and it was this Schyron whom Rabelais chose as his patron in much the same manner that Nostradamus, as his matriculation record shows, chose Antoine Romier.

Whether Nostradamus and Rabelais got to know each other at Montpellier must remain conjectural, since any hard documentary evidence for an association is lacking. Nonetheless it is through Rabelais' literary eyes that we are able to glimpse something of the lighter moments that the two would have enjoyed during their time there. Much as at colleges in the present-day universities of Oxford and Cambridge, staff and students alike attended regular university feasts, at with large quantities of food were washed down with highly regarded local wines such as Mirevaulx. Such occasions provided the opportunity to stage home-grown theatrical performances, in which the different faculties of university men – for this was of course long before the admission of women to universities – lampooned each other mercilessly. The physicians of the Medical School would poke fun at the pomposity of the lawyers from the Law School. The lawyers in their turn would ridicule the doctors for smelling of glisters 'like old devils', and their sampling of patients' urine and faeces. As Rabelais would later recall in his *Pantagruel*, Montpellier staff and students, Rabelais among them, staged *The Man who married a Dumb Wife*, of which this was the plot:

The good husband wanted to have her [the dumb wife] speak. She did speak, by the skill of the doctor and the surgeon, who cut off a restricting cord under her tongue. With her speech recovered she talked and talked so much that her husband went back to the doctor for a remedy to shut her up. The doctor replied that he had indeed in his craft remedies to make women talk, but none to shut them up; the only remedy for this interminable talking by his wife was deafness in the husband. The rascal became deaf, though I know not what spell they cast. His wife, seeing that he had become deaf, that she was talking in vain, he wasn't hearing her, went mad. Then, when the doctor asked for his fee, the husband replied that he really *was* deaf and couldn't hear his request. The doctor cast over his back some powder or other by virtue of which he went crazy. Thereupon the crazy husband and the mad wife joined

The satirist François Rabelais, a
fellow-student of Nostradamus at
the Montpellier Medical School.
From an early engraving.

forces together and beat up the doctor and surgeon so badly that
they left them half-dead. I've never laughed so hard as I did at that
crazy farce...[13]

Rabelais provided the names of some of those who played alongside
him, from which list it is clear that even some of Montpellier's most
illustrious academics did not hold back from letting their hair down –
literally, for women's parts necessarily had to be played by men – and
from making fools of themselves. The *Dumb Wife*'s cast included
Antoine Saporta, physician to the King and Queen of Navarre, and
Pierre Tolet, who wrote medical treatises in French.

Nostradamus goes unmentioned by Rabelais, and as the former left
no memoir of Montpellier's entertainment in his own writings it can
only be inferred that he had less taste for this kind of frivolity. Evident
from his publications, however, is that he indeed knew some of the
very same *illustrissimi* as those mentioned by Rabelais and others. Thus
in his discussion of a recipe for a laxative syrup which he included in
his later *Treatise on cosmetics and jams*[14] he remarked:

The famous city of Montpellier is graced by a number of erudite
individuals in the perfect Faculty of Medicine. There this [disci-
pline] is brought to perfection. Also there at the present are individuals who practise the science of medicine somewhat curiously.
Among them are a number who work tirelessly, preparing written

works to perpetuate their memories for eternity. These include Antoine Saporta junior, of whom I can't be sure the spirit of Hippocrates has passed into him. Guillaume Rondelet, for whom Aelianus Massarius, or Dioscorides the Freckled could not have left a more divine reincarnation of Euphorbius within him. Also Honoré du Chastel who is still in the east, for it is not permitted to exercise the Iatric [i.e. medical] faculty of setting anything to memory while they are in the west.[15]

Some of Nostradamus' asides in this passage seem to be sardonic witticisms that are near-impossible for us of the twenty-first century to appreciate. Nonetheless, it is readily apparent that Nostradamus here speaks favourably of the same Guillaume Rondelet who as 'procurator' appeared to have struck his name from the medical faculty some time after October 3 – which leads me to the possible alternative explanation for this otherwise strange excision. For it is known that after Rondelet received some earlier medical training in Paris, he had enrolled at Montpellier only four months before Nostradamus, which makes it rather strange that he should already hold a position of sufficient authority to dismiss another incoming student.[16] Montpellier students were notorious for having their own elected leader, a kind of Lord of Misrule, whom they would anarchically parade around the town in much the manner of rebel students today; a possible interpretation of the whole deletion of Nostradamus' registration is that it was some undergraduate prank. Whatever happened, Rondelet was a serious enough scholar who qualified in 1537, went on to be physician to the Cardinal of Tournon, to write a number of books, and ultimately to be appointed Chancellor of the Montpellier Medical Faculty between 1560 and 1566.

Also on Nostradamus' list as worthy of special mention can be seen Antoine Saporta, the very same man whom Rabelais described as having taken part in the 1532 performance of the *Dumb Wife* farce. Like Rondelet one of the younger members of the faculty in Nostradamus' time, Saporta went on to succeed Rondelet as Chancellor in 1566,[17] and he left a posthumous treatise on tumours, which his son published in 1624.

Unquestionably, then, Nostradamus rubbed shoulders with some distinguished medical men at Montpellier. We may envisage him gravely discussing with them the works of the revered ancient Greek and Arab physicians – those of the Arab Avicenna took up some half of the lecture syllabus – and eagerly absorbing all that they could teach him of the worthy profession that he had chosen for himself.

But despite the suggestion by a number of Nostradamian authors that he achieved a medical expertise ahead of his time, any such idea is hardly borne out by the evidence. In some medical matters, the sixteenth century was surprisingly advanced, Nostradamus being directly contemporary, for instance, with the Flemish physician Andreas Vesalius (1514–1564), who revolutionised the teaching of anatomy. However, the discovery of key concepts such as the circulation of the blood lay decades in the future, and all the evidence shows that Nostradamus and his peers still entertained a lot of ideas and treatments at which the modern mind can only baulk, aghast.

Thus there was a near-universal medical supposition that all creation was governed by the four elements of earth, air, fire and water, complemented by the four humours. These latter consisted of 'hot' blood (in Latin *sanguis*), from which we get the adjective sanguine; 'cold' phlegm, from which we get 'phlegmatic', 'moist' black bile (Greek *melan chole*), from which comes 'melancholic'; and 'dry' yellow bile (*chole*), giving us the term 'choleric'. Because blood was believed to be 'hot', the routine medically favoured remedy for the relief of many conditions such as fevers and inflammations was the reduction of the amount of blood in the patient's body, either by the incision of a vein or artery, or by the application of leeches. Physiologically such a loss of blood would cause a light-headedness which might give patients the illusion of some improvement to their condition. The actuality, however, was that the lowering of blood volume and pressure weakened the patient's resistance to whatever was ailing him or her, the medical intervention prescribed thereby being positively harmful to recovery.

Another popular medical procedure was 'cupping', involving the application to the problematic body area of cups from which the air has been sucked out, again in order to draw off blood. Some inflammations were treated in this manner. Others were treated by 'seton', an acupuncture-like counter-irritation of the skin using bristles or threads of silk or cotton. Yet a further variant was 'moxa', consisting of the cauterising of a selected area of the body by the application of something red-hot, such as the heated top of a cylinder of wool. Later, thanks to the unique survival of a medical prescription drawn up by Nostradamus, we will find him prescribing precisely this form of treatment to a gout-stricken cardinal.

Equally astonishing to our scientifically-minded age is the extent to which astrology and astrological theory were mixed in with medical training, Nostradamus in particular taking this doctrine very seriously indeed. Historically, both in France and elsewhere, astrology was almost unquestioningly regarded as one of the most fundamental principles upon which all medical understanding needed to be founded, much as knowledge of mathematics underscores modern-day physics or an understanding of the telescope and radio-telescope underpins astronomy.

Thus when King Charles V of France, in the second half of the fourteenth century, founded a medical school at the University of Paris, this was specifically accorded the motto: 'A physician without astrology is like a blind eye.' At this same period there flourished the English poet Geoffrey Chaucer, who in his famous *Canterbury Tales* penned this image of a contemporary English 'Doctor of Physic', or physician:

> *In all this world was there no one like him*
> *To speak of physic and of surgery;*
> *For he was grounded in astronomy*
> *He kept his patient a full great deal*
> *In hours by his natural magic*
> *Well could he [cast a] fortune [by] the Ascendant*
> *Of his [horoscope] images for his patient*
> *He knew the cause of every malady*
> *Were it of hot, or cold, or moist, or dry*
> *And where they engendered, and of what humour.*[18]

In a manner that at the time was regarded as far less 'fringe-ish' than it would be today, physicians of the astrologically-minded variety believed that every part of the body was ruled by a particular sign of the zodiac. They used anatomical charts much like those used by modern-day acupuncturists, except that these showed the head to be ruled by Aries the Ram, the neck by Taurus the Bull, the chest by Cancer the Crab, the genitals by Scorpio the Scorpion, and so on. During the early adult part of Nostradamus' life France's ruling monarch was King François I, whose mother Louise of Savoy was so devoted to astrology that she appointed an astrologer, Henry Cornelius Agrippa, as her personal physician. When she ultimately dismissed Agrippa it was because she felt him insufficiently astrological in his approach.[19]

Yet contemporary with Nostradamus were also individuals who had very little time for many of the superstitious ideas, chained to the old classical authorities, that were still being perpetuated amongst the medical establishments of Nostradamus' time. In 1543 there appeared at Basle the ground-breaking textbook *The Structure of the Human Body*. Illustrated with plates and woodcuts by the great pioneer anatomist Vesalius, this was a work which was to have far-reaching implications for the study of medicine. The Swiss physician Paracelsus (c.1493–1541), described by some as 'the Luther of Medicine', refused

Zodiacal Man, illustrating the belief in Nostradamus' time that different zodiacal signs ruled different parts of the human body. Detail of a miniature from the manuscript 'Très riches heures du duc de Berry', Musée Condé, Chantilly.

to lecture in Latin, and burnt the works of Galen and Avicenna in the streets of Berne, declaring of physicians:

Your science is founded upon lies! You are not professors of the truth but professors of falsehood. It is not the opinion a person holds, but the work he performs, that constitutes a physician.[20]

A particularly outstanding example of someone who was in advance of his time was the French surgeon Ambroise Paré, who was born in 1510 and lived on to 1590. The son of a poor cabinetmaker as a youngster Paré supplemented his income by work as a barber to the local seigneur. This led him into a career as barber-surgeon (a common combination at the time), except that because he had not been educated in Latin and Greek he had no way of being indoctrinated in the works of Galen in the way that Nostradamus was at Montpellier. Paré thereby learned his skills by practical experience and common sense, adopting the philosophy, which he repeated several times in his writings, 'I dress it. God cures it.'[21] Paré developed the precise application of a ligature to arrest a haemorrhage, instead of red-hot cautery. He designed a number of surgical instruments, and devised the method of turning a child in its mother's womb in case of mal-presentation.

Nostradamus' fellow student at Montpellier, Rabelais, played his part too. Indeed, the record of Rabelais' time at Montpellier is as well documented as it is illustrious. As earlier remarked, he had received some medical training from Jules-César Scaliger at Agen immediately prior to his arrival at Montpellier, and this seems to have enabled him drastically to reduce the normal two-year interval between his enrolment and his qualification as a Bachelor of Medicine. Thus the Montpellier Medical School record is clear that on November 1, 1530, a mere six weeks after his original admission, he had conferred upon him the Degree of Bachelor of Medicine, his examination having apparently been presided over by the Jean Schyron who had been Scaliger's former pupil.[22] The very next year Rabelais is documented from his own writings as lecturing 'before a good-sized audience'[23] on the original Greek texts for the medical authors Hippocrates and Galen, in which he had found many mistakes in the Latin translations then being used at Montpellier and other medical schools.

Tempting though it is to envisage Nostradamus among Rabelais' audience in one of the Montpellier lecture halls in 1531, the plain fact is that the record of Nostradamus immatriculating or enrolling at Montpellier on October 23, 1529, also constitutes the last record that we have for him at that medical school. While the association of individuals such as Rabelais with Montpellier is well documented, also that of many of the other medical school *illustrissimi* mentioned earlier in this chapter, over Nostradamus and Montpellier there hangs a mysterious pall of silence. As the Canadian scholar the late Professor Pierre Brind'Amour has pointed out,[24] there are plenty of other individuals, including very illustrious ones, for whom there are major gaps in their documentation. Even so, such an extensive pall of silence cannot be dismissed lightly.

NOTES

1 '*Il fut envoyé en Avignon pour apprendre les lettres humaines. De là il vaqua fort heureuseme[n]t à la Philosophie, & theorie de medecine dans l'université de Montpellier jusques à ce qu'a l'occasion d'une pestilence qui survint au pays, prist sa route devers Narbonne, Tholouse, Bourdeaux; ausquelles villes & citez donnant ses premiers coups d'essay, tira premierement fruict de ses labeurs, & lors il menoit lá 22. de son eage. Ayat sejourné quatre ans en ces quartiers pratiquant la Medecine, il luy sembla bon retourner à Montpellier, pour se recuire & passer au Doctorat ce qu'il fist en peu de temps, nó sans prevue, loüange & admiration de tout le College.*' Jean-Aimé Chavigny, *Brief Discours sur la Vie de M. Michel de Nostre Dame*, reprint, Les 7 Fontaines, Verna, Eric Visier, 1995

2 His only other potentially relevant remark is to be found in a letter of 1561, in which he described himself as having been studying medicine and astrology throughout the last forty years. See Jean Dupèbe, *Nostradamus Lettres Inédites...*, op. cit., Letter XXX, p.96

3 '*Apres avoir consumé la plus grande part de mes jeunes ans... en la pharmaceutrie & la cognoissance & perscrutation des simples; par plusieurs terres et pays depuis l'an 1521 jusques en l'an 1529, incessament courant, pour entendre et scavoir la source & origine des plantes et autres simples concernans la*

27

fin de la faculté iatrice'. Nostradamus, *Traité de fardemens et confitures...*, op. cit., quoted in Leroy, p.57

4 Michelet is a diminutive of Michel, roughly equivalent to 'Micky'. It seems to have been characteristic among the Provençals of Nostradamus' time to render their name, even on official documents, by such diminutives

5 *'Quem vides hic – audi Lector – obliteratum fuit apotecarius sive pharmacop* [written incorrectly in Greek as 'pharcapop'] *et probavimus per Chante, apotecarium Urbis huius per scolasticos qui illum male dicentem de doctoribus audiverunt, quare decreto per statutum mihi in [iusis]sent ut illum dellerem de libro scolasticorum. Guillelmus Rondelletus procurator.'* Quoted in Pierre Brind'Amour, *Nostradamus Astrophile*, Ottawa, University of Ottawa, 1993, p.114, after Marcel Gouron, 'Documents inédits sur Université de médicine de Montpellier (1495–1559), in *Montpellier Médical*, 99th year, 3rd series, t.L no 3, November 1956, p.375

6 *'Ego ~~Pet~~ Michaletus de nostra domina, natione provintie vile sancti Remigii, Avinion. Dyocess, veni in han[c] universitatem montis pessulany studere dy [i.e. dei] gratia in actu et promito me observat[urum] jura et statuta et priviligia edita et edenda; sorluy[?] jura ejusdem et eligo un[u]m patrum ut pote dominum Antonium Romerium, dye XXIII mensis octobris 1529, millesimo quingentesimo visesimo nono die, ut supra 1529.'* The text of the full original register, which is conserved in the archives of the Faculty of Montpellier University, has been published in Marcel Gouron (ed.), *Matricule de l'Université de Médicine de Montpellier, 1503–1599*, Geneva, Librairie Droz, 1957. Nostradamus' registration appears as entry 943, on p.58

7 Preface to the *Traité de fardemens et confitures* quoted in Brind'Amour, *Nostradamus Astrophile...*, op. cit., p.113

8 Such was Italian veneration for him that in 1485 his remains were taken back to Venice for a suitably elaborate reburial there

9 Jean Plattard, *Life of François Rabelais*, trans. Louis P. Roche, London, Frank Cass & Co., 1968, after A. Germain, *Les anciennes écoles de Montpellier*, Montpellier, 1881

10 For useful background, see articles by A. Germain collected in his *Les anciennes écoles*, op. cit.

11 Rabelais' registration appears as entry 964: Franciscus Rablesus, Chinonensis, dioc. Turonensis (Schyron), September 17...

12 There is some uncertainty whether Rabelais was born in 1483 or 1494

13 François Rabelais, *Pantagruel*, Bk 3, Ch. 34, trans. Donald M. Frame, *The Complete Works of François Rabelais*, Berkeley, University of California Press, 1991, p.3

14 Nostradamus, *Traité de fardemens et confitures...*, op. cit.

15 *'Montpellier cité fameuse est locupletée d'un nombre de sçavans personnaiges en la parfaite faculté de medecine, & en y à qui à toute perfection parachevent & la font: Aussique la y à de present personnaiges ou toute la doctrine de medecine es curieusement exercée: & d'entre eux sont plusieurs qui continuellement labourent, redigent par escrit pour perpetuer leur memoire à jamais: comme sont Antonius Saporta filius, que je ne say si l'ame de Hyppocrates seroit point transformée in luy: de Guillaume Rondelet, à qui Aelianus Massarius, ou Dioscorides le lentilleux luy auroient point laissée par une divine mutation de Euphorbi en luy: & Honorius Castellanus*

qui est encores au soleil levant: car il n'est permis à exerceant la faculté Iatrice de rien rediger par memoire quilz ne soient au soleil couchant.' Nostradamus, *Traité de ... confitures*, op. cit., facsimile reprint of edition of Christopher Plantin printed in Antwerp 1557, Ch. XXX, p.5

16 Pierre Brind'Amour, *Nostradamus Astrophile...*, op. cit., p.117, note 34

17 ibid., p.117, note 33, after Gouron, no.709, p.42

18 Geoffrey Chaucer, Prolouge to the *Canterbury Tales*

19 D.C. Allen, *The Star-Crossed Renaissance, the quarrel about astrology and its influence in England*, Durham, North Carolina, Duke University Press, 1941, p.51, after L.-F.A. Maury, *La Magie et L'Astrologie dans l'Antiquité et au Moyen Age ou Étude sur les Superstitions Païennes qu se sont perpétuées jusqu'à nos jours*, Paris, 1877

20 Quoted in John Leaney, 'Medicine in the Time of Shakespeare', *History Today*, March 1963, p.170

21 *'Je le pansait; Dieu le guérit'*

22 Jean Plattard, *The Life of François Rabelais...*, op. cit., p.92 after Marty-Laveaux, vol. III, p.308: *'Ego Franciscus Rabelaesus diocesis Turonensis, promotus fui ad gradum baccalaureatus, die prima mensis novembris, anno domini millesimo quingentesimo trigesimo, sub reverendo artium et Medicinae professore magistro Joanne Scurronio, Rabelaesus.'*

23 Donald M. Frame (trans.), *Complete Works of François Rabelais, ...*, op. cit., p.743

24 Pierre Brind'Amour, *Nostradamus Astrophile...*, op. cit., p.114–15

CHAPTER 3

'A Complete Atheist'

According to his later secretary Jean-Aimé de Chavigny, the culmination of Nostradamus' studies at the Montpellier Medical School was that he 'retook and passed his Doctorate, which he achieved in a short time, not without the approval, praise and admiration of all the College.'[1] Most writers on Nostradamus have happily taken this statement at face value. As if all were well-documented fact they have described him as first going through the various oral 'disputations with professors' by which he could gain his *baccalaureat* or Bachelor's degree, his licence to begin practice as a novitiate physician. According to the 1940s author James Laver[2] Nostradamus then underwent 'a whole new series of examinations' culminating in a colourful ceremony in the church of St Firmin at which the medical faculty, dressed in their finest robes, conferred on him his doctorate proper, thereafter fully qualifying him to practise medicine among the general populace.

It is perfectly possible that this is what happened. A problematic fact to be overcome, however, is that the process of getting a medical licence from Montpellier, the *crème-de-la-crème* of its field, normally took a full nine years.[3] Furthermore, while the Montpellier Medical School's records are mostly well preserved (certainly for this period), they are curiously blank on the subject of Nostradamus after his enrolment in 1529. There is also a lack of any other independent contemporary testimony. While the medical registers' silence cannot be taken as proof that Nostradamus did not gain his degree from Montpellier – for, as historians acknowledge, the records cannot be regarded as comprehensive[4] – the contrast with Rabelais is a telling one. Thus the Montpellier Medical School Register, which we have already noted as recording Rabelais' 1530 *baccalaureat*, also shows him paying his fees for the degree of Licentiate in Medicine on April 3, 1537. Following this we know that his Degree Ceremony proper was held on May 22 of the same year, the register of the Faculty of Medicine duly carrying the appropriate entry in Latin:

I, François Rabelais, of the diocese of Tours, have taken my degree as doctor [*suscepi gradum doctoratus*], under Dean Antoine Griffe in the illustrious Faculty of Medicine, May 22 of the year of our Lord 1537.[5]

As was the prescribed custom on full graduation, Rabelais would then have been presented with his doctor's insignia of 'a gold ring, a gilt belt, a copy of Hippocrates and a black cloth cap surmounted by a scarlet silk tassel'.[6]

In the case of Nostradamus, however, while he appears at some undetermined time post-1529 to have obtained from somewhere a licence to practise medicine, there is absolutely nothing to show that this was at Montpellier. The only secure fact is that some time around 1533/4 at which period he should still have been working his way through the Montpellier medical curriculum, he turned up some 170 miles (280 km) distant at Agen, a town notable principally as a market for the local agricultural produce. As Chavigny related:

> Passing by Toulouse, he [Nostradamus] came to Agen, a town on the river Garonne.[7]

Agen is located not too far from Bordeaux in western France, and to reach it from St-Rémy in Nostradamus' time demanded several days' hard riding across the rugged Massif Central. It was hardly the sort of place for anyone to visit without some definite purpose in mind. On this point biographer Chavigny, in his very next words, sheds the crucial light:

> [Here] Jules-César Scaliger, an individual of well-known and exceptional learning, caused him [Nostradamus] to stay.[8]

Jules-César Scaliger of Agen, it may be recalled, was the very same medical *savant* under whom François Rabelais had studied medicine before his arrival at Montpellier. Rabelais' Montpellier tutor Jean Schyron had similarly been a pupil of Scaliger. Originally hailing from the tiny Alpine town of Riva in northern Italy (where his family name was Scaligeri, though he claimed to descend from the noble Della Scala family of Verona), Scaliger was nearly twenty years older than Nostradamus. After initially pursuing a military career, then turning to medicine because of poor health, he had first arrived at Agen in 1524 in the train of the town's new Italian bishop Antonio della Rovere. He must have quickly grown to love the place, for two years later, at the age of forty, he married a beautiful local sixteen-year-old,

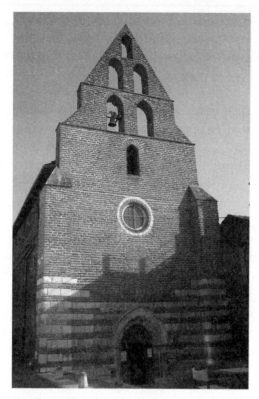

Church at the market town of Agen in S.W. France, to which Nostradamus moved in the aftermath of his studies at Montpellier.

Audiette de Roques-Lobéjac, who proceeded to bear him no less than ten daughters and five sons. The couple set up house in the rue saint-Georges, near the church of St-Hilaire, in which vicinity there is today a commemorative Boulevard Scaliger. The family home became his medical school. And whether as fully fledged or as still a would-be doctor, it is to this establishment that we may envisage the thirty-year-old Nostradamus arriving, no doubt rather hot and dusty after the long ride, no later than 1533/4.[9]

It may be useful at this point to remind ourselves what was happening on the world stage around this time. A string of years with cold, dry summers had been responsible for repeated failures of European grain harvests – which must have meant some bad times for Jaume de Nostredame in St-Rémy – prompting famines and severe economic hardship. Religious argument and discord were rife. For some years the highly respected Dutch scholar Desiderius Erasmus, having two decades earlier made a definitive translation of the New Testament from its original Greek into Latin, had been very politely showing that the Roman Catholic Church's 'official' Latin texts of the Bible had

Jules-Cesar Scaliger, the medical teacher much admired by Nostradamus. From a contemporary woodcut.

some serious flaws. The year 1531 had seen the publication of the so-called Confession of Augsburg, the burgeoning Lutheran Protestantism's equivalent of America's Declaration of Independence. In 1532 England's King Henry VIII redoubled his determination to divorce his wife Katherine of Aragon, thereby making his split from the Roman Catholic Church inevitable. In the Mediterranean, Suleiman the Magnificent's Ottoman Turks, having only narrowly been beaten back from Vienna in 1529, repeatedly raided ports all along southern Europe's coastlines as far west as Nice, continuing relentlessly year after year.

Against the backdrop of such traumas a definite 'end of the world is nigh' mood flourished in Europe, heightened by the fact that according to some contemporary calculations Easter 1533 marked the exact 1500th anniversary of Jesus' crucifixion. The German painter Hans Holbein's masterpiece *The Ambassadors*, notable for its enigmatically distorted skull, was painted in this very year, and has recently been shown to be shot through with so many numerological pointers to the world's ending at exactly 4 pm on Good Friday, April 11, 1533, that there can be no doubt that many believed this to be a serious possibility.[10] Despite this 'doom' date passing without incident, it is notable that the commissioning and preparation of Michelangelo's *Last Judgement* began the very next year.

In all this, why Nostradamus should have gone so far out of his way to seek Jules-César Scaliger, and why at this particular point in time, is by no means easy to determine. That he held Scaliger in high regard there can be no doubt. Later in life he would speak of him as a 'wise and learned man'[11] and (most intriguingly) as one 'to whom I remain more indebted than to anybody else in the world'.[12] Yet Rabelais, it will be recalled, had studied under Scaliger before going on to Montpellier. Some comments that he made in 1532 make it unlikely that he would have gone out of his way to recommend Scaliger's medical tuition to his fellow-student Nostradamus, even assuming that the two were on more than nodding acquaintance while they were at Montpellier.

For in 1531 Scaliger had written a virulent pamphlet attacking the famous New Testament scholar Erasmus for some criticisms that he had made of Italians with an over-purist attitude towards the Latin language. As a result of this Rabelais in November 1532 wrote a letter to Erasmus from Lyons (where he was then in practice as a junior doctor), drawing his attention to the attack, and sympathetically imparting his own 'insider's' information on Scaliger:

Scaliger…was originally from Verona: he belongs to the exiled family of Scaliger, and he too is an exile. But for the time, he is

*practising medicine around Agen. I know him well, and by Zeus,
that calumniator does not have a good reputation. To put it briefly,
he has some knowledge of medicine, but in other respects he's a
complete atheist without his like anywhere.* [Italics mine][13]

Clearly conscious of the libellous nature of the remarks that have here
been italicised, Rabelais took the precaution of switching the language
in which he was writing these from Latin to Greek, no doubt in order
to limit the danger of his letter being read by unauthorised eyes. It is
important for us to be aware that for the sixteenth century the term
'atheism' did not have quite the same meaning as it does for our own
scientific age. At that time, it would have meant some kind of hostility
towards the established Catholic religion, rather than necessarily an
outright denial of any supernatural deity's existence.

In fact at this time doctors in general tended to be regarded as atheists. This was because they studied anatomy, which was forbidden by
the Church. Likewise they practised dissections also forbidden. And
similarly severely frowned upon was their reliance on medical texts
written by Islamic Arabs.[14] The Middle Ages had a proverb: *ubi tres
medici, duo athei* – wherever you get three doctors, two will be atheists.

It so happens that there is some hard documentary evidence that the
doctors Scaliger, Nostradamus and a further physician local to the Agen
area, Philibert Sarrazin, all came into serious conflict with the might of
the established Catholic Church at Agen at precisely this point in time.
As part of a suppression of the perceived growth in anti-Catholic sentiment which the rise of Protestantism was provoking, in January 1538
King François I of France dispatched from Toulouse to Agen one Louis
de Rochet, Grand Inquisitor for the Languedoc and Guyenne regions.
When Rochet arrived at the end of February he swiftly delivered a forceful sermon at the church of St-Phébade in the course of which he urged
all faithful Christians to denounce any of their friends and neighbours
who might have been expressing opinions hostile towards the Catholic
Church. A number of informants duly came forward, and when their
evidence was heard between March 6 and April 30, three of those
accused turned out to be Scaliger, Sarrazin and Nostradamus.

Scaliger cleverly wriggled out of whatever charges had been brought
against him by getting his case transferred to the jurisdiction of Briand
Vallée, President of the Court at Saintes, a large town to the north
of Agen. Vallée, clearly already well known to Scaliger, helpfully
dropped the case, arguably because he was of much the same
independent persuasion.

Sarrazin, who was regent at Agen's schools from 1535 to 1538 and
would later be described by Nostradamus as 'a notable personage of

incomparable knowledge',[15] was apparently accused of sympathies towards Lutheranism sufficiently serious for a warrant to be issued for his arrest. He therefore took the only prudent course and fled the town before the arresting party arrived. As he turned up in Geneva in 1551 to become physician to the French Protestant leader Jean Calvin,[16] there can be no doubt that he was an individual strongly inclined to some form of Protestantism. It must be borne in mind that Calvinism and Lutheranism were not entirely the same brand of this, however.

As for Nostradamus, the charges against him show that in 1538 he was living and working as a doctor at Port-Sainte-Marie, a small village on the Garonne twelve miles (20 km) to the west of Agen. This village still has some quaint houses dating from the time. Nostradamus' accusers were three Franciscan friars from Agen, who testified that around 1533 or 1534, when he had apparently been living in Agen, he had made some ill-considered criticisms of the Roman Catholic Church's cult of saints. (This is incidentally our sole, and thereby highly important, historical confirmation that Nostradamus had arrived at Agen no later than this time.)

In particular, observing the making of a bronze statue of the Virgin Mary, Nostradamus had reportedly remarked that this was little short of idolatry.[17] In actuality the comment was not at all heretical, given the biblical second commandment of Moses: You shall not make yourself a carved image or any likeness of anything in heaven above or on earth beneath' (Exodus 20: 4), an injunction that the Church in general has chosen sometimes to take seriously, at other times to ignore. Agen's Franciscan friars, however, were apparently not prepared to see Nostradamus' remarks in any such favourable light.

So exactly what type of 'atheism' was it that Scaliger, Sarrazin and Nostradamus might have fomented together during the 1530s? Nostradamus himself may well have provided us with the clue. By way of explanation of the adulatory 'wise and learned man' comments that he made in the 1555 edition of his Treatise of Cosmetics and Jams he pointedly added that Scaliger was 'a second Marsilio Ficino in Platonic philosophy'.[18] This might not seem particularly contentious to us. However, it is notable that in the further edition of this same Treatise, which was published only two years later, Nostradamus went to the trouble of completely rewriting this passage, now dropping any such association of Scaliger with Ficino, and substituting instead a remark that Scaliger's soul was:

...for all I know...that father of eloquence, Cicero; in his perfect and supreme poetry a second Maro,[19] in his medical teaching worth any two of Galen.[20]

So who was Marsilio Ficino, since although Nostradamus believed Scaliger to be an individual in much the same mould, he seemingly felt such an allusion rather too 'sensitive' to be retained? A protegé of the great fifteenth-century Florentine patron Duke Cosimo de'Medici (1389–1464), in 1462 Ficino had been hard at work translating into Latin some Greek texts of Plato when the now elderly Cosimo urged him to put this to one side and to work instead on another manuscript that he specially wanted to see translated, the *Corpus Hermeticum*. Modern scholarship's assessment of this work is that it is a piece of esoterica that had probably been composed around the second century of the Christian era. But in the late fifteenth and early sixteenth century it was regarded as a highly potent 'magical' text that had been handed down via Plato, Pythagoras and Moses from the ancient Egyptian god Thoth, the fount of all wisdom and healing, known by the ancient Greeks as Hermes Trismegistus. Reputedly the *Corpus* embodied some hugely ancient 'Cabbalah', or arcane Jewish wisdom deriving from the tree of all knowledge that had been enjoyed by Adam and Eve before the Fall.

As Ficino's translation duly revealed, the *Corpus Hermeticum* text is undeniably one of appeal for anyone with a taste for the so-called paranormal and the occult. It opens with Thoth/Hermes, in a state of spiritual uplift, experiencing a vision of an enormous Being 'completely unbounded in size'.[21] Introducing himself as 'Mind of Sovereignty' (or in modern parlance 'Supermind'), this Being promises knowledge of all 'the things that are', together with an understanding of their nature. He then becomes transformed into 'an endless vision in which everything became light', from which there proceeds 'an inarticulate cry like the voice of fire'. The Being then imparts the promised revelation of the 'secret of the Universe' to Hermes:

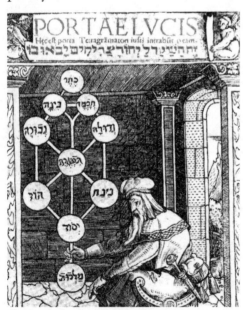

Scholar pondering the Cabbalah. From a 1516 edition of a thirteenth century cabbalistic work.

I am the light you saw, Mind, your God who existed before the watery nature that appeared out of the darkness. That in you which sees and hears is the word of the Lord. But your mind is God the Father. They are not divided from one another.[22]

To any conventional sixteenth-century Roman Catholic thinking, here was some dangerously 'atheistic' theology, and it surfaced in translation at a time when religious toleration had about as much appeal as the idea of wild-life conservation would have had amongst the former British Empire's big-game hunters. Making matters worse, further on in the *Hermetica* are words that can only be regarded as the very essence of the state that Nostradamus later affected to be in when he wrote his verse prophecies:

> Consider this for yourself: command your soul to travel to India, and it will be there faster than your command. Command it to cross over to the ocean, and again it will quickly be there, not as having passed from place to place, but simply as being there...See what power you have, what quickness!...Make yourself grow to immeasurable immensity, outleap all body, *outstrip all time, become eternity* and you will understand God...[23]

Ficino's Latin translation of the *Hermetica* was first published in 1471, and almost inevitably it and some of Ficino's related activities led to him being charged with practising magic, charges which he succeeded in brushing aside, though not without difficulty. Such was the interest his *Hermetica* work aroused, however, that by the mid-sixteenth century the translation had gone through two dozen editions and had also been translated into several vernacular languages.

Other writers carried on the interest in this mystic, Cabbalistic lore, thereby further fuelling the controversy. Notable amongst these was the German scholar-magician Cornelius Agrippa (1486–1535), mentioned already as the astrologer-physician to King François I's mother. In 1531, after a delay of twenty years, Agrippa released his masterwork *Of the Occult Philosophy*,[24] which he had written when he was just twenty-four. This publication would therefore probably have reached Agen at around the same time that Scaliger and Nostradamus were first getting to know each other. Much like the original author of the *Hermetica*, Agrippa claimed magic to be the route to understanding God and nature, and he affected to explain everything in the world in terms of Cabbalistic and numerological analyses of Hebrew letters. Predictably, the religious establishment of the time imprisoned him and branded him a heretic.

That Jules-César Scaliger's household had a copy of Ficino's translation of the *Hermetica* when Nostradamus came to be associated with it in the 1530s and was also aware of Cornelius Agrippa and others, there can be very little doubt. Quite aside from Nostradamus' own allusion to Ficino in association with Scaliger, none other than Scaliger's son Joseph Justus Scaliger would go on to help produce a new, improved version of the same *Hermetica* in 1574.[25] Arguably therefore it was Scaliger who introduced Nostradamus to this whole area of magical knowledge, which readily explains Nostradamus' later grateful description of him as the individual 'to whom I remain more indebted than to anybody else in the world'.

The Inquisition record of 1538 which described Nostradamus as living at Port-Sainte-Marie notably also referred to him as practising medicine in that town, and this is therefore history's first known reference to the fact. We may infer that wherever and however he qualified as a doctor, whether this was at Montpellier, or somehow via Scaliger's teaching school, by 1538 he was definitely in practice. Given the still unresolved fact of his omission from the Montpellier record, however, there hangs a serious question over the exact worth of that qualification, even by the prevailing standards, let alone those of our own time.

In this context it is notable that Rabelais, on June 3, 1532, at which time he was technically still only a Bachelor of Medicine practising at Lyons, had these depressing comments to say of the medical scene:

> ...in almost all classes of society people have begun to realise that if you examine closely those who are physicians or who pass as such, you will find them void of knowledge, honesty and good counsel, but full of arrogance, envy and squalor. They perform their experiments...by killing people, and are a good deal more dangerous than the maladies themselves. Now at last those in high places are beginning to give much heed to those who follow the purified ancient ways of medicine.[26]

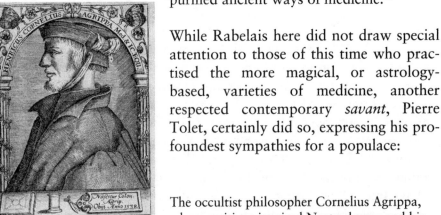

While Rabelais here did not draw special attention to those of this time who practised the more magical, or astrology-based, varieties of medicine, another respected contemporary *savant*, Pierre Tolet, certainly did so, expressing his profoundest sympathies for a populace:

The occultist philosopher Cornelius Agrippa, whose writings inspired Nostradamus and his circle. From a contemporary engraving.

...deceived by a horde of charlatans (*laterniers*) who come to France from several foreign countries, some of them professing the art of magic, others dressed in white, green, gray or red.[27]

Furthermore, as we have already learnt, Rabelais, one of France's wittiest writers ever, and Nostradamus, one of the world's all-time greatest forecasters of the future by the stars, both happen to have been students together at the same medical school at exactly the same 1530–1 period. It seems surely therefore rather more than coincidence that within two years of this association – and specifically during the 'end of the world' year of 1533 – Rabelais released his *Pantagrueline Prognostication*, a hilarious send-up of the very kind of astrological almanacs by which Nostradamus would later make himself so famous.

Mimicking the contemporary hyperbole of introductions for such works, Rabelais vaunted this publication as:

> *Certain, Veritable and Infallible*
> *For the Perpetual Year*
> *Newly Composed for the Profit and Edification*
> *Of natural-born Dimwits*
> *By Master Alcofibras.*

Here it does not need too much deduction to recognise 'Alcofibras' as an anagram of Fr[an]ço[is] Rabalais,[28] such anagrams, as we will discover later, being a favourite device of Nostradamus for adding mystification to his prophetic utterances.

Still emulating exactly the same style that we will find Nostradamus using right up to his death, we find Rabelais then proceeding tongue-in-cheek to pronounce his most solemn predictions for the coming year:

Of this year's Eclipses:
This year there will be so many eclipses of that sun and moon that I fear, not wrongly, that therefore our purses will suffer inanition...And a lot of other planets will not go as you command.

Wherefore this year crabs will go sideways, ropemakers backward, footstools will climb up on benches, spits upon andirons and caps upon hats. Many men's ballocks will hang down for want of game-pouches. Fleas will for the most part be black. Bacon will shun peas in Lent. The belly will lead the way...

Of this year's Maladies

This year the blind will not see much. The deaf will hear rather poorly. Mutes will not talk much. The rich will be a little better off than the poor and the healthy will stay better than the sick. Many sheep, oxen, hogs, goslings, chickens and ducks will die… Old age will be incurable this year because of the past years… People who have diarrhoea will often go to the close-stool… And there will reign over almost all the universe a most horrible and dreadful malady, malign, perverse, frightening and unpleasant, which will leave everyone stunned, and many at their wits' end… I tremble with fear when I think of it, for I tell you, it will be epidemic… *lack of money.*[29]

For anyone wedded to the business of star-gazing, Rabelais' *Prognostication* was a very cruel parody indeed. And it shows just how closely Rabelais had his finger on the pulse of the astrological almanac business, as if he had observed a strong interest in it from someone who had been close at hand to him.

Conceivably that person observed was none other than Nostradamus. If it was, however, for the moment he had other matters on his mind. Not least, it would seem, he was looking at the prospect of a marriage as happy as that which he, for his part, had observed in the Scaliger household.

NOTES

1 '…*se recuire & passer au Doctorat qu'il fist en peu de temps, nó sans prevue, loüange & admiration de tout le College*', Chavigny, *Brief Discours sur la Vie*…, op. cit.

2 James Laver, *Nostradamus, or the Future Foretold*, 1973 edition, Maidstone, George Mann, p.28

3 See Hastings Rashdall, *The Universities of Europe in the Middle Ages*, ed. F.M. Powicke & A.B. Emden 3 vols., Oxford 1936, vol. III, p.156

4 Pierre Brind'Amour remarks on p.115 of his *Nostradamus Astrophile*…, op. cit.: 'Les exemples ne manquent pas de médecins dont nous savons qu'ils furent diplômés de Montpellier et dont les noms ne paraissent pas dans ces registres.' [Examples are not lacking of doctors whom we know to have been graduates of Montpellier and whose names do not appear in its registers.]

5 After French translation in Leroy, *Nostradamus, Ses Origines*…, op. cit., p.59

6 Jean Plattard, *The Life of François Rabelais*…, op. cit., p.185

7 '*Passant à Tholouse, vint à Agen, ville sur la riviere de Garone*', Chavigny, *Brief Discours*…, op. cit.

8 '…*Jule Cesar Scaliger l'arresta, personage de signalée et rare eruditió*', ibid.

9 These dates are determined solely from evidence given in the legal charges brought against Nostradamus, as described later in this chapter. See note 17.

10 John North, *The Ambassadors' Secret*, London, Hambledon, 2002. Holbein's painting *The Ambassadors*, one of the London National Gallery's most prized masterpieces, has long been famous for its distorted image of a skull. North,

emeritus professor in medieval philosophy and science at the University of Groningen in the Netherlands, has shown that the angle at which this skull has to be viewed in order for it to appear undistorted is 27 degrees. A line drawn at this angle leads to the eyes of Jesus in a partly hidden crucifix in the painting's top left corner. At 4 pm on Good Friday, April 11, 1533 the sun would have been at 27 degrees over London. A cylinder dial, a sundial on the shelf behind the ambassadors, indicates the same date and time.

11 'homme savant et docte', Nostradamus, Traité de fardemens et confitures..., op. cit., 1555 edition, quoted in Leroy, Nostradamus, Ses origines..., op. cit., p.60

12 'de qui je me tiens plus redevable, que de personnaiges de ce monde', Nostradamus, Traité de fardemens et confitures..., op. cit., 1557 edition, quoted in Peter Lemesurier, The Essential Nostradamus..., op. cit., p.29

13 Quoted in translation in Donald M. Frame, Complete Works of François Rabelais..., op. cit., p.746. On the outside the letter was addressed to one Bernard Salignac, Salignac apparently being the third party who would direct it to the intended recipient. By common scholarly consent the intended recipient was Erasmus

14 See Muriel Bowden, A Commentary on the General Prologue to the Canterbury Tales, New York, Macmillan, 1948, p.208

15 Traité des fardemens et confitures..., op. cit., Confitures, ch.XXX

16 Pierre Brind'Amour, Nostradamus Astrophile..., op. cit., p.117, n.35

17 'Enquête sur les commencements du protestantisme en Agenais' with note by M.O. Fallières & Canon Durengues, Recueil des travaux de la Société d'agriculture, sciences et arts d'Agen, 2nd series, t.XVI, Agen 1913

18 'Julius Squaliger homme scavant & docte, un second Marcile Ficin en Philosophic Platonique', Nostradamus, Traité des fardemens et confitures..., op. cit., 1555

19 Here Nostradamus meant the Roman poet Virgil (70–19 BC). Virgil's full name was Publius Vergilius Maro, Maro being his family name

20 'que je ne sçay si son ame seroit point le pere de l'eloquence Cicero, en la parfaite & supreme poësie un second Maro, en la doctrine de medicine deux Galiens...', Nostradamus, Traité des fardemens et confitures..., op. cit., 1557 edition

21 Brian P. Copenhaver (trans.), Hermetica: The Greek Corpus Hermeticum and the Latin Asclepius in a new English translation, Cambridge, Cambridge University Press, 1992, p.1

22 ibid.

23 ibid., p.41

24 Cornelius Agrippa, De occulta philosophia..., 1531

25 Joseph Justus Scaliger was one of the editors of an edition of the Hermetica published this year

26 Donald M. Frame (trans.), The Complete Works of François Rabelais..., op. cit., p.742

27 Pierre Tolet, Chirurgie de Paulus Aegineta Lyons, Dolet, 1540, quoted in Jean Plattard, The Life of François Rabelais..., op. cit., p.108

28 In sixteenth-century France, as in England, the spelling of names was not standardised

29 Donald M. Frame (trans.), The Complete Works of François Rabelais..., op. cit., pp.749–50

CHAPTER 4

Plagued Interlude

As we have seen, Jules-César Scaliger married soon after moving to Agen, showing every sign of domestic happiness. Nostradamus would appear to have done the same not long after his arrival in the town, though in his case the happiness was rather more short-lived. According to secretary Chavigny's succinct, but mostly helpful, biography:

> There [i.e. at Agen] he took as wife a most reputable young woman, by whom he had two children, a boy and a girl. They died, and finding himself alone and without companionship, he decided to return to Provence, his country of origin.[1]

One of the hard facts to be faced about Nostradamus is that this bald, unsubstantiated statement represents virtually the sum total of our knowledge of his first marriage and its offspring. In all his own surviving writings, including the Bibliothèque Nationale's Latin manuscript of some of his correspondence, he makes not the slightest mention of even having had a first wife and children, nor anything of this tragedy, let alone giving any explanation of how it may have happened. Two French novelists have somewhat unfairly imagined him having 'assassinated' his young family, alleging some dark history of adultery.[2] The kinder and more commonly favoured scenario, passed from one Nostradamian writer to another, though with no reliable contemporary evidence to back it up, is that after beginning work as a fully fledged physician he was called away from Agen to deal with an outbreak of plague at another town. When he returned, he found his wife and children fatally stricken with this same disease. The British Nostradamian author James Laver and others have added a further cruel twist, that in the wake of the bereavement 'the family of his late wife started a lawsuit against him for the recovery of her dowry'.[3] If only the papers for such a lawsuit existed, we might at least know the name of the Agen family into which Nostradamus married. However, as acknowledged even by Laver, 'her [Nostradamus' first wife's] name is not mentioned', and although there has been a recent suggestion that she was one Henriette d'Encausse, this has yet to be properly substantiated.

Similar uncertainty shrouds the exact reason for Nostradamus' leaving Agen. Secretary Chavigny, as we have seen, suggested that this was due to his loneliness following his bereavement, minding him to return to his Provençal roots, though there is no evidence of his making such a return at this stage of his life. Chavigny also mentioned some kind of fierce quarrel breaking out between Nostradamus and Scaliger 'as often happens between doctors'.[4] The puzzle here is that Nostradamus continued to be highly laudatory about Scaliger – the man 'to whom I am more indebted than to anybody else in the world' – long after this quarrel is supposed to have divided the pair. There is also Laver's completely unsubstantiated claim that the first wife's family started a lawsuit. It is important not to forget, either, the Inquisition proceedings of 1538. The outcome of these in Nostradamus case is by no means certain, there being a strong suggestion that, like Sarrazin, he decided to leave town rather than to face whatever justice Inquisitor de Rochet might be expected to mete out to him.

The one certainty, with King François I's government continuing a harsh crackdown on Protestant sympathisers and others challenging the official Roman Catholic status quo, is that very soon after the 1538 Inquisition hearings Nostradamus took to the road again, now apparently fully able to practise medicine. And adding a certain credence to the suggestion that his first wife and children had died of plague is the fact that – with admirable courage – he seems to have made the prevention and treatment of plague his medical speciality.

Chavigny, in his biographical *Brief Discourse*, represented Nostradamus as having practised medicine along the route 'Narbonne, Toulouse, Bordeaux'[5] *before* (theoretically) becoming fully qualified in medicine at Montpellier. With characteristic vagueness Nostradamus himself, in his 1555 *Treatise of cosmetics and jams*, spoke of having '*once* [*autrefois*] practised in the cities of Bordeaux, Toulouse, Narbonne and Carcassonne',[6] adroitly avoiding a clear indication of when that 'once' was. Given the fact that all these cities are located either along, or (in the case of Bordeaux) some way beyond, a logical route for travelling between St-Rémy and Agen there has to be a good case for Nostradamus' more significant time in these cities coming *after* his departure from Agen, that is, during the six-year period between 1538 and 1544 when his movements are otherwise unaccounted for.

And certainly, in the case of Bordeaux, for instance, Nostradamus would later specifically mention in his *Treatise on cosmetics and jams* that he had visited this city in 1539. Indicative of his continued strong leaning towards the 'pills and potions' branch of medicine, he described how while he was there he had called upon an apothecary called Léonard Bandon.[7] A local peasant had brought Bandon some specimens of ambergris,[8] an intestinal product of the sperm whale which had undoubtedly been washed up on one of the Bordeaux region's Atlantic coast beaches. This develops a pleasant odour after exposure to the air, and is used to fix fine perfumes; it provided Nostradamus with a relished opportunity to expound on how it originated.

A number of non-contemporary, semi-legendary anecdotes about Nostradamus suggest that he also wandered far to northern regions of France at about this time. One story associates him with Fains, near Bar-le-Duc in north-eastern France,[9] another with Brittany, a third with Belgium. For one reason or another these stories are mostly highly suspect, and not worth recounting.

It is from 1543 on, not long after Nostradamus' fortieth birthday, that the biographical trail warms up. In *Treatise on cosmetics and jams* Nostradamus spoke of having, at Vienne, just south of Lyons, resumed acquaintance with an individual who is known to have been a contemporary of his at the Montpellier Medical School, François Valériolle. In recounting this, Nostradamus went out of his way to praise Valériolle for his 'singular humanity, his prompt knowledge and tenacious memory'.[10] The Medical School records show that Valériolle received his medical licence from Montpellier in 1531, two years after Nostradamus' enrolment there. Valériolle is known then to have taken up practice in Vienne where he remained until 1544. Then, on being asked to help deal with a plague outbreak at Arles, he ended

Typical scene of an outbreak of plague in the 16th century. At the centre a physician checks a patients urine. From a contemporary woodcut.

up staying permanently there. So the meeting with him in Vienne is unlikely to have been after 1544.

It is precisely this same plague epidemic of the mid-1540s that gives us our first detailed historical glimpse of Nostradamus at work as a physician. In November 1544 a prolonged spell of exceptionally heavy rains caused the river Rhône to rise well above its normal levels. Besides causing widespread structural damage the heavily swollen waters even broke down part of Avignon's sturdy city walls. Cemeteries became flooded; corpses were washed out of their graves. Throughout the predominantly flat delta country south of Avignon the flooding was so severe that the only way to reach many of the scattered townships, including St-Rémy, was by boat.

Even when the water level dropped the serious disruption to housing and sanitation, combined with an inadequate understanding of the principles of hygiene, maximised the likelihood of a major epidemic, which indeed broke out in the region during the next two years. In 1544 Nostradamus seems to have been at Marseilles, specifically studying the treatment of plague under the veteran physician Louis Serre, to whom he accorded the accolade of 'Hippocratic perspicacity and know-how'.[11] Serre was another Montpellier man, though of a much earlier generation, having first enrolled when Nostradamus was but a four-year-old.

Then in 1545 Nostradamus' brother Jéhan became a civic lawyer at Aix-en-Provence, just a few miles to the north of Marseilles. Whereupon, just as the consuls or civic leaders at Arles called upon Vienne's François Valériolle to help deal with their city's epidemic, so in 1546 Nostradamus – arguably at his brother Jéhan's instigation – was summoned to deal with the 'horrible, dangerous and unparalleled'[12] contagion that had broken out at Aix. As Nostradamus' son César subsequently described in his *History and Chronicle of Provence*:

All of a sudden the city [i.e. Aix] became uninhabited and [near] deserted. Those who were struck down by the fury of the disease straight away gave up all hope of cure...Houses were left abandoned and empty. Men were disfigured. Women were ravaged. Children were given up for lost. Old men were left aghast. Even the strongest were overcome...The palace was closed and locked up. The law courts were silent and deserted. Themis [goddess of law and order] became absent and mute, and porters and grave-diggers were the only people in business. Market stalls were shut down. Arts ceased. The churches were empty and their clergy in confusion.[13]

The sixteenth century's equivalent of AIDS in our time, plague was altogether worse in a number of respects, not least because of its repulsive symptoms, its contagiousness, and the breathtaking speed with which it could become lethal. Black, egg-sized swellings, or buboes (hence 'bubonic' plague), would appear in the armpits and groin, oozing blood and pus. Black blotches would follow all over the skin, accompanied by severe pain, and within five days the victim would usually be dead. A second variety of the disease, often running hand-in-glove with the first, presented as an intense feverish delirium with much coughing up of blood. Death from this form could be even swifter, in as little as twenty-four hours or less, and there were instances of doctors found dead alongside the patients whom they had been called to attend. In both varieties patients quickly lapsed into despairing of survival, with all their body fluids, whether blood, sweat, pus or urine, smelling absolutely foul.

As modern-day science now knows, the root cause of plague was a bacillus, *pasturella pestis*, which was transmitted to humans from the bites of fleas and rats, these creatures carrying it in the stomach and bloodstream respectively. The first form of the disease was spread from fleas that had just left the body of a host rat, thereupon transfer-ring their attention to a human. The second, pneumonic form occurred when the bacillus invaded the respiratory system. There were also rarer septicaemic and enteric varieties that with unerring fatality attacked the blood and digestive systems. Nostradamus, whose payment for attending the plague at Aix is recorded in the town's trea-surer's accounts for June 1546, has left a harrowing and convincingly clinical description of what he witnessed at first hand, confirming the genuine hands-on part that he played as a medical professional, and his humanitarian concern to do what he could to help the sufferers:

It [the plague] began at the end of May and it lasted altogether nine months. Irrespective of their ages people died even while eating and drinking. The cemeteries became so full of dead bodies that there was no more consecrated ground in which to bury them. The greater number became delirious on the second day. Those who suffered the delirium did not get the spots, but those afflicted with spots died quickly after.

All were found to be covered in black spots after dying. The epi-demic was so violent and so evil that no one could approach nearer than five paces from victims without becoming struck down them-selves. Many had carbuncles front and rear. These people lived no more than six days. Blood-letting and medicaments had no more effect than doing nothing at all. Each time that the city was inspected and the plague victims thrown out, yet more would be found the next day.

Death was so sudden that fathers took no heed of their children. Many, covered in plague spots, were tossed into pits. Others were thrown out of their windows. Yet others who had the affliction behind the shoulders and on the front of their chests suffered nose-bleeds which lasted night and day, until they died. In brief the desolation was so great that often even those with gold and silver to offer might die for lack of a glass of water.

Among the most moving sights that I witnessed I think must be counted one woman who called to me from her window. I saw that single-handedly she was sewing a shroud around herself. I could see that she had the *alarbres* (as we call the plague spots in our Provençal language). When I made up my mind to go into this woman's home, I found her dead, laid out in the middle of the house, with her shroud half-sewn...[14]

Nostradamus had, of course, no idea of what caused plague. Nor, as he candidly admitted, had he any clear notion how to cure it. But what he could and did offer to those who had not yet contracted the disease was something he claimed as a first-class preventative – a special rose-pill for which he supplied the recipe in his *Treatise on cosmetics and jams*:

Take some sawdust or shavings of cypress-wood, as green as you can find, one ounce; iris of Florence, six ounces; cloves, three ounces; sweet *calamus* [cane palm], three drams; aloes-wood six drams. Grind everything to powder and take care to keep it all air-tight. Next, take some furled red roses, three or four hundred, clean, fresh and culled before dewfall. Crush them to powder in a marble mortar, using a wooden pestle. Then add some half-unfurled roses to the above powder and pound the mixture vigor-ously all over again, while sprinkling on it a little rose juice. When all the above has been mixed together thoroughly, fashion it into little flat pastilles as you would pills and let them dry in the shade. They will smell good.[15]

Arguably harking back to the enthusiastic sales pitches that he had made during his days as an itinerant pedlar, Nostradamus spared no hyperbole in his claims for this preparation:

No other medicament is to be found which is more protective against the plague than this recipe. All those who swallowed it were protected.[16]

As is evident from Nostradamus' claims for other of his remedies, such hyperbole was typical. In his *Treatise* he published a remedy that he had prescribed for the bishop of Carcassonne which included the exotic ingredients '*aurum potabile*', that is, drinkable gold (seemingly powdered gold leaf), together with coral and lapis lazuli. Of this he boasted:

> This composition rejuvenates the person who uses it. If he is sad or melancholy it makes him light and joyful. If he is timid it makes him audacious. If he is taciturn it renders him affable by changing his qualities. If he is surly it makes him sweet and kindly, as if he were but thirty years old. If his beard is turning grey it retards old age by much, preserves the colour in spite of the years, rejoices the heart and the whole person... preserves from headaches and constipation, and augments the sperm in such abundance that a man can do whatever he wishes without damaging his health; and conserves the four humours in such symmetry and proportion that if a man had it from birth, he could live forever.[17]

Nostradamus was by no means alone in his enthusiasm for such exotic remedies. A whole breed of sixteenth-century physicians offered their wealthier clients concoctions with self-evidently rare and expensive ingredients in order to inflate their fee proportionately. The revered Greek medical authority Galen together with the Persian Avicenna (980–1036) had prescribed drinkable gold, together with 'unicorn horn', thought to have been ground-up rhinoceros horn, and bezoar, a poison antidote made from a concretion found in the stomachs of mountain goats. England's College of Physicians had in its official pharmacopoeia crabs' eyes, partridge feathers, buttered live spiders, ants' eggs, powdered human skull and Egyptian mummy. Not everyone of the time was impressed by such remedies. The French essayist Montaigne, who suffered from stones in the bladder, commented of the elaborate cocktail that his physician had prescribed for him; 'No rock could withstand so great a battery; yet I hear that the least atom of gravel will not stir for it.'[18] But those living in the sixteenth century had little alternative but to make the best of whatever was available to them from the qualified medical practitioners of their time.

Whatever wealth a patient might possess and however good his physicians might be, mortality comes to everyone. Across the Channel in England the beginning of the year 1547 saw the death, after a reign of thirty-eight years, of the fifty-five-year-old King Henry VIII, to be succeeded by his sickly ten-year-old son Edward VI. Two months later, after a reign of thirty-two years, France's fifty-three-year-old

King François I followed suit, to be succeeded by his eldest surviving son Henri.

And in the new Henri II's France one city that, thanks to the *Treatise on cosmetics and jams*, Nostradamus is definitely known to have at least passed through during 1547 is Lyons, on the mighty Rhône, some 160 miles (260 km) north of St-Rémy, and even then one of France's largest cities after Paris. Here Nostradamus would again seem to have sought out the company of the local pills and potions specialists, for he specifically remarked of one preparation: 'René the mortar pounder grew [it] at Lyons at the time I was there in 1547.'[19]

But Lyons was not the only town in which Nostradamus was to be found during 1547. His father Jaume had died around the beginning of the year, and as Nostradamus seems to have stayed closely in touch with his brothers, who remained locally based, he very probably hurried back to St Rémy for the funeral. Furthermore, there was another domestic consideration which either prompted or ensured his return to southern Provence. As secretary Chavigny later recorded...

> Coming to Salon de Crau, a town only a short distance from Aix and halfway between Avignon and Marseilles, he married for the second time.[20]

Salon de Crau is today the picturesque, plane-tree-shaded town of Salon-de-Provence, seventeen miles to the south-east of St-Rémy and centred on a district noted for its olive-growing. In Nostradamus' time, as now, it was dominated by the imposing Château de l'Emperi, one of the residences of the Bishop of Arles. At that time Salon was dubbed 'de Crau' because of the arid terrain in its vicinity, a desolate area known locally as the Crau. According to a number of authors, Nostradamus' reason for going to Salon was again to treat plague, which could well have been the case, though there is a lack of any firm contemporary corroboration.

Although secretary Chavigny, in his *Brief Discourse*, again omitted to name Nostradamus' new wife, in this instance independent contemporary documentation has not failed us. The bride whom he married in Salon was Anne Ponsarde, known as *Gemelle*, 'the Twin', presumably because she had been one of twins. She was the widow of one Jean Beaulme, as a result of which, together with her well-to-do birth, would have enabled her to bring a substantial dowry to the union. Local records show that the couple's wedding took place on November 11, 1547, with Anne's first cousin, the lawyer Étienne Hozier, as one of the officiants.[21] At that time Nostradamus was within a month of his forty-fourth birthday. Anne, however,

The town where Nostradamus settled down to married life. Present-day Salon-de-Provence, seen looking towards the Porte de l'Horloge.

must have been considerably younger, for although her birth-date is unknown, she would go on to bear him six healthy children over the next fourteen years.

But as yet the birth of even the first child lay four years into the future, for, temporarily at least, Nostradamus had not given up his old 'wandering Jew' habits. He went off to Italy, with Venice, Genoa and Savona all apparently on his itinerary, though whether he took his new bride with him is unrecorded. It was in Savona, around a year after his marriage, that he reported – again in *Treatise on cosmetics and jams* – meeting yet another colleague in the 'pills and potions' trade. This was Antonio Vigerchio, whom he acclaimed as worthy of a laureate in the pharmacy business.[22] Vigerchio's speciality, apparently, was the preparation of an excellent 'rose syrup laxative'[23] which had proved most efficacious for relieving constipation among the gentle-folk of Savona. According to Nostradamus' characteristically upbeat recommendation, this preparation was equally good for helping along pregnant women 'in their first and last months, at any age and at any time' without the slightest danger to their health.[24]

A picture accordingly emerges of Nostradamus wandering from town to town fraternising, not so much with doctors, but with 'spicers' and pharmacists with whom he was always ready to try out, or swap, some new recipe conducive to general well-being, or to alleviate some minor health irritation. He also made a point of seeking out some rich client. For another individual whom he appears to have charmed while he was at Savona was the aristocratic Signora Benedetta, sister of the Marquis of Finat. Especially for her, in the year 1549, he concocted a *confiture* or jam called 'Pignolat en roche'. His recipe for this, later duly published in his *Treatise on cosmetics and jams*, used pine-nuts, enjoyed in the Mediterranean since the Roman era. Nostradamus' recipe involved cooking these in Madeira sugar, then a rather more scarce and expensive ingredient than it is now.

Yet another Italian port of call was Milan. It was from this city that Nostradamus appears to have obtained the recipe for a 'Trivulzio soup' that a member of the city's wealthy and aristocratic Trivulzio family had offered to his guests in the fifteenth century as part of a 'sumptuous and pontifical' banquet. Marshal Trivulzio was a client for whom Leonardo da Vinci was asked to design an equestrian statue, only for this to prove one of the projects Leonardo never took further than the drawing board.

But alongside all these wanderings, and some undoubted indulgence in delights of the senses, Nostradamus had not forgotten his taste for the more esoteric. It would appear to have been around this period that he composed a work that he grandiosely entitled 'Horus Apollo, son of Osiris, king of the Nile's Egypt, from notes of two hieroglyphic books set in the form of rhythmic epigrams'.[25] Comprising 182 verse-epigrams, the original manuscript is today preserved in the Paris Bibliothèque Nationale as Manuscript no. 2594.

Exhibiting much the same tendency towards hyperbole that we noted earlier, Nostradamus self-confidently proclaimed this work as one of unbelievable and admirable learning and antiquity, translated by Michel Nostradamus of Saint-Rémy-en-Provence'.[26] Since the manuscript carries no date, the main clue to when it was composed is its mention of St-Rémy, which suggests that it was written some time before he had begun to settle down in Salon, therefore before 1547. If this is correct it probably represents the first instance of Nostradamus' literary usage of the Latinised *nom-de-plume* 'Nostradamus' in lieu of his normal surname 'de Nostredame'. It is important to note, however, that the authenticity of this particular manuscript cannot be considered beyond question. Faked manuscripts attributed to Nostradamus are not uncommon. There has been insufficient serious scholarly attention to Nostradamus for truly reliable assessments of such material to be made. And one puzzle is the manuscript's partial indebtedness to a Latin-Greek version by Jean Mercier which was not published until 1551, when Nostradamus was definitely established in Salon.

Whatever the answer, if *Orus* is genuinely the work of Nostradamus' pen, then via Mercier's Greek text he affected to have been able to interpret ancient Egyptian hieroglyphs. This claim, it should be pointed out, was much more than two centuries before the French scholar Jean-François Champollion, during the era of Napoleon, succeeded in a true decipherment with the crucial aid of the famous bilingual Rosetta stone (not discovered until 1799, and today in the British Museum). And whatever other prophetic or time-

Detail from the Orus Apollo manuscript,
which purports to be of Nostradamus'
authorship. Its authenticity is far from assured.

travelling powers Nostradamus might or might not have possessed, in the case of *Orus* neither did he succeed in convincing anyone of its worth at the time, nor has anyone subsequently been any more impressed. The *Orus* languished unpublished for centuries, at one time being acquired by Jean-Baptiste Colbert, finance minister to King Louis XIV, and has been resurrected by Nostradamian enthusiasts only in our own era. It continues to deserve oblivion.

But *Orus* – always assuming it is genuinely from his hand – was very far from the sum total of Nostradamus' literary ambitions. And in another genre altogether he was about to become a lot more successful.

NOTES

1 '*Là prist à femme une fort honorable Damoiselle, de laquelle il eut 2 enfans, masle & femelle. Lesquels decedez, se voyat seul & sans compagnie, delibera soy retirer du tout en Provence son naturel pays.* Chavigny, *Brief Discours...*, op. cit.

2 Jean-Charles Pichon, *Nostradamus et le Secret de Temps*; Geoffroy Cadres, *L'Etrange Docteur Nostradamus*

3 James Laver, *Nostradamus, or the Future Foretold...*, op. cit., p.30

4 '*apres en forte simulté & pique, ainsi qu'advient souvent entre les doctes'*. Chavigny, *Brief Discours ...*, op. cit.

5 '*prist la route devers Narbonne, Tholouse, Bourdeaux...'*. For full text see Chapter 2, note 1

6 '*J'ai autrefois pratiqué en la cité de Bordeaux, de Thoulouse, de Narbonne et de Carcassonne'*, Nostradamus, *Traité des fardemens et confitures*, op. cit., ch. XXX

7 '*en la cité de Bourdeaux...une foys al'an mil cinq cents trenteneuf estant en la boutique d'un apoticaire nommé Leonard Bandon...'*, Nostradamus, *Traité des fardemens et confitures...*, op. cit., fol. 31r

8 Nostradamus, *Traité des fardemens et confitures*, op. cit., ch. XXX

9 See James Laver, *Nostradamus, or the Future Foretold*, op. cit., pp.32–3

10 '*Pour sa singuliere humanité & pour son sçavoir prompte & de memoire tenaeissime me contrainct de le remorer*'

11 '*perspicacité & savoir Hippocratique*', Nostradamus, *Traité des fardemens et confitures...*, final chapter

12 *horrible, dangereuse & inouye* – César de Nostredame, *Histoire et Chronique de Provence...*, op. cit., p.772B

13 '*La cité en est tout-à-coup deshabitee & deserte. Les personnes attaintes de la fureur de ceste maladie chassent incontinent toute esperance de salut... les maisons sont abandonnees et vides, les hommes desfigurez, les femmes esplorees, les enfans esperdus, les vieillards estonnez, le plus forts vaincus & les animaux poursuivis: le Palais clos & fermé, la Justice en silence & desertion, Themis absente & muette & les portefaix & sandapilaires en credit: les boutiques fermees, les arts cessez, les temples solitaires & les Prestres tous confus*'. César de Nostredame, *L'Histoire et Chronique de Provence...*, op. cit., p.772B

14 '*[Elle] commença le dernier de may et dura neuf mois tout entiers, où mourait de peuple sans comparaison, de tout aages, en mangeant et buvant, tellement que les cimetières estoyent si pleins de corps morts que l'on ne sçavoit plus lieu sacré pour les enterrer. La plus grande part tomboyent en phrénésie au second jour: ceux auxquels la phrénésie venoit, les taches ne venoient point, et à ceux à qui les taches venoyent, mouroyent subitement. Après la mort, toute personne estoit couverte de taches noires. La contagion estoit si violente et si maligne que seulement si l'on approchait cinq pas près d'un qui fut pestiféré, tous ceux qui ce faisoyent, estoyent blessez; et plusieurs avoient charbons, devant et derrière; et ne vivoyent que six jours. Les saignées, les médicaments cordiaux n'estoyent pas efficaces. Quand on avoyt faict la visitation par toute la cité et jetté hors les pestiférés, le lende-main, y en avoit plusqu'au paravant. La mort estoit tant subite que le père ne tenoit pas compte de son enfant. Plusieurs, entachés de peste, se sont jettiés dedans les puits; d'autres se sont précipités de leurs fenestres. D'autres qui avoient le charbon derrière l'epaule et devant la mamelle, leur venoit une saignée du nez qui duroit nuict et jour, tant qu'ils mouroient. A brief parler, la désolation estoit si grande qu'avec l'or et l'argent à la main, souventes fois, mourait-on, faute d'un verre d'eau. Entre les choses admirables que je pense avoir vues, c'est une femme qui m'appela par la fenestre. Je vis qu'elle-même, toute seule, se cousoit le linceul sur sa personne, (en) commençant aux pieds. Je vis venir les alarbres (comme nous appelons, en notre langue provençale, ceux qui ensevelissent les pestiférés). Je voulus entrer dans la maison de ceste femme. Je la trouvai morte, couchée au milieu de la maison, avec son suayre demi-cousu...*' Nostradamus, *Bastiment de plusieurs receptes...Remède pour la peste*. Published in combination with *Traité des fardemens et confitures*, edition of D. Rigaud, 1590

15 '*Prenés de la sieure ou le rayment du boys de cyprés, le plus verd que vous pourré trouver une once, de Iris de Florece six onces: de giffles 3 onces: calami odorati 3. dragmes; ligni aloes 6. dragmes, faites le tout mettre en poudre, qu'il ne essuente: & puis prenés de roses rouges incarnées trois ou quatre cets, qui soyent bien mondées toutes fraiches, & ceuillies avat la*

rosee: & les ferés fort piller dedans un mortier de marbre, avec un piloir de bois: & les roses à y dedens la poudre susdicte, & derechef le pillés fort, en l'arrousant un peu de suc de roses: & quand le tout sera bien meslé, faictes en de petites balottes plattes, faictes en la mode de trociques et les faictes seicher à l'ombre, car elles sont de bonne odeur.' Traité des fardemens et confitures, op. cit.

16 'on ne trouva aucun médicament qui fût plus préservatif de la peste que cette composition. Tous ceux qui en portoyent à leur bouche en estoyment préservés.'

17 Nostradamus, *Traité des fardemens et confitures*, op. cit., ch. XXVI, translation from James Laver, *Nostradamus, or the Future Foretold*, p.26

18 Quoted in John Leaney, 'Medicine in the Time of Shakespeare', *History Today*, March 1963, p.172

19 '*René le pillier verd à Lyon du temps que je y estois l'an mil cinq cens quarante sept ...*', Nostradamus, *Traité des fardemens et confitures...*, op. cit., fol. 75

20 '*Venant a Saló de Craux, ville distáte d'Aix d'une petite journée, & mi chemin d'Avignon & Marseille, il se maria en secódes nopces.*' Chavigny, *Brief Discours...*, op. cit.

21 Louis Gimon, *Chroniques de la ville de Salon, depuis son origine jusqu'en 1792*, Aix, 1882, reprinted Laffitte Reprints, Marseilles, 1974, p.197

22 '*bien messer Antonio Vigerchio espicier de Savone, homme de bien, auquel veritablement en lafaculté de la pharmaceutrie luy est deüe la palme, ou le laurier*'. Nostradamus, *Traité des fardemens et confitures ...*, op. cit., ch. XXX

23 '*sirop laxatif de rosat*'

24 '*bailler aux femmes enceintes, ès premiers et derniers mois, en tout age et en tout temps, sans danger nul que ce soyt*'

25 '*Orus Apollo, fils d'Osiris, roi de Aegipte niliaque, des notes hiéroglyphiques livres deux, mis en rithme par épigrammes*'

26 '*oeuvre de incredible et admirable érudition et antiquité, traduit par Michel Nostradamus de Saint-Remy-en-Provence*'

CHAPTER 5

Almanac Entrepreneur

In the late nineteenth century the French archivist Louis Gimon, combing Salon-de-Provence's land registers for a history of the town through the centuries, turned up a hitherto unnoticed property document for 'Monsieur the Doctor Nostradamus'.[1] This showed that in 1552 Nostradamus possessed at Salon, in the Farreiroux district, a house that had been acquired at some undetermined time since his marriage with Anne Ponsarde. This was described as 'facing the windmill of Estienne Lassale and the house belonging to Juanette Texier's heirs.'[2]

Though the town of Salon, still walled in Nostradamus' time, has undergone many changes, today what is said to be this same house is a four-storeyed, rather plain-fronted Renaissance-style edifice that since 1992 has been tastefully if somewhat theatrically converted into the town's Nostradamus Museum.[3] It is operated under the management of the waxworks specialists Musée Guimet, France's equivalent of Madame Tussaud's. While in recent decades Salon-de-Provence's civic authorities have renamed the road the Rue Nostradamus in honour of their local hero, formerly it was the rue du Moulin-d'Isnard, that is, the road of Isnard's windmill, thereby confirming that a windmill was indeed once a landmark in this road.

The house's interior includes a surprisingly spacious entrance hall which currently features a wealth of mostly replica 'Nostradamiana' specially brought in to create the museum. Not least of these is a waxwork of a bearded Nostradamus himself, seated and with quill pen in hand. Notwithstanding these items, precious little that is truly original survives from Nostradamus' century except for an impressive spiral stone staircase, which visitors ascend level by level in order to follow the Musée Guimet's entertaining multi-language 'sound-and-light' presentation of his life. Nonetheless, on the basis of the Gimon document and other local records there is a very reasonable likelihood that this house was indeed Michel and Anne de Nostradame's home from the early 1550s, in which Nostradamus would produce all the published writings that would bring him such enduring fame.

Of those writings, in actuality the work by which Nostradamus became best known in his own lifetime was not the famous *Prophecies*, as is so often supposed. Instead it was a series of popular throwaway Almanacs that he composed annually prior to each new year, in the manner of present-day diaries and calendars. Direct ancestors of the *Old Moore's Almanac* that I can recall from my post-World War II boyhood, these Almanacs – or 'Prognostications', as they were alternatively titled – contained his predictions of the main news and weather events that he anticipated happening day by day during the forthcoming year. Taking his inspiration from pre-ordained astrological tables for calculating the planetary positions for each day, and noting any unusual conjunctions these might involve, Nostradamus would compose and write up his forecasts in the top-floor study of his Salon-de-Provence house. Then, as there was no printing press in Salon, the manuscript would be sped northwards by courier to Lyons or, in some later instances, Paris, for the necessary typesetting printing and distribution.

In the early 1550s it had been only a century or so since the development of Europe's first printing presses, yet Nostradamus' Almanacs and Prognostications were far from the first of their kind. We may

recall from an earlier chapter how François Rabelais had published a lampoon Almanac in 1533. The very fact that fun was already being poked at the almanac industry shows it to have become well established. In fact, the earliest-known printed French *Calendrier*, discovered in 1804 in the archives at Mayence, is said to be dated 1457, that is, almost concomitant with the very beginning of printing in France.[4] And throughout Nostradamus' boyhood during the first half of the sixteenth

Nostradamus' house in Salon-de-Provence, today converted into a waxworks museum.

century, France's equivalent of England's *Old Moore's* was the *Great Shepherds' Calendar…with their Astrology and many other items*.[5] From as early as 1503, the year of Nostradamus' birth, this publication even had a similar, regularly produced English-language edition entitled *The Kalendar of Shepherdes*.

Subject to minor variations, such publications mostly comprised three essential elements, usually interwoven. First, there was an Almanac proper. This comprised all the year's known astronomical movements, eclipses, conjunctions and so on in relation to the zodiac, the notional moving band that is the basis of all astrology. As envisaged as far back as Babylonian times, the zodiac, divided into twelve 30-degree sectors from Aries to Pisces, represents the sun's annual path through 'houses', arbitrarily divided segments of an unmoving background sky. It is important to note that in Nostradamus' time, when the invention of the telescope lay more than a century into the future, the only known major heavenly bodies were the sun, the moon, and the planets Venus, Mars, Mercury, Saturn and Jupiter.[6] In the second century AD the Graeco-Egyptian astronomer Claudius Ptolemy had set down a system of mathematical laws by which the positions of the planets in relation to the zodiac could be calculated both back into the past and forward into the future. While mathematically satisfying, this Ptolemaic system was accurate only up to a point, since due to precession, that is, a gradual shift in the earth's axis that was unknown to the Greeks, by Nostradamus' time the signs and stars had significantly shifted their alignment. The accruing error, which essentially reduces all astrological calculations to the status of fictional notions, today amounts to a full star-sign, with true spring actually starting in Pisces, not Aries. If Nostradamus was aware of this, it certainly did not trouble him, any more than it apparently does his modern-day counterparts.[7]

The second element the publication incorporated was a Calendar, showing, in relation to the Almanac, how the days of the week, from Sunday to Saturday, would fall for each month throughout the coming year, and noting the scheduled dates for moveable feasts such as Easter, together with saint's days, etc. This was presented in essentially near-identical manner to that which we are accustomed to see in the calendars and diaries of today, except that, at the first half of the sixteenth century, all calendars again embodied a fundamental and long-accumulated error. From its beginnings as an official religion, Christianity had continued using the Roman calendar that had been devised by Julius Caesar in 46 BC. By this so-called Julian Calendar the length of each year had been calculated with an impressive accuracy, though not quite exactly enough, since by the early sixteenth century there had accrued an error of no less than ten days. Though calendrical experts had come to recognise this error in Nostradamus' time, it took until 1582, that is, a decade and a half after his death, before Pope Gregory XIII issued the necessary reform. Gregory formally reduced by ten the number of days in that particular year and brought in our present so-called Gregorian Calendar, which by a leap-year adjustment avoids the recurrence of the error. Non-Catholic England, to its shame, delayed for a further seventeen decades before it yielded to the Gregorian revision, while the Greek Orthodox Church, which has never adopted the reforms, is now thirteen days out of true in its calendar.

The third element incorporated a 'Prognostication', that is, a section in which an author-compiler such as Nostradamus assembled his forecasts for the year's most notable events. These he would first have devised mathematically, based on the astrologically predicted angles that the planets formed day by day with the earth. For instance, when two planets were 60 degrees apart astrologers regarded this aspect as having only a mild influence. However if they were in square, that is at 90 degrees, or in opposition, at 180 degrees, then strife was expected. For the interpretation of the nature of this and any other impending traumas the astrologer looked to each individual planet's personality attributes. From ancient times each planet had become associated with certain characteristics, hence the English language's adjectives such as martial, after Mars; mercurial, after Mercury; saturnine, after Saturn; and jovial, after Jove or Jupiter. As followers of present-day newspaper horoscopes are well aware, zodiac signs were also associated with certain personality types, with each 'house', or section of fixed sky through which the zodiac moves, likewise being thought to have its own distinctive mood or theme. The first house represents personality, the second, money and wealth, the third, peer groups, and so on. This 'prognostication' section of the almanac was thus the one in which each astrologer had the opportunity really to show his individuality and true predictive mettle.

Finally, the printer might decide to add certain filler items such as road distances between towns, gardening tips, a mini-chronicle of world history from the Creation, the dates of forthcoming fairs, and suchlike. This was partly to provide the almanac's purchaser with extra value, but also, given that printing then, as today, was done in multiples of eight or sixteen pages, to fill in any pages that might otherwise be blank.

Much like modern-day newspapers, Almanacs and Prognostications were relatively cheaply produced, throw-away printed ephemera. This is why the entirety of Nostradamus' very first publications of this kind perished long ago. And of even his later versions, dating from when he had become more famous, mostly only one or two have survived from each year. However, secretary Chavigny, at the end of his brief biography, remarked:

> We have from him [i.e. Nostradamus]...portents [*présages*] in prose, drawn up for the years between 1550 and [15]67, the majority collected and edited by me in twelve books, which are worthy of being commended to posterity.[8]

In 1991 there turned up at Dijon, to become swiftly acquired by the Municipal Library at Lyons, a very tattered manuscript, dated 1589 and entitled 'Compilation of the Prose Portents of M[onsieur] Michel de Nostredame'.[9] Though it has yet to be edited and published, this seems to be Chavigny's actual original manuscript. In it he compiled, from what was then a still complete collection of almanacs, the 'portents' or pithy forecasts that Nostradamus had composed for each month of each year, from when he started producing almanacs to when he died. From this manuscript, and from the closing remarks in Chavigny's biography, Nostradamus would therefore appear to have compiled his first published Almanac in the year 1549 (for the year 1550), and then to have kept this up each year for the rest of his life. As we will later learn, he even, most conscientiously, had the 1567 edition all ready for the printers at the time of his death in mid-1566.

But it was one thing to dream up an Almanac, quite another to get it typeset, printed and widely distributed – particularly as Salon was far too small and off the beaten track to have any printing establishment of its own. The identity and whereabouts of the printer who produced Nostradamus' 1550 Almanac is unknown. However, from surviving correspondence, and from actual specimens of Nostradamus' earliest surviving Almanacs, one of the earliest and most faithful of his printers was one Jean Brotot of Lyons.

To this day Lyons, at the confluence of the Rhône and Saône some 290 miles (460 km) south of Paris, is France's third largest city. In Nostradamus' day it was likewise a city of great wealth and sophistication, its four annual fairs, instituted by Louis XI in 1462, attracting merchants from Italy, Spain, Germany and even further afield. It was also very conscious of its long and distinguished past. As Roman Lugdunum it had been the birthplace of no less than three of Rome's most famous emperors: Claudius (10 BC–AD 54), Marcus Aurelius (AD 121–180) and Caracalla (AD 188–217). All sorts of goods flowed into it to be sold in the stalls lining its riverside quays – cloths, hides, tapestries, lacework, musical instruments, pots and pans, also, not

16th century printing shop. Nostradamus' annual Almanacs would have been printed at premises resembling this one. From a contemporary woodcut.

least (as we noted in the last chapter), pills and potions.

In the early sixteenth century Lyons had the distinction of being, in terms of France, second only to Paris for printing, along with the ancillary industries of papermaking, ink manufacture, type manufacture and bookselling. In the 1520s two German printers, the Juntes and the Greyffs (or Griffes), set up shop in the rue Thomassin. Some time later in the same decade the native French printer Jean Brotot installed himself in premises in the rue Tramassac, on the right bank of the Saône. In time he would publish the works of the contemporary poet Charles Fontaine, the court astrologer Gabriele Simeone and Nostradamus himself. And the Junte, Greyffe and Brotot presses were far from alone among Lyons printing establishments. As Fontaine wrote of the city in 1557:

> *Inside a thousand houses*
> *A huge million of black teeth*
> *A million of black teeth*
> *Work during and out of fair days.*[10]

By 'black teeth' Fontaine was referring to the inked typographical characters that printers used right up to (and still in some cases during) our own computer era. In this regard France's printers were particularly far-sighted, since they opted for classic, readily legible Roman type (that is, the kind of typeface that is still used for most general printing, including this book), rather than for the ornate and altogether less legible Gothic type that their German counterparts favoured. Nostradamus' works, as published in his lifetime, would all be set in Roman type. It should also be appreciated that at around this time French and other printers effectively doubled as publishers. Of necessity, they would make their own shrewd editorial assessments of any works submitted to them, since the laborious and expensive printing process, together with the publication's subsequent marketing, would often be at their commercial risk.

By chance, amongst the Latin manuscript cache of Nostradamus letters preserved in the Paris Bibliothèque Nationale there has survived what appears to be the text of Jean Brotot's first ever letter to Nostradamus. Although the latter's son César, in his later transcription from the original into Latin, dated this to 1557, he seems to have misread the date, the more likely date being 1553. This may be considered near-certain for, as is evident from works that have survived in hard print, Brotot and Nostradamus had long been in business by 1557, whereas the content of Brotot's letter shows it to be a response to two 'Prognostications' that Nostradamus had sent Brotot on spec, before the two had got to know each other.

One of these Prognostications was apparently dedicated to Claude de Savoie, Governor of Provence, the other to Joseph des Panisses, Provost of Cavaillon, and the hope that Nostradamus had apparently expressed to Brotot was that he might publish them for the following year. On September 20, that is, only one day after the manuscripts' receipt, but clearly after having looked through them both very carefully, Brotot responded to Nostradamus:

Most learned sir, on 19 September I received the two Prognostications so carefully enclosed in the packet that you sent me...To be frank, I must admit being a little taken aback by your tendency to verbosity. Candidly – and you should not be surprised by this – I am concerned about the deterrent effect of such wordiness on a lot of readers. These days, most learned Michel, the fashion is for brevity. As everyone says: "Why use a lot of words when fewer will serve the same purpose?"...

In all honesty, I very much want to be able to carry out what you have in mind. And I have no wish for all your hard labours to be wasted. But I do urge you to be realistic. What do you think your readers will make of two separate Prognostications, especially when the two derive from one and the same source? Who wouldn't suspect you of trying to have your cake and eat it too?

You must make up your mind on the soundness of what I propose. This is that I have decided to print just one of the Prognostications (...In the case of the other one, I want to hold it back for a while...). When I have finished the first version, I will add the name of the second dedicatee to that of the first...I will finish off the astronomical tables...with the list of the saints, the phases of the moon and their meanings. Also I will add the French verses. Using this formula, I believe the work will be a great credit to you. Relevant sayings by philosophers will be added to each month.[11]

Brotot apparently appended to his letter an Almanac that had already been produced by another Lyons printer, Antoine de Rosne – known as 'Lizerot'. This was presumably to give Nostradamus an idea of the competition that he faced, and how he (Brotot) envisaged treating the version that Nostradamus had supplied. Brotot's forthright letter has all the air of a busy printer (or, today, a respected editor) totally unabashed about telling a would-be author, even a Nostradamus, that he was too verbose. He is also commendably decisive in making some shrewd commercial judgments in both his and his author's best interests. Nostradamus, for his part, appears initially to have had the good sense to accept Brotot's advice, only to become horrified a few weeks later when he received his first proofs. Though it was already late in the day to publish an Almanac in time for the next year, he apparently decided on a drastic course of action.

Amongst the papers of Etienne d'Hozier – the notary or lawyer cousin of Anne Ponsarde's who had officiated at her wedding with Nostradamus in 1447 – the Salon archivist Louis Gimon discovered a power of attorney that had been made out on November 11, 1553, on behalf of Nostradamus. This empowered 'Lizerot' – the printer of the Almanac of which Brotot had sent Nostradamus a specimen copy – to take over from Brotot the printing of what is specifically described as the *Prognostication for the Year 1554*.[12] Nostradamus' apparent reason for such intervention was that Brotot had 'made a copy corrupt and mutilated, such that the contents could only be judged to be inept and made by an ignorant man, thus doing the author a serious disservice'.[13]

Whoever eventually printed Nostradamus' 1554 Almanac, no copy of it is known to have survived. Exactly what transpired next is therefore unknown. Very possibly Antoine de Rosne/Lizerot, as the new year was already close, and he was already producing a rival Almanac for a different author, turned Nostradamus down, which might have persuaded him that Brotot had rather more sense than he had credited him with.

Whatever happened, somehow or other Brotot and Nostradamus must have patched up their differences – and relatively soon. For Brotot certainly produced for Nostradamus a particularly splendid Almanac for 1555. And the individual to whom this was dedicated was 'Monseigneur le Révérend Prélat Monseigneur Joseph de Panisses', i.e. Joseph des Panisses, Provost of Cavaillon, the person to whom Nostradamus had intended to dedicate the second version of the 1554 Almanac. Just a single copy of this 1555 Almanac has survived. It was preserved in the private library of the late South American collector Daniel Ruzo up to the time of Ruzo's death in 1991.[14] Since then, however, a veil of obscurity has fallen over its current whereabouts.[15] From photographs and other data that Ruzo made available before his death the Almanac's cover reads in translation:

> *New PROGNOSTICATION and portentous prediction*
> *For the year 1555*
> *Composed by Master Michel Nostradamus*
> *Doctor in medicine, of Salon de Crau in Provence,*
> *Named by Ammianus Marcellinus SALUVIUM.*[16]

Below this a woodblock shows 'M. de Nostradame' (this name is set on a shield) with long beard and doctor's hat, seated in his book-lined study, surrounded by signs of the zodiac, and gazing out of a window at the sun, moon and planets. This is probably the earliest known depiction of Nostradamus, and it can only have been made specially. Below this appears the printer's byline: 'At Lyon, by Jean Brotot'.[17]

Brotot would also appear to have done well with the distribution and sales of the Almanac, since its publication caused a perceptible buzz throughout France. On December 12, 1554 one 'de La Tourette', who appears to have purchased a number of copies to send to his friends, wrote from Lyons to Jean de Morel, a noted patron of contemporary writers at the court of King Henri II of France: 'I am sending you new almanacs, prognostications and marvellous predictions by Nostradamus in three forms.'[18]

Likewise Claude Haton, the curé of Provins, an attractive little town some fifty miles (80 km) south-east of Paris, wrote in his *Mémoires* for the end of 1555:

The earliest known depiction of Nostradamus. Woodcut illustration from the title page of his 1555 Almanac. The signs of the zodiac appear all around the border. In the central panel Nostradamus is seen in his book-lined study, writing with quill pen at his desk, drawing his inspiration from the sun, moon and five planets.

> At this time there entered the scene, with great clamour, an astrologer-mathematician from Salon de Crau in Provence named Master Michel Nostradamus, doctor in medicine, maker of prophecies and almanacs. His almanacs and prophecies predict much of moment about to happen for Christianity, even its desolation, particularly in the countries of France and Germany.[19]

As we will learn later, much of great moment was indeed about to happen to Christianity in France. The country was shortly to be torn apart by decades of bloody religious differences. Nor, certainly, would Germany go unscathed.

But whatever fame and potential prophetic success Nostradamus might have been enjoying at this time with his Almanacs, creatively he was on fire in all departments. As an indication that his marriage with Anne Ponsarde was a happy one, some time around the year 1551 Anne produced for him their first daughter, Madeleine. This was followed on December 18, 1553 – be it noted, just four days after Nostradamus' fiftieth birthday – by their first son César, this choice of name surely a mark of his indebtedness to Jules-César Scaliger.[20]

The year 1552 saw Nostradamus finishing the writing of his *Treatise of cosmetics and jams*, known from the fact that in its preface he characteristically recorded the date of its completion as on April 1 of that year. This little book was in two parts. In the first he offered prescriptions and recipes for various types of cosmetics and perfumes to accentuate and beautify the face'.[21] It is difficult to avoid detecting, in the hyperbole that Nostradamus attached to some of these preparations, a harking back to his days as a pills and potions pedlar. In the second part he provided, again by means of recipes, 'ways and means of making many varieties of jams, cooked variously in sugar, honey and wine'.[22] The very practical recipes supplied, which can be followed to this day, make evident Nostradamus' delight in collecting such items on his travels, and trying them out when he got back home. This prompts the suggestion that the Nostradamus Museum really should add to its presentation a scene of the learned doctor at work in his kitchen, enthusiastically utilising all Anne Ponsarde's pots and pans for yet another sticky, sweet creation. In the event it would take Nostradamus a three further years, to 1555, to see this particular work in print, the printer in this instance being Antoine Volant of Lyons, perhaps because the subject matter more suited Volant's particular readership market.

Locally Nostradamus' literary talents were finding recognition, as a result of which in 1553 he was invited to compose a Latin inscription for a new addition to Salon's attractive public water fountains, of which examples are still to be seen scattered in town squares and on street corners. Though this inscription has presumably been effaced by time, its wording has been preserved. And this clearly reveals the side to Nostradamus that, as we have seen earlier, could get him into trouble from time to time, his sardonic sense of humour:

If human ingenuity were capable in perpetuity
Of providing Salon's citizens with a supply of wine
The Senate and Magistrates of Salon would not have needed
At great cost, during the consulships of Paul Antoine and Palamède
Marc
To erect this nondescript water fountain
Which you see before you
M. Nostradamus
To the immortal gods
For the people of Salon
1553.[23]

Thankfully it would seem that Palamède Marc, a local aristocrat and one of Salon's consuls or mayors at this time, was a close friend of Nostradamus and his wife, and would therefore have appreciated the joke. Nostradamus' son César, in his *History and Chronicle of*

LE VRAY ET
PARFAICT EMBEL
LISSEMENT DE LA FACE,
& conseruation du corps en son
entier, contenant plusieurs Receptes secretes & desi-
rées non encores
veûes.
&
LA SECONDE
PARTIE, CONTENANT
LA FAÇON ET MANIERE
de faire toutes confitures liquides,
tant en sucre, miel, qu'en
vin cuit.

Ensemble deux façons pour faire le syrop rosat laxatif: & pour
faire le sucre candi, penites & tourrons d'Hespaigne.

Par M. Michael Nostradamus.

Title page of Nostradamus' Treatise of
Cosmetics and Jams. In this Nostradamus
exhibits a clarity and directness quite
different from his prophetic writings.

Provence, specifically attested to his father's friendship with Marc.[24]
And this is further evident from the fact that Marc was later one of the
witnesses to Nostradamus' will and was one of three local worthies
who would be entrusted with the keys to the seer's personal fortune.[25]

Likewise Nostradamus would seem to have been on cordial terms
with Provence's governor, Claude de Savoie, Count of Tende, hence
his dedication of the lost 1554 Almanac to Tende. When on March 10
of 1554 Nostradamus, along with many others in the locality,
observed some kind of falling meteorite, nine days later he wrote to
the governor about this, speaking of:

A horrible yet marvellous spectacle [that] was witnessed by many
people, on Jewish Saturday March 10 between 7 and 8 o'clock in
the town of Salon in France.[26]

It would in fact be via the intermediacy of Claude de Savoie that in the
very next year Nostradamus would receive a life-changing summons
to the royal court in Paris.

But before this, and undoubtedly the fruits of an idea that had been welling in his creative consciousness for some long time, was his production – and completion to publication by May 1555 – of the work that would subsequently give him enduring international fame, his *Prophecies*.

NOTES

1 '*Monsur le Docteur Nostradamus*' – Louis Gimon, *Chroniques de la ville de Salon*, op. cit., p.199; Archives of Salon, land register (*cadastre*) 1552, fol. 70, verso

2 '*se confronte ambe* [avec] *lo mollin de Estienne Lassale et la maison des hers* [héritiers] *à Juanete Texier*'

3 For tourism purposes it is known as La Maison de Nostradamus', i.e. The House of Nostradamus

4 Leroy, *Nostradamus, Ses Origines…*, op. cit., p. 147

5 *Grand Calendrier et Compost des Bergiers, avec leur Astrologie et plusieurs autres choses* – Leroy, op. cit., p. 147

6 Uranus, Neptune and Pluto were yet to be discovered. Uranus was first noted in 1781, Neptune in 1846 and Pluto only as recently as 1930

7 These mostly continue to follow the Ptolemy-based tables, ignoring astronomical truth

8 *Nous avós de luy d'autres presages en prose, faits puis l'an 1550 jusques à 67 qui volligez par moy la plus part & redigez en xii livres, sont dignes d'estre recommandez à la posterité.* Chavigny, *Brief Discours*, op. cit.

9 *Recueil des présages prosaïques de M. Michel de Nostredame*

10 *En million maisons, au dedans*
Un grand million de dents noires
Un million de noires dents,
Travaille enfoires et hors foires.
Charles Fontaine, *Ode de l'antiquité et excellence de la vile de Lyon*, 1557, translation from Plattard, *Life of Rabelais*, p. 106

11 '*Praedictiones duas, vir peritissime, hoc undevigesimo Septemb. abs te accepi, quae fasciculo non indiligenter erant inclusae…Harum ut prolixam demiratus sum farraginem, perculsa mens est mea non parum, quodque mirum tuo candori videri non debet, remorata est animum meum, offensura etiam multos (ut conjicio) nimia ista prolixitas. Gaudent adprime, mi doctiss. Michael, huiusce tempestatis ingenia Laconismo: in ore enim est omnium, frustra id pluribus fieri, quod paucioribus potest, modo aequé bene…Utinam mihi esset integrum tuis obsequi iussis! Non committerem certe ut huc tuae frustra lucubrationes adferentur. Sed quaeso, dispice, an aequa fronte candidi lectores accepturi sint duas praedictiones, ab eodem praesertim manates fonte? Quis non reformidet una fidelia duos parietes de albare? Boni tamen consules quae ad te scribo. Mihi vero decretum est quamcumque iusseris typis commitere, ex altera (à qua exudenda super-sedebo), quae utilia erunt adiecturo, cunque dimidiatum numerum explevero, prioris heroïs nomen mutabo, alterum praefigam, tuaque sic prae-dictio utrius nomine decorabitur. Ipsum diarium…respicit, ditabo catalogo Sanctorum, et signis Lunaeque significationibus; rithmos item adjiciam Gallicos, eritque institutum hoc meum honore non parvo nomine tuo, mea*

quidem opinione. Accedent etiam unicuique mensi decreta philosophorum'.
Jean Dupèbe, *Nostradamus, Lettres Inédites ...*, op. cit., Letter II, p.31

12 *Pronostication pour l'année 1554*

13 *'une copie corrompue et mutilée, tellement que l'on jugeroit la matière estre inepte et facile à homme ignare, ce qui porteroit un tort grave à l'auteur'*, Actes du notaire d'Hozier, année 1553, fol. 569, quoted in Leroy, *Nostradamus, Ses Origines ...*, op. cit., p.148, after Louis Gimon, *Chroniques de la ville ...*, op. cit., p.199, note 1

14 Mentioned by Jean Dupèbe, *Nostradamus, Lettres Inedites ...*, op. cit., p.29, n.1, after D. Ruzo, *Le testament de Nostradamus*, tr. fr. Paris 1982, p.340

15 I am indebted for this information to the German scholar Dr. Elmar Gruber

16 *'Prognostication nouvelle & prediction portenteuse pour Lan M.D.L.V. Composée par maistre Michel Nostradamus, docteur en medicine, de Salon de Craux en Provence, nommée par Ammianus Marcelinus Saluvium'*

17 *A Lyon, par Jean Brotot*

18 *'je vous envoye de nouveaulx almanachz, prognostications et presaiges merveilleux de nostradamus en troys sortes'.* Letter quoted in Jean Dupèbe, *Nostradamus, Lettres Inédites ...*, op. cit., p.172, note 1. The sender appears to have been Alexandre de la Tourette, a metallurgist described in 1575 as *'President des généraux maistres des monnoyeurs de France'*

19 *'Pour ce temps entroit en grand bruict ung astrologue mathematicien de Salon de Craux en Provance, nommé maistre Michel Nostradamus, docteur en medicinne, faiseur de propheties et almanactz, lequel par ses ditz almanacz et propheties prédisoit mout de cas a advenir en la chretiente, mesmement la desolation d'icelle et nommement es pays de France et Allemagne.'* Quoted in Pierre Brind'Amour, *Nostradamus Astrophile ...*, op. cit., p.437, after Claude Haton, *Mémoires de Claude Haton, contenant le récit des événements accomplis de 1553 à 1582, principalement dans la Champagne et la Brie, publiés par M. Félix Bourquelot*, 2 vols., Paris, Impr. Impériale, 1857, p.26. The original manuscript is in the Bibliothèque Nationale, Paris, as BN fonds français 11575, folio 17rv

20 This date has been deduced from letters written by César to his cousin Pierre Hozier in 1617 – see Brind'Amour, *Nostradamus Astrophile ...*, p.23, n.9

21 *'traicte de diverse façons de Fardemens & Senteurs pour illustrer & embellir la face'*

22 *'nous monstre la façon & maniere de faire confitures de plusieurs sortes, tant en miel, que sucre, & vin cuict'*

23 SI HUMANO INGENIO PERPETVO SAL-
LONAE CIVIB. PARARI VINA POTVISSET
NON AMOENVM QVEM CERNITIS FON-
TEM AQVARVM S.P.Q. SALON. MAGNA
IMPENSA NON ADDVXISSET
DVCTA N. PALAMEDE MARC
O. ET ANTON. PAVLO CONSS
M. NOSTRADAMVS
DIS IMMORTALIBVS
OB SALONENSES
M.D.LIII

Text reproduced in Leroy, op. cit., p.78, after L. Gimon, *Chroniques de la ville de Salon*, p.199

24 César de Nostredame, *Histoire et Chronique de Provence* ..., op. cit., p.775, quoted in Leroy, *Nostradamus, Ses Origines* ..., op. cit., p.77

25 See chapter 16

26 Text preserved in German translation published at Nuremberg by Joachim Heller, as follows: '*Ein Erschrecklich und Wunderbarlich zeychen/so am Sambstag für Judica den zehenden tag Martij zwischen siben und acht uhrn in der Stadt Schalon in Franckreych/ von vielen leuten geseehen worden*', quoted in Pierre Brind'Amour, *Nostradamus Astrophile* ..., op. cit., p.475. The letter was apparently published in the form of a placard

CHAPTER 6

Prophecies on the Presses

In the early part of 1555, King Henri II of Valois, the bellicose second son of François I, had held the French throne for eight years, in the company of his plain, though astute, Florentine Queen, Catherine de Medici. At war with the now veteran Holy Roman Emperor Charles V, whose vast domains sprawled across the Netherlands, Germany and much of eastern Europe as well as Spain, Henri had armies on his eastern frontiers and in Italy, the latter with little success helping the Sienese and Florentines in their struggle against Charles' mainly Lutheran occupying troops. Like his Queen Catherine a devout Roman Catholic, Henri was continuing his father's policy of suppressing Protestantism, the promulgation of which, directed by the theologian Jean Calvin from the safety of Geneva, was particularly strong in Nostradamus' Provence.

King Henri II of France and his Italian-born Queen Catherine de Medici, as Nostradamus would have seen them at the palace of St Germain-en-Laye. From their tomb sculpture in the Basilica of St. Denis, Paris.

Henri and Catherine had accordingly welcomed the news, received eighteen months earlier from Protestant England, that Henry VIII's fifteen-year-old son Edward VI, a puppet in the hands of his Protestant councillors, had died, to be succeeded by the fiercely pro-Catholic Mary Tudor. Mary, thirty-seven years old and appalled at the damage that the Protestants had inflicted upon England's old churches and monasteries, was now none too gently setting about restoring her country to Roman Catholicism. Meanwhile, on Europe's eastern borders and along its Mediterranean coasts, Islamic Turkish forces under Suleiman the Magnificent were continuing to pose a most formidable invasion threat to all Christendom, by both land and sea.

It therefore hardly needed a prophet or seer to perceive that, in 1555, much of Europe was a tinderbox of religious and political dissensions all too likely to be sparked off into any number of bloody conflicts. Nonetheless Nostradamus' secretary Chavigny had this to say of his master's writing of the *Prophecies*, published that same year:

He [Nostradamus] saw in advance the remarkable shifts and changes that were about to happen throughout Europe. Also the bloody civil wars and the pernicious troubles that would be so fatal to this Gallic monarchy. Entranced, and as if filled with some all-new fervour he set himself to write the 'Centuries'[1] and other predictions, beginning thus:

> *When the divine spirit takes over the prophetic soul*
> *Trouble, famine, plague, war are unleashed*
> *Water, arid desert, earth and sea are tinged with blood*
> *Peace refuses to be born; prelates and princes die.*[2]

Chavigny went on:

For a long time he kept everything to himself without wanting to publish them. He anticipated – quite correctly as events turned out that the very novelty of such subject-matter could not fail to arouse numerous mis-reportings, falsehoods and venomous criticisms. But eventually, and with his urge to be of public profit uppermost, he brought everything out into the open ...[3]

Modern-day sceptics may well find it difficult to avoid a wry smile upon reading Chavigny's naïve-sounding assurances that Nostradamus' motives were above all 'to be of public profit'. As James Randi for one would argue, rather nearer to the mark might be Nostradamus' intentions to profit *from* the public.

This said, the *Prophecies* was a remarkable publication from the inception of its very first 1555 edition, even though this was much shorter than the expanded versions that followed. This remarkableness was not least due to this edition's Preface, dated March 1, 1555, taking the form of an open letter written by the author to his baby son César. Even the most sceptical must admit that this demonstrates some impressive prescience on Nostradamus' part, given that at this plague-ridden period it was all too common for children to die in infancy. Had Jean Brotot been the printer/publisher, he would no doubt have ruthlessly abridged the letter as far too long-winded. In the event the printer was Macé Bonhomme, also of Lyons, who, despite his author's verbosity, worked fast. On April 30 he obtained from the royal Lieutenant of Lyons the necessary official 'privilege' or approval, and by May 4 the book was in print.

And despite parts of the Preface that are often tortuously long-winded, from the very opening sentence Nostradamus' sardonic sense of humour is again apparent, as when he chides his hapless infant son for his 'late-coming' into the world. This is unmistakably an allusion to the near seven years that he, as an already elderly father (he was now in his early fifties), along with his wife Anne had impatiently waited for César:

> Your late coming, César Nostredame my son, has prompted me to set down in writing all that has come to me from my long hours of uninterrupted night vigils. This is so that you have a way of remembering after I, your physical progenitor, have breathed my last. It is also for humanity's common profit with regard to the knowledge that the Divine Essence has bestowed upon me from astronomical cycles.[4]

Time and again in his later writings Nostradamus would allude to the long vigils that he kept in the small hours of the night in order to facilitate his 'receiving' of the visions in which he time-travelled far into the future. And in the very first two quatrains, or four-line verses, which start the 353 prophetic verses of the first–edition, he made readily apparent what may be best described as the 'Delphic oracle' manner in which he performed his forecasting:

> *Being seated by night studying in secret*
> *In lone repose on the brazen tripod*
> *A faint flame springs from the solitude*
> *Causing to flourish that which is not to be believed in vain.*[5]
> *[C.I, q.1]*

PROPHETIES
DE
M. NOSTRADAMVS.

CENTVRIE PREMIERE.

ESTANT afsis de nuit fe-
cret eſtude,
Seul repoulé ſus la ſelle d'æ
rain,
Flambe exigue ſortant de
ſolitude,
Fait proferer qui n'eſt à croire vain.

Laverge en main miſe au milieu deBRANCHES
De l'onde il moulle & le limbe & le pied.
Vn peur & voix fremiſſent par les manches,
Splendeur diuine. Le diuin prés s'aſſied.

2

Opening quatrains, or four-line verses, of Nostradamus' *Prophecies*.
In these verses he likened the method by which he drew his inspiration
to that used by the Delphic oracle of the ancient Greeks.

The Delphic oracle seated on her tripod.
From a 5th century BC red-figure vase in
the State Museum, Berlin.

Here in this first quatrain Nostradamus' reference to the 'brazen tripod' represents the key to our understanding of how – theoretically at least – he induced his 'seeing' into the future. In the State Museum in Berlin there is a Greek red-figure cup of the fifth century BC that bears in its bowl a striking depiction of the ancient Greek Pythia, or priestess of Apollo at Delphi, in the process of giving a divinely inspired oracular prophecy. Although the Pythia's client Aigeus appears to be standing directly before her, it is known that the entranced priestess actually induced the prophecy alone in the secrecy of her inner sanctuary. And as the vase-painting accurately shows, she specifically did so 'seated...on the brazen tripod'. Furthermore, equally specifically she framed her prophecies in much the same cryptic, poetic way that Nostradamus used. A few years ago the highly respected classical scholar Peter Levi commented that with the ascendancy of Christianity around the fourth century AD the Delphic tradition of 'oracular wisdom' became 'broken', and was never revived'.[6] Yet Nostradamus, albeit temporarily and single-handedly, certainly revived it in the mid-sixteenth century.

The second quatrain with which the *Prophecies* began is as revealing as the first:

> *The wand is put in hand in the midst of Branchus*
> *In the water he moistens hem and foot*
> *Fear, and a voice cause trembling in his arms*
> *Divine splendour. The Divine Being assumes proximity.*[7]
> [C.1, q.2]

Here Nostradamus' choices of words make it possible even to determine the particular books that he had read in order to become a second Delphic oracle. We referred in Chapter 3 to Marsilio Ficino, the fifteenth-century Florentine Neoplatonist who translated the *Corpus Hermetica* from Greek into Latin for Duke Cosimo de'Medici. Ficino was the individual to whom Nostradamus admiringly likened Jules-César Scaliger. Another of Ficino's translations was Iamblichus' *Of the Mysteries of the Egyptians*. And this work not only contains a strikingly familiar-sounding description of the Delphic oracle, it also refers to a similar oracle of the priests of Branchus at the modern Didyme (Yenihisar) on the Aegean coast of Turkey:

The sibyl [i.e oracle] at Delphi received the divinity in two ways. One, by a certain faint breath and flame which sprang from the verge of a cavern. The other ensconced in her sanctuary on a brazen three- or four-legged seat and consecrated to the divinity. In one or the other place she offered herself to the divine spirit, thereby becoming illumined by divine flame...Another such woman who produced oracles is at Branchus. Seated on an axle (of a wheel), she holds in her hand a divine wand. She moistens her feet and her hem in water, and by this means is filled with the divine splendour. Assuming the divinity, she prophesies.[8]

As has been pointed out by the late Canadian scholar Pierre Brind'Amour,[9] from clues such as a telltale mis-spelling, 'in Brancis' instead of 'in Brancidis', the fact that Nostradamus drew from the controversial Ficino's translation can be considered certain. Except that Nostradamus may not necessarily have read this in the original, but rather at second-hand. For another Florentine, the sixteenth-century author Peter Crinitus, reproduced the very same passage in his book *De honesta disciplina*.[10] And Nostradamus most definitely had a copy of this volume, which was reprinted in 1543, in his personal library, for his son César would specifically mention inheriting it from his father. Further, some of Nostradamus' remarks in his ostensibly original and personal letter to César in the *Prophecies* Preface can be seen to be lifted almost word for word from Crinitus, complete with misspellings and grammatical errors, a point which incidentally indicates that Nostradamus was far from being as original as some Nostradamians claim.

This said, in conceiving the project of the *Prophecies* Nostradamus can hardly be accused of lacking ambition, intelligence, or courage. Indicative of his ambition is the impressive number of quatrains, or four-line prophetic verses that he composed, and the sheer chronological sweep of time that he claimed for his prophetic rovings:

> With the aid of lengthy calculation deriving from night-time studies...I have compiled these books of predictions, each containing 100 prophetic astronomically-derived prophetic quatrains, for from now [i.e. 1555] until the year 3797.[11]

Printer Bonhomme created the 1555 edition of the *Prophecies* in sextodecimo format, that is, sixteen pages to the printed sheet. From six such sheets Bonhomme made up a book of ninety-six pages containing just the first 353 of what, with later editions, would become no less than 942 'genuine' Nostradamus quatrains.[12] This is not counting a number that would subsequently be invented and/or forged in his name, of which we will hear more later. Nostradamus conceived the book in groups of a hundred quatrain verses, each group of a hundred being termed a 'Century'. The fourth 'Century' of his first edition should therefore have contained a full hundred verses, in the manner of the first three 'Centuries', except that printer Bonhomme opted to keep the book at ninety-six pages, so that there was no space for the last forty-seven verses. Had the paging been increased to the next multiple of sixteen, that is, to 112, then six pages would have been left blank, so Bonhomme parsimoniously opted for the cheaper, less wasteful alternative. In the event later editions would supply those verses which had been so arbitrarily omitted.

Since Nostradamus claimed to have time-travelled into the future at least as far as the year 3797, he evidently had a rather more optimistic view of how much time mankind had before Judgement Day than many of his fellow-astrologers. Some of these contemporaries had voiced the gravest forebodings, in particular for the year 1583. Astrologically this marked the end of a 200-year epoch known as that of the watery trigon, followed by a return through all twelve signs of the zodiac to the primal epoch of the fiery trigon. To the more pessimistic of the sixteenth century's astrologers, among these the Czech Cyprian Leowitz, such a shift in the heavens had to mean that some momentous things would happen in that year, just as had earlier been so erroneously expected of 1533. As Leowitz would predict for 1583: 'Undoubtedly new worlds will follow, which will be inaugurated by sudden and violent changes.'[13]

This leads us in turn to consider Nostradamus' intelligence. For one of the undoubted secrets of his success in the devising of the *Prophecies*, both for the short term and for the much longer term, was his clever avoidance of a mistake committed by so many doomsters, in the sixteenth century and in virtually every century since. Time and again other so-called 'prophets' have pronounced that it would be on a clearly and unequivocally specified date that some earth-shattering event such as the end of the world would occur. Of course, it goes without saying that the expected event has never transpired, leaving such 'prophets' one after another with egg on their faces.

Not so Nostradamus. Rather than being caught out by being totally explicit about any particular date, on his own admission he quite deliberately obscured his predictions. As he told the infant César:

> ...of that which I have perceived, in order to avoid any actual human eventualities scandalising the fragility of what has been sensed by oracle, I have expressed everything nebulously, rather than as clear prophecy.[14]

Later in the same letter to César, when referring to arranging everything in quatrains grouped into hundreds, he repeated: 'I have quite deliberately arranged [these] a trifle obscurely.'[15]

As he also made clear, the verses of the *Prophecies* are in no special chronological order, so that any one verse can be applied to any year of the reader's fancy, thereby hugely increasing their credibility on the part of the already credulous.

And a further cleverness on his part – albeit for his own self-protection – was his extremely careful avoidance ever to make any statement or prediction that might land him in serious political or religious trouble. Specifically in order to give himself the best possible defence in any such hostile circumstances, we find him repeatedly insisting that everything he was knew or stood for came from God. For, as he could not fail to be acutely conscious, in an era when witches were commonly burnt at the stake, if any of his prophecies were seen to be too obviously successful, he would face the very real danger of success backfiring on him. He might find a populace ever suspicious of 'atheist' doctors once again hauling him before the Inquisition as some kind of wizard deserving execution for breaching the biblical laws stated in the Book of Deuteronomy 18: 10: 'There must never be anyone among you ... who practises divination, who is a soothsayer, augur or sorcerer.' In such circumstances he could find himself saying goodbye to his promising new family for a very long time indeed.

It was not without a certain courage, therefore, that Nostradamus set down in hard print, in 1555, his famous verses looking as far into the future as 3797. He wrote them in what was for him 'modern' French, laced with occasional flourishes of Latin and Provençal. Nonetheless his terminologies and meanings are often obscure, both for the Frenchmen of his time and for their descendants to this day. As part of his 'obscuring' policy, he made fairly obvious anagrams of certain names, such as Rapis', for 'Paris', and 'Eiovas' when he meant Savoie, or Savoy. Overall the style in which he composed his quatrains was unmistakably poetic and cryptic, deliberately different from the direct, matter-of-fact explicitness that he used for his recipes, as in his *Treatise on cosmetics and jams*, and that we will later see from his personal correspondence.

In fact, even where, in quite a number of the quatrains, the sense is expressed clearly enough, they are so lacking in any landmark or period that they could be applied to any time, any place. For instance there is Century I, q.67:

> *The great famine that I sense approaching*
> *Often changing direction, then becoming universal*
> *So great and so prolonged that from the tree*
> *The root will be torn, and the infant from the breast.*[16]

Famines have occurred in virtually every century and on every continent for as long as humankind has been deriving sustenance from tilling the soil. The application of this particular quatrain to any one historical famine would therefore be the purest guesswork.

Other quatrains, while they are often commendably full of readily identifiable landmarks, are still open to the widest possible interpretation with regard to the century to which they should be applied. Take for instance this example, quatrain 72 from Century I:

> From all Marseilles the inhabitants changed
> Course in running flight nearly as far as Lyons
> Narbonne and Toulouse by Bordeaux become outraged
> Those killed and taken prisoner [number] almost a million.[17]

Nostradamian authors Erika Cheetham, John Hogue and Henry Roberts have interpreted this as forecasting events during the Second World War when German troops marched into Paris, and Marshal Pétain's Vichy regime occupied Toulouse, Lyons and Narbonne (along with much else of France). Peter Lemesurier sees it as forecasting a Muslim invasion of Europe between the years 2005 and 2006.[18] In essence, it is anyone's guess. Small wonder, then, that in time there would grow up in the English language the saying 'as good a prophet as Nostradamus'. The meaning of this, according to *Brewer's Dictionary of Phrase and Fable*, was 'so obscure that your meaning cannot be understood', due to the 'very ambiguous language' in which the Nostradamus prophecies were couched.

Yet the plain fact to be faced is that there was something in Nostradamus' verses which persuaded not only his own generation, but umpteen generations since, that these were uncanny insights into the future worthy of serious consideration, as the extraordinary attention that he received in the wake of September 11, 2001 bears witness.

Confronted with this phenomenon, the sceptic James Randi has resorted to casting serious doubt upon whether Nostradamus truly got himself into print with the *Prophecies* as early as 1555. As he has mused, could the 1555 edition have been a fiction invented by later writers, beginning with Nostradamus' son César, who conceivably composed 'prophecies' in his father's name after some of the events had actually happened? At the very end of his 1990 book *The Mask of Nostradamus* Randi devoted a special Appendix to describing how he found in the New York Public Library a 'twelve-page manuscript-style typewritten essay, circa 1930 by an anonymous author' specifically arguing that there has never been a 1555 edition of the *Prophecies*.

On the basis of this one unpublished essay of unknown

authorship Randi cited 'one celebrated Nostradamian...Count von Klinkowström' who apparently at the beginning of the twentieth century 'had travelled over Europe searching for a first edition of Nostradamus, only to be disappointed'. As Randi further pointed out:

> Klinkowström, apparently, was unable to find any trace of the *Privilege du Roy* (royal permission to print) for the first edition, in Lyons or elsewhere. That permit would have been required, and would certainly be on record.[19]

In his typical 'voice of commonsense' manner, Randi gave the reader clearly to understand that there is no 'unobjectionable, genuine first edition' of Nostradamus in existence. He also expressed serious doubt that from 1555, or indeed from any time within Nostradamus' lifetime, any published copy of the *Prophecies* had ever existed. It has therefore fallen to me, with no axe to grind for Nostradamus or his Nostradamian devotees, to set the matter straight in the interests of fairness and truth.

The true facts are that in the time of 'Count von Klinkowström' and of Randi's anonymous, unknown informant of the 1930s the survival of any original 1555 edition of the *Prophecies* was indeed uncertain. While nineteenth-century French library catalogues show that a Nostradamus copy of this description was kept in bay Y4621 of the old library at the Paris Hôtel de Ville, the whole massive public building went up in flames during the Communard Insurrection in Paris of May 1871,[20] taking the library and inevitably the Nostradamus first edition with it. Likewise, although nineteenth-century sources record a 1555 edition as having been stored in Bay 28614 in Paris' Mazarine Library, this copy similarly disappeared without trace, and has been presumed stolen, some time after June 1887.

In 1982, however, well before the publication of Randi's *Mask of Nostradamus*, an exhaustive trawl by the French organisation *Les Amis de Nostradamus* was made of European libraries specifically in search of any 1555 edition of the *Prophecies* that just might have survived. There came to light two precious copies which, though they had long been kept in public collections, had simply lain unknown to any active Nostradamians. The first of these was housed in the Imperial collection in the main Library at Vienna. The second was in the public library in the picturesque French town of Albi, straddling the river Tarn on the edge of the Massif Central region and about equidistant between Montpellier and Agen.

At the end of October 2001, while my wife and I were en route between Montpellier and Agen pursuing researches for this book, we decided to make a slight detour to Albi specifically to seek out this particular copy. To our surprise Albi's main public library had only recently been renamed and rebuilt as a very modern-looking Mediathèque, and at first sight it looked a rather unlikely location for conserving books from the sixteenth century. However an enquiry quickly led us to the very helpful chief conservator Marielle Mouranche, who confirmed that a 1555 edition of the *Prophecies* was indeed under her care. When I asked her how the Albi public library had come to own this particular volume she explained that it was one of several thousand collected by the late eighteenth-century French explorer and hero Henri Paschal de Rochegude. Rochegude, born in Albi, had returned to his home city during his retirement, whereupon eventually his entire book collection was bequeathed to the library.

Madame Mouranche very kindly brought out the Nostradamus volume for our inspection. At first sight the preservative red calf rebinding which Rochegude had provided for it gave it a disquietingly modern appearance. But inside was the totally authentic-looking title-page from the original printing, reading in translation:

THE PROPHECIES
OF M. MICHEL
NOSTREDAMUS
AT LYON
The house of Macé Bonhomme
1555
The permission is inserted on the page that follows
WITH [ROYAL] PRIVILEGE[21]

Below the title was a new woodcut that printer Macé Bonhomme appears to have had specially made for this particular book. Much like the title-page woodcut that was regularly used for the annual Almanacs, this version shows a bearded Nostradamus seated in his study. In this instance, however, the frame of zodiac symbols has been omitted and Nostradamus is depicted gazing at a model or 'theoretick' of the Universe with an unearthly glow appearing to emanate from it. Plain as a pikestaff, the date is clearly reproduced in Latin letters as 'MDLV' or 1555. From the title-page wording 'AVEC PRIVILEGE' ('WITH PRIVILEGE', i.e. royal permission), and the reproduction of the official details of this on the book's second page, Randi's argument that 'Count von Klinkowström' could find no such permission is blown to smithereens. And Henri Rochegude's distinctive red stamp on the title-page shows that this particular copy's whereabouts can be reliably tracked from the time of the French Revolution onwards.

As Marielle Mouranche confirmed, there is not the slightest reason to believe that this slim volume is anything but what it appears to be: a surviving copy from Macé Bonhomme's very first, 1555 printing of Nostradamus' *Prophecies*. It thereby confirms that any Nostradamus prophecy within its pages, that is, the first 353 of the now famous 'Centuries' verses, was genuinely framed by Nostradamus in or before the year 1555. Further, it underlines that any of James Randi's suggestions to the contrary are now utterly worthless.

But there is another reason for dismissing Randi's suggestion that Nostradamus' prophecies may have been a fiction later faked up by his

Left Title page of the exceptionally rare 1555 edition of Nostradamus' *Prophecies* preserved in Albi, southern France.

Below Privilege and Preface from the 1555 edition of the *Prophecies*.

Extraict des regiſtres de la
Seneſchaucée de Lion.

S.VRCE que *Macé Bonhomme Imprimeur demeurant à Lyon*, ha dict auoir recouuert certain liure, intitulé, LES PROPHETIES DE MICHEL NOSTRADAMVS, qu'il feroit volentiers imprimer s'il nous plaiſoit, luy permettre ce requerāt: & outre ce defenſes eſtre faictes à tous Imprimeurs & autres de ne l'imprimer, ou faire imprimer de deux ans. Et apres que le dict liure ha eſté par nous veu en aucūs poincts d'iceluy & que le dict Macé Bōhōme ha affermé en tout icelui liure n'auoir aucune choſe concernant la foy prohibée. Auons, ouy ſur ce le procureur du Roy permis, & permetons au dict Macé Bonhomme de pouoir imprimer, & faire imprimer le dict liure. Et ſi auons faict defences de par le Roy à tous imprimeurs d'icelui n'imprimer dès deux ans à conter du iour & date de la preſente à peine de confiſcation deſdicts liures: et d'amende arbitraire.

Faict à Lyon par nous *Hugues du Puis*, ſeigneur de la Mothe, Conſeillier du Roy, & Lieutenant particulier en la Seneſchaucée de Lyon: le dernier iour d'Apuril, l'an mil cinq cents cinquante cinq.

Collation faicte.

Signé,   Du Puys,   I. Croppet.

PREFACE

DE M. MICHEL
NOSTRADAMVS
à ſes Prophecies.

Ad Cæſarem Noſtradamum filium
VIE ET FELICITE.

 ON TARD aduenement CESAR NOSTRADAME mon filz, m'a faict mettre mon long temps par continuelles vigilations nocturnes reſerer par eſcript, toy delaiſſer memoire, apres la corporelle extinction de ton progeniteur, au commun profit des humains de ce que la Diuine eſſence par Aſtronomiques reuolutions m'ont donné congnoiſſance. Et depuis qu'il a pleu au Dieu immortel
A ij

son César. This is that, even before printer Macé Bonhomme had been able to begin properly getting the *Prophecies* on to the market stalls, the fame that Nostradamus had already generated, even by his Almanacs alone, had caused him to be summoned to King Henri II and Queen Catherine de Medici's royal court in Paris.

NOTES

1 The *Prophecies* ('*Prophéties*') were composed in blocks of one hundred verses called 'Centuries'

2 '*Où prevoyat les insignes mutations & changemes advenir en l'Europe universellement, & mesmes les guerres civiles & sanglantes, & les troubles pernicieux de ce Royaume Gaulois fatalement s'approcher plein d'un enthusiasme, & comme ravi d'une fureur toute nouvelle, se mist à escrire ses Centuries, & autres presages commençant ainsi:*
D'esprit divin l'ame presage atteinte
Trouble, famine, peste, guerre courir
Eau, siccite, terre & mer de sang teinte:
Paix, trefue, à naistre, Prelats, Princes mourir.'
Chavigny, *Brief Discours...*, op. cit.

3 Ibid.

4 '*Ton tard advenement Cesar Nostredame mon filz, m'a faict mettre mon long temps par continuelles vigilations nocturnes reserer par escript, toy delaisser memoire apres la corporelle extinction de ton progenitor, au common profit des humains de ce que le Divine essence par Astronomiques revolutions m'ont donne congnoissance.*'

5 '*Estant assis de nuict secret estude*
Seul repouse sus la selle d'aerain
Flambe exigue sortant de solitude
Faict proserer qui n'est à croire vain'

6 Peter Levi, *Atlas of the Greek World*, London, Phaidon, 1980, p.78

7 '*La verge en main misc au milieu de BRANCHES*
De l'onde il moulle & le limbe & le pied
Un peur & voix fremissent par les manches
Splendeur divine. Le Divin prés s'assied'

8 '*Sibylla in Delphis duobus modis suscipiebat deum, vel per spiritum quendam tenuem igneumque, qui erumpebat alicubi ex ore antri cuiusdam; vel sedens in adyto super sedem aeneam, habentem tres aut quatuor pedes & deo dicatam, & utrobique exponebat se spiritui divino, unde radio divini ignis illustrabatur...Femina quinetiam in Brancis fatidica, vel sedet in axe, vel manu tenet virgam ab aliquo deo datam, vel pedes, aut limbum tingit in aquam, vel ex aqua quadam vaporem haurit & his modis impletur splendore divino, deumque nacta vaticinatur...*', Iamblichus, *De mysteriis*, 3, 11, fol. 9v of edition of 1516

9 Pierre Brind'Amour, *Nostradamus Astrophile...*, op. cit., p.455 n.66

10 Petrus Crinitus, *De Honesta Disciplina*, Lyons, Seb. Gryphius, 1543

11 '*par longue calculation rendant les estudes nocturnes... jay composé livres de propheties contenant chascun cent quatrains astronomiques de propheties...pour d'yci à l'année 3797*'

12 Theoretically there should be 10 × 100 quatrains, each 'Century' containing a hundred quatrains. However, in later editions Centurie 7 stops at quatrain 40 in the 1557 edition, and at 42 in an edition of 1568

13 Cyprian Leowitz, *De Coniunctionibus magnis insignioribus superiorum planetarum*, London, 1578

14 'celles que j'ay apperceu, quelque humaine mutation que adviene ne scandalizer l'auriculaire fragilité, & le tout figure nubileuse, plus que du tout prophetique'

15 'j'ay un peu voulu raboter obscurement'

16 'La grande famine que je sens approcher
Souvent tourner, puis estre universele
Si grande & longue qu'en viendra arracher
Du bois racine, & l'enfant de mammelle'

17 'Du tout Marseille des habitans changée
Course & pursuitte jusques au pres de Lyon
Narbon, Tholoze par Bourdeaux outragée
Tués captifz presque d'un million'

18 Peter Lemesurier, *The Nostradamus Encyclopaedia…*, op. cit., p.188

19 James Randi, *The Mask of Nostradamus…*, op. cit., p.228

20 John Roberts, 'The Myth of the Commune', *History Today*, May 1957, p.293

21 LES PROPHETIES
DE M. MICHEL
NOSTREDAMVS
A LYON
Chés Macé Bonhomme
M.D. LV
La permission est inserée à la page suivante
AVEC PRIVILEGE

CHAPTER 7

A Tricky Invitation

Much as history is indebted to Nostradamus' son César and to his secretary Chavigny for their efforts to perpetuate their hero's memory, both have also been responsible for some serious historical errors that crept into the Nostradamus literature at a very early stage and have been too often perpetuated by Nostradamian authors to this day. Chavigny, speaking of the 'noise and fame' that the publication of Nostradamus' *Prophecies* had generated, wrote in his *Brief Discourse*:

> The very powerful Henri II, King of France, sent to him to ask if he could come to court in the year of grace 1556.[1]

Directly as a result of this and of other misleading statements,[2] there has arisen a widespread supposition, shared not least by the truth-seeking James Randi,[3] that 1556 was the year in which Nostradamus made his historic visit to Paris.

In actuality, as can be determined from clues that have mostly become available only within the last two decades, the true date of this visit was during the summer of 1555: that is, very shortly after the publication of the *Prophecies*, yet (importantly) not prompted by any reactions to it, despite many assumptions to the contrary. Rather, its springboard was a number of disturbingly cryptic remarks, directed specifically at the royal household, that Nostradamus had made in the Almanac for 1555 (the one entitled *Prognostication*), which he had prepared, and the Lyons printer Jean Brotot had published, at the end of 1554.

As we know from extracts from this *Prognostication*, which one of Nostradamus' sternest critics, his fellow-astrologer Laurens Videl of Avignon, would later quote back to him, for the period immediately following the full moon of January 7, 1555 Nostradamus declared that he dared not state openly what was about to happen during this

year. And if that was not enough to make anyone even mildly suscep-
tible to astrology sit up and take notice, he solemnly forecast that for
the month of July:

> The King should watch out for himself that one or more individu-
> als do not pursue carrying out that which I dare not put into
> writing, a matter on which the stars are showing accordance with
> occult philosophy.[4]

As remarked by Videl, did Nostradamus really think that the King
would not want to know what this meant? Certainly not this King –
nor, especially, his Queen. Besides the arts of war King Henri II's principal preoccupation was dalliance with his alluring mistress, the long-
widowed Diane de Poitiers, elegant, highly intelligent and twenty
years his senior. For Henri any mention of 'occult philosophy' was
likely to raise unpleasant memories of Cornelius Agrippa, the sorcerer-
like German magician whom his grandmother Louise of Savoy had
sacked as astrologer-physician. His book, specifically entitled *Of
Occult Philosophy*, had been put on the banned list by the Indices of
Venice and Milan, predecessors of the subsequent, fearsome papal
Index of Prohibited Books.[5] Henri II's attitude towards any astrological matters was probably much the same as that of the biblical King
Saul towards the witch of Endor.[6] That is, while as a practical-minded
soldier and a crowned head of one of Europe's leading countries he
felt duty-bound to stamp heavily on any seriously heretical superstition, curiosity gave him a sneaking urge to find out whatever he could
from this controversial art.

In the case of Queen Catherine, by contrast, anything and everything to do with astrology had long had a serious fascination for her,
which stemmed from her Medici roots in Florence. Orphaned at three
weeks old, forced out of Florence by Charles V's German troops at the
age of eight, married in her mid-teens to a husband who preferred a
substantially older woman, and childless throughout the first ten years
of her marriage (she then made up for it by producing ten children in
the space of thirteen years), Catherine could hardly avoid a deep sense
of insecurity. Understandably, therefore, she became driven to search
for life's meaning in the stars, for which her Medici genes provided
plenty of precedents.

As we may recall, it had been Duke Cosimo de'Medici, Catherine's
great-great-great-uncle, who had paid for the upkeep of Nostradamus'
hero Marsilio Ficino during the long years that he laboured on his
translations of ancient works of magic and mystery such as the *Corpus
Hermetica*. Figuring high in the Medici folklore was Ficino's casting of

an astrological horoscope for Catherine's great-uncle Giovanni when he had been but a child, specifically predicting that he would become pope, as indeed he did under the name Leo X.[7] Another of the Medici family's astrologer protégés was the Neapolitan Luca Gaurico, who had deeply impressed everyone by predicting that Catherine's cousin Giulio de'Medici would have some serious political difficulties and beget many children. True to Gaurico's forecast, Giulio became Pope Clement VII (pontificate 1523–34); he lost England for the Catholic Church, and fathered twenty-nine illegitimate children. Gaurico also reputedly predicted the pontificate of Clement's successor Pope Paul III, who more modestly fathered only three sons and a daughter, and had died only six years earlier.

So when Catherine's husband Henri had become France's Dauphin, or heir apparent, on his brother François' unexpected death in 1536, she lost no time in calling for Gaurico, who prophesied that Henri would have his accession to the throne marked at both its beginning and its end by a sensational duel. Just nine days before his coronation, Henri duly witnessed a dramatic and fatal duel between two aristocrats, Gui Chabot Jarnac and François Vivonne la Châtaigneraie.

As Queen, therefore, Catherine enthusiastically attracted to her entourage a number of professional astrologers, among them the Italians Cosimo Ruggieri and Gabriele Simeoni, the latter who in 1555 was away with the French army in Italy, though only temporarily. So when someone brought to Catherine or to Henri a copy of Nostradamus' admonitory *Prognostication* for 1555, the royal interest in yet another promising astrologer could be virtually guaranteed. For just what might this intriguingly named Provençal have foreseen that he dared not commit to paper?

In the manner often employed by Britain's royals to this day, French protocol of the time dictated that any royal communication to a lowly commoner had to be conveyed via the intermediacy of that commoner's local governor or county lieutenant. In Nostradamus' case this was Provence's governor Claude de Savoie, Count of Tende. As later described by Nostradamus' son César:

> The Queen sent impatient letters by express to Count Tendé, commanding him to send her this individual [i.e. Nostradamus] whom the King wished to see.[8]

It had, of course, been Count Claude to whom, only a little over a year before, Nostradamus had dedicated his 1554 Almanac and had also communicated the information about the meteorite sighting. There are good grounds for believing that the two knew each other quite well socially through Anne Ponsarde's high-born Hozier family connections. So Count Claude would have had no difficulty locating Nostradamus and conveying to him that his presence was needed in Paris, and with some urgency.

Many authors have understandably supposed that Nostradamus would have interpreted this royal summons as his big break and a great honour, and that his mood would therefore have been one of pride and elation. His socialite son César, in his later writings about him, certainly tried to convey that impression. In actuality it is highly doubtful that Nostradamus himself saw it at all in this way. In 1555 he was fifty-two and the nearly five-hundred-mile (800 km) journey northwards from Salon to Paris demanded around a month in the saddle, with ever-present dangers of robbery or a fall from horse or mule along the way.

For any such journey north, the city of Lyons had to figure large on the itinerary, and thanks to a dedicatory notice that would later appear in Nostradamus' 1558 Almanac[9] we know more or less exactly where, and with whom, he lodged overnight while in the city. His Lyons host was Guillaume de Guadagne, a former Florentine merchant's son who was then the city's seneschal, or royal representative, and whom Nostradamus, in his later dedicatory notice, warmly thanked for the:

> ...great hospitality that Your Excellency extended to me at your Lyons house, on my way to Court, with such great and sumptuous conviviality, in the company of such a number of important people, all of honour, learning, nobility and wisdom.[10]

Guadagne's house was the then forty-year-old Hôtel de Gadagne [sic], still to be found amongst the narrow streets of Lyons' old quarter. And amongst the 'important people' so convivially dining there on that occasion was the local merchant Jean Guéraud, with whom, perhaps under the influence of Guadagne's liberal liquid hospitality, Nostradamus appears to have fallen into particularly deep and meaningful conversation.[11] Whether or not Nostradamus realised it, Guéraud kept a diary, which has survived. And thanks to this we have a unique insight into Nostradamus' distinctly apprehensive state of mind at this stage, one third completed, of his travels northwards. On a date some time around the last week of July 1555 (which happens to provide one of the several clues that 1555 was the true year of Nostradamus' visit to the Paris court), Guéraud recorded:

> At this same time there passed through the city an astrologer called

Michel de Nostre Dame of Salon de Crau in Provence. A man very knowledgeable in palmistry, mathematics and astrology, he talked of great things and of matters as much from the past as to come, and to the extent of reading thoughts, just as if they were spoken. He was on his way to the Court of the King to which he had been summoned. And he greatly feared that some evil might happen to him, for he said that he was in great danger of having his head cut off before the 25th day of the August coming.[12]

Guéraud's account is highly interesting, not only because of Nostradamus' obvious garrulousness on this occasion, indicating his interest in otherwise undiscussed matters such as palmistry and telepathy, but also because of his clearly serious concern that he might have his head cut off, specifically before August 25th, by which time he could be expected to have reached Paris. So why such apprehension, and why associated with a particular date? It is virtually certain that prior to embarking on such a long journey, at (for the time) an advanced age, leaving behind two very young children, Nostradamus would have cast a horoscope for himself as a check on what hazards the venture might hold for him. So had this self-motivated dabble into his own future proved seriously unfavourable, warning him specifically that he could lose his head on or before August 25? Had he perhaps not even confided this grim portent to his wife Anne, in order not to cause her undue worry during his long absence? Whatever the answer, Guérard's diary information provides a most significant indicator that Nostradamus seemed genuinely to believe in his powers of seeing into the future: so much so that he could be seriously spooked by them, rather than being an all-out cynical pretender, in the manner that a James Randi would have us believe.

According to César de Nostredame (who was only eighteen months old when his father made his court visit), the date that Nostradamus had bade farewell to his wife was July 14, 1555, and that of his arrival before the walls of Paris was August 15, 'the day of the Assumption of Our Lady, she whose name he bore'.[13] The journey had taken just over a month, an average of some sixteen miles (25 km) a day, and would therefore have been ridden very cautiously, rather than at a gallop. One curiosity that César noted is consistent with the remarks about the Virgin Mary for which Nostradamus two decades earlier had been hauled up before the Inquisition at Agen. Rather than immediately going to his namesake cathedral, the famous Notre Dame on the Seine, to give thanks for his safe arrival, Nostradamus instead paid his respects to the standard of his other namesake, St Michael the Archangel, helper of the Chosen People.[14]

The Paris that Nostradamus would have encountered at the time of his visit in 1555. Detail from a 16th century map, showing the Cathedral of Notre Dame.

So far as can be determined, this was Nostradamus' first ever visit to Paris. The city's population at the time has been calculated at around 200,000. Its central area, the Île de la Cité in the middle of the Seine, was dominated then, as now, by the ancient Cathedral of Notre Dame, the island being connected to the right and left banks by fine bridges, among them the Pont Nostredame and the Pont Michel. At this time two small islands just north of Notre Dame had not yet been joined to the Île de la Cité, the more southerly of these being the Isle Nostre Dame. So Nostradamus, although his Provençal accent would have marked him out as a southerner, ought to have felt at least a little at home in this chilly northern city, far though it was from his beloved Provence.

When Nostradamus, crossing one of the Seine's bridges, looked downstream he would have gazed on sixteenth-century Paris's right bank, an area over-spilling the old walls. This was the sector for business and commerce, where each main trade had its own quarter and each business its own distinctive sign, much in the manner of today's advertising logos. Rich merchants had fine houses here, and the shops and booths of money-changers, goldsmiths and drapers crowded the Pont au Change. On the left bank lay the city's university quarter, which was also the haunt of its many booksellers and printers. Amongst the latter, at the sign of the two cockerels, was the printing shop of Jacques Kerver, upon whom Nostradamus may well have called during his visit, since Kerver would later, in association with Brotot of Lyons, publish his 1557 Almanac.

No doubt reminding Nostradamus of his home town, throughout much of Paris safe drinking water was supplied in abundance from public fountains fed from aqueducts. In the more well-to-do areas the streets were wide, paved and kept clean and well-swept, though in poorer districts they were narrow and reeked of human and animal excrement. It was certainly a city receptive to astrologers, since the contemporary diarist Pierre l'Estoile estimated that there were some 30,000 touting for business among its streets. While L'Estoile's estimate must surely have been an exaggeration, for Nostradamus to have been summoned to the royal presence over the heads of anything like so many local practitioners should be reckoned as some kind of accolade in itself

According to César, on his father's arrival in Paris he was first received by 'Monsieur le Connestable', to whose headquarters he had no doubt been told to report. This was Constable Anne de Montmorency, a veteran soldier who had spent his long life in the royal service, and was a particularly trusted adviser and confidante to Queen Catherine. If Montmorency truly received Nostradamus in person, then the seer was indeed honoured, for the court buzzed with any number of lesser flunkeys, amongst them some ten chamberlains, seven *maîtres d'hôtel*, four masters of the wardrobe, five doctors, thirty-seven pages of honour, twenty-eight *valets de chambre*, twenty-two ladies in waiting, three apothecaries, four barbers, two laundresses, plus numerous porters, grooms and other attendants.

In a manner that was not uncommon throughout Europe at the time, the French court had a number of royal palaces, with no one fixed abode among them. As financial accounts of the time indicate, on a typical day the royal household might consume 250 loaves of bread, eighteen joints of beef, eight sheep, four calves, twenty capons, 120 chickens and pigeons, three deer, six geese and four hares.[15] Accordingly, it only needed the court to tarry for just a few weeks in any one palace for it to accumulate a displeasing and odorous superfluity of waste and litter. In such circumstances the recognised solution was for the entire household and its permanent attendants to move lock, stock and barrel on to the next palace that had been cleaned and prepared for them.

Surviving records of the time indicate that in the second half of August and early September 1555 the chosen palace was one a few miles to the north, the magnificent Saint Germain-en-Laye.[16] Pierre Chambiges, architect to King Henri's father François I, had only three decades earlier transformed this former fortified castle into a magnificent pentagonal Renaissance château surrounded by acres of superbly laid out gardens. So it was to this that Montmorency would have escorted Nostradamus for the prescribed royal audience, the goal of his long and arduous journey north.

Sadly, while the Saint Germain-en-Laye palace is still extant, an ill-conceived transformation of it in the nineteenth century, turning it into a distinctly drab prehistory museum, has deprived us of any meaningful glimpse of the once glittering throne-room to which Montmorency would have led Nostradamus in August 1555. Of whatever discussion Nostradamus might have had with the King and Queen on this occasion, César recorded nothing, and Chavigny merely noted that they 'conversed together on great things'.[17] The only indication of any kind of favourable impression that Nostradamus might have made is that, according to César, King Henri ordered that he be lodged at the palace of the Cardinal of Sens.

On the Seine's right bank, and now known as the Hôtel de Sens, the Cardinal of Sens' residence is one of only three great medieval private

The Palace of St. Germain-de-Laye, where Nostradamus had his audience with King Henri II and Queen Catherine.

residences left in Paris. Through its porch and across its courtyard the visitor comes to an attractive spiral staircase winding its way up a square tower. This must surely have reminded Nostradamus of the spiral staircase that he had left at home in Salon. And such splendid lodgings seem to have pleased him, since in his next, expanded edition of the *Prophecies* he would devote a special quatrain to the Cardinal of Sens.

In this regard we may now recall that Nostradamus had a very good reason for wanting comfortable and, most importantly, secure lodgings at this particular time. For the dreaded deadline of August 25, the date by which, according to what he had told Guéraud, he feared suffering some method of decapitation, had not yet come. Given therefore that we know Nostradamus arrived in Paris on August 15, that his royal audience was arranged almost immediately, and that neither César nor Chavigny appear to have been aware of his forebodings, this makes all the more interesting César's information concerning the days leading up to and just beyond the 25th.

> There [i.e. in the palace of the Cardinal of Sens] a surprise attack of gout *detained him for ten or twelve days* [italics mine], during which time his Majesty sent him a hundred gold crowns in a velvet purse and the Queen nearly as much.[18]

Now ten to twelve days would conveniently have taken Nostradamus to just beyond the danger period. So was this 'surprise attack of gout' contrived to enable him to stay in circumstances of maximum security and comfort until the decapitation danger could be considered past?

Maybe this is an unworthy suggestion, since in later years we will find this gout, or some similar condition, recurring in indisputably genuine circumstances. Nonetheless it is quite certain that César de Nostredame's account of the later events of his father's visit to Paris definitely suffers from some serious further departure from the truth. According to César:

> He [Nostradamus] was hardly free of these severe ills when by the King's express orders he set off for Blois, to examine the children of France [i.e. the royal children], which he managed very happily. As for honours, royal largesse, most pleasing and magnificent presents which he received from their Majesties, from the Princes, and from the greatest in the Court, I would prefer to rest my pen, fearing that to speak of them with too great a pride might cause me to say more than modesty permits.[19]

As earlier mentioned, the first ten years of Catherine's marriage to Henri had been childless. This was due not to any sterility on her part, but to Henri's dalliance with the glamorous and beautiful Diane de Poitiers. Then at last the ever-sensible Diane herself advised Henri that he really ought to do his duty by his country, whereupon between 1544 and 1555 Catherine gamely bore him ten children. Three of these failed to survive infancy, nothing exceptional by the medical standards of the time. The rest, as at the late summer of 1555, comprised the sickly heir-apparent, eleven-year-old François, then already getting to know his future Scottish bride Mary Stuart; and the second eldest son, Charles, later to be Charles IX, aged five. Then came four-year-old Henri (then known as Edouard Alexandre, but later to be Henri III), and four other princes and princesses. These were the 'children of France' to which César referred. And on the strength of his description one author after another has envisaged Nostradamus solemnly journeying over a hundred miles (160 km) down the Loire valley to examine them astrologically at their magnificent 'royal nursery' château at Blois. There even survives an engraving that has been commonly interpreted as a contemporary depiction of this scene. Nostradamian biographers then assume that Nostradamus would have hurried back to Paris to report his predictions of the children's future to Henri and Catherine before at last being free to return to his family in Salon. As César's account further relates, his father's eventual send-off from Paris was a correspondingly impressive one, the seer's travel-bags reportedly being packed with the largesse that his country's grateful rulers and their court had showered upon him.

Yet that this is utterly fictional is made clear in a crucial letter by Nostradamus which has long been preserved in the Bibliothèque Nationale,[20] and was first brought to scholarly attention as long ago as 1895. Composed in 1561, that is, six years after the Paris visit, it was addressed to Jean Morel, the very same individual whom we noted only months earlier reporting the success that Nostradamus' 1555 *Prognostication* had enjoyed. Peter Lemesurier, aware of this letter, has assumed that Morel was a mere money-lender to whom Nostradamus had forgotten to repay a debt he had incurred while in Paris.[21] In fact Morel was rather more illustrious, none other than Jean Morel d'Embrun (1511–81), a one-time disciple of Erasmus and highly respected *maître d'hotel* to Henri II's court who specialised in helping poets, scholars and writers with any problems that they might incur while at the royal court.[22]

So what had transpired between Nostradamus and Morel? Although Morel's letter of 1561 has not survived the gist of it is easy enough to gather from Nostradamus' response to it. Apparently

Nostradamus' travel expenditure during the long outward journey to Paris had considerably exceeded his expectations. On his arrival in the capital, therefore, he had been in urgent need of money, and Morel had generously lent him some to tide him over. As Nostradamus freely admitted: 'When I was in Paris and went off to make obeisance before her Majesty the Queen, you [i.e. Jean Morel] lent me two Rose nobles and two crowns'.[23]

So far, nothing seems particularly untoward, except that, as the same letter makes clear, Nostradamus then had to leave the capital in such a hurry that he had no time to recompense Morel with the money that he had received from Henri and Catherine. To make matters far worse, once safely back in Provence he completely failed either to communicate or to make any attempt to repay his debt until an extremely irate Morel caught up with him late in 1561.

Clearly caught on the wrong foot, Nostradamus in his letter to Morel made a lengthy explanation of how and why it was that he had to leave Paris so quickly in 1555. And in doing so he cast his entire visit in an entirely different light from the rose-tinted version that has been provided by César. First, he told Morel:

> Please understand, Monsieur, that immediately I arrived at the Court, after my having spoken a little time with her Majesty the Queen, I told her myself of your nobleness of heart, and of your Caesarean generosity making me the loan. And it was not just one time that I said this to Her Majesty, but it was reiterated by me four more times.[24]

It is not altogether clear from this whether Nostradamus had just one royal audience, during which he repeated himself four times to Queen Catherine on the matter of the loan, or whether he had four separate audiences. Either way, instead of meeting King Henri, as claimed by César, he throughout mentions only meeting Queen Catherine.

Secondly after effusively assuring Morel of his good character, he cryptically remarked:

> I thought that my visit to the court was because I had been commanded to go there. But there were also counter-orders by others of an opposite variety, that I should not go there at all.[25]

Immediately the question is raised: if Nostradamus had been commanded to go to Paris by none other than the Queen, a point on which all sources are agreed, who was it who had authority to issue counter-orders? Was it Henri himself or, at the very least, some high-placed courtiers hostile to astrology, acting with his full approval?

Thirdly, rather than having been showered with an embarrassing number of farewell gifts as described by César, the actuality would seem to have been a downright royal stinginess, at least by Nostradamus' estimates of his personal worth:

> As a fine recompense for my attendance at Court I fell sick. The King sent me a hundred crowns. The Queen sent me thirty. There's a handsome reward for my having come two hundred leagues! It cost me a hundred crowns to get there, so I made thirty![26]

Fourthly, postively contradicting César's account of a visit to the 'children of France' at Blois under a halo of royal approval, or an honourable departure from Paris showered with gifts, Nostradamus told Morel:

> After my arrival back in Paris from Saint Germain[en-Laye], that same night there came to see me a very becoming great lady. I do not know who she was, but her appearance showed her to be most worthy, and a woman of honour. She spoke of certain matters – I cannot say what these were – and she left late that same night. The next morning she came to see me again. After Her Ladyship had spoken to me of more discreet matters than previously she told me that men from the Paris Justice department were planning to seek me out to question me about what science I use, and how I make my predictions. My response to her was that they need not trouble do any such thing, since I would save them the bother. I had already decided to leave the next morning for my return to Provence, and this I did.[27]

This short passage is so melodramatic that my first reaction to it was to dismiss it as Nostradamus telling the tallest story that he could think of in order – still unconvincingly – to wriggle out of his dishonourable behaviour in taking so long to pay off a debt. After all, according to him, he did not even know this 'great lady's' identity, yet she came to him unannounced, stayed with him far into the night, then returned the next morning to tell him the highly sensitive information that the Justice department was planning to arrest him. So just who could this beautiful aristocrat have been, that she was able to stay out so late at night unchaperoned with a man whom she had never met before, and yet be party to decisions that were being taken at the highest level by the King's legislature?

Historically there seem to be only two alternatives. Either

Nostradamus' mysterious night-time visitor? Royal mistress Diane de Poitiers depicted as the Roman goddess Diana, from a contemporary painting in the Louvre.

Nostradamus was indeed spinning a fantastical story to Morel, though one wonders why he should go to so much trouble when he could have settled the matter with an abject apology plus restitution of the loan, both of which he appears to have attended to anyway. Or he was telling the truth, and the mysterious 'great lady' was very real, being none other than the King's mistress Diane de Poitiers. To the best of my awareness, no one has ever suggested this before. And by the very nature of the evidence we have absolutely no proof that Nostradamus ever met the beautiful Diane on either this or any other occasion. But the royal mistress not only perfectly fits Nostradamus' description of a very becoming 'great lady' visitor, she also makes sense of Nostradamus' air of mystery surrounding her identity. While he may genuinely have been unaware of who she was, she alone, far more than any woman at the royal court other than Queen Catherine, could have been party to what was going on amongst her lover King Henri's chief legal and religious advisers, and been in a position to warn Nostradamus accordingly.

But overall, whoever this mysterious lady visitor may have been, the gist of the Bibliothèque Nationale's undeniably genuine letter from Nostradamus to Morel is that once Nostradamus had been warned of the danger he was in, he left Paris immediately – not with any warm and well-rewarded farewell from the King and Queen, but in great haste, indeed in abject fear for his life. César's colourful account of his departure showered with gifts may therefore be dismissed as a fiction. Likewise fictional, whether Nostradamus himself later put it about verbally, or whether César perhaps invented it to boost his father's importance, has to be the story of examining the royal children at Blois. On this point, the engraving that has been vaunted as a contemporary depiction of Nostradamus making this examination has been convincingly shown to be nothing of the kind. As has been explained by Dr Edgar Leroy, the architecture depicted bears no resemblance to that of the château at Blois. And in fact the scene is nothing to do with Nostradamus. Instead it is the third 'Age' from the 'Seven Ages of Man', a series of prints produced in Antwerp in 1577. Nostradamus' association with this print arose from a totally mistaken attribution made by an over-imaginative Bibliothèque Nationale print room conservator in the mid-nineteenth century.[28]

It is important to point out that none of these adverse findings should necessarily be taken either to contradict, or to detract from, Nostradamus' reputation as a genuine seer or prophet of his time. They most certainly warn us, however, never to be too trusting of any information coming from César de Nostradame, or from secretary Chavigny, however close in time and place they may have been to their hero.

NOTES

1 '...le tres puissant Henry II Roy de France, l'envoya querir pour venir en Cour l'an de grace 1556'

2 César, for instance, spoke of his father making the journey when he was fifty-three years old, which would again put it in 1556

3 James Randi, *The Mask of Nostradamus...*, op. cit., p.233

4 'le roy se gardera de quelcun ou plusieurs qui ne pourchassent que de faire ce que je n'ose metre par escrit, selon que les astres accordéz a l'oculte philosophie demonstrent' – quoted by Laurens Videl, *Declaration des abus ignorances et seditions de Michel Nostradamus...*, Avignon, Pierre Roux & Ian Tramblay, 1558; see Jean Dupèbe, *Nostradamus – Lettres Inédites*, op. cit., p.30, n. 3. Of the *Prognostication* itself, as earlier remarked, only one copy survives, which was owned by the late Daniel Ruzo, and has since become inaccessible following his death in 1991. Accordingly it has not been possible to check Videl's quote against this sole original. However I am greatly indebted to Dr Elmar Gruber for providing a transcript of the relevant section from Chavigny's *Recueil* manuscript, in which the same wording appears, except that the phrase 'selon que les astres...demonstrent' has been omitted, which it may be assumed was one of Chavigny's many known abbreviations from the original almanacs

5 Lynn Thorndike, *A History of Magic and Experimental Science*, New York, Columbia University Press, vol. VI, p.146

6 See the Bible, I Samuel, chapter 28

7 See Jakob Burckhardt, *The Civilization of the Renaissance in Italy*, trans. S. G. C. Middlemore, London, Phaidon, 1944

8 'la Royne qui en a le vent mande incontinent lettres expresses au comte Claude de luy envoyer ce personnage que le Roy desire voir.' César de Nostredame, *Histoire de Provence...*, p.776

9 *Pronostication Nouvelle pour l'An mil cinq cens cinquante & huict. Composée par maistre Michel Nostradamus de Salon de Craux en Provence*, Paris, Guillaume le Noir, 1557

10 '*du bon acceuil que vostre excellence me feit dans vostre maison à Lyon, allant à la court, en tant grand & sumptueux convive, accompagné d'un nombre de graves personnages, tous d'honneur, de doctrine, de noblesse & erudition*'

11 I have here inferred that Guéraud was present at the banquet held by Guadagne, which, though it seems likely, cannot be taken for certain. Likewise it is possible that Guadagne's hospitality towards Nostradamus, though it certainly comprised a very impressive banquet, did not include overnight lodgings

12 '*En ce mesme temps fust et passa par cestre ville un astrologue nommé Michel de Nostre Dame en Sallon de Craulx en Provence, homme très scavant en chiromancye et mathématicque et astrologie, qui à dict de grandes choses à aulcungs particulliers tant du pasé que de l'advenir et jusques à deviner les pensées, ainsy qu'on disoit: et alloit à la cour du Roy où il estoit mandé et craignoit grandement qu'on luy fist maulvais party, car luy mesme disoit qu'estoit en grand danger d'avoir la teste couppée devant le XXV jour d'aoust ensuyvant...*', Jean Gérard, *La chronique lyonnaise de Jean Guérard 1536–1562*, ed. Jean Tricou, Lyons, 1929, p.85, para 132, quoted in Brind'Amour, *Nostradamus Astrophile...*, op. cit., p.63. This particular part of Guérard's chronicle concerns the period May 20 to July 27, 1555. Since César records his father's departure from Salon as on July 14, Nostradamus probably arrived in Lyons around July 24 or 25

13 '*le quinze du mois d'Aoust, jour de l'Assumption nostre Dame, luy qui en portoit le nom...*'

14 See the Bible, Daniel 10.3 ff and 12: 1

15 Antonia Fraser, *Mary Queen of Scots*, after Alphonse de Ruble, *La première jeunesse de Marie Stuart*, 1891, p.19

16 Jean Dupèbe, *Nostradamus, Lettres Inédites...*, p.172, n.5, after *Registres du Bureau de la ville de Paris*, vol. 4, pp.380, 384

17 '*avec iceluy communiqué de choses grandes*'

18 '*...la goutte qui le surprend le detient dix ou douze jours, pendant lesquels sa Majesté luy envoye cent escus d'or dans une bource de velours, & la Royne presques autant*', César de Nostredame, *Histoire et Chronique de Provence...*, op. cit., p.776

19 '*Hors de ces violentes douleurs...par l'exprez commandement du Roy il prend le chemin de Blois, pour voir les enfans de France: ce qu'il fit tres-heureusement. Quant aux honneurs, despouiles royales, joyaux & magnifiques presents qu'il receut de leurs Majestés, des Princes & plus grands de la Cour, j'ayme mieux les laisser au bout de ma plume, que de les dire par trop d'esquise vanité, craignant d'en avoir plus dit que ne requiert la modestie.* César de Nostredame, *Histoire et Chronique de Provence*, op. cit., p.776

20 Paris, Bibliothèque Nationale, ms.lat.8589. The full text of this letter, in the original French, is given in Jean Dupèbe, *Nostradamus, Lettres Inédites...*, op. cit., pp.169–71

21 Peter Lemesurier, *The Nostradamus Encyclopaedia*, op. cit., p.172

22 M. Gerard Davis, 'A Humanist Family in the Sixteenth Century', *The French Mind. Studies in honour of Gustave Rudler*, Oxford, 1952, pp.1–16

23 '*moy estant a Paris m'en allant voyr faire la reverence à la maieste de la Royne me prestatez deux nobles a la Roze et deux escus.*' Paris, BN, ms.lat.8589, op. cit.

24 '*Devez entendre, Seigneur, que tout incontinent que je feuz arrivé a la cour apres avoir parlemente quelque peu a la maieste de la Royne je luy diz mesmes la noblesse vostre et vostre plus que Caesaree liberalité de ce que m'aviez presté. Et ce ne fut pas une foys que le diz a sa maiesté, mais assuerez vous que il feut reiteré par moy de plus de quatre foys.*' Quoted in Dupèbe, *Nostradamus, Lettres Inédites...*, op. cit., p.169

25 '*Je pensois mon allee estre a la court que j'estois mandé pour y aller. Mais aussy a l'opposite par aultres contremande de n'y aller poinct.*' Quoted in Dupèbe, *Nostradamus, Lettres Inédites...*, op. cit., p.170

26 '*...pour bonne recompense que j'euz de la court, je y vins malade, la maiesté du Roy me bailla cent escuz, la Royne m'en billa trente et voila une belle somme pour estre venu de deux cens lieues, y avoir despendu cent escuz, j'en ai trente.*' Quoted in Dupèbe, *Nostradamus, Lettres Inédites...*, op. cit. p.170

27 '*Apres que je feuz arrivé a Paris du retour de Saint Germain, une fort honneste grande femme que je ne scay quelle estoit, a son apparence demonstroit estre dame grandement honneste et dame d'honneur, quelle que fut qu me vint veoir le seoir que je feuz arrivé et me tint aulcuns propos, je ne scaurois dire quelz c'estient, et print congé qui estoit asses nuict. Et le lendemain matin me vint veoir et apres que sa noblesse m'eust tenu quelques propos tant de ses affaires particulieres que aultrement, a la parfin elle me dist que Messieurs de la justice de Paris me debuoient venir a trouver pour me interroger de quelle science je faisois et presageois ce que je faisois. Je luy diz par response qu'ilz ne prinsent pas de penne de venir pour telz affaires, que je leur ferois place, que aussy je avois delibere m'en partir le matin pour m'en retourner en Provence, ce que je feiz.*' Quoted in Dupèbe, *Nostradamus, Lettres Inédites...*, op. cit., p.170

28 Leroy, *Nostradamus, Ses Origines...*, op. cit., pp. 81–2

CHAPTER 8

Dealing in Futures

That some time around late August or early September of 1555 Nostradamus left populous Paris and hurried back home to Salon fearing for his life is corroborated from another source, the Avignon-based fellow-astrologer Laurens Videl. According to Videl, on passing through Lyons Nostradamus made no attempt to seek a repeat of the royal seneschal Guillaume de Guadagne's hospitality. Instead he called only on his regular Almanac printer Jean Brotot, specifically insisting that he should not spread it about that he was in town.[1]

Of the rest of Nostradamus' return journey, and of his arrival in Salon, there survives no word. All that is known is that when he was safely back home he lost very little time getting back to his forecasting, and with renewed vigour. During the winter of 1555/6 there flowed from his quill pen no less than three predictive works, all intended for 1557.

Those to whom Nostradamus dedicated these works are very interesting, considering the circumstances in which he had left Paris. One of the works was *The Marvellous Predictions for the Year 1557, dedicated to the very Christian King Henri, the Second of that Name*.[2] The first of any of Nostradamus' works that he had dedicated to the King, this set of prophecies for 1557 was clearly inspired by his royal audience of August 1555. The chosen printer was the hitherto untried Jacques Kerver of Paris, which indicates that while in the capital Nostradamus must have called on Kerver's premises in the Rue St-Jacques and come to some special publishing arrangement, thereby giving his writings a wider distribution than the Lyons-based Brotot alone could provide.

A second production was an *Almanac for the year 1557*, dedicated 'to the most Christian and most serene Catherine Queen of France'.[3] This, according to the date of its dedication, was completed on January 13, 1556, and shows that Nostradamus' impression of his meeting with Catherine were similarly favourable. For this the vital 'privilege', or royal permission, is however dated October 14, the long delay in obtaining it apparently due to extended communications. This was because this particular publication was a co-edition between the Parisian Jacques Kerver and the faithful Jean Brotot of Lyons, these printers being jointly named in the 'privilege'.

The third work, apparently a second Jacques Kerver 'exclusive', was *The Grand New Prognostication with portentous predictions for the year 1557*.[4] This is internally dated as completed May 20, 1556, and Nostradamus dedicated it to the 'King of Navarre, Antoine de Vendôme',[5] described in court circles as First Prince of the Blood on account of his Bourbon lineage, which made him and his descendants next in line to the throne after Henri II's Valois dynasty. Highly interesting about this unexpected choice of dedicatee is that both Navarre, and more particularly his Queen, Jeanne d' Albret, King Henri II's cousin, had been falling under increasing suspicion of Protestant leanings because they sheltered exiled Calvinist preachers, a suspicion that would later turn out to be well justified. So for Nostradamus to have issued two Almanacs in a single year, one dedicated to the very Catholic Queen Catherine de Medici, the other to the probably Protestant King of Navarre, smacks just a little of what Brotot would have called 'having your cake and eating it too'.

Although copies of all three Almanacs have survived to our own time, the single extant copy of *Marvellous Predictions for the year 1557* was privately acquired and is no longer available for scholarly study, a circumstance regrettably, all too commonly encountered in respect of Nostradamus' Almanacs. In all cases, however, the images and wording for at least the title-pages are known. And one hitherto unprecedented element common to all three title-pages is a line clearly referring to the murky circumstances in which Nostradamus had made his hurried departure from Paris: 'Against those who many times would have had me dead'.[6]

This seems to have been a none too subtle allusion to certain shadowy individuals, among them at least one jealous rival astrologer, whom Nostradamus suspected of being behind the moves to have him arrested while he was in Paris As has been suggested by Pierre Brind'Amour, the inaccessible *Marvellous Predictions for the Year 1557* may well carry some clues to the identities of these individuals, though in the present state of our knowledge this can only be a guess.

Nonetheless, even though Nostradamus had some influential enemies, he still had some highly placed friends, even among rival astrologers. And, as is evident from another letter amongst the Bibliothèque Nationale's vitally important Latin manuscript of

Nostradamus' correspondence, one who certainly seems to have been well-disposed was the Italian-born court astrologer Gabriele Simeoni, who happens to have been another author published by Brotot of Lyons. As noted earlier, when Nostradamus visited the Paris court Simeoni had been away with the French forces at Volpiano in Italy. However, some time in the course of correspondence Nostradamus appears to have asked Brotot about him, whereupon when Simeoni returned from Italy, on February 1, 1556, he got in touch with Nostradamus, remarking with seemingly unfeigned amity:

> Immediately upon my return from the war in Volpiano – fortunately unharmed – I was greatly pleased to hear of your success at court, with the King, the Queen and other notables.[7]

Importantly, the date of this letter from Simeoni agrees with, indeed positively confirms, our earlier indicators that Nostradamus' visit to Paris had been in 1555, not 1556. Furthermore, Simeoni's unprompted mention of Nostradamus' 'success' with both the King and the Queen suggests that the royal audiences in Paris may possibly have been rather warmer and more productive than he was prepared to admit in his later apologetic letter to Jean Morel. Unclear, however, is whether Simeoni's response was based on what he had heard at court when he arrived back in Paris, or simply gathered secondhand from what Brotot had told him, from Nostradamus' description.

In any event, also evident from other letters amongst the same Bibliothèque Nationale manuscript is that the general public's interest in Nostradamus and his prophetic capabilities increased very sharply from this time on. From both near and far individuals of all ages and walks of life became increasingly keen to contact him, asking him to cast their horoscopes, to advise them on business decisions, to tell them how long they had to live, and much else about their futures.

Despite the biblical injunctions against 'soothsayers and augers' one such enquirer was the Italian-born churchman Bishop Pierre de Forlivio, then, like Nostradamus, a long-time resident of Provence. In the early 1530s Forlivio had been a regent at Avignon University, and for the previous sixteen years he had held the see of Apt, a small town east of Avignon. A family man, with a strong interest in certain nephews or grandchildren – frustratingly, the Latin does not allow us to differentiate which – at the time he contacted Nostradamus in November 1557 he was going through some kind of mid-life crisis. As he asked of the seer:

> My Nostradamus, if you care for me, consult my stars. Would

Roman soil be more rewarding for me than that of Provence? Which of the two is more suitable for me? Can I expect to be better favoured in the city? Is a persecution about to happen? Or some other adversity? I also want to know how my nephews/grandsons will treat me. Do I have a long or a short time to live? Advise me also whatever happinesses or sorrows may befall the children, also any other relevant matters that you may be able to add.[8]

The same month that Forlivio was writing from Apt, another of Nostradamus' correspondents, the Italian Giovanni Cibo Boerius, contacted him from Sturlano, the territory of the river Sturla that runs south-east of Genoa. Boerius had some similarly pointed questions concerning his future. He began on a flattering note, telling Nostradamus how far his fame was travelling.

Most illustrious doctor, the brilliance of your virtue has shone out not only to your country's borders, but has become extended to all Frenchmen everywhere. And flying above the high peaks of the Alps it has penetrated gloriously into Italy, to arrive at last in our own Liguria [the Genoa–Savona region of Italy].[9]

Having thus, with luck, attracted Nostradamus' attention, Boerius then proceeded to pose five leading questions that would seem almost ridiculous directed at anyone but an astrologer:

First, is my sister still alive at St Bridget's convent in England? Second, how many years do I have to live? Third, would it be better for me to sell or to retain my property at Sturlano? Fourth, is there any buried treasure in this property, which is amongst the ruins of an old palace? Fifth and last, might I be able to find any veins of spring-water here at Sturlano?[10]

Absurdly naive as such questions might seem to any sceptic, they were quite literally meat and drink to sixteenth-century astrologers – and indeed continued to be so during the subsequent centuries. If a satis-factory-sounding answer could be provided by the astrologer, a suit-ably satisfactory financial reward could be expected from the client. As the mid-twentieth-century English professional astrologer Phyllis Naylor once remarked of her clientèle, the two stock questions that they would ask her were: 'Will I inherit any money?' and 'When do you think my husband/wife will die?' As she commented of this: 'What people want is an inexpensive act of magic, preferably one that does not cost more than a guinea or two!'[11]

Helpful though it would have been to know Nostradamus' responses to his eager 'clients' Bishop Forlivio and Cibo Boerius, they have not survived. In the case of Bishop Forlivio all we know is that shortly after writing to Nostradamus he accepted the post of titular abbot at the Cistercian abbey of Sénanque, just outside Avignon. This posting turned out to be very shortlived, for by February 5, 1559 he was dead,[12] so whether Nostradamus had told him of his short life-expectancy, or had specially recommended his move to Sénanque, must remain purely conjectural.

However, a third letter amongst the manuscript's collection, from Sigismund Woyssel, a twenty-five-year-old man from Bratislava whom Nostradamus may have met in Paris, was evidently written *after* advice that Nostradamus had given in earlier (lost) correspondence. And this letter not only shows something of what Nostradamus recommended, but also how even the most credulous clients could sometimes react with not altogether unstinting gratitude. By way of introduction Woyssel, like Boerius, praised Nostradamus for his spreading fame:

> You asked me to give you information about any astrologers, should I come across any well-known ones while in Italy. The fact is that I have not heard of any here. There is just one person who is famous with everyone: Nostradamus. Not a word about anyone else.[13]

Woyssel then turned to the case of a bankrupt Hungarian whose creditors had had him thrown in jail, a matter on which, via Woyssel, Nostradamus had apparently offered some earlier advice. The bad news was that this advice had caused rather more confusion than been of any help. In Woyssel's words:

> He [the Hungarian] could be let out of prison, and everyone satisfied, if only we knew what we were looking for. He regards the response that you [Nostradamus] gave him as far too obscure. He pleads that you explain things more clearly. He promises that you will be truly and liberally rewarded for your efforts.[14]

Reinforcing his critical stance, Woyssel, whose letter was written from Padua, turned to some apparently more explicit advice that Nostradamus had earlier given him personally, directing him to seek his fortune in Italy:

> Without wanting to criticise your earlier work, some does not seem to be altogether accurate. For example, you stated: 'Your fortune

lies in Italy.' But so far since my being here I have suffered more setbacks than any good luck. I think it possible that your error derived from my not having given you the correct time for my birth. The date that I gave you before was December 19 in the year of grace 1534, an hour before sunset. In actuality it was half an hour after sunset… Another point puzzles me a great deal. Earlier I had thought you had predicted that a lot of good things would happen to me in 1559. Now what I read is that this [year] will be unfavourable rather than favourable. Here I have your exact words: 'Beware the year 1559, the 23rd day' But the 23rd of which month? It saddens me that the month in which this 23rd falls has not been specified. I urge you, write to me diligently on this and the other matters, and you will have no need to doubt my faith.[15]

As is evident from other, similar letters, such criticisms of Nostradamus' forecasting and obscurity of expression were far from exceptional. Other clients repeatedly complained that he provided them with exasperatingly incomplete information and, not least, that he set it down in well-nigh illegible handwriting.

Yet, in his defence, the very same Bibliothèque Nationale manuscript containing such samples from his correspondence also contains a lot of evidence to indicate his conscientiousness in his craft. For Forlivio, for Woyssel and for a number of others, Nostradamus prepared elaborate astrological birth-charts, based on information that each had supplied to him concerning the date, time and place of their births. From this information, and from the various ephemeris charts and tables available to him, Nostradamus calculated the planetary positions at the time and place of each birth. He also calculated what was astrologically termed the Medium Coelis, or Mid-heaven – that is, the degree of the zodiac culminating at any given minute – together with its related Ascendant, the degree of the zodiac simultaneously rising on the eastern celestial horizon. He also had to take into account any relevant 'aspects', that is, the angles of the planets to each other, and whether one happened to be directly opposite another at the relevant moment. All such calculations demanded a significant degree of technical expertise and mathematical skill. The data obtained were set down on a special chart – Nostradamus used a squarish form, other astrologers a round one – variants of which continue to be used for astrological forecasting to this day. Once such a chart had been prepared, interpretations of the future could then be drawn from it, much in the manner that Tarot readers draw inspiration from a particular layout of Tarot cards, or palmists from the lines on a client's hand.

It is often assumed that Nostradamus must have been outstanding amongst his fellow-astrologers at making all the necessary preliminary mathematical calculations Yet this was certainly not how many of his contemporaries saw it. Rather, they were horrified at his sloppiness. Early in the last chapter Laurens Videl was mentioned as the astrologer who had pointed out to Nostradamus how his 1555 Almanac, with its warnings of dangers to the French monarchy, could hardly have failed to attract the King and Queen's attention. Videl had a particular interest in Nostradamus' almanacs because he himself produced very similar publications. But what seems to have particularly stung him is that, though Nostradamus was many times more successful than he was, his astrological methodology was incompetent, even a disgrace.

Early in 1558 Videl issued from his home town of Avignon a powerful pamphlet, with an impressive print-run of 6,000 copies,[16] entitled *A Declaration of Michel Nostradamus' Ignorant Abuses and Sedition*.[17] In this he pulled absolutely no punches. He expressed the suspicion – very likely to have been well founded, according to the astrologically proficient modern scholar Professor Brind'Amour[18] – that Nostradamus used ephemeris tables prepared for the meridian of Venice, and consistently failed to adjust them to make his calculations applicable to the meridian of Lyons. He also accused Nostradamus of going through mere pretences of observing the night sky for the writing of his almanacs, remarking, 'It is certain that you have no idea how to calculate by the sky, nor by any tables'.[19] Referring to one of Nostradamus' calculations, Videl went on a little later:

> You show yourself to be so ignorant that it is impossible to find anyone to whom you are second in ignorance. You put that it should be around one hour after midnight, and then when you make your chart, you make it sunrise where the line should be for midnight or a little after. Think about it, you great ass. You want the sun to be at midnight and in the east all at the same time? For what should be in the fourth house, you put in the first. And for that which should be in the first, you put in the tenth.[20]

According to Videl, amongst innumerable other technical blunders, in creating his almanacs Nostradamus located the sun at the moment of vernal equinox, not at 0°0' of Aries, as he ought.

At least Videl identified himself by his true name in his attacks. And his accusations were at least properly argued and, as such, relatively mild compared to those of another critic who adopted the pseudonym 'Hercules le François'. The anonymous tract was entitled The First

Invective of Lord Hercules the Frenchman against Monstradamus,[21] and was published from Paris in both 1557 and 1558.[22] Hercules' insulting adulteration of Nostradamus' name was quite deliberate, but far more serious was his charge that Nostradamus was promulgating 'execrable heresies' and abrogating powers that pertained only to God:

> like a prophet of superlative degree he ['Monstradamus'] predicts the conditions of Kings and Emperors; of their life, of their death; of the thrills of wars, treacheries, and their outcome; of peace and alliance, of local governments and republics; changes of monarchy; plagues, famines, in short, all that pertains to God's will and ultimate power.[23]

To 'Hercules' Nostradamus was a 'twenty-four-carat liar' who:

> ...preys so well upon people's simple credulity...that by his babble, his double meanings and double entendres...he reduces to superstitious events the days for getting married, for travelling, for transacting business, even for when to wear a white shirt.[24]

With no let-up to his stridency Hercules ended his 'Invective' with an eight-line verse:

> *Decry, my muse, by your trumpet blast*
> *(like silver of a bad alloy)*
> *This sorcerer who deceives the world*
> *Under the pretext of good faith*
> *Remember to protest*
> *That if his cackling were to take hold*
> *The laws [of nature] would all be changed*
> *And he would invent us another God.*[25]

Incredibly, the years 1557–8 that is, the period within eighteen months of Nostradamus' abruptly terminated visit to Paris, brought to the fore yet more virulent anti-Nostradamus publications. Another, issued under the pseudonym Jean de la Daguenière, was entitled *The Monster of Abuse*, in the original French '*Le Monstre d'abus*', yet another insulting play on Nostradamus' name. In this 'Daguenière' particularly stressed the ambiguity and obscurity, already remarked upon, in which Nostradamus couched his prophetic utterances. These, he insisted, were 'naked of all truth', going on:

> ...nothing can disguise your ignorance by which you complicate

your utterances with obscure, ambiguous and rarely used language. In place of a little knowledge you have come to give us none at all.[26]

Again pulling no punches, 'Daguenière' felt obliged to make known to a still highly anti-Semitic world Nostradamus' ancestral Jewishness, pointing out that the seer's annual almanacs, filled as they were with 'evident lies', were 'still steeped up to their neck in Judaism'.[27]

Someone even composed a witty anti-Nostradamus Latin ditty:

Mich. Nostradamus: Nostra damus cum verba damus, quia fallere Nostrum est. At cum verba damus nil nisi Nostra-damus.[28]

This loses a lot in translation, being essentially a piece of word-play on '*damus*' (the Latin for 'we give'), and '*damnus*' ('damned'). But the basic intention seems to have been something along the lines of:

> *Michel Nostradamus:*
> *We give/damn ourselves when we give out words,*
> *for deceiving comes naturally to us;*
> *and when with words we give/damn ourselves,*
> *no one does it better than Nostradamus.*

Even Nostradamus' ostensible old friend from Agen, Jules-César Scaliger, joined in the fray, presumably jealous of the great fame that his former pupil had attracted. Callously echoing 'Daguenière' in reiterating the allusions to his Jewishness, Scaliger composed the following verse as part of three anti-Nostradamus Latin epigrams which, though not published until 1574, can date no later than October 1558, since Scaliger died during that same month:

> Credulous France, what do you hope for, what are you waiting for, hanging on to the words that are hurled out with such fury by his [Nostradamus'] Jewish art? ... Don't you see how much the language of this vile driveller is inane? How can you support this man who mocks you with his self-confidence? Who in the end is the dumber – this evil buffoon, or you who spend too much time fawning on his impostures?

When Nostradamus, presumably in an attempt to air his medical expertise, made a rather free translation of Menodotus' *Paraphrase of Galen*, published by the Lyons printer Antoine du Rosne in 1557, this too came in for some severe criticism. Nostradamus had made his translation into French from Erasmus' earlier translation of the original Greek into Latin, and a cousin of his, Olrias de Cadenet well-educated in Greek, happened to comment somewhat unfavourably on it to Nostradamus' brother Jéhan in Aix. The rather pompous Cadenet then showed off by writing a letter in Greek to Nostradamus, enraging the latter so much that he fired off a seriously insulting letter of response. Nostradamus' letter has not survived, but something of its intemperance can be gathered from Cadenet's response to him:

To Dr Michel Nostradamus 'APPRATEIN!' [seemingly a corrupted form of the Greek 'eu prattein', 'bad luck!']
　　The letter that I wrote to you in Greek, Michel, ought to have been enough to pacify your hostility. But this time maybe it's worth using Latin in an attempt to convey to you that your slanders are as delirious as they are 'over the top'. You wilfully accuse me of ignorance and, particularly annoyingly, of being an illiterate. My education was not strictly elementary, but thank God it includes literature, the humanities and the liberal arts... My letter written in Greek was an attempt to demonstrate to you the truth of my attestation of my literacy. It's too bad if you yourself cannot comprehend Greek.

What the Cadenet letter shows is that at least some of the anti-Nostradamus propaganda that was being hurled about got under his skin. And when the seer hit back, as he did in this instance, he could do so extremely intemperately. Yet that he was watching his back at around this time is evident, not least from the changing, noted earlier, of his references to Scaliger between the 1555 edition of *Treatise on cosmetics and jams* and the 1557 one. As may be recalled, in the 1555 version he had spoken of Scaliger as a 'second Marsilio Ficino in Platonic philosophy', suggesting that at that time he felt safe enough to associate himself with the ever-controversial subject of Hermetic magic. But two years later after the attacks he was clearly much more on guard, hence the pointed dropping of his reference to Ficino, substituting instead the altogether less contentious comparison to 'that father of eloquence, Cicero'.[30] Perhaps thankfully, Nostradamus seems to have been blissfully unaware of the dying Scaliger's change of attitude towards him

　　Ironically, whether or not Nostradamus himself fully appreciated this at the time, the extraordinary fusillade of vicious attacks upon him, far from destroying his fame and popular success, only served to increase them, just as so often happens with those who attract the media spotlight in the present day. One of the perennial themes to be found in the letters that Nostradamus' 'clients' sent to him is that of remuneration. And letter after letter in the Bibliothèque Nationale Latin manuscript collection promised him a suitably handsome reward for this or that item of astrological advice.

The fact that Nostradamus was thereby becoming comfortably off, so much so that he could look to the future in a rather more down-to-earth manner than just astrologically, is quite evident from his investment at this time in a particularly ambitious local project.

Until the late 1550s the so-called 'Crau', the terrain that surrounded his adopted home town of Salon-de-Crau, was just a desolate, desic-cated, stony wilderness, useless for agriculture and inhabited by little more than lizards, snakes, scorpions and birds of prey. But a brilliant young local engineer, Adam de Craponne, had a most forward-looking dream for it.

Born in Salon in 1525, and therefore more than twenty years younger than Nostradamus, Craponne had already created quite a stir in 1552 when he was employed as military engineer to the French army under Henri II's fiercely pro-Catholic general François, Duke of Guise. Thanks largely to Craponne's expertise, the Duke of Guise was able successfully to defend the town of Metz from a particularly deter-mined siege personally led by France's arch-enemy, the Holy Roman Emperor Charles V.

When Craponne's military service ended and he returned to Salon his restless energy minded him to try to implement an idea that Raymond, Bishop of Arles, had first suggested in the twelfth century.

This was to bring much-needed irrigation to the Crau region by digging a canal from the river Durance, which fed into the Rhône, all the way to Salon. Craponne had studied canals and lock systems in Italy, and he had a very clear idea of what engineering work needed to be done. The

Engineer Adam de Craponne, originator of the pioneering Provenal canal system that still bears his name. From a bust in the Hotel de Ville, Salon-de-Provence.

more difficult preliminaries were obtaining the necessary local government approval and finding financial backing.

The hoped-for breakthrough came in 1554 when Craponne's elder brother Frédéric became Salon's First Consul or mayor. This created the right political climate for the scheme to be approved by the town council. The local landowners readily agreed to the canal being driven through their properties, knowing that the irrigation thereby provided would be bound to increase their productivity and thus the value of their land. All that the scheme therefore needed was sufficient investment to fund the engineering operations.

Craponne went to all his family and friends seeking their financial help – to his brother Frédéric, to his brother-in-law Alphonse de Cadenet, of the same family as Nostradamus' correspondent Olrias, to his uncle, and to all others whom he could persuade to see the scheme's benefits. Amongst those were Nostradamus and his wife Anne, since a surviving document drawn up by Salon's notary M. Laurent on July 27, 1556 shows that Nostradamus duly invested the very substantial sum of 200 crowns in the project. Since this represented more than ten years' rent for a substantial family house,[31] it was a very significant investment indeed. And it was followed by some similarly large sums in succeeding years.

The finance thus raised from Nostradamus and others enabled the work to go ahead, the canal scheme's first stage being completed by April 20, 1559, when the town's entire population turned out to watch the magical joining up of the waters. Everyone of any note was there, so it is surely no undue stretch of the imagination to envisage Nostradamus and his wife amongst them, the family now swelled to seven, the eldest daughter Madeleine now eight, César, five, followed by three-year-old Charles and two-year-old André, with Anne, the newest arrival, barely a year old.

Even for all those who watched in awe as the great waterway cut by Craponne's workmen filled with water from the Durance, it was difficult to foresee that this was the start of further schemes that would steadily enable the hitherto arid desert surrounding Salon to be transformed into highly productive market gardening land. Even in the canal's first year of operation the town council of the time was able to record:

By the irrigation works which he – Craponne – has made in the present year, the town has benefited in excess of seven to eight thousand gold crowns.[32]

In present-day Salon-de-Provence – the old 'de-Crau' name interestingly,

The Craponne canal, seen alongside the Rue Jean Moulin, northwest of Salon-de-Provence.

long dropped – Adam de Craponne's contribution to the tranformation of the region's prosperity is much remembered and honoured, not least by a fine life-size nineteenth-century statue of him that surmounts a fountain opposite the town hall. It is much to Nostradamus' credit, therefore, that he had the indisputably genuine foresight to have shared Craponne's dream for Salon's future, and to have used some of the wealth that he had accrued from his astrological future-gazing to help make that vision a reality.

But as we are about to see, far to the north, at the royal court, the same year of 1559 would witness some altogether different dramas, with Nostradamus' future-gazing again heavily involved.

NOTES

1 Laurens Videl, *Declaration des abus ignorances...*, op. cit., fol. C4v–DIr
2 *Les Presages Merveilleux pour lan. 1557. Dediés au Roy tres chrestien, Henri deuxiesme de ce nom*, Paris, Jacques Kerver, 1557
3 'à la christianissime et Sérenissime Catherine reine de France'
4 *La Grande Pronostication nouvelle avec portenteuse prediction, pour l'An M.D.LVII...*, Paris, Jacques Kerver, 1557
5 'Roy de Navarre, Anthoine de Vandosme'
6 'Contre ceulx qui tant de foys m'ont fait mort'
7 'maximeque gavisum esse quod intellexissem, statim et bello Vulpiciano incolumis reversus, res tibi in aula cum Rege, Regina et caeteris magnatibus ad votum contigisse' – full text in Dupèbe, *Nostradamus, Lettres Inédites...*, op. cit., p.29
8 'Consule, mi Nostradame, astra, si me amas, an foecundius sit solum Romanum, an Provinciale, utrum meae naturae accommodatius, et si in urbe expectandus favor, necne, et si persecutio immineat, vel sinistra sors aliqua. De nepotibus qualiter nobiscum sese habebunt velim etiam scire. De longitu-

dine vel brevitate vitae nonnihil. Postremo de liberorum felici vel infelici successu, et de reliquis huiusmodi ad nos pertinentibus, quae tu ipse per te commode adjicere poteris.' Quoted in Dupèbe, *Nostradamus, Lettres Inédites…*, Letter III, p.33

9 *'Clariss. Doctor…splendor virtutis tuae non solum infra patrios limites vagaretur, sed et per universas Gallias disparsus…in Italiam usque gloriose penetrarit, atque adeo etiam in nostram Lyguriam tandem delatus sit.'* Quoted in Dupèbe, *Nostradamus, Lettres Inédites…*, op. cit., Letter XLII, p.144

10 *'Primum hoc erit: Utrum vivat soror mea incoenobio S. Brigidae in Anglia Deo dicata. Secundum quaesitum, vitae meae periodum definire. Tertium, Utrum melius mihi sit praedium meum Sturlanum vendere an retinere. Quartum, Utrum interveteres ruinas cuiusdam antiqui palatii diruti in dicto meo praedio aliquid lateat subterraneum. Quintum et ultimum, Utrum in loco mihi designato in eodem Sturlano venam aquae vivae potero adipisci et reperire.'* Dupèbe, *Nostradamus, Lettres Inédites…*, op. cit., p.144

11 Quoted in Ellic Howe, *Urania's Children, The Strange World of the Astrologers*, London, William Kimber, 1967, p.20

12 Dupèbe, *Nostradamus, Lettres Inédites…*, op. cit., p.33, n.1

13 *'Rogabas ut certiorem te redderem de Astrologis, si quos in Italia celebres invenissem; verum ego de nullo adhuc audire potui: tantum unus est in ore omnium celebratissimus ille Nostradamus, de aliis ne verbum quidem'.* Dupèbe, *Nostradamus, Lettres Inédites…*, op. cit., Letter VII, p.37

14 *'posset liberare, et omnibus satisfacere, si illud quod quaerimus inveniretur. Responsum tuum nimis obscurum illi videtur: petit ut clarius rem explices; pollicetur se labori tuo liberaliter et honeste satisfacturum.'* Ibid.

15 *'Priora illa non vitupero, sed tamen minus convenire videntur, praesertim illud: FORTUNA TUA IN ITALIA EST. Nam hactenus potuis adversam, quam bonam sum expertus. Credo erratum contigisse propter tempus navitatisminus exacte datum. Nam illic tempus hoc scriptum est, Anno Domini M.D.XXXIIII. XIX Decembr. Hora prima ante occasum Solis. Sed verum tempus est hora media ante Solis occasum. Quare ut figuram erigas rogo, satisfaciam labori tuo pro viribus. Miror valde unum aliud: solebas mihi praedicere sub finem anni M.D.LIX. bonum maximum at ibi pro bono malum scriptum est. Sic enim habet ad verbum: Cave ab hoc anno M.D.LIX.XXIII die, maximum nescio quid: non expressum cuius mensis diem XXIII cadere debeam valde doleo. De his et aliis ut ad me scribas diligenter, summopere te rogo, nec de fide mea dubites.'* Dupèbe, *Nostradamus, Lettres Inedites…*, op. cit., Letter VII, p.37

16 This is known from an account that happens by chance to have survived

17 Laurens Videl, *Declaration des abus ignorances et seditions de Michel Nostradamus, de Salon de Craux en Provence*, Avignon Pierre Roux & Ian Tramblay, 1558

18 Brind'Amour, *Nostradamus Astrophile…*, op. cit., p.71

19 *'il est certain que tu ne says calculer ny au ciel, ni par tables aucunes.'* Videl, op. cit., fol. B3v, quoted in Brind'Amour, *Nostradamus Astrophile…*, op. cit., p.72

20 *'… tu te mostres le plus ignare qu'il n'est possible en trouver un qui te seconde en ignorance: tu metz que c'estoit environt la minuit & une heure, &*

quant tu fais ta figure, ce que devoyt estre a la ligne de minuit ou un peu apres, tu le metz aux soleil levé. Regarde un peu, gros asne: tu veux que le soleil soit a minuit & en orient tout en un mesmes temps: car ce que doit estre a la quatriesme maison, tu metz a la premiere, & ce que doit estre a la premiere, tu le metz a la dixiesme.' Quoted in Brind'Amour, *Nostradamus Astrophile...*, op. cit., p.74

21 *La Premiere Invective du Seigneur Hercules le Fraçois contre Monstradamus,* Paris, Simon, Calvaria, 1558

22 The 1557 edition was published by Roux of Lyons the 1558 by Simon Calvarin, rue St-Jean de Beauvais, Paris

23 *'...comme prophete en superlatif degré, il predit des estats des Rois et Empereurs, de leur vie, de leur mort, de l'emotion des guerres, seditions: de l'issue d'icelles, de la paix & alliance, du gouvernement des villes & republiques, changemens de Royaumes, pestes, famines: & en bref, de tout ce que Dieu veult, & peult de Puissance absolüe.'* From facsimile reprint of the Simon Calvarin 1558 printing as preserved in the Bibliothèque Municipale, Lyons, Eric Visier, Verna, 1995, A iij.

24 *'menteur a vingt quatre carrats, si bien empatronné de la simple credulité des personnes...Qu'il semble bien...de son babil a double revers & double entente...[il] assigne aux superstitieux esventez, les jours de se marier, voyager, traffiquer, & vestir leur chemise blanche.'* Ibid.

25 *'Descrie, ma muse à son de trompe*
(Comme argent de mauvais alloy)
Ce sorcier qui le monde trompe
Soubs pretexte de bonne foy.
De remonstrer souvienne toy,
Que si son caquet avoit lieu
Il fauldroit tous changer de loy,
Puis qu'il nous forge un aultre Dieu.'

26 *'neud de la verité, pour ne pouvoir farder ton ignorance qu'avecques ces involutions de propos et langaiges obscurs, ambigus & inusités, tu nous viennes donnes a entendre l'incogneu pour le moins congneu...',* Le Monstre d'abus Composé premierement en Latin par Maistre Jean de la Dagueniere, Paris, Barbe Regnault, 1558. Quoted in Pierre Brind'Amour, *Nostradamus Astrophile...*, op. cit., p.78

27 *'Et que ou vous esteignies du tout de dessein que vous avez faict, de nous vouloir persuader de tant evidentes menteries descrites en vos petitz pacquectz annuelz, qui sentent encores leur Judaisme en plain gorge.'* Quoted in Pierre Brind'Amour, *Nostradamus Astrophile...*, op. cit., p.79

28 This was first reproduced in 1568 in the *Xenia* of the poet Charles Utenhove, but as pointed out by Professor Brind'Amour, it must surely have been composed during Nostradamus' lifetime. See Pierre Brind'Amour, *Nostradamus Astrophile...*, op. cit., p.85

29 *'Credula quid speras; quid spectas pendula verbis Gallia, Judaea quae blatit arte furor?...Nonne vides linguam impuri nebulonis inanem? Huncne tuam pateris Iudificare fidem? Utrum futilius, pectusne nocentis Agyrtae? An tu, quae toties fasla fovere potes?* Jules-César Scaliger, *Iulii Caesaris Scaligeri viri clarissimi poemata...* Anno M.D.LXXIII. Quoted in Pierre Brind'Amour, *Nostradamus Astrophile...*, op. cit., p.86

30 Nostradamus, *Traité de fardemens et confitures*, op. cit.
31 In 1561 Nostradamus would rent a house for his family in Avignon for an annual payment of 18 crowns – see chapter 11
32 '*par les arrosages qu'il – Craponne – a facts en la presente année de son eau, la Ville en valut plus de sept à huit mile escus d'or*'. Deliberation of the Communauté de Salon, May 1559

CHAPTER 9

On Martial Field

Already apparent is that much of Nostradamus' surprisingly widespread fame during the 1550s derived from the short-term predictions that he made in his annual Almanacs, rather than from the theoretically longer-term ones in his book of *Prophecies*. As attested by his Italian correspondents such as Cibo Boerius, his fame had spread far into Italy. This was almost inevitably fanned by the publication of Italian-language editions of his almanacs.

His 1557 *Prognostication*, for instance, was published in Italian by Innocentio Cicognera of Milan.[1] And in the environs of Turin, the large northern Italian city which in the sixteenth century was part of the domains of the Dukes of Savoy,[2] is an intriguing piece of evidence suggesting that Nostradamus made a visit there in 1556, perhaps *en route* to arrange this Milan edition. Two miles from the city centre, on a marble plaque on the wall of an ancient farmhouse[3] located in a hilly

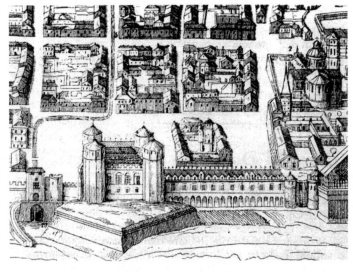

Turin as Nostradamus would have known it.
Detail from a 16th century map.

district with glorious views of the Alps, is to be found an enigmatic inscription in Roman capitals reading:

1556
NOSTRADAMUS LODGED HERE
WHERE HEAVEN, HELL AND PURGATORY RESIDE
I AM CALLED VICTORIA
GLORY WILL COME TO WHOEVER HONOURS ME
RUIN TO WHOEVER SCORNS ME[4]

During its history Turin has been under French domination for significant periods, with French being widely spoken to this day. Linguistically, however, it was, and is, predominantly Italian. The language of the inscription, however, is in an arcane-sounding sixteenth-century French, and the lines that follow after 'Nostradamus lodged here' have a sibylline tone suggesting that they were composed by Nostradamus himself. As we saw when he coined an inscription for one of Salon's fountains, he derived a certain satisfaction from such exercises in word-spinning. Although the building with the inscription is today known as the Farmhouse[5] Morozzo, it seems earlier to have been called the Villa Victoria. The best guess concerning the inscription's origins is that Nostradamus penned the lines as a 'thank-you' for his overnight stay, which then prompted the Villa Victoria's owners to immortalise them in stone as a souvenir of the great man's visit.[6] Whatever the explanation, it certainly further corroborates Nostradamus' growing fame.

But if in the late 1550s Nostradamus was best known for his almanacs, his by now far more famed *Prophecies* had already attracted more than sufficient interest to encourage the creation of further, expanded editions. Historically, given the friability of such publications' survival, the difficulty is in tracking down these earliest editions and determining just when they first appeared. In the early twentieth century James Randi's favourite Nostradamian researcher, the wonderfully named Count Klinkowström, claimed to have found a copy of an otherwise unknown 1557 edition of the *Prophecies* in the Library of Munich.[7] This 1557 version reportedly incorporated 'three hundred [prophecies] never before printed',[8] showing that even as early as 1557 Nostradamus had added another 300 prophetic verses to those in his 1555 edition. Puzzlingly, instead of Nostradamus having used his 1555 *Prophecies* printer Macé Bonhomme, who should have had the type of the original 353 verses still standing, this particular edition was apparently the work of Antoine du Rosne. This was the same Lyons printer, nicknamed 'Lizerot', whom, it may be

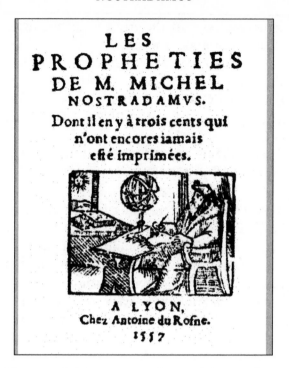

Title page of the rare 1557 edition of the *Prophecies*.

recalled, Nostradamus had tried to persuade to print one of his earlier Almanacs when he was in dispute with Brotot. Unfortunately, amidst the massive bomb damage that Munich suffered during the Second World War its main Library's apparently unique copy of the 1557 edition vanished without trace. This aroused considerable suspicion that it may never even have existed, a position that has continued to be espoused by James Randi.

However, in 1983 the very same trawl of European libraries that produced the two hitherto unknown copies of Macé Bonhomme's 1555 edition also brought to light two similarly surviving copies of the 1557 edition.[9] These latter were indeed printed by Antoine du Rosne of Lyons, thereby confirming that Count Klinkowström's information had been correct after all. One of these copies was found in the National Szechenyi Library, Budapest,[10] the other identical, in the Lenin Library in Moscow. Again confirming Klinkowström's information, these 1557 copies, prefaced as previously with Nostradamus' open letter to his son César, contain a further 300 quatrains extra to those in the 1555 edition. These consist of the forty-six quatrains of Century IV which printer Bonhomme had omitted for lack of space, plus a complete complement of all-new quatrains for Centuries V and VI, plus the first forty verses of Century VII. With regard to Century VII's arbitrary truncation, clearly du Rosne exercised every bit as much Procrustean ruthlessness towards Nostradamus' verses as his predecessor. It is difficult to avoid the impression that however hallowed the seer's words might have seemed to his public, to his printer-publishers, along with his fellow astrologers, they were held in altogether lesser awe.

Because the majority of the new prophetic verses were composed after the 1555 visit to the royal court, Nostradamus was able to reflect and honour in them some of the illustrious individuals whom he had met while in Paris. It had amused his near-contemporary Michelangelo, during the painting of the *Last Judgement* some twenty years earlier, to portray as located in heaven or hell various individuals who had either pleased or crossed him respectively. And Nostradamus appears to have been of somewhat like mind when dreaming up this further set of quatrains.

Thus, clearly in honour of the plain but agreeable Queen Catherine de Medici, to whom he had already dedicated one of his 1557 almanacs, Nostradamus composed the commensurately explicit Century V, quatrain 39:

> *Sprung from the true branch of the fleur de lys*
> *An Etruscan heritage has been placed and lodged.*
> *Her ancient blood from a long lineage*
> *Will make Florence flourish in the coat of arms*[11]

Such a linking of 'Etruscan' Florence with France's royal heraldic symbol of the *fleur de lys* can only refer to Catherine de Medici, the verse thereby surely having been specifically calculated to please her. Because Florence's Medici family originated as mere merchants, many amongst the French aristocracy regarded Henri II (who at the time of his marriage to Catherine had been only second in line to the French throne) as having been more than a little short-changed in the selection of Catherine for him as a bride. At the time the political advantage for King François I was that Catherine's cousin Giulio de Medici was Pope, as Clement VII. However, Clement died almost immediately the deal was sealed and delivered, prompting the King to comment tartly on Catherine's arrival: 'I have received the girl completely naked,'[12] a remark which had deeply humiliated the young woman. So by alluding to her Florentine roots as actually gracing the *fleur de lys* symbol of French royalty, Nostradamus arguably scored one of his greater diplomatic triumphs.[13]

Similarly, mindful of the splendid Paris lodgings in the Hôtel de Sens where he had rather overstayed his welcome on account of his attack of gout (whether feigned or unfeigned), Nostradamus also gratefully acknowledged his host of that time, the Cardinal of Sens, bestowing upon him Century VI, quatrain 86:

> To the great prelate, one day, after his dream
> Interpreted contrary to its sense
> From Gascony a monk will come
> Who will be elected the great prelate of Sens.[14]

This second, 1557 edition of the *Prophecies* also included verses that, whatever one's opinion of their prophetic worth, would later become widely interpreted as predicting, in the short term, Catherine de Medici's widowhood,[15] and in the longer term, the rise of Napoleon.

But even while this second, 740-verse edition of the *Prophecies* was still being churned out on du Rosne's presses in Lyons, to the south in Salon Nostradamus was already at work – to all appearances at least – on an edition of nearly 300 more quatrains in order to round the final number up to 1,000. For this final, all-inclusive version of the *Prophecies* Nostradamus apparently decided to abandon the former Preface addressed to his son César in favour of an open letter to 'the most invincible, most powerful and very Christian' King Henri II. At the start of this he alluded in the most sycophantic terms to his recollections of having been granted an audience with Henri at the royal court in 1555:

> O very Christian and very victorious King, ever since my long beclouded countenance became presented before your Majesty's immeasurable deity I have been perpetually bedazzled. I have never ceased to honour and venerate that day when first I became presented before so singular yet humane a Majesty.[16]

Nothing exceptional by the standards of subject-to-monarch communications of the time, this passage provides the clearest surviving indication that King Henri had definitely been present with Queen Catherine when in August 1555 Nostradamus was received at St Germain-en-Laye, even if, as indicated by his letter to Jean Morel, his more meaningful dialogue on this occasion may have been with the Queen. As Nostradamus declared to Henri, he had been 'long uncertain as to whom I should consecrate these three remaining Centuries of my Prophecies, making up the thousand'.[17] Then inspiration had struck that 'his Majesty' was the obvious choice.

> I have dedicated my night-time prophetic computations to a most prudent and wise Prince. These have been composed rather more

by natural instinct, mixed with a certain poetic fervour, than by the rules of poetry. And they have mostly been composed and astronomically calculated according to the years, months and weeks of the regions, countries and for the greater part the towns and cities throughout Europe, together with Africa and part of Asia where most of these circumstances are due to take place.[18]

Historically, not least of the insights offered by this Letter to Henri II is that it shows Nostradamus as more than a little shaken by the various published attacks on him, as described in the last chapter. He therefore took the opportunity openly to address some of these. Without referring to his Jewishness as such, he clearly had in mind his hostile critics' savage allusions to it when he wrote that the means by which he made his prophecies was:

> ... by my natural instinct for predicting which was bestowed on me by my ancestors, by calibrating this natural instinct with my long computations, and by freeing soul, spirit and courage of all care, anxiety and worry.[19]

Exactly as he had explained in the very first two quatrains with which he had opened his prophecies, he described himself receiving his futuristic glimpses Delphic oracle-style, seated 'on the brazen tripod'.[20]

Mindful of those such as the anonymous 'Hercules le François' who had accused him of abrogating powers pertaining only to God, he rejoined: 'There are a number of people who would attribute to me that which does not belong to me at all.'[21] Affecting complete religious orthodoxy, he appealed to the one true God to protect him against such evil-minded tittle-tattlers: 'Sole God eternal, who sees into human hearts, who is pious, just and merciful, the one true judge, I pray to you to defend me against evil ones who spread slander.'[22] Particularly tellingly, he pointed out to King Henri II that those who accused him, Nostradamus, of abrogating divine gifts could easily turn next to attacking even the King. For did not King Henri himself following a time-honoured royal custom begun many generations back, claim to be able to work a certain 'magic' of his own, in curing certain diseases, such as scrofula, by the 'royal touch'?

> 'These evil-minded individuals would want to ask, equally as slanderously, by what means all your ancient ancestors the Kings of France cured scrofula.'[23]

Emphasising his religious orthodoxy by describing how he made his

Nostradamus' defence against those who accused him of practising magic. King Henri II using the royal touch for curing scrofula, from the contemporary manuscript Les Heures de Henri II, as preserved in the Bibliothèque Nationale, Paris.

reckoning 'solely by the holy scriptures', Nostradamus summarised for Henri his chronology for the history of the past:

The first man Adam preceded Noah by around 1242 years ... After
Noah and the universal Flood Abraham came around 1080 years
later.[24]

Then he launched into a summary of the events that he saw happening
in the future, foreseeing times of grave crisis for the Christian Church.
In this instance, however, instead of providing any exact dates or year
intervals, he declared having virtually deliberately muddled everything
up: 'by this discourse I throw these predictions almost into confusion
with regard to when they can happen'.[25] Somewhat unconvincingly, he
claimed that while he could have put a date to everything he predicted
– 'If I had wanted to put a date to each quatrain, that would have been
possible to do'[26] – he quite deliberately refrained from doing so
because it would have made him vulnerable to those who wished him
harm. And in fairness to him, it was far from unknown for sixteenth-
century monarchs to put to death those who brought bad tidings to
them, whether prophetic or hard fact.

Yet while Nostradamus mostly shrank from giving hard dates and
locations for the fulfilment of his prophecies, he was nonetheless characteristically punctilious in recording the date on which he wrote the
early part of his Letter to Henri as March 14, 1557, and the date of
completing it as 'From Salon this 27th June, 1558'. Just so long as we
can believe the truth of these dates, then the *Prophecies* should certainly have reached its final 942 verse form by the end of June 1558.
And there are reasonable grounds for believing in Nostradamus'
honesty in this instance – not least because a number of seventeenth-
century sources positively suggest the existence of a 1558 publication,
apparently produced by yet another Lyons printer, Benoit Rigaud,
containing both the Letter to Henri II and the 'Centuries VIII, IX and
X, which have never before been printed'.[27] Frustratingly, however,
while we have seen hitherto unknown copies turn up for the 1555 and
1557 editions, there has been no such luck in the case of this 1558
edition. And after 1557, the earliest surviving version of the
Prophecies, and therefore the earliest to contain all 942 verses plus the
letter to Henri II, is dated 1568: that is, two years after Nostradamus'
death, and nine after the King's.

Given that the royal interest in astrology is usually attributed
almost exclusively to Queen Catherine, it was noticeable that the King
was exhibiting a surprisingly close interest in Nostradamus' predictions at least as early as 1558. As already remarked, Henri II was one
of the more bellicose of France's kings. And in June 1558, his vigorous
and resourceful army supremo François, Duke of Guise – the same
Duke for whom Adam de Craponne had worked as engineer, and who

was now a national hero for having recently recaptured Calais from the English – was in the process of besieging the fortress of Thionville, on France's heavily disputed northeastern border. At this time Thionville was still held by German troops of Charles V's brother and successor, the new Emperor Ferdinand I. But by June 21 French sappers under the direction of Guise's best general, Blaise de Monluc, were on the brink of undermining the town's great Tour des Puces, or Tower of Fleas, which had originally been built by the counts of Luxembourg. Noting that the fortress's defenders were becoming altogether more disheartened and lack-lustre in their resistance, the Duke of Guise sensed the imminence of victory. Whereupon, as Blaise de Monluc subsequently recorded in his memoirs, the Duke immediately:

> ... sent a courier to the King, for he otherwise held back from his superiors any news that they might not want to hear. His Majesty had been reading Nostradamus' predictions the day before, and read for the next day 'good news for the King'. The courier arrived on this same day and the next day the town was taken. Some say that these are just dreams but I have seen a number of such things from this man [i.e. Nostradamus].[28]

The first surprise from this account is just how much an addict of Nostradamus' almanacs King Henri had become, actually reading the seer's prediction of the day even before members of his court. In today's terms this might have entitled Nostradamus to display the royal warrant. The second surprise from these memoirs is the healthy respect that so veteran and practical-minded a campaigner as Monluc should have had towards Nostradamus and his powers of prophecy – as evident from his enigmatic remark 'I have seen a number of such things from this man' – despite this particular prophecy taking the utterly vague form of 'good news for the king'.

In accordance with his normal practice, Nostradamus prepared his Almanac for 1559 early in 1558. In this instance no original French copy has survived, only thirteen preliminary 'Presages' or Predictions for each month that were collected decades later by secretary Chavigny and recorded in his *Compilation* manuscript.[29] But the English edition of the same 1559 Almanac has survived. This was entitled '*The Prognostication of Master Michael Nostradamus, Doctor in Physic, in Provence, for the year of our Lord 1559, with the predictions and presages of every month*'.[30] It was published from Antwerp, and reveals some vintage Nostradamian predictions for what would indeed turn out to be a landmark year.

The English King Henry VIII's eldest daughter, the Catholic Queen

'I have seen a number of such things from this man.'
The French general Blaise de Monluc was one of
Nostradamus' contemporaries awed by his
apparent prophetic powers. From a
contemporary engraving.

Mary Tudor, in whose reign England
had most humiliatingly lost Calais to the
French, had died childless in mid-
November 1558. Mary's twenty-five-
year-old half-sister, the Protestant
Elizabeth, succeeded as England's new
Queen. And since Mary had left England
with badly-neglected defences and a seriously impoverished treasury, the prospect of
yet another turnabout of religious denomination
was just about as welcome to the country as a military defeat.

Accordingly, at the beginning of 1559 it would have needed a very
optimistic prophet indeed to predict that Elizabeth's reign could be at
all successful. And Nostradamus, who had composed his 1559
Almanac before Mary's death, certainly exhibited no such optimism in
his forecasts for England's future. All that he foresaw for the country
was 'divers calamities, weepings and mournings' and 'civil sedition'
that would make the 'lowest' rise up against the 'highest'. France, by
contrast, seemed positively at an apogee in its fortunes. The old
enemy, the Emperor Charles V, had died in September 1558. On his
retirement his empire had been broken up. Spain went to his son, the
thirty-one-year-old Philip II, a chronically cautious man, just widowed
by Mary Tudor's death, and far more inclined to diplomatic compro-
mise. To this end, in April 1559 Europe's leading ambassadors bro-
kered the so-called Peace of Cateau-Cambresis by which a number of
territories that had been the subject of expensive border disputes were
handed back to their rightful owners. This freed up huge numbers of
troops to return to their normal occupations and cease being a drain
on the royal finances of several nations.

To seal the deal, King Henri and Queen Catherine agreed that their
attractive and intelligent fourteen-year-old daughter Elisabeth should
become affianced to Philip II. She would be a most welcome replacement for Mary Tudor, who had been forty-two at the time of her death.
Likewise it was agreed that Henri's sister Marguerite should be affianced to the dashing thirty-year-old Emanuel-Filibert of Savoy. It was
planned that a double wedding be held in Paris in the late June and early
July of 1559, the sort of occasion that the French loved to stage, with
days of feasting, dancing and pageantry, tournaments and jousting.

For anyone astrologically inclined, one potential cloud hung over the festivities, albeit perceived by precious few. The much revered Italian astrologer Luca Gaurico (who, it will be recalled, had warned that Henri II's reign would begin and end in a duel), had died in March 1558. Just two years before, however, he had sent Henri a stern reiteration of his earlier warning. As later recalled by France's Secretary of State Claude de l'Aubespine, in February 1556 'there was a dispatch from Rome containing the horoscope of the king, composed by Gaurico. I translated it from the Latin into French in order that the King might understand it.'[31] Gaurico's message warned Henri that he should:

> ...avoid all single combat in an enclosed field, especially around his forty-first year, for in that period of his life he was threatened by a wound in the head which could bring about blindness, or death.[32]

Thanks to a contemporary courtier, the Seigneur de Brantôme, there survives a very vivid account of what transpired at the court upon the receipt of the letter:

> Monsieur the Constable was present there, to whom the King said, 'See, my friend, what death is predicted for me.' 'Ah Sire', replied the Constable. 'Would you believe these rascals? They are nothing but liars and babblers. Throw it in the fire.' 'My friend,' replied the King, 'Why so? They sometimes tell the truth. I care not if my death be in that manner more than any other. I would even prefer it, to die by the hand of whomever he might be, so long as he was brave and valiant, and that I kept my honour.' And without paying any heed to the Constable's words, he gave the prophecy to M. de l'Aubespine to keep for him until he should ask for it.[33]

A number of Nostradamian writers, including James Laver, have envisaged the receipt of this letter, on February 5, 1556, as the cue for Queen Catherine de Medici to summon Nostradamus to the court, as a check on Gaurico. However, the revised dating of his visit to summer 1555 makes this impossible, and there is no reason to believe that Nostradamus himself had anything to do with this particular prophecy.

Nonetheless there are very good historical grounds for believing that Gaurico genuinely lodged this as a prophecy before his death in 1558, in which case the events that followed represent a most remarkable fulfilment of his prediction. By June 1559 the now forty-year-old Henri II had reached the forty-first 'danger' year that Gaurico specifically warned him of. On June 22 his daughter Elizabeth was married to Philip II of Spain, which, although by proxy (issues of security made it too difficult for Philip to attend in person), was nevertheless cause for great celebration. A six-day pause was needed for the marriage contract between Henri's sister and Emanuel-Filibert of Savoy to become formalised. Then all was set for a week-long programme of celebratory festivities leading up to the marriage ceremony proper, the preliminaries including balls, dances, masques – and the holding of Henri II's favourite participatory sport, spectacular jousting tournaments.

Relics of an era that passed with the invention of the gun, tournaments in the mid-sixteenth century were splendid occasions in which the intention was to show off heraldic finery and physical prowess, not to risk serious injury. Despite a touch of corpulence the King was still at near-peak fitness and full of enthusiasm for such activities, much like the present Prince of Wales who so keenly engaged in polo until recently. The joustings were held in the courtyard of the Tournelles, the Paris equivalent of London's Horseguards Parade, just off the wide rue de St Antoine on Paris' east side, a short walk from where Nostradamus had stayed at the Hôtel de Sens.

Throughout most of the programme for the first three days Henri triumphed in every joust, the only individual to match him, and then on the third day, June 30, being the young Jacques de Lorges, Count of Montgomery and captain of the archers of his Scots guard. With honours even Henri positively insisted that Montgomery should joust with him one final time. The highly informative English envoy Sir Nicholas Throckmorton was the only ambassador to be present, and he had a grandstand view. According to the report that he sent back to London, as the two richly caparisoned riders thundered towards each other, Montgomery's lance:

> ... first lighting on the King's head and taking away the pannage (whereupon there was a great plume of feathers) which was fastened to his headpiece with iron, did break his staff; and with the rest of the staff hitting the King's face, gave him such a counterbuff as he drove a splinter right over his eye on the right side; the force of which stroke was so vehement, and the pain so great, that he was much astonished and had great ado to keep himself on horseback, and his horse also did somewhat yield.

Henri's aides were with him almost immediately, helping him off his horse and stripping him of his armour just in front of where Throckmorton sat. Throckmorton's first impression was that although 'a splint [was] taken out of a good bigness' the King's 'hurt seemed not to be great' and that 'he is but in little danger'. He added, however, that on the King 'being carried away … nothing covered but his face, he moved neither hand nor foot but lay as one amazed'.[34]

Henri was taken to the nearest suitable residence, the Hôtel des Tournelles, no longer extant but in the vicinity of what is today the Place des Vosges, Paris' oldest square. The house's associations were not exactly auspicious, as it was where Henri's grandfather Louis XII had ended his days three years before Henri's birth. Nonetheless the country's best doctors and surgeons were hastily summoned, while key notables such as the army chief, François Duke of Guise, Constable Anne de Montmorency, the Duke of Savoy and others kept vigil, along with some emotional court ladies. Though the programme of celebrations was put on hold, throughout much of the next nine days the medical reports mostly maintained optimism, insisting that there was 'no danger', even that 'it was doubted that the King would lose his eye'. On July 9, at Henri's insistence, the marriage of his sister Marguerite with Emanuel-Filibert of Savoy was held, albeit in an extremely low key, at midnight, in a darkened chapel, before a minimum of witnesses.

The moment a prophecy was fulfilled? The fatal joust between King Henri II and Jacques de Lorges, Count of Montgomery, June 30, 1559. From a contemporary woodcut.

The fact, however, was that splinters from Montgomery's broken lance had penetrated deep into Henri's brain. In desperation, the royal surgeons, among them the eminent Paré, made dissections of the heads of recently executed criminals in order to give them some guide to the extent of the King's terrible injury, the pain of which he reportedly bore with heroic fortitude. But all efforts proved useless, and on July 10 Henri breathed his last. A month later, after a funeral service in Notre Dame, his body was solemnly interred in the Basilica of Saint-Denis. The renowned sculptor Germain Pilon would later create for his tomb monument a highly realistic sculpture of him as he had looked in death, stripped of royal dignity, the great wound readily evident over his right eye.

Few royal courts can ever have felt themselves more stricken by a fulfilled astrological prophecy than that of Henri II and Catherine de Medici. Secretary of State Claude de l'Aubespine remarked of the repeat warning that had been received three years earlier from Gaurico:

> This...was neglected until the day of the King's wound, when I showed the copy which caused much astonishment.[35]

Luca Gaurico, as the author of this prophecy, was of course no longer around to receive either opprobrium or acclaim. But Nostradamus, from the same astrological stable, was still very much alive. Furthermore, quickly recognised was the appositeness of Nostradamus' quatrain 55 of Century III, committed to hard print in the 1555 edition of the *Prophecies*:

> *In the year when France shall have a one-eyed King*
> *The Court shall find itself in a very troubled state.*[36]

Later, in his *Prognostication* for 1562, composed early in 1561, Nostradamus would reproduce a letter that he had received from one Jean de Vauzelles, clearly recognising the relevance of this particular quatrain.[37] Considerably later his son César would also point to the appositeness of quatrain 35 of Century I, which had similarly been committed to hard print in 1555:

> *The young lion shall overcome the old*
> *On martial field in single combat*
> *In a golden cage his eyes will be put out*
> *Two into one, then to die a cruel death.*[38]

Tomb-sculpture of Henri II, showing the wound over his right eye. From his tomb in St. Denis, Paris.

To this day this particular quatrain enjoys a high reputation amongst Nostradamians as among the most compelling of all Nostradamus prophecies. The thirty-year-old[39] Montgomery is identified as the 'young lion'. King Henri II, at only forty, is identified as the old one. And the 'golden cage' is interpreted as the visor that Montgomery's lance so cruelly penetrated. What few Nostradamian authors care to dwell on is that if Nostradamus had genuinely known the date that this terrible accident was going to happen – knowledge of the kind that in his letter to Henri he certainly claimed to be capable of – he gave absolutely no recognisable hint of it, either in his letter, or in his predictions for June/July as published in his 1559 *Prognostication*. While, as earlier noted, the French language version of this *Prognostication* has not survived, it is most unlikely to have contained anything of moment, since no one of the time remarked on anything of this kind, either for the day of Henri's accident, June 30, or for the day of his death, July 10. The closest that the English-language version comes is a line for July:

> Some great prince lord and ruler to die, other to fail and decay, and others to be in great danger.[40]

And since Nostradamus liberally sprinkled his almanacs with any number of forecasts of this degree of vagueness, this particular line is about as convincing in its applicability to Henri II as Rabelais' satirical prophecy that 'crabs will move sideways'.

Yet, whatever we may make of this, as Luca Gaurico's obvious heir apparent, there can be absolutely no doubt that following July 10, 1559 Nostradamus' stock as prophet reached a new height.

NOTES

1 *Pronostico e tacoyno francese, fatto per Maestro Michel Nostradamus...*
  Tradutto de lingua Francesca, in lingua Italiana. Milan, Innocentio
  Cicognera

2 It became the capital of Savoy from 1578

3 See Coraddo Pagliani, 'Di Nostradamus et di sue una poco nota iscrizione
  liminare torinen', *Torino, della Rassegna mensile municipale*, Turin, no.1,
  January 1934, XII, pp.3–20

4 1556
  NOSTRE DAMUS ALOGE ICI
  ON IL HA LE PARADIS LENFER
  LE PURGATOIRE IE MA PELLE
  LA VICTOIRE QUI MHONORE
  AURALA GLOIRE QUI ME
  MEPRISE OVRA LA
  RUINE HNTIERE

5 In the original Italian, 'Cascina'

6 It is, however, our only indication that Nostradamus visited Italy during
  1556

7 ref: 8° Astr. P 98

8 '*dont il en y à trois cents qui n'ont encores jamais esté imprimées*'

9 *Les Prophéties de M. Michel Nostradamus. Dont il en y [sic] à trois cents qui
  n'ont encores jamais esté imprimées*, Lyons, Antoine du Rosne, 1557. Editions
  Michel Chomarat made a facsimile reprint from the Budapest copy in 1993

10 ref Ant 8192

11 *Du vray rameau de fleur de lys issu,*
   Mis & logé heritier d'Hetrurie
   Son sang antique de longue main issue
   Fera Florence florir en l'armoirie.

12 '*J'ai reçu la fille toute nue.*' Quoted, without source, in J.H.M. Salmon,
   'Catherine dei Medici and the French Wars of Religion', *History Today*, May
   1956, p.298

13 César de Nostredame, it should be noted, later interpreted this quatrain as
   referring to Marie de Medici, in his time the Queen to King Henri IV

14 '*Le grand prélat, un jour, apres son songe,*
   Interprêté an rebours de son sens
   De la Gascogne luy surviendra un monge [i.e. *moine*, or monk]
   Que fera eslire le grand prélat de Sens

15 For example, Century VI, q.63

16 '*Pour icelle souveraine observation que j'ay eu, ô Tres-Chrestien et tres victo-*
   rieux Roy, depuis que ma face estant long temps obnubilee se presente au
   devant de la deité de vostre Majesté immesuree, depuis en ça j'ay esté per-
   petuellement esblouy, ne desistant d'honorer et dignement venerer iceluy jour
   que premierement devant icelle jeme presentay comme á une singulière
   Majesté tant humain.'

17 '*j'ay esté en doute longuement à qui je viendrois consacrer ces trois Centuries*
   du restant de mes Propheties, parachevant la miliade'

18 '*Mais à un tresprudent, à un tressage Prince j'ay consacré mes nocturnes et*

Prophetiques supputations, composées plutant d'un naturel instinct, accompagné d'une fureur poëtique, que par reigle de poesie et la plus part composé et accordé à la calculation Astronomique, correspondant aux ans, moys et sepmaines des regions, contrees, et de la pluspart des Villes et Citez de toute l'Europe, comprenant de l'Affrique et une partie de l'Asie par le changement des regions, qui s'approchent la plus part de tous ces climats...'

19 *'...par mon natural instinct qui m'a esté donné par mes aiules ne cuidant presager, ...adjoustant iceluy naturel instinct avec ma longue supputation uny, et vuidant l'ame, esprit et le courage de toute curem solicitude et fascherie par repos et tranquillité de l'esprit.'*

20 *'Le tout accordé et presagé d'une partie trepode aeneo.'*

21 *'ils sont plusieurs qui m'attribue ce qu'estant antant à moy comme de ce que n'en est rien.'*

22 *'Dieu seul eternel, qui est prescrutateur des humains courages pie, juste et misericordieux, en est le vray juge, anquel je prie qu'il me vueille defendre de la calumnie des meschans.'*

23 *'[des meschans]...voudroyent aussi calumnieusement s'enquerir pour quelle cause tous vos antiquissimes progeniteurs Rois de France ont guery des escronelles.'*

24 *'Le premier homme Adam fut devant Noé environ mille deux cens quarante deux ans...Apres Noé, de luy et de l'universal deluge, vint Abraham environ mille huictante ans.'*

25 *'...par ce discours je mets presque confusement ces predictions, et quand ce pourra estre et l'advenement d'iceux.'*

26 *'...so je voulois à un chacun quatrain mettre le denombrement du temps, ee pourroit faire'*

27 *'Centuries VIII, IX, X. Qui n'ont encore jamais esté imprimées'*

28 *'...s'en alla despescher un courrier au Roy, car il tarde aux grands que les nouvelles ne volent. Sa Majesté faisoit lire les presages de Nostradamus le jour devant, et lisoient pour le lendemain bonnes nouvelles au Roy. Le courrier y arriva ce jour mesmes, et le lendemain y avoit ville rendeue. On dira que ce sont des resveries, mais si ay-je veu plusieurs telles choses de cest homme.'* Quoted in Brind'Amour, *Nostradamus Astrophile...*, op. cit., p.33, after *Commentaires de Blaise de Monluc*, ed. Paul Courteault, t.II, 1913, pp.346–7

29 See chapter 5, page 73

30 In the original spelling, 'THE PROGNOSTICA-tion of maister Michael Nostredamus, Doctour in Phisick. In Province for the yeare of our Lorde 1559. With the predictions and presages of every moneth.'

31 Claude de l'Aubespine, 'Histoire particulière de la Cour de Henri II', manuscript reproduced in *Archives curieuses de la France*, 1st series, vol. III, pp.295–6, 1835, quoted in James Laver, *Nostradamus or the Future Foretold...*, op. cit., p.48

32 *'...contre tout combat singulier en champ clos et notamment aux environs de la quarante et unième année, parce qu'à cette époque de sa vieil était menacé d'une blessure à la tete qui pouvait entrainer la cécité ou la mort.'* Quoted in Leroy, *Nostradamus, Ses Origines...*, op. cit., p.86

33 Quoted in translation in James Laver, *Nostradamus, or the Future Foretold...*, op. cit., p.48, after Brantôme, *Oeuvres, publiées et annotées par*

Ludovic Lalanne. Edition de la Société de l'Histoire de France, vol. III, p.280

34 *Calendar of State Papers, Foreign, Elizabeth*, ed. J. Stevenson, 1863. Vol. I, p.256

35 When Constable Anne de Montmorency, who had been present when Gaurico's message had arrived from Italy, was told of Henri's death he is reported to have exclaimed of Nostradamus: 'O wicked prophet, to have predicted this so evilly yet so well' ('*O le méchant devin qui prédit et si mal et si bien*'). But this appears to have no contemporary foundation, and must be counted amongst the legends created by later Nostradamians.

36 '*En l'an qu'un oeil en France reguera*
La court sera à un bien fascheux trouble. C. III, q.55. Translation Laver.
Later editions of the *Prophecies* have '*sera en un bien fascheux*

37 Nostradamus, *Pronostication nouvelle*, 1562, p.22, reproduced in Brind'Amour, *Nostradamus Astrophile*..., op. cit., p.268

38 *Le lyon jeune le vieux surmontera*
En champ bellique par singulier duelle
Dans cage d'or les yeux luy crevera
Deux classes une, puis mourir, mort cruelle
'*Deux classes*', which nearly every interpretation translates differently, is a typical Nostradamian piece of obscurity which even Nostradamus' fellow Frenchmen mostly do not pretend to understand – see Leroy, *Nostradamus, Ses Origines*..., op. cit., p.85, n.3

39 See Leroy, *Nostradamus, Ses Origines*..., op. cit., p.85, n.3

40 In the spelling of the original 'Some greate prince lorde and ruler to dye, other to fayle and decaye, and others to be in great daunger'

CHAPTER 10

Continent in Thrall

I t is difficult to over-estimate the impact upon European society of the outcome of Henri II's jousting accident. Whether this tragedy truly fulfilled anyone's prophecy, either Gaurico's written warning to Henri, or one of Nostradamus' published quatrains, is anyone's guess. What is undeniable is that the superstitious all around Europe were strengthened in their belief that at least some of the more reputable prophets needed to be taken seriously, with Nostradamus suitably high on the list. And exactly as occurred in the wake of the 2001 World Trade Center attack, this feeling was intensified by a dramatically heightened sense of insecurity.

For the political effect of Henri's untimely death was that France, which under his vigorous rule had been one of Europe's more stable monarchies, changed course under its new ruler, a seriously under-developed boy of fifteen-and-a-half. More inclined to hawking than to statecraft, and with a physical appearance so unhealthy-looking, that it was rumoured he had leprosy, this was Henri and Catherine's eldest son François, who just over a year before, in a glittering ceremony in

the Cathedral of Notre Dame, had been married to the beautiful and generally healthier Mary, Queen of Scots. Old enough to make at least some decisions of his own, King François II immediately declined to appoint as regent the Protestant-tinged Antoine King of Navarre, even though by

The sickly teenager King François II, from a pencil portrait by François Clouet in the Bibliothèque Nationale, Paris protocol this role should have fallen to him as First Prince of the Blood. Similarly marginalised was the Queen Mother, Catherine, who for all her late husband's philandering found herself genuinely mourning his loss. Likewise sidelined was Constable Anne de Montmorency, the veteran official who had greeted Nostradamus in Paris.

Instead the sickly teenager King François effectively handed over the reins of his country to the army commander, François, Duke of Guise, and his brother Charles of Guise, Cardinal of Lorraine. François was already related to the Guise family through his marriage to Mary Queen of Scots, whose mother was Mary of Guise, so to him it would have seemed a wise enough choice. As a war hero and proven leader, the Duke of Guise commanded considerable popular support, while the Cardinal was a similarly proven administrator. However, the great problem with the Duke, his brother and indeed all members of the Guise family was that they were Catholic ultra-extremists. While Henri II had been alive he had found France's Protestants difficult enough to control, but at least he had behaved relatively moderately towards them, and thereby maintained a reasonable status quo. The Guises, by contrast, quickly proved so repressive that they stimulated the most vigorous Protestant counter-reaction. It was at this time that Jean Calvin's supporters took on the name Huguenots, to denote their distinctively French brand of Protestantism. Furthermore, hardly had Henri II's body been lowered into its tomb when the Vatican announced the death, at eighty-three, of the pro-French pontiff Pope Paul IV. This necessitated the immediate summons of all cardinals to Rome to elect his successor.

In England the tension between Catholics and Protestants was so great that Queen Elizabeth's inexperienced Protestant government was having a most difficult task even finding a suitable individual to accept the post of Archbishop of Canterbury. To their frustration, their most favoured candidate, the scholarly and moderate-minded Matthew Parker, repeatedly declined the offer of the post. As for Spain, while the very Catholic King Philip II had relatively few sectarian religious problems there, this was far from the case in the northernmost part of his dominions, the Spanish Netherlands, where he had been with his army at the time of Henri II's death. As will be recalled, it was at this time that Philip had been married by proxy to Henri II's daughter Elisabeth, elder sister of François II. Feeling that he had already spent far too much time in the Netherlands, Philip was eager to get back to Spain as quickly as possible in order to prepare a suitably lavish reception for his new bride. One small problem, however, prevented him and his fleet from leaving the port of Antwerp – unfavourable meteorological forecasts, as published in the current annual astrological almanac.

And just whose almanac was responsible for holding up the mighty King of Spain and his entire fleet? In the English-language version of Nostradamus' Almanac for 1559[1] can be found his weather forecast for August, the very time that Philip wanted to set sail through the unpredictable English Channel and Bay of Biscay. This indeed reads most alarmingly:

> *August 7*: Changing of weather
> *August 8*: Treacherous for shipping[2]
> *August 9*: Bewailing for [ships'] captains[3]
> *August 11–12*: For shipping, cold, evil weather[4]
> *August 13*: Changeable. Tempest
> *August 14*: Cold, changeable weather
> *August 15*: Drowning
> *August 16*: Shipwreck[5]

Chronically over-cautious about virtually everything, King Philip heeded these warnings, as a result of which his fleet's departure from Antwerp was seriously delayed for what turned out to be an utterly groundless fear. This is historically attested by no less an authority than Sir Thomas Challoner, England's envoy in the Spanish Netherlands, who on August 26, 1559 drily reported from Antwerp back to London:

> On Friday last [i.e. August 25] the king [Philip] embarked with his whole fleet towards Spain, with an easterly wind, very small, next to a calm, but such as most gladly he embraced, as irked of his long abode here. The number of his ships was twenty Spanish and Biskaynes, thirty hulks, Hollanders, and forty sail of less sort. The first part of Spain he can recover he will land at... *The foolish Nostradamus, with his threats of tempests and shipwrecks this month, did put these sailors in great fear* [italics mine].[6]

As an indication of just how much Nostradamus' words were being followed in rural France we may cite the diary of a Norman country farmer, Gilles de Gouberville, whose lyrically rustic life revolved around growing cereals, keeping some sheep and cattle, hunting a little, and looking after the apple trees from which he produced an excellent Normandy cider. Between 1558 and 1562 Gouberville mentioned Nostradamus four times, of which the following two concern the 1558–60 period:

29 November 1558
Saturday 29th, I did not budge from my seat. I am going to start sowing at the Haulte-Vente, on the two sides of the Capplier. Nostradamus said in his almanac that it will be good to work on this day.

19 November 1560
Sanson was at Bayeux...and brought back a lamp of copper from Lambert's haberdashery, for which I have paid nothing, and an almanac by Nostradamus, which cost 8d.[7]

It is important to note, despite the Netherlands envoy Thomas Challoner's deprecatory suggestions to the contrary, that it was not just the credulous Continentals who were mesmerised by Nostradamus. The facts are that even England had fallen under much the same astrological spell. Records of the country's publications for the politically precarious late 1550s and early 1560s show the printing of an unusually high number of almanacs and prognostications quite aside from the translations of Nostradamus' annuals. An English astrologer named Cuningham issued such material every year between 1558 and 1561, another named Vaughan in 1559 and 1561, and a third, Low, every year from 1558 to 1560.[8] Yet another English astrologer, Francis Coxe, under government pressure turned from poacher to gamekeeper at much the same time. In a short booklet entitled *Short Treatise declaring the Detestable Wickedness of Magical Sciences* Coxe described the English in the year 1559 as being so mesmerised by astrologers and their almanacs that they were 'loath to ride or go on any journey unless they consulted either with these blind prophets, or at least their prophecies'. And as he went on, they did:

> ...so waver, the whole realm was so troubled and so moved with blind enigmatical and devilish prophecies of that heaven-gazer Nostradamus...that even those which in their hearts could have wished the glory of God and his Word most flourishing...doubted God had forgotten his promise.[9]

Even the highly esteemed Protestant cleric Dr Matthew Parker, in enumerating the reasons for his reluctance to become Archbishop of Canterbury – not least, a disability following a fall from a horse, and England's parlous lack of suitable Protestant clergy – felt obliged positively to deny that Nostradamus' gloomy prognostications for 1559 had anything to do with his hesitancy. Confiding to his friend Sir Nicholas Bacon, he remarked:

Nostradamus prophecies were a 'fantastical hodge-
podge' according to Church of England Archbishop
Matthew Parker. From a contemporary engraving.

I pray you think not that the prognostication of Mr Michael
Nostre Dame reigneth in my head. I esteem that fantastical hodge-
podge not so well as I credit Lucian's book *De veris narrationibus*
['Of True Stories' – in actuality a pack of lies! – I.W.]; nor yet all
other vain prophecies...[10]

Meanwhile in the same year, far to the south in Provence,
Nostradamus' long-suffering wife Anne was pregnant again. This
time, after a run of three sons, she was carrying their second daughter,
to be named Anne after her, to whom she would give birth in mid-
December of 1559.[11] Yet even when Anne was quite far advanced in
this pregnancy Nostradamus, clearly on a career high, seems to have
felt sufficiently confident about his wife's health – perhaps because he
had cast a favourable horoscope for her and her unborn daughter? –
to go on travelling locally.

Thus at Montpellier has been preserved a letter dated October 20,
1559 which shows that on that date Nostradamus was several days'
ride distant from Salon, at the picturesquely-sited wine-trade town of
Béziers, beyond Montpellier on the Mediterranean coastline southwest towards Spain. As it happens, we know from Nostradamus' son
César's monumental *History and Chronicle of Provence* that plague
was raging in Béziers at that particular time. According to César 'in
the month of October [1559] the plague spread to seven or eight

thousand bodies in the town of Béziers'.[12] Quite possibly, therefore, Nostradamus had gone there to help with this outbreak. However, this was not the malady suffered by the illustrious patient to whom Nostradamus addressed his letter.

For the patient in question was none other than a Cardinal, thirty-six-year-old Lorenzo Strozzi, bishop of Béziers. He was one of the four sons of an Italian-born couple related to the Queen Mother, who had been her devoted servants in her childhood days in Florence. On becoming Queen of France Catherine had graciously ensured worthwhile careers for the Strozzi sons, though only the year before Lorenzo's gunnery expert brother, Piero, had been killed at Thionville, during the ultimately successful preparations to take this fortress. In October 1559 Cardinal Lorenzo should have been on his way to attend the papal conclave in Rome, but he had apparently been prevented from doing so by pains in his head, shoulders, stomach and limbs, hence his call for Nostradamus.

From the symptoms described, the likeliest nature of the Cardinal's ailment was gout, possibly from a certain over-indulgence in Béziers' abundant wine production. Not least of the letter's interest value, therefore, is that it is effectively a medical prescription, and unique as such in affording us insights into Nostradamus' medical methodology. By way of introduction Nostradamus impressively told Strozzi that he had considered his ailment from three different approaches, 'medicine, surgery and judicial and natural astrology'.[13] Then he launched into the prescription proper:

First, on Sunday[14] around one o'clock, after having lunched as normal, you should apply a red hot button in the place(s) which I have indicated, and touched with a finger. And this button should be as follows [Here Nostradamus supplied a drawing of a rod bent at right-angles, with a handle and a little ball at the far end]. The depth should be no more than carried by the circuit of the head of

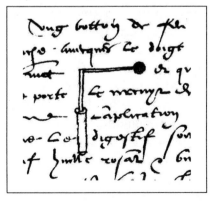

Nostradamus' 'hot button' technique for curing a Cardinal of his malady. Detail from a prescription Nostradamus prepared for Cardinal Lorenzo Strozzi, as preserved in the Departmental Archives of the Herault at Montpellier, ref.G.262.

the button. After heat has been applied a cauterisation will be effected.[15]

Arrant quackery though it might sound to us, the medical procedure prescribed was one quite widely used during the Middle Ages and later. Known as 'moxa', the principle behind it was the creation of a new irritant calculated gradually to reduce and alleviate the problem being tackled, along lines somewhat similar to acupuncture. For treating what would appear to have been at least two blisters inflicted by the searing hot 'button' Nostradamus prescribed a once-a-day application of a soothing mixture of egg, rose oil and butter, together with some leaves of *hedera parietis*, the climbing variety of ivy, promising:

> Every night when you go to bed there will be an improvement. You should carry out this treatment continually for around seven months, but be assured, my lord, that there will not have passed seven or eight days…without all of a sudden feeling a great relief… You should not feel any more pain from the head, or the brain, no fever, nor any shoulder pain, nor that of the stomach, the limbs, nor any other part of the body,… Also don't fail to use the distillation which I have prescribed for you, which you will find a really sovereign remedy. Rub it on yourself morning and night rubbing all the nape of the neck, the vertebrae of the back up to the end, and part of the joints. Praying to God, my lord, that he will grant all that you wish for. Made at Béziers on my journey through Provence to Narbonne, October 15, 1559. [Latin] Made by M. Nostradamus, Béziers, October 20, 1559. Your humble servant M. Nostredame.[16]

As is evident from definite examples of Nostradamus' handwriting, such as his registration at Montpellier, he did not personally write the prescription's main text. Possibly he dictated it to one of Cardinal Strozzi's secretaries, since he had not yet begun employing a secretary of his own. By general agreement, however, the Latin signing-off and the signature are genuinely in Nostradamus' own hand. Though no record exists of whatever business it was that was taking him from Béziers on to Narbonne, the general impression is of a man currently much in demand.

Because he was away from Salon at the time, Nostradamus missed the excitement as Duke Emanuel-Filibert of Savoy and his retinue fleetingly passed through the town during October. The Duke had dutifully lingered in Paris for his new brother-in-law Henri II's funeral, duly followed by François II's coronation in Reims on September 18. By this stage he was in a tearing hurry to get back to his long-neglected realms, and rode too fast for his new bride the Princess Marguerite to keep up with him. Yet the Duke need not have rushed, because before entering his main territory, Piedmont (the environs of Turin, at the foot of the Italian Alps), he learnt that the region, like Béziers, was in the grip of plague. He therefore tarried in Nice, where his bride, travelling at her own, more ladylike pace, joined him in due course.

Meanwhile, back at the royal court in Paris, Nostradamus' prophecies were far from forgotten. The late King Henri, shortly before his death, had imprisoned for suspected Protestantism Councillor Anne du Bourg, a greatly respected member of the Paris Parlement. Had Henri lived he would probably have released Bourg after a cautionary period. Much to Protestant anguish, however, the repressive Guise brothers coldly sentenced him to death. Then, while they held the councillor in an iron cage awaiting execution, someone noticed that Nostradamus had written in his Almanac for that very month of October a verse which included the line 'the good Bourg will be far'.[17] Immediately Cardinal Charles of Guise suspected a plot to spring Bourg from their clutches. As noted by the contemporary royal adviser and historian Régnier de la Planche:

> And because Nostradamus, astrologer and summoner of devils, had put into his prognostications 'the good Bourg will be far', the Cardinal wanted the hide of this individual. So fearful was he that he had the number of guards doubled, while anyone so much as passing the prison was arrested, held captive and terrorised, even if they had so much as looked at the place.[18]

In any event Nostradamus, aided by his characteristic double meanings, was right either way, for poor Bourg indeed did go far, to his death by execution.

Given Cardinal Charles of Guise's angry remarks about wanting his hide, it was perhaps fortunate that Nostradamus was living so far to the south. Even so, for quite independent reasons, a 'send for Nostradamus' air seems to have gripped certain more well-disposed members of the Paris court. According to a letter of November 24 sent to Nostradamus from his correspondent Lorenz Tubbe – a Bourges-based German of whom we will hear more in a later chapter – when Tubbe called on Nostradamus' brother Jehan in Aix, Jehan told him that Nostradamus had just been sent for by 'the Queen' and was 'preparing to leave for Paris'. Technically 'the Queen' at this time was none other than Mary Queen of Scots, bride of young François II. Far more likely, however, is that Tubbe meant the Queen Mother, Catherine de Medici, and it is not too difficult to understand why she should have felt deeply in need of the best astrological guidance at this particular time.

For when François II was crowned in Reims in mid-September – amidst wild weather of the very sort that Nostradamus had predicted for the previous month – the young king's physical frailty, unhealthy pallor and general debilitation had been all too painfully obvious. It was even openly doubted that François had the physical capability to consummate his marriage to the beautiful Mary Queen of Scots. As was again noted by Regnier de la Planche: 'His [François'] testicles were undescended and incapable of fulfilling their function.'[19]

If Nostradamus, as we suspect, had been reluctant to travel to Paris during the summer of 1555, his reticence at the end of November 1559 was even more justified. It was winter, then, as now, not a good time for long-distance travel north, and besides, he had one very good reason for staying which even a royal, and particularly a royal woman, would be bound to respect, the imminent birth of his child. And – all credit to him – this latter consideration seems to have prevailed, for he did not make the journey. He was therefore at home when in December the Princess Marguerite, *en route* south to join her new husband Emanuel-Filibert, stopped overnight at Salon. In the manner customary for all distinguished visitors, she and her large entourage used the imposing Château de l'Empéri for their lodgings. As César, who was but five at the time, recorded in his *History and Chronicle of Provence*:

> Michel de Nostredame my father, who was asked by the magistrates and principal nobility to perform the honours for the town, composed some brief Latin verses, in heroic rhyme, amongst which were 'Born of Trojan blood and of Trojan stock. And Queen of Cyprus'.[20]

Busy though he was, Nostradamus had done his homework well. 'Queen of Cyprus' referred to a title that the Dukes of Savoy liked to claim through their Lusignan inheritance, though it was actually an empty one, Cyprus being under Venetian control throughout Nostradamus' lifetime. As César went on:

> And as I have been assured by a gentleman who was present throughout, this Princess entertained him [Nostradamus] for a very long time, and he accorded her great honour, tracing in her the lineage and royal virtues of the great François [I] her father.[21]

As we have learnt throughout this book, there is often a need to be cautious about César de Nostredame's descriptions of the royal honours and favours bestowed on his father, since he undeniably revelled in their reflected glory. Even so there is good reason to believe that Princess Marguerite was almost as impressed by Nostradamus' alleged prophetic powers as her more obsessive sister-in-law the Queen Mother. Certainly Nostradamus would have further cordial associations with her and her husband when the couple began to raise a family. And in his Almanac for 1561,[22] which he is likely to have prepared no later than two months after her visit, he devoted a particularly fulsome Latin dedication to her:

> To the divine Marguerite, Jewel of the French, Great Daughter of François, Sister of Henry the Very Good and Great, Bride of the most victorious and invincible King of Cyprus and Duke of Savoy, Born to leave an eternal memory in mankind's history, Your most devoted Michel Nostradamus offers this gift.[23]

Within the Almanac's text proper Nostradamus even included a particularly favourable 'presage' for Marguerite and her husband's land of Savoy:

> The land of Savoy will be in the greatest joy, gladness and rejoicing, and will be mostly moved in some glory of honour and superb abundance, well serving their Prince and Princess. They will be established in glory and honour, convalescing[24] and in the greatest contentment and sublimation.[25]

The cynic might very understandably dismiss such hyperbole as just Nostradamus flattering a visiting blue-blood because she had shown some interest in him. Yet whatever else may be said about Nostradamus' prophetic powers, it is an inescapable fact that this particular 'prognostication' proved surprisingly accurate. Virtually throughout the previous century the Savoy family's fortunes had been extremely unsettled. Their realm had suffered serious disruptions from French invasions. A succession of dukes had died tragically young. And in 1532 the family's pre-eminent religious relic, the Shroud of Turin, had come within a whisker of being destroyed in a chapel fire. By contrast, from virtually the moment of Emanuel Filibert's marriage to Marguerite a bright new era dawned for Savoy. And the couple's son Charles Emanuel I, 'the Great', who would be born to them in January 1562, would take the family's fortunes to yet greater heights and the small dukedom to a golden age.

But if all augured well for Savoy, it did not need a Nostradamus to perceive that France was in for an altogether bumpier ride. In the February of 1560 the English ambassador Sir Nicholas Throckmorton reported 'factions in religion springing up everywhere' in France. In March, when the court had made one of its moves to the dramatically-sited château of Amboise on the Loire, a group of a hundred anti-Guise horsemen stormed the courtyard under cover of an early morning mist along the river. Their first pistol shots woke the guard, who returned fire, sending the would-be invaders disappearing back into the gloom. Badly shaken by their narrow escape, the Guises swiftly arrested a number of individuals whom they suspected of having taken part in the insurrection, tortured them and publicly hanged them in front of the château windows. During this same month the Spanish ambassador Perronot de Chantonnay reported, 'The affairs of this kingdom are in such confusion that one cannot hold anything for certain'.[26]

For Catherine de Medici such expressions of anti-Guise sentiment had the effect of enhancing her status politically, since her very presence brought back memories of more stable and moderate times. But for Nostradamus' credibility the continuing insecurity was even more potent. At the end of March, France's most senior political post, the Chancellorship, fell vacant upon the death of its incumbent, François Olivier. The new appointee was the highly respected and poetically inclined Michel de L'Hôpital. At this very time L'Hôpital had been preparing a beautiful Latin poem featuring some of the places he had visited, amongst which were these words about Salon-de-Provence:

There appear from afar the roofs of stony Salon.
Here Nostradamus conjures up ambiguous prophecies for people who ask him for these.
Already – what madness! – his utterances govern the spirits and the hearts of the sovereigns and nobility.
This seeing into the future does not come from God. For it is forbidden for mortals to know in advance the events that are to come.'[27]

These were serious criticisms expressed by an individual who had just become equivalent to France's Prime Minister, yet so far as can be determined Nostradamus shrugged off this sort of remark like water from a duck's back. For him what was all-important was that whether in Spain, in England, in France, in the Netherlands or in Savoy even the very greatest in the land knew his name and made their own choices as to whether or not they followed his predictions.

'What madness!' Michel de L'Hôpital, Chancellor of France in 1560, was an arch-sceptic towards Nostradamus' prophecies, commenting 'This seeing into the future does not come from God.' From a contemporary portrait.

Located as he was so far to the south, there can be little doubt that Nostradamus took a certain comfort in this remoteness, a major factor in his and his young family's protection. Indeed, such was his confidence that during the drama-torn year of 1559 he invested a further 200 crowns in Adam de Craponne's canal project. But as events soon transpired, even far-flung Provence was not immune from the forces of deep religious discord now running amok throughout all France. In and around Salon on May 1 of 1560 large bands of ultra-Catholic local peasants, dubbed Cabans after the capes that they wore, assembled in mobs and began hunting down local people suspected of Protestantism. César de Nostredame, in his capacity as local historian, would later chronicle the events as follows:

> Emblazoned with crosses of paper, and long cock feathers in their caps... vineyard workers gathered outside the houses of those whom they suspected to be sympathetic towards, and tainted with, Lutheranism... Taking their suspects with threats, abuse and violence, they dragged them amidst terrifying shouts and screams to the archbishop's castle [i.e. the Château de l'Empéri].[28]

One local landowner, Pierre Roux, deputed to keep law and order, tried to arrest one of the rioters, only to find himself a fresh victim of the mob:

> Some four or five hundred of the peasants... threw themselves furiously against him with foul language, evil intent and violent abuses, calling him a supporter of heretics and of the Lutheran rabble, and even being Lutheran himself. Around six o'clock at night... they brought [dry] vine branches and straw to set fire to the house in which he was taking refuge... It was a horrible thing to see their manner and their doings, and to hear the chants that

A mob of militant Catholics marching in procession during the 16th century's civil wars in France. From a contemporary engraving.

the Cabans shouted out extremely loudly, rough and confused, amongst the streets, with the branches, the bundles of straw and torches…crying out 'To the fire! To the fire! Long live the Cabans. Death to the Lutherans!'[29]

After a few days the mob elected their own leader, one 'Villermain, popularly called Curnier', a most 'arrogant and rebellious' individual according to César. Curnier's mortal enemy was Antoine Marc, 'suspected of the religion' – that is, of harbouring Protestant/Huguenot sympathies. As may be recalled, it had been Antoine and Palamède Marc, close neighbours of Nostradamus in Salon's Farreiroux district, who had been the consuls for whom Nostradamus had composed the water fountain inscription during happier times a few years earlier. Since Nostradamus would later make Palamède Marc a trustee of his personal fortune his closeness to the Marc family, and his sympathy towards their religious stance, can be considered certain. One evening in July someone, probably Antoine Marc, fatally wounded Villermain, and although there was a fresh wave of rioting, with threats of putting all the town's 'Lutherans' to death, this had the effect of restoring local order, at least for a while.

There can be little doubt that Nostradamus would have been badly shaken by such violence right on his own doorstep. As well as his friends the Marcs, even his own family circle was affected. The Salon lawyer Etienne Hozier, who was his wife's first cousin, and who had officiated at his marriage to Anne, was another of those whom the Cabans 'suspected of the New Religion'. When the mob caught up with Hozier they coldly murdered him.[30] Nostradamus' astrological dabbling was too well known, and he had too many links with individuals of Protestant leanings – not least having dedicated one of his Almanacs to Antoine King of Navarre – for his own religious orthodoxy not to come under suspicion. Such concern was inevitably heightened when in October 1560 Antoine and his brother the Prince of Condé, likewise a Protestant sympathiser, were summoned to the court, then at Orléans. Condé was thrown into prison, then sentenced to death for treason, and Antoine held under virtual house arrest.

But before 1560 was out yet another tragedy was to strike at the very heart of the French monarchy, and this time it was even more strongly linked with Nostradamian prophecies. On Saturday November 16, while the court was still at Orléans, the now sixteen-year-old King François, after going hunting with his brothers, returned complaining of severe pain in his ear. Soon the ever-observant foreign ambassadors were noting a lump behind the ear as large as a walnut'. Although the tumour was lanced, and the usual blood-letting carried out, this did little either to lessen the young king's pain or to improve his health, and he was described as 'almost out of his mind' with pain. On November 29 Throckmorton reported back to London, 'Great lamentation is made at the court, for they mistrust the King will not recover.'[31]

Whereupon there immediately broke out amongst Throckmorton's fellow ambassadors talk of a quatrain in the third and final section of Nostradamus' *Prophecies*. This has to refer to the 1558 edition, of which no published copy has survived, yet which must have already existed, and been in circulation, because of the ambassadors' very discussion of it. As the Venetian ambassador Michele Suriano reported back to Venice in a dispatch sent from Orléans on November 20, 1560:

And they [the court] discussed also a prophecy made by the astrologers, to the effect that he [Francois II] *would not reach the eighteenth year of his age* [italics mine]. And each then expressed their concerns, in making these reckonings, that some sinister misfortune was about to happen at this time.[32]

There can be absolutely no doubt that ambassador Suriano was referring to Nostradamus' Century X, quatrain 39, from the *Prophecies'* third and final section, the content of which was otherwise known only from the 1568 edition:

The first son of the widow, of an unhappy marriage
Without any children, two Isles in strife
Before the age of eighteen [will die] a minor
Of the nearest other even younger there will be accord.[33]

At the same time another Venetian ambassador, Giovanni Michieli, even quoted the exact chapter and verse for this prophecy, thereby confirming that the tenth and last 'Century' must have been in print: 'Each courtier remembers the thirty-ninth quatrain of *Centurie X* of Nostradamus and comments upon it under his breath.'[34]

All this is secondary, however, to the import of the prophecy itself. For since François was born on January 19, 1544, on November 20 1560 he was just two months short of his seventeenth birthday. He was the eldest, or 'first son' of a 'widow', Catherine de Medici. He was 'without any children'. And if he were to die he would indeed cause strife for 'two Isles', since his young wife was Queen Regent of Scotland almost from birth as well as Queen Consort of France. Although Nostradamus' last line is relatively obscure compared to the rest, there had been an 'accord' that Catherine's 'nearest other' son Charles, though aged only ten, i.e. 'even younger', should marry Princess Elizabeth of Austria.

Yet even more prophetically pertinent was a line in the 1560 Almanac for the very month in which François' life hung on such a slender thread. Although this particular Almanac is another that has not survived to our own time, the Tuscan ambassador Niccolò Tornabuoni quoted from it in a letter to his overlord Duke Cosimo on December 3, 1560:

> The King's state of health remains ever uncertain... This is what the people are saying. And in particular Nostradamus, by prophecy, for in his predictions for this month he says 'One most young will lose the monarchy because of an unexpected illness.'[35]

The fulfilment of both of these unusually explicit prophecies had but little time to run. Within forty-eight hours of ambassador Tornabuoni's message François lapsed into a coma. By the evening of December 6, seven weeks before his seventeenth birthday, he was dead. For France's monarchy this would mean yet another huge political turnabout. For Mary Queen of Scots, after innumerable interim adventures, it would ultimately bring about her tragic death by execution. But for Nostradamus, his stock as a star prophet could hardly have stood higher.

NOTES

1 Nostradamus, *An Almanacke for the yeare of oure Lorde God 1559*. Quoted in Brind'Amour, *Nostradamus Astrophile...*, op. cit., p.35
2 In the original 'Schipping tresshnesse
3 In the original 'Bewailyng of capt.'
4 In the original 'Schipping cold evel wether'
5 In the original 'Shypwracke'
6 *Calendar of State Papers Foreign, Elizabeth, 1558–59*, ed.Joseph Stephenson, London, 1863, pp.503–4
7 '*29 Novembre 1558: Le sabmedi XXIXe, je ne bougé de céans. Je fys commencer à semer du fourment à la Haulte-Vente, des deux costés du Capplier. Nostradamus disoyt en son allemanac qu'il faisoyt bon labourer ce jour. 19 novembre 1560: Sct-Sanson fut à Bayeulx quérir l'acte des derniers plès de Tour contre Grandval, et apporta une lampe de cuyvre de chez Lambert, mercyer, que je n'ay poynct payée, et ung almanac de Nostradamus qui cousta VIII d...*'. From Bibliothèque Nationale manuscript 4°Lc^{19}. 13 [31]. Published as *le journal du sire de Gouberville publié sur la copie du manuscrit original faite par M. L'Abbé Tollemer avec une introduction et un appendice par M.E. de Robillard de Beaurepaire*, coll. Mémoires de la Societé des antiquaires de Normandie, 4th series, vol. 1, Caen–Rouen–Paris, 1892
8 See D. Cameron Allen, *The Star-Crossed Renaissance...*, p.196
9 Francis Coxe, *Short Treatise declaringe the Detestable Wickednesse of Magicall Sciences*, London, 1561
10 Letter of Matthew Parker, March 1, 1559 in J. Bruce & T.T Perowne (eds.), *Correspondence of Matthew Parker*, Cambridge, The Parker Society, 1853, pp.59–60
11 A handwritten note in the Bibliothèque Nationale's Latin manuscript 8592 of Nostradamus letters bears the words '*1559...le 15 decembre nasquit ma soeur ane*' – '1559...On the 15th December was born my sister Anne'. There is good reason for believing this note to have been written by César de Nostredame
12 César de Nostredame, *Histoire et Chronique de Provence...*, op. cit., p.783
13 '*par voye de medecine, chururgie ensemble, les accords de l'astrologie judicielle et naturelle*'
14 This would have been Sunday October 22, 1559 – see Brind'Amour, *Nostradamus Astrophile...*, op. cit., p.451, n.43
15 '*Premierement dimenche, a une heure apres-midy, ayant disné a votres acoustumée, que vous soyt apliqué ung botton de feu au lieu ou je vous ay monstré et touché avecques le doigt. Et que le boton soyt comme s'ensuict et que l'on ne le proffonde pas plus que porte le circuyt de la teste dudit boton, que apres comme l'aplication de cauthere ardant sera faicte.*' Manuscript preserved at Montpellier, in the archives for Hérault, ref. G.261, reproduced in Brind'Amour, *Nostradamus Astrophile...*, op. cit., p.451, after Gouron, *Documents inédits*, pp.376–7
16 '*Touteffoys le soir par lors que vous yres couchez sera le meilleur, et le porteres continuellement environ l'espace de sept moys: mais assurez-vous, Monseigneur, que vous n'aures pas porte l'espace de sept a huict jours*

lesdites ouvertures aux deux jambes, que vous sentirez tout aung coup ung souverain allegement: et la plus part d'icelle froydeur incluse dedans se perdra. Et cela non tant seulement vous proffictera a icelle maladie que vous pretendes, mais aussi tant que portres lesdites fontaines ouvertes, ne sentires ne dolleur de teste, de cerveau, de fieuvre aulcune, ne mal d'espaules, d'estomach., ne de jambes, ne d'aulcune partie du corps, car a cecy, ne s'approche medecine que soyt au monde convenant principallement ce faict. Je ne vous en fays plus long discours des vertus et efficaces que vous mesmes en peu de temps cognoistres plus ample tesmoinaige de la verité. Aussi ne failhires de user de la distilation que vous escriptz, que vous y trouveres ung souverain remede, vous en frotant matin et soir toute la nuque et tous les spondilles du dos jusques au dernier et une partie des joinctures. Priant a Dieu, Monseigneur, que vous doinct ce que vous desires. Faict a Besiers en faisant mon chemyn de Provence a Narbonne ce XVe octobre 1559. Faciebat M. Nostradamus. Biterris, XX octobris 1559. Votre humble serviteur. M. de Nostre-Dame. As previous note

17 'le bon Bourg sera loin'

18 Biliothèque Nationale 8°L⁴⁵.10, Régnier, sieur de la Planche, *Histoire de l'estat de France, tant de la République que de la Religion, sous le regne de François II*, Re-edition, Paris, 1836, p.64

19 '*Il avoit les parties génératives du tout constipées et empeschés sans faire aucune action.*' Regnier, sieur de la Planche, *Histoire de l'estat…*, op. cit., p.75

20 '*Michel de Nostredame mon pere, qui avoit esté prié des Magistrat & principaux Nobles de faire l'honneur de la ville, avoit poser quelques breves inscriptions Latins, en vers heroiques, entre lesquels furent ceux-ci*
   Sanguine Troiano, Troiana stirpa creata,
   Et Regina Cypri.'
César de Nostredame, *Histoire et Chronique de Provence…*, op. cit., p.783EF, quoted Brind'Amour, *Nostradamus Astrophile…*, op. cit., p.35

21 *Et si m'a asseuré un Gentilhomme qui fut present toutes ces choses, que ceste Princesse l'entretint fort longuement & luy fit beaucoup d'honneur, suyvant in cela les traces & les vetus Royales du grand François son geniteur.*' César de Nostredame, *Histoire et Chronique…*, op. cit., p.783EF, quoted Brind'Amour, *Nostradamus Astrophile…*, op. cit., p.35

22 *Almanach pour L'an 1561, Composé par Maistre Michel Nostradamus Docteur en Medicine, de Salon de Craux en Provence.* Paris, Guillaume le Noir. According to Brind'Amour, *Nostradamus Astrophile…*, op. cit., p.480, a copy is preserved in the Library of Sainte-Geneviève as Z 4° 1711 INV, 1721 rés.

23 *Divae Margaretae, Galliarum Gemmae,*
   Francisci Magnae filiae, Henrici Opt. Maxi. Soror,
   Cypriorum Regis, & Sabaudiae Ducis,
   Victoriosiss. & Invictiss. Coniugi, natae
   Ad Aeternitatem perpetui hominis,
   Michaël Nostradamus deditiss. D.D.
D.D. is a recognised abbreviation in inscriptions of Roman monuments, standing for 'Donum dedit' – 'he/she offers this gift'

24 'convalescing' – Marguerite had been suffering from a long illness at this time – see Brind'Amour, *Nostradamus Astrophile…*, op. cit., p.36, n.63

25 'Le pays de Savoe sera en supreme joye, allegresse & resjuissance, & seront la plus part esmeux en quelque gloire d'honneur & abondante superbe, bien servant leur Prince & Princesse, seront constituez en gloire & honneur, convalescence, & grandissime contentement & sublimation.'

26 Quoted in Irene Mahoney, *Madame Catherine*, New York, Coward, McCann & Geoghegan, 1975, p.62

27 'Apparent longe lapidosi tecta Saloni:
Hic mendax contorta dabat responsa petenti.
Nostradamus populo, iam (quae dementia!) regum
Dictirs nobiliumque animos & corda regebat,
Haec aliena Deo prudentia: namque futuras
Prospicere eventus mortalibus ille negavit.'
Michel de L'Hôpital, *Ad Iac. Fabrum Iter Nicaeum*, p.266, quoted in Brind'Amour, *Nostradamus Astrophile...*, op. cit., p.37

28 'Les vignerons alloyent, emblastonnés avec des croix de papier et de longues plumes de coq en leurs barrètes...Par les maisons de ceux qu'on doutoit oingts et contaminés du luthérianisme...prendre les suspects avec menaces, outrages et violences, qu'ils entrainoyent avec huëments et crieries', César de Nostredame, *Histoire et Chronique de Provence...*, p.786

29 ibid.

30 Leroy, *Nostradamus Ses Origines...*, op. cit., p.94

31 *Calendar of State Papers Foreign, 1560–61*, op. cit., item 744

32 'Et è venuto anco in consideratione un pronostico fatto da astrologhi, che ello non sia per passare li xviij dieciotto anni de vita. Et cosi ogn'uno discorre secondo le sue passioni, facendo li suoi conti, che se accorresse qualche sinistro accidente a questi tempi...'. Quoted in Brind'Amour, *Nostradamus Astrophile...*, op. cit., p.39, after Paris, Bibliothèque Nationale MS fonds Italien 1721, an 18th-century copy from the original collection of documents of which this particular report formed part

33 Premier fils vefve malheureux manage
Sans nuls enfans deux Isles en discord
Avant dixhuict incompetant eage.
De l'autre pres plus bas sera l'accord.

34 Quoted by James Laver on p.66 of his *Nostradamus or the Future Foretold...*, op. cit., though unhappily without the proper source details

35 'La salute del Re è sempre incerta...Questi sono i discorsi; e quello di Nostradamus par profezia, che, nelle sue predizioni di questo mese, dice che il più giouane perderà la monarchia di malattia opinata'. Quoted in Brind'Amour, *Nostradamus Astrophile*, op. cit., p.40, after Abel Desjardins, *Négociations diplomatiques de la France avec la Toscane, documents recueillis par Giuseppe Canestrini et publiés par Abel Desjardins*, t.III, Paris, 1865, pp.427–8

CHAPTER 11

Seeking The Lost

The Queen Mother, Catherine de Medici, was now in her early forties, and the portraits of her from this time show her much as she would appear for the rest of her life, dressed in mourning black relieved by a simple white collar, with the beginnings of a double chin, her heavy-lidded eyes with the characteristic Medici bulge. When her husband had died, and her eldest son François had succeeded him at an age not far short of his majority, she had been too genuinely grief-stricken to attempt to take charge herself. She had watched helplessly as the repressive Guise regency led the country to the very brink of civil war. And during this uneasy period she took to heart the advice given her by Chancellor Michel de L'Hôpital that if she ever had the opportunity she should make herself France's mistress, and not be dependent on evil councillors.

So when upon François' death the crown fell to his younger brother, the ten-year-old Charles, still very much a child under her tutelage, Catherine swiftly took control as Regent. Acting with confidence and decisiveness, she recalled the redoubtable Anne de Montmorency as Constable. She exhibited religious tolerance by appointing Antoine of Navarre as her first councillor. Just one week after François' death she presided over France's equivalent of Parliament, the Estates General, making great show of having the extravagantly dressed, almost doll-like figures of the new King, his two brothers and sister Margot seated on high beside her. And she ensured that the proceedings included a repeal of the Prince of Condé's death sentence and his release to return to his domains in Picardy. At a stroke it was the hitherto powerful Guise family who became marginalised, having Mary Queen of Scots – who upon François' death had instantly lost all political clout to her title as Queen of France – with little option but to leave and take up her other, less alluring crown in the land of Scotland.

But even with the Guises no longer in power, for France the chill hand of fate still had plenty of cards up its sleeve. The very next day

Catherine de Medici,
from a pencil portrait by
François Clouet preserved
in the Bibliothèque Ste-
Genevieve, Paris.

after François' death, the royal line's last in succession, the twelve-
year-old Marquis de Beaupréau, was killed in strange circumstances.
As the ambassador Perronot de Chantonnay reported back to Spain in
January:

> It is noted that in a month both the first and last [in line of succes-
> sion] of the royal house have died. The day after the passing away
> of the King there passed near him [the young Marquis] a ruffian on
> a great horse who [mortally] wounded him by raining blows on his
> head. These tragedies have amazed the court, along with the warn-
> ings by Nostradamus, which it would be better to suppress, rather
> than to let his prophecies have free sale, encouraging every vain
> and superstitious belief.[1]

For a child of ten the new King, henceforth to be known as Charles
IX, could and did hold himself regally enough. Yet, mindful of his
deceased brother, the foreign ambassadors disquietingly noted him to
be 'not very robust'.[2] This inevitably fuelled discussion of a verbal prediction that Nostradamus had apparently made to Catherine de
Medici – presumably during his visit to the royal court in 1555 – that
she would live to see all her sons become kings. Felicitous as this might
sound, its underlying implication was that either Catherine would be
extremely long-lived or that her sons would have unusually short
reigns. In the words of the Venetian ambassador Suriano:

> There are no lack of suspicions. One such is derived from the
> astrologer Nostra Adam [clearly a corruption of the name
> Nostradamus] who for some while has been predicting numerous
> calamities for the realm of France, and has acquired the confidence
> of many. He has told the Queen that she will see all her sons

[become] kings. As she has already seen two, François and Charles, this leaves two, Alexander, Duke of Orleans, and Henri, Duke of Anjou, the one ten years old, the other seven. The Queen needs to understand that this setback could quickly cause the monarchy's total destruction. For things could continue for too long with just children, failing to achieve adult age, and being governed by tutors. [Much needed] is the coming of a king furnished with supreme authority who can command his subjects' obedience, be respected by his neighbours, be feared by all, and by his signal appropriate actions can bring back to this Crown its [former] reputation and grandeur.[3]

Catherine was far too astute not to be conscious of such dangers herself. When but a child of eight she and her formerly illustrious family had been brutally expelled from Florence, so she knew all too well the fickleness of dynastic fortune. All she could do, however, was handle the reins of power as best she could until at least one of her sons was old enough to take them over from her, in the interim perhaps feeling herself fortified by the sixty-third quatrain of Nostradamus' Century VI:

> *The Lady shall be left alone in the kingdom of her only spouse*
> *Dead before her on the field of honour.*
> *After mourning him for seven years*
> *She shall live long for the welfare of the kingdom.*

Predictably, the ultra-Catholic faction of which the Guises were still leaders baulked at Catherine's regime as being far too tolerant towards the 'new religion' for their own tastes. The Protestants, for their part, were equally dissatisfied, regarding this same toleration as mere lip-service paid to their cause. Fulfilling prophetic warnings that Nostradamus had percipiently issued during the previous decade, there thus began to gather momentum the religious wars that would greatly impoverish and debilitate France throughout the rest of Catherine's life and beyond, for three decades.

Meanwhile, in Provence, still in some shock from the Caban anti-Protestant local riots of the previous year, Nostradamus seems to have been unusually anxious to demonstrate his adherence to the prevailing Roman Catholic orthodoxy. In early 1561 his self-appointed task, as in every year, was to prepare his Almanac for the following year, i.e. for 1562. This time his choice of dedicatee was none other than Pope Pius IV, the Paris-educated son of a Milanese family who had been made Pope during the conclave held in the month of François II's death. Pius' predecessor Paul IV had instituted the Index of Prohibited Books, which included many works of astrology, but never any of Nostradamus' publications. And this was a situation that Nostradamus fervently hoped to see perpetuated under his successor.

For the handling of this particular Almanac Nostradamus had chosen as his printers the Parisians Guillaume le Noir and Jehan Bonfons, and from a surviving copy of their edition we know that they obtained the royal privilege on February 1, and that Nostradamus signed off his dedication to Pius IV on March 17. In it he lauded the Pope as 'the Atlas of our Christian Republic'. In his classic manner he pointed out for the coming May a conjunction of Saturn and Mars in Cancer, followed later in the year by Saturn and Jupiter in the same sign, then in September 1563 by the same planets in Leo. To his astrological eye this meant, in terms of the humours, three water signs and three fire signs, one of the worst such conjunctions throughout the previous 960 years, and therefore of great concern in the context of the present religious unrest. Confirming his great affection for Catherine de Medici, he spoke most warmly of having communicated his calculations to 'Her Most Serene Majesty the Queen Mother, Regent of France, monarch of an incomparably noble disposition'.[5]

But this particular *New Almanac for the Year 1562*[6] shows many signs of having been interrupted during its composition, the predictions after March suddenly becoming much simpler than normal, and the book being printed with a number of blank pages. The explanation for this is in fact not hard to find. At the Easter of 1561, right on Nostradamus' doorstep, there had erupted a fresh outbreak of Caban ultra-Catholic mob fury, with Nostradamus, for all his attempts to display Catholic orthodoxy, now under deep suspicion for harbouring Huguenot or 'Lutheran' Protestant sympathies. From one of his letters to his German correspondent, Lorenz Tubbe, there has survived a particularly vivid first-hand description of what he experienced:

> Amongst us in this town [i.e. Salon], as everywhere arguments and hatred are growing on matters of faith and religion...A certain Franciscan, quite an orator when he gets in the pulpit, is always inflaming opinion against the Lutherans, inciting people to violence and even to full-scale massacres. On Good Friday [1561] 500 ruffians armed with iron rods burst into the church. Along with a number of Lutherans they named Nostradamus. Everyone thus suspected left the town. In my case, in the face of such disturbing rage, I fled to Avignon...I was absent for two months or more until the governor of Provence, the Count of Tende, an individual of great humanity, restored the peace.[7]

In a town of only some 3,000 people, for an armed mob 500-strong to go on the rampage would have been a fearsome sight indeed. And undoubtedly heightening Nostradamus' concerns for his own and his family's safety would have been the fact that his wife Anne was yet again pregnant. In 1561 Good Friday fell on April 4, and since their sixth and last child Diane was born in the September Anne would already have been some four months into her term at the time of this unrest. Direct evidence for the family's seeking refuge in Avignon survives in the archives of France's *département* of Vaucluse. A legal document recorded that on April 14, 1561 the lawyer Géraud de Rippe rented for one year to Michel de Nostredame, from the town of Salon, the front of a house situated in Avignon's rue de la Servellerie.[8] The cost of the year's rent was eighteen gold crowns. The Avignon notary Antoine de Béziers drew up the contract and received twelve crowns for his services.

However, the danger that had necessitated this move from Salon was short-lived. Within a few weeks the rental for the Avignon house became transferred to Jean Payot, called Dorgellet. Nostradamus was certainly back home in Salon by April 20, 1561, for he recorded that date and that location on completing a second copy of the letter to Pope IV for a second version of the Almanac.[9] This latter Almanac was the work of the Lyons printers Antoine Volant and Pierre Brotot, Pierre's father Jean Brotot having apparently died shortly before.

In his letter of July 15, 1561 reporting the fresh Caban violence Nostradamus also told Tubbe – then a resident of Bourges, a town south of Paris along a logical route between Salon and the capital – of having just received another request to visit the royal court:

> While I have been writing this, a message has just arrived from a great Prince, summoning me to court, where he is. If I go (it would have to be brief), I will be sure to visit you … May Christ let you be the first person whom I meet in Bourges.[10]

In the event Nostradamus once again did not make the long journey north, either to Bourges or to Paris, and again we do not know the reason. Perhaps the 'summons' from the mysterious 'great Prince' was not quite as grand or as positive as he had made it appear to Tubbe. Perhaps he had a guilty conscience about his now long-standing debt to the court *maître d'hôtel* Jean Morel. Perhaps he could not face so many days on horseback at an age not far short of sixty. Perhaps this time he was simply anxious to be on hand during his wife's pregnancy.

Whatever the reason, the message from the court also appears to have included a request for him to prepare a horoscope for the new

King, Charles IX, and this he actually did. Accordingly, in a letter to Tubbe written only three months later, during which time his wife Anne had given birth to their daughter Diane, he reported:

> I do not intend to make that journey to the court of which I wrote to you [previously]. I have been working on a birth chart for King Charles IX. This has been costing me long night vigils and an incredible amount of work, as so great an undertaking demands.[11]

Nostradamus' horoscope as prepared for Charles IX has not survived amongst France's royal archives; more than likely it was destroyed during the French Revoluton. However, from the only such royal horoscope of his which has survived, a 119-page one that he later made for Prince Rudolf of Austria (to be discussed in a later chapter[12]), there can be no doubt that the one for Charles IX would have been an exhaustive document, specifically covering such matters of national interest as the young King's likely longevity, what illnesses he would suffer, whom he would marry, how many children he would have, what diplomatic alliances he would make or break, and much else.

Indicative that the lost horoscope was indeed so exhaustive is the fact that Nostradamus was still working on it intensely that same October. In the document's absence it is difficult even to guess at the identity of the 'great Prince' supposed to have 'summoned' Nostradamus to the court. Whoever the approach came from, logically the likeliest person ultimately to have been interested would have been Regent Catherine de Medici, because of both her known astrological leanings and her strong anxieties for the young Charles IX's future. For when Charles had undergone the royal anointing in Reims on May 13, though he had appeared a little stronger than his late brother during this same ceremony, his frailty was even so a major cause for concern. Tubbe, in his letter of November 15, told Nostradamus that the child-king had fallen ill on October

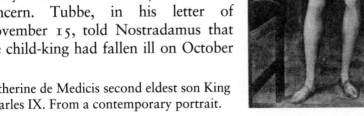

Catherine de Medicis second eldest son King Charles IX. From a contemporary portrait.

1, and that when he was seen again in public a few days later 'he seemed rather sickly and suffering from I don't know what weakness'.[13]

But another 'great Prince' who certainly called on Nostradamus' services at around this time was the Duke of Savoy, Emanuel-Filibert, together with his wife the Duchess Marguerite. Nostradamus and Marguerite, of course, had met during the latter's relatively recent sojourn in Salon. Thanks to the plague relaxing its grip in Savoy the ducal couple had eventually been able to return to Turin, where Nostradamus was duly summoned, apparently pleasing them greatly by predicting that Marguerite would give birth to a son. Pinpointing a time in 1561 when Nostradamus may have made such a visit is by no means easy. However, Turin is only some 150 miles (240 km) from Salon, a much shorter journey than to Paris, and it is a matter of firm historical record that Marguerite did give birth to a son, the future Charles Emanuel I of Savoy, at Rivoli, just outside Turin, on January 12, 1562.

But mixed with all the honour and glory of predicting the destinies of Europe's royalty, and the headiness of becoming a father again at the age of nearly sixty, the year 1561 had some further knocks for Nostradamus, on top of those he had already suffered from the Caban violence. As a number of instances in the Bibliothèque Nationale Latin correspondence manuscript indicate, he had found immensely useful the printer Jean Brotot's regular courier service between Lyons and Salon. Over his eight-year association with Brotot, the blunt printer who had dared tell him he was too verbose had proved rather more loyal to him than the other way round. Despite Jean's son Pierre quickly taking up his father's mantle, remarks that Nostradamus later made to other correspondents show that the old printer's death had struck him quite hard.

This same year, as would emerge from later correspondence, an arrogant German aristocrat named Jerome Schorer took great exception to a horoscope that Nostradamus had prepared for him, after 'a great deal of work', in his own handwriting. As Nostradamus later recalled:

> He contemptuously sent it back to me complaining that it was virtually illegible. I then had it properly done by a calligrapher, but still he was not satisfied.[14]

These seem to have been the circumstances in which Nostradamus was persuaded to employ a secretary, since Chavigny, a well-educated young man who had otherwise found no suitable employment, entered his service around now.

Duke Emanuel-Filibert of Savoy, for whose realms Nostradamus predicted a particularly prosperous period. From a drawing of c.1560 in the Bibliothèque du Conservatoire National des Arts et Métiers.

On November 29 there caught up with him, thanks, it seems, to the news that he might be visiting the court, Jean Morel, the Parisian arts patron and *maître d'hôtel* who had lent him money at the time of his first visit to Paris in 1555, and who had never been repaid. Clearly uncomfortable at having been found very much in the wrong, Nostradamus hastily provided promissory notes to make good this old debt.

Potentially the most serious blow of all that year, however, was an apparent omission by the Lyons printers Antoine Vollant and Pierre Brotot to obtain the necessary royal privilege for their second edition of Nostradamus' 1562 Almanac. Exactly how or why this happened is by no means clear. Possibly it was an oversight by the still inexperienced Pierre Brotot on taking over from his late father. Possibly there was some procedure that Nostradamus had overlooked amidst the flurry of moving his family backwards and forwards between Avignon and Salon earlier in the year. Whatever happened, Nostradamus as the Almanac's author seems to have borne ultimate responsibility, whereupon when the illegal copies appeared on the streets of Paris around November 23, 1561, the judiciary in Paris immediately sent orders to the Count of Tende in Provence for his arrest. These Tende carried out on December 16, when Nostradamus was taken to the Count's castle at Marignane, a few miles from Salon. As we have already seen, Tende and Nostradamus were on friendly terms; he is most unlikely to have received any harsh treatment, and on December 18 Tende reported back to Paris:

With regard to Nostradamus, I have seized him and he is with me, having been forbidden to make more almanacs and prognostications. This he has promised me. Please let me know what it would please you should be done with him?[15]

Certainly it all appears to have been a misunderstanding, and the whole matter was swiftly resolved and Nostradamus released. Nor did it appear to do his standing amongst his clientèle any perceptible harm. They continued to pester him not only for horoscopes, of which he would have provided markedly shorter versions than those created for royalty, but also for astrological guidance even on pursuits such as treasure-hunting.

Thus amongst the Nostradamus correspondence preserved in the Paris Bibliothèque Nationale Latin manuscript is a letter that Nostradamus sent on January 20, 1562 to two Toulouse-based clients, Dominic de Saint-Etienne and Jammot Panthon. Though their original letter of enquiry has not survived, the context in which they had approached Nostradamus is evident enough from his response:

As soon as I received your letter on a treasure hidden somewhere in Spain, I drew up an astronomical chart. I discovered the Ascendant XIII in Aries in the opposite part of the middle of the sky, which undoubtedly means that there is a quantity of gold and silver [to be found], as large as your own reckoning. The region is Tarragonese Spain, today called the kingdom of Aragon, and the place is known as Batestan, from the name of the town or colony of Batestan. It is not far from Saragossa ... This territory was the theatre for the fighting between the dictator Julius Caesar and Sextus and Gnaeus, the sons of Pompey. When these latter were defeated, they hid their treasure. I am going to show you very clearly where this is to be found. To the west can be seen ruins, statues and vases. Under the debris of an ancient temple a very deep pit lies hidden. The opening to this pit is concealed by a stone that was quarried to an extraordinary thickness. This was to prevent anyone who struck it from discovering it. An urn and a lamp with an everlasting flame will be found inside. Without any doubt not far from the urn there lie antique coins of the purest gold, silver, heavy bronze, also gems and precious stones.[16]

This response reveals him as thoroughly at home in the guise that he most revelled in – as magician *par excellence*, capable of 'seeing' even deep into the earth. After the short introductory flourish of astrological flummery he gave his Toulouse clients just what they wanted, the encouragement to go off gold-seeking in Spain, complete with some impressively precise-sounding directions. He recommended that they make their trip between mid-June and mid-July, since astrologically this was the most favourable time. He composed for them six accompanying *Prophecies*-like verses by way of further clues to their quest, which even featured the client-name 'Jamot' in a couple of the lines. And he concluded his calculations, for which no doubt he charged a significant fee, with the confident assurance:

> These are my judgments which I send you, made from astronomical calculations of the maximum certitude and truth…Farewell, you lucky ones, and when you find your treasure, don't forget your mortality.

History has no record of what happened to Dominic de Saint-Etienne and Jammot Pathon and whether they ever did set out for Spain armed with Nostradamus' instructions. For all we know their bodies might still be lying somewhere on the wild-goose chase that, wittingly or unwittingly, he sent them on. While Saragossa is in north-eastern Spain, 'Batestan', the modern-day Baza, is in the southern province of Almería, not far from Granada. And the battlefield of Munda, where Caesar did indeed defeat Pompey's sons, is hundreds of miles to the west, in what is today southern Portugal. So whatever judgement anyone may make of Nostradamus' astrology, he could and did get seriously confused in both his geography and his history.

But Nostradamus' reputation was such that even churchmen continued to call upon his astrological 'lost and found' services, as most certainly did the venerable canons of the ancient Cathedral of Notre Dame at Orange, the quaint old Roman town some thirty-five miles (56 km) to the north of Salon. On the night of December 20, 1561, during outbreaks of sectarian violence similar to those at Salon, a mob broke into the cathedral's treasury and stole its most sacred treasures. These included the main crucifix, the great chalice and a number of sacred statues, all in gilded silver. With Nostradamus just a day's ride away down the road the canons swiftly sought his guidance to help them recover the valuables.

And in exactly the manner that he had used for the Toulouse treasure-hunters, on February 4, 1562 Nostradamus drew up an astrological chart for the missing items, together with a written appraisal of where these were to be found. As with so much Nostradamian material, the original of this letter and chart disappeared long ago, but fortuitously a copy was made in 1714 by Orange's provost at the time. From the distinctive style this document seems unmistakably to derive from a genuine Nostradamian original,[17] but it is the content that is a revelation, since in it Nostradamus accused outright some amongst the cathedral's own hierarchy of perpetrating an 'inside job':

As you can readily see from the astrological chart shown above [Nostradamus provided the chart of his calculations], it shows that the sacrilegious outrage was [perpetrated] with the collusion of two of the brothers of your own Church. Do you not remember their private counsel on several occasions as to what had happened to your silver? One giving you one opinion, the other, another. One said it had been taken to Avignon, another that it had been taken somewhere else. Both were of the opinion that it had been sold.[18]

Nostradamus went on to describe three clerical miscreants as locking the silver away in one of their houses, with a lot of discussion and disagreement then taking place on how best to melt the metal objects down so they could sell them without arousing suspicion. Nostradamus advised these secret felons that by far their best course was quietly to return the stolen objects to their rightful place. If they did not, divine vengeance would see to it that they and their families incurred the greatest misfortune, and to cap it all, Orange would suffer the greatest plague that it had ever known. Nostradamus even had a plan for how the honest canons could themselves flush out the culprits from within their own midst, recommending:

Let this letter of mine be read with everyone present, as if it had not been previously opened until all were assembled. Immediately the faces of those who took part will change due to their being unable to hide their deep shame and confusion.[19]

Horoscope as prepared by Nostradamus for the canons of Orange, to help them trace their lost valuables. Drawing after Edgar Leroy.

Whatever the truth or otherwise of Nostradamus' astrological percep-
tions in this instance, by any gauge it was a most audacious piece of
human psychology. Historically it would be fascinating to know
whether the Orange canons ever held a chapter meeting to flush out
their miscreants along the lines that Nostradamus advised; or whether
he ever received any fee for his services; or whether the cathedral's
treasures ever did mysteriously reappear. No Nostradamian researcher
appears to have tried to find out such details. All we do know is that
today the building which was the scene of the theft is no longer a
cathedral, and but a pale shadow of its one-time glory.

As for Nostradamus, he had become preoccupied with some much
furtherflung locations upon which to focus his metaphorical crystal
ball.

NOTES

1 'Ha se notado q. en un mes muniéron el primero y el postro del casa Real. El
diá siguiente yendo el Rey a passear passo cerca del un moco en un cavallo
grande el qual no herro un xeme de dar le un par de coces en la cabeça, estos
desastres tienen esta corte atonita, con las amenazas de aquel Nostredamus,
al qual seria mejor castigar, q. dexar vender sur prognosticos que unduzen a
credulidades vanas y superstitiosas.' Quoted in Brind'Armour, Nostradamus
Astrophile..., op. cit., p.40, after manuscript K1494, 27 in the General
Archives at Simancas, Spain

2 Reported by one of the Venetians – see Irene Mahoney, Madame Catherine,
op. cit., p.74

3 'Mà quello che dà non manco sospetto, è che il nostro Adamo Astrologo, il
quale da molto tempo in qua hà sempri predetto il vero di molti calamità del
Regno di Francia, conchi' s'è aquistato fede appresso de molti, hà detto à la
Regina, che'lla vedrà tutti li duoi figliuoli Rè, due de quale hà visto
Francesco, et Carlo, restano due Alexssandro duca d'Orliens et Heredi dica
d'Angiò, secundi dieci, l'altro di sett'anni, li quali s'ella hà da veder bisogna,
che questa mora presto, chesaria la total destruttioni del Regno, perche con-
tinouando frà tanto tempo in putti, che sino all'età perfetta bisogna che siano
governati da Tutori, tarariasi troppo ad hauer'un Rè con autorità suprema,
che fossitenuto da sudditi, respettato da vicini, et temuto da tutti, et que con
qualisi attioni segnalata rendessi la reputationi et la grandessa à quella
Corona. Brind'Amour, Nostradamus Astrophile..., op. cit., after M.N.
Tommaseo, Relations des ambassadeurs vénitiens, vol. I, pp. 542–5

4 The translation in this instance is that given in James Laver, Nostradamus or
the Future Foretold..., op. cit., p.62. The original French reads:
La dame seulle au regne demourree
L'unic estaint premier au lict d'honneur
Sept ans sera de douleur exploree,
Puis longue vie au regne par grand heur.

5 'la serenissime Majesté de la Royne mère, Regente de France, monarque d'incomparable débonnaireté.'

6 *Almanach Nouveau Pour l'An. 1562, Composé par Maistre Michel Nostradamus, Docteur en Medecine, de Salon de Craux, en Provence.* Paris, Guillaume le Noir & Jehan Bonfons

7 'Apud nos in hac ipsa urbe, ut ubique, inter praecipuos cives tanta est controversia et latens odium ob fidem et religionem susceptum...Franciscanus quidam miré vocalis in pulpito plebem quotidie animabat in Lutheranos, vim ut eis inferrent, et ad unum occidione occiderent. Parum itaque abfuit, quin die Veneris sancta quingenti fere in templum prodierint armati velut buffones, scipionibus ferratis acutissimis tamen. De numero Lutheranorum, uti aiebant, erat Nostradamus; caetere fere omnes suspecti urbe fugerunt; hoc ego tumultu et rabie commotus Avenionem secessi, hac illac fugiens populi tam furibundi fuorem abfuique à mea domo duos menses et amplius. Tandem supervenit Provinciae praefectus Comes a Tenda, qui ut est humanus, composita pace...Letter XXVII, Dupèbe, *Nostradamus, Lettres Inedites*..., op. cit., p.87

8 Arch. Dép. Du Vaucluse, *Fonds de notaires*, Beaulieu no. 1145, fol. 147, quoted in Leroy, *Nostradamus, Ses Origines*..., op. cit., p.96

9 *Pronostication nouvelle, Pour l'an mille cinq cents soixante deux. Composee par maistre Michel Nostradamus, Docteur en Medicine, de Salon de Craux en Provence.* Lyons, Antoine Volant & Pierre Brotot

10 'Interea dum haec scriberem, ecce mihi nuntius à magno quodam Principe, qui me ad aulam regiam ubi est accersit; ad quam si mihi profisceendum est, (ut certe est brevi) disperam nisi te viso...Faxit Christus, ut tu mihi primus occurras Biturigum. Letter XXVII, Dupèbe, *Nostradamus, Lettres Inédites*..., op. cit., p.86

11 'Nolui me viae dar et in aulam profisci, ut ad te scribebam. Nisi perfecta plane atque absoluta Caroli IX Francorum regis genitura: quod hisce diebus fecimus, non sine magnis vigilis et labore incredibili, ut res tanta postulabat.' Letter XXXI, Dupèbe, *Nostradamus, Lettres Inédites*..., op. cit., p.99

12 For details of this, see chapter 15

13 'itaque visus est mihi post macilentior et nescio quo modo imbecillior' – Letter XXXIII, Dupèbe, *Nostradamus, Lettres Inédites*..., op. cit., p.107

14 'qui ut debet animo esse elato cum nescioquo contemptu remisit, causatus lectionem eius esse difficulem. Itaque dedi operam ut transcriberetur his paulo elegantioribus characteribus; quae etiam fecit minimi.' Letter LI, Dupèbe, *Nostradamus, Lettres Inédites*..., op. cit., p.163

15 'Au regard de Nostradamus, je l'ay faict saisir et est avecques moy, luy ayant deffendu de faire plus almanacz et prognostications, ce qu'il m'a promise. Il vous plaira me mander ce qui'il fous plaist que j'en fasse.' Reproduced in Brind'Amour, *Nostradamus Astrophile*..., p.43, after MS. BN fonds français 15875, fol. 421r

16 'Acceptis vestris literis quam primum ad illam vestram interrogationem de thesauro abscondito in nonnullis Hispaniae partibus, figuram Astronomicam erexi, offendique ascendens XIII gradum Arietis in parte opposita medii coeli, qui sine dubio significavit magnam ibi inesse et numerosam auri atque argenti congierem, et maiorem etiam quam vos putatis. Plaga illa est Hispaniae Tarraconensis, quae hodie regnum Aragoniae appellatur; ager Batestanus dicitur, non longe ab Caesarea Augusta, ab oppido Batestano, sive colonia sic dictus...illa imperii Romani aetate bellum gestum est à Caio

Iulio Caesare Dictatore contra Sextum et Cneum Pompeios Cnei illius magni filios, qui multis profligati praeliis, re tandem desperata, quidquid habebant pretiosi, ne in manum hostium deveniret, aurum argentumque omne, facta scrobe, unum in locum congesserunt…indicabo sine ullo errore, nodo aut sermonis involutione. Is est versus occidentalem agri partem; ad quam plurima etiam num hoc die videntur fragmenta marmorea, et ila quidem animalium sculptura…sunt urna, sunt vasa fictilia…Sed vel inter caetera, rudera sunt antiquissimi templi et subtus puteus profundatis maximae et amplitudinis, in cuius ambitu et operculo lapis est quadratus proportione aequali quadrilaterali, sed mirae crassitudinis, eo consilio profecto ne percussus signum daret concavitatis. Ibi urnam videre licebit et lampadem ardentem purissimo quodam liquore perpetuum fomitem vi igneae subministrante. Ad urnam non longe…repositum est sine dubio ingens illud numismatum antiquorum ex auro purissimo, argento, aere pondus atque etiam gemmarum et lapidum preciosorum.' Letter XXXVI, Dupèbe, *Nostradamus, Lettres Inédites…*, op. cit., p.122

17 *'A mes venerables Seigneurs Messieurs les Chanoines de l'Eglise Cathedrale de lantiquiss. Cité D'aurange'*, ms. Mediathèque d'Arles 96

18 *'Comme vous pouvez le voir amplement, jouxte la figurine astronomique ci-dessus, il est manifeste que le ravissement sacré l'a été par le consentement de deux de vos frères de l'Eglise même. Souvenez-vous du conseil privé que vous fites par plusieurs fois: qu'est ce qu'on ferait de votre argenterie? Qui dict une opinion. Qui en dict ung aultre. Qui disoit de les porter en Avignon. Qui disoit de porter en aultre part. Puis, deux furent l'opinion de la vendre.'* Quoted in Leroy, *Nostradamus, Ses Origines…*, op. cit., p.90

19 *'Que cette mienne lettre soit lue, à la présence de tout vos Messieurs et qu'elle ne soit ouverte que tous ne y soient que lors continent, la face des Consentants changera de haute vergogne; et de confusion qu'ils auront, [ils] ne se pouront contenir.'* Ibid.

CHAPTER 12

A Satisfied Client

From the perspective of our sceptical twenty-first century it might be easy to suppose that the majority of those who sought Nostradamus' astrological services were impractical, rather credulous individuals, likeliest to be of Latin extraction from southern France and Italy. Yet one major client who certainly did not fall into any such category was the German mining magnate Hans Rosenberger, for whom Nostradamus' correspondent Lorenz Tubbe, mentioned earlier, acted as agent and intermediary.

Today the inhabitants of the picturesque, lake-studded Kitzbühel Alps in Austria's far western corner live mainly by the winter sport of skiing and by summer tourism. In the sixteenth century, however, when the region was part of the Holy Roman Empire, first under Charles V, then under his brother Ferdinand I, its atmosphere was akin to that of the Klondike. For beneath the verdant Alpine hills there had been found since prehistory some surprisingly rich seams of gold, silver, copper, lead and iron. During Nostradamus' lifetime the science of mining and metallurgy had developed rapidly – the pioneering German scientist Georg Bauer, writing under the Latin name Georgius Agricola, had produced his definitive treatise *Of Things Metallic* within the same decade that Nostradamus produced his *Prophecies*.[1] And under the supervision of enterpreneurial German magnates such as Rosenberger, encouraged by political overlords like Ferdinand I and his son Maximilian II, tens of thousands of miners had flocked into the Kitzbühel and similar regions in the hope of making their fortunes, along with those of their employers.

Hans Rosenberger was seven years younger than Nostradamus and, due to his upbringing in Augsburg, Southern Germany, ostensibly well fitted to cope with the daunting entrepreneurial risks that sixteenth-century mining involved. At that time Augsburg was one of Europe's premier financial capitals. Local families such as the Fuggers had become billionaires by acting as lending-banks and mints to Europe's crowned heads in return for commercially advantageous mining leases, customs exemptions and other concessions. And for Alpine mining operations the 1550s had been a high-point: in 1557, for instance, the mines around Salzburg alone yielded 850 kilograms of pure gold and 2,723 kilograms of pure silver.[2]

But in the late 1550s an altogether sharper economic wind blew. It became evident that nearly every monarch in Europe, and most particularly those of France, England and Spain, had been spending well beyond their means, maintaining expensive armies in the furtherance, or defence of their political ambitions. One of the benefits of the 1559 Treaty of Cateau-Cambrésis, following which thousands of army reservists had been laid off, was a marked stemming of this financial haemorrhage. Nonetheless some serious general restraint was needed, forcing the great banking houses to curb their more run-of-the-mill lending. Unfortunately for Rosenberger, who had pumped a great deal of money into his mines in and around Fieberbrunn, where he also maintained a fine mansion called Rosenegg, he found himself financially over-stretched at precisely this belt-tightening time.[3]

Rosenberger had long had a fascination with astrology, almost certainly inherited from similarly inclined parents. A manuscript in the Paris Bibliothèque Nationale's collection[4] has a list of fifty-two prominent individuals for whom birth-chart horoscopes were created during the early sixteenth century. Along with King Christian of Denmark, Pope Paul III, and the Holy Roman Emperors Maximilian and Ferdinand I we find the name Hans Rosenberger.[5] Locally, Rosenberger's astrological consultant was the highly-rated Bohemian Cyprian Leowitz – whom we saw earlier casting gloom and doom for the year 1583 – whose illustrious clientele included the bankers Georg and Ulrich Fugger. But once the Fieberbrunn mining productivity began faltering and the very real prospect of bankruptcy stared him in the face, Rosenberger asked his Bourges contact Lorenz Tubbe urgently to put him in touch with Nostradamus. Tubbe had a German merchant associate in Lyons who was able to pass the message on to Nostradamus' printer Brotot, via whose courier service to Salon the mining magnate's plight was eventually conveyed to Nostradamus himself.

Initially, probably on Rosenberger's express instructions, Tubbe was tantalisingly vague about the individual on whose behalf he was making the approach. Omitting any mention of the name, he simply described him as an 'owner of metal mines', and provided just the bare minimum information of birth date, time and latitude that were universally recognised as necessary for the creation of any horoscope. Nostradamus was assured that Tubbe would personally guarantee suitable financial reward, and that if all went well other advantageous German clients might follow. He then asked Nostradamus to predict what future this particular client might expect from his mines, what honours he might receive, and what might be his future 'health, fortunes and misfortunes'.[6]

Exhibiting a distinctively saturnine side to his personality, of which we have seen hints before, Nostradamus' initial reactions were dilatory and offhand almost to the point of rudeness. First he ignored Tubbe's repeated reminders to produce the horoscope. Then when Tubbe at last received a first version of it, March 1560 (therefore definitely before secretary Chavigny had been hired), it was to discover that the handwriting was execrable. And rather than use the scholarly *lingua franca* of Latin, Nostradamus had written in French, which Tubbe had told him he needed the help of friends to translate, and which, as he also pointed out, Rosenberger could neither speak nor write.

At the beginning of December 1560, that is, when François II lay dying, Tubbe received two more letters from Nostradamus. Though these have not survived, their contents certainly pleased him rather more than anything he had received hitherto. In particular he noted that while they were still in French, they were now much more legible, which would enable him to expedite their translation first into Latin, then German, for Rosenberger's benefit. With other clients such as Jerome Schorer having earlier complained about Nostradamus' handwriting, this improvement could well be attributable to secretary Chavigny being at least tried out some time around now.

Thus encouraged, Lorenz Tubbe became far more forthcoming about the German mining entrepreneur for whom he was acting as intermediary. In an immediate response he told Nostradamus:

> His name is Hans Rosenberger, his mother is Klara, daughter of Ulmen Ehinger. His city is Augsburg but he has mines in the Tyrol and also new ones in Styria, which produce gold, and from which he hopes for great things. Among other mines in the Tyrol he has an important one called St George, for which he has particularly high expectations. Of this he has written to me seeking your guidance and advice. He has this question of the St George mine. In which direction should he tunnel, and to what depth?[7]

From a twenty-first-century perspective the mining magnate was clearly expecting from Nostradamus, at a distance of hundreds of miles, nothing less than the service that today's mining companies expect from their on-site geologists. However, geology's foundation

Sixteenth century use of a divining-rod to locate veins of metal.
Engraving from Georgius Agricola's *De Re Metallica*.

as a formal science lay centuries into the future. Georgius Agricola, in his otherwise extremely practical *Of Things Metallic*, showed water-divining rods in the woodcuts of sixteenth-century prospectors, so why not metal prospecting via the stars?

Certainly, though Nostradamus' horoscope for Rosenberger has not survived, the German magnate was sufficiently impressed by Tubbe's translation of it that on March 11 of 1561, he penned Nostradamus an enthusiastic direct acknowledgement. Opening with much the same sort of flattery that we have noted Nostradamus' other clients also using, he told the seer that his fame had become widespread amongst the German-speaking world,[8] and that his obvious astrological expertise richly justified this. He continued that his Jewish ancestry (of which Rosenberger had apparently become aware) was being discussed as responsible for his remarkable gifts:

I have consulted many mathematicians [in Nostradamus' time, an alternative term for an astrologer] not only in Germany but also in

Italy ... but I do not know any one but you in whom are combined such painstaking qualities for dealing with occult and mathematical science. I wonder if it derives from your ancestors?[9]

Rosenberger confirmed that some of the troubles that Nostradamus had apparently astrologically perceived as having already befallen him were, sadly, only too true. He accepted that this was due to the stars currently not being in his favour. In forecasting his and his mines' prospects for the next twelve years, i.e. to 1573, Nostradamus had also evidently warned him that his current woes could well get worse before they got better. To this he responded stoically:

I will not lose hope of my fortunes improving. Nor will I abandon my enterprises, even if these continue to lose money. I will try to follow your wise advice, that is, to patiently let time and a few more adversities take their course [ever hopeful that] 'Good things will arrive suddenly at an hour when they are not expected'.[10]

This last line, a quotation from Horace,[11] Nostradamus had presumably offered Rosenberger by way of encouragement in the face of his difficulties.

Mindful that, even when clients are in adversity, astrologers still expect to be paid, Rosenberger had thoughtfully included with his letter a medallion bearing his portrait on one side and a representation of one of his mines on the other. This, he explained, was merely a preliminary token of appreciation. He promised that there would follow 'by the next courier' a more significant remuneration, a handsome silver-gilt goblet specially created by a German craftsman, which was decorated with his family coat-of-arms. In the interim he wanted some further work from Nostradamus, notably horoscopes for his two sons, twenty-seven-year-old Karl and seventeen-year-old Hans, whose birthdate details he provided.

As good as his word, Rosenberger duly followed up with a further letter written on April 8, 1561,[12] including with it the promised silver-gilt goblet, explaining that this had been carefully wrapped in oil-cloth and packed in a vase in order to protect it during its long journey from Fieberbrunn to Salon. In the same easy conversational manner of his earlier letter he mentioned his continuing study of Nostradamus' forecasts for him and for his mines to 1573, and he just wondered whether the seer might be prepared to be a little less ambiguous in some of his remarks? Even if secretary Chavigny's arrival had improved Nostradamus' handwriting, he was clearly powerless to improve his clarity.

Rosenberger in his second letter also elaborated more on why he was so anxious to receive the horoscope for his elder son Karl. While returning from a trip to Italy around 1558 Karl had contracted plague, apparently from the very same Savoyard outbreak that the following year had prevented Duke Emanuel-Filibert from returning to his territories. Though Karl had come very close to death, in the event he had survived. Then only last March, that is, March 1560, he had suffered a bad fall from his horse while making a routine visit to one of his father's mines. This had been followed in May, during a similar mine visit, by an ambush by certain individuals with whom he had earlier been in dispute. They had knocked him to the ground, thrashed him mercilessly with sticks, and left him for dead. Again he had survived, albeit extremely badly bruised both in body and spirit, only two weeks later to be attacked by yet another enemy. This latter assailant, armed with a sword, had inflicted several further injuries, including completely severing Karl's right thumb. With admirable philosophical poise Rosenberger expressed to Nostradamus his gratitude to the stars that for all the seriousness of these adversities that had befallen his son, they had always stopped just short of fatality.

In the case of modern-day postal services the expectation is that letters dispatched a month apart will mostly arrive about a month apart. Sixteenth-century communications, however, were very much more precarious. The early part of the route between Fieberbrunn and Salon involved some long, complicated traverses of Alpine passes, and Rosenberger's financial standing vis-à-vis courier services would have seriously deteriorated, along with the rest of his fortunes. From a surviving letter from Tubbe to Nostradamus dated June 7 we learn that it was only the previous day that Rosenberger's March 11 and April 8 messages both arrived together at Tubbe's Bourges address, still to be forwarded on to Lyons, then to Salon. The silver-gilt goblet accompanying the second letter had apparently reached Lyons independently, but it was accompanied by strict instructions that its onward dispatch was to be at Tubbe's express direction.

Before forwarding Rosenberger's letters south Tubbe had of course to translate them from German into Latin for Nostradamus' benefit. In what was a long covering letter of his own, he also advised him that Rosenberger's troubles were worsening. Rosenberger's younger brother Marquard,[13] though not involved in mining, was apparently beset with much the same financial problems as Hans. In the event, therefore, it was not until the end of June that Nostradamus – who had only recently returned to Salon from his family's temporary refuge in Avignon – at last received both the accumulated Rosenberger correspondence and the silver-gilt goblet.

Two weeks later, on July 15, Nostradamus responded to Tubbe. He acknowledged safe receipt of the goblet and medallion, commenting of the portrait on the latter that the physiognomy perfectly matched 'the person for whom I made my astronomical calculations'.[14] He observed that, just as he had expected, Rosenberger's features were typical of an individual with a preponderance of black bile, or the 'melancholia' humour. Expressing his sympathies over the misfortunes suffered by Karl, he sagely remarked that these were only to be expected atrologically, due to 'the malefic aspect of Jupiter with the Tail of the Dragon in the twelfth house.'[15] As for Rosenberger's mild criticisms of the ambiguities to his forecasts, Nostradamus acknowledged that in some of the eventualities that Rosenberger could expect, he had been 'rather pessimistic'. But he vigorously denied any obscurity:

Our master [Rosenberger] has nothing to fear concerning any ambiguities, riddles and equivocations. All my [predictions of] the future are clear as daylight. Nothing will be enigmatic. I will obscure nothing by allegory.[16]

To this end, after describing the outbreak of violence in Salon that had caused him and his family recently to take refuge in Avignon, Nostradamus gave Tubbe a commendably clear and unambiguous pledge. He was to pass on to Rosenberger that in due time, and so long as he persevered, he would genuinely see a marked improvement in his present adversities:

I beseech you that if you visit our master you must greet him and wish him well from me, telling him that success and good fortune really are shortly in store for him. Within one year, as from today, he will be surprised by an eventuality that will be as happy for him as it is unexpected. I solemnly vow him this, from all that the stars show me. This is why I urge you to persuade him, whatsoever may happen in the interim, that he should on no account give up his enterprises. Time and again I have repeated: 'Do not give up your enterprises'. What he has dreamed of will come to pass, and with the greatest joy and satisfaction, thanks to an unexpected eventuality. All that my innermost being tells me of will take place, to the death and confusion of his enemies.[17]

On September 9 Nostradamus reiterated much these same sentiments in a letter addressed directly to Rosenberger. We can now be virtually certain that this letter reveals secretary Chavigny's involvement, for Nostradamus noted in passing, 'So that my work may be more legible I

The drilling mineshafts and tunnels, as practised
in the Austrian Alps in Nostradamus' time. Engraving
from Georgius Agricola's *De Re Metallica*.

have given it to a young Frenchman to copy out, who offered himself to us recently.'[18] Clearly bent on offering his client every encouragement he could, Nostradamus assured Rosenberger that there were significant astrological indications for his mines that discoveries of silver were imminent, including the finding of one particularly rich vein. He also predicted that, associated with one such find, the miners would have a frightening, ghostly experience. Once again he urged Rosenberger, whatever the adversities that he might suffer in the interim, to hold tight and 'Don't give up your enterprises'.

Nostradamus was beginning to invest in this one rich but financially precarious client rather more time and effort than business and common sense might have deemed prudent. He surprisingly followed up his September 9 missive, well before he could expect any reply, with a further long letter dated October 15. Again this was addressed directly to Rosenberger, and this time he boldly predicted that the earlier prophesied silver find might well occur in the very month in which he was writing. He also said that he had been doing some further work on all the horoscopes and that these showed a real turning of the corner in his run of misfortunes, with the fifth zodiacal house, that of children, looking particularly good for Rosenberger's sons and their descendants.

With such explicit and forceful astrological promises Nostradamus could hardly have put his reputation more on the line. This was particularly so given that both Hans and Marquard Rosenberger, as had not been made entirely clear to him, had been effectively bankrupt since March 1560. In order to escape being thrown into jail by their creditors they had had on one occasion to seek sanctuary in the monastery of Saint Ulrich at Augsburg. Hans had then fled to his Austrian eyrie of Rosenegg near Fieberbrunn. There must therefore be a very strong suspicion that the attacks on Karl Rosenberger had come from angry people to whom Hans owed money. Indeed it would seem to have been due only to the direct intervention and protection of the Emperor Ferdinand I, one of the few individuals who was his debtor rather than his creditor, that Hans Rosenberger still clung to liberty.

Just as Nostradamus had warned, things did actually get worse before getting better. As Rosenberger informed Nostradamus in a letter of December 15, 1561, a rogue employee had robbed him of several thousand crowns. And only recently a fire had broken out near one of his mines, in which all the buildings servicing this mine were gutted.

Yet ever since Nostradamus' last letter, the one dated October 15, which Rosenberger acknowledged he had received, the prophesied turnabout in his fortunes had begun to occur. As Rosenberger told Nostradamus in his December 15 letter:

You should know, most excellent lord Nostradamus, that since you last wrote to me there has been discovered in my mine a seam of mixed silver and copper, which seems mediocre so far, but from which I hope for further, more long-lasting seams. In the same mountain in which my buildings were destroyed by fire I have found a seam of silver which although meagre, nevertheless I have great hopes of and am pursuing with great diligence and effort, much as you urged of me.[19]

Rosenberger further indicated that even Nostradamus' prophecy of a ghostly apparition had been most strikingly fulfilled:

On another mountain I have another mine in which a ghost appeared to the miners during eight days and one single night. When the miners had come out of the mine, grease which was used on the walls in place of candles combined with the stones and set off a great explosion in the mine. From this and from similar experiences the miners have great hopes that they will find bigger seams. And without doubt your prophecy has been fulfilled, since the ghost which appeared in the mineshaft caused terror amongst the miners, then vanished.[20]

Just over two months later, on February 24, 1562, when the Austrian hills would still have had their winter covering of snow, Rosenberger was able to send Nostradamus yet a further positive report, his tone now firmly upbeat:

You have been so helpful to us that I can allow myself to impart to you some of our news. We are doing well. With regard to the mines, some of them are already giving me satisfaction, others are looking promising. We started again digging one of them, Saint Sigismund, which has narrow seams of silver, which my miners neglected, so that nearly five months elapsed in which the whole mine was abandoned. Now it has been started up again and is being diligently explored. It is growing bigger and bigger, and is being driven deep into the mountain. This is the meagre seam which you mentioned in your letters. And new work is under way on another one, Saint Rudolph, which has been abandoned for the last six years. This seam falls eastwards in the mountain to a great depth, and for this I have great hopes. In the case of the mine called Saint Vitus, however, in which the ghost was heard that I mentioned in my last letter, no metal ore has been discovered. We hope that this will be brief, for the spirit of the earth is often heard, and the miners

Part of the process of refining silver, as this would have been
practised by some of Hans Rosenberger's mining technicians.
Engraving from Georgius Agricola's *De Re Metallica*.

regard this as a sign that ore cannot be far away. As for the seam of
lead, of which I wrote to you, this is getting bigger and bigger.[21]

It was the American sceptic James Randi, to his credit, and to most
Nostradamian authors' shame, who first introduced extracts from the
Rosenberger correspondence into the English language. However,
Randi used only Dupèbe's very bald French summaries of the letters'
content, and he thereby missed much of the salient detail which Dupèbe
had not translated from the Latin, as given in some of the extracts
quoted above. And from this hitherto omitted material – which would
certainly not have suited Randi's argument – what is now clear is just
how uncannily accurate, albeit not without a few relatively minor discrepancies, Nostradamus' predictions actually were, and just what a sat-
isfied customer Hans Rosenberger was by the beginning of 1562.

Also further omitted by Randi, and so far not explored by any
English-language pro-Nostradamian writer, was any investigation of
exactly what subsequently happened to the Rosenberger business –
that is, whether it ultimately foundered after all, despite the promising
strikes in late 1561 and early 1562; or whether, against all the earlier
appearances of imminent failure, it actually successfully made the
turnabout that Nostradamus had so stoutly predicted for it.
Frustratingly, Rosenberger's letter of February 24 was the very last
item in his correspondence with Nostradamus that has come down to

us. As for the always informative Lorenz Tubbe, who by now was mainly concerned with getting Nostradamus to work on his own horoscope, he blandly told him on April 13, 1562: 'I hope soon to be seeing our Rosenberger, whose mines, I hear, are gradually beginning to flourish'.[22] Thereafter, all lapsed into silence from him as well.

Luckily, however, it so happens that the subsequent history of the Rosenbergers of Fieberbrunn has been recorded. And from local later records, as is known quite independently of any Nostradamian spin on them, what is certain is that members of the Rosenberger family continued to flourish at their Rosenegg eyrie late into the sixteenth century and beyond. In 1591 Hans Rosenberger's residence is referred to in local documents as the 'alto Rosenegg' or 'high Rosenegg', and is clearly still in the family's possession. In 1613 Hans Marquard Rosenberger, proudly bearing the names of the two trauma-racked brothers of the early 1560s, rebuilt Rosenegg on a grander scale and at around this same time founded a factory. He did so because he had developed a special process by which the iron ore from his inherited mines could be converted into what became called Pillersee steel. And this product brought great prosperity not only for the Rosenberger family but for all Fieberbrunn, achieving a worldwide reputation for its quality and suppleness.[23] Overall there can be no doubt that Hans Rosenberger's descendants actually achieved the enduring prosperity which Nostradamus had so emphatically predicted for them.

Unmistakably, therefore, in 1561 Nostradamus had made some unusually specific predictions, at an impressively long distance, and in the teeth of some seriously troubled circumstances. These had not only deeply impressed his German entrepreneur client at the time, but had proved to be true in the long term. But was this all just a lucky guess on Nostradamus' part? What do we know about what was happening to Nostradamus' predictions for France's equally troubled rulers, the Valois dynasty?

NOTES

1 Georgius Agricola, *De Re Metallica*, Basle, 1556. Agricola had in fact died in 1555, and is thought to have completed the manuscript in 1550

2 These exact figures derive from Hans Goldseisen, an official in the employ of Salzburg's Archbishop, whose precise records, written in five thick folio volumes, are deposited in the Salzburger Landesarchiv, Salzburg, Austria

3 For a history of the Rosenberger family in the years leading up to Nostradamus' encounter with them, see Ilse Lutzmann, *Die Augsburger Handelsgesellschaft Hans und Marquand Rosenberger* (1535–60), Kallmunz, 1937

4 Bibliothèque Nationale BN Rés. V. 1300

5 See Lynn Thorndike, *A History of Magic and Experimental Science*, New York, Columbia University Press, vol. VI, p.105

6 Letter X, sent January 1, 1560 reproduced in Dupèbe, *Nostradamus, Lettres Inédites...*, op. cit., pp.43–4

7 '*Ipsius nomen est Ioannes Rosenberger, matris eius Clara, filia Ehinger Ulmensis. Ipse civis est Augustanus, sed fodinas habet in Comitatu Tyrolensi et alias novas in Styria, quae aurum proferunt et in quibus spem magnam habet. Quas in Tyroli havet inter eas una est fodina praecipua, cui nomen est ad S. Georgium, de qua praecipué egregié speraverat; de ea nuper ad me scripsit, ut tibi indicarem et consilium peterem. Est autem haec quaestio: fodinam ad S. Georgium hactenus versus occasum et meridiem tentavit et scrutatus est venas ad magnam profunditatem deorsum.*' Letter XVIII, reproduced in Dupèbe, *Nostradamus, Lettre inédites...*, op. cit., p.64

8 '*...quae omnem prope iam orbem pervagata est*'

9 '*ego quidem Mathematicos non tam in Germania, quam Italia...quorum consuetudine...Sed...nesciam an aviti tui, a quibus olim hauseris diligentissimo calculo scientiam tuam, te magis hoc in genere studiorum illustrent, an tu illos.*' Letter XXI, reproduced in Dupèbe, *Nostradamus, Lettres Inédites...*, op. cit., p.69

10 '*Non tamen adeo, ut omnino spe deiiciar melioris fortunae, aut an incoepto desistam, ac si impensae periturae essent. Sed iuxta consilium tuum prudentissimum, cedo paululum tempori et, quod fideliter admones, patientia vincere conor, quod mihi ferendum sinistra fortuna obtrudit. GRATA SUPERVENIET QUAE NON SPERABITUR HORA.*' Letter XXI, op. cit.

11 Horace, *Epodes*, 1, 4, 14

12 Letter XXI, reproduced in Dupèbe, *Nostradamus, Lettres Inédites...*, op. cit., pp.69–71

13 Marquand Rosenberger is not actually named as such in the letter, but his identity is well known from other sources, cf. Lutzmann, *Die Augsburger Handelsgesellschaft...*, op. cit.

14 '*cuius physionomia multa profecto cognovi quae cum calculo Astronomico conveniret.*'

15 '*Hoc fecit Iupiter male affectus cum cauda in XII. Iuxta illud apotelesma.*'

16 '*Non est quod Dominus noster timeat de ambagibus, aenigmatibus vel amphibologiis: omnia futura sunt vel ipsa luce lucidiora. Nihil 'en ainigmois' erit, nihil 'allegoriais' obscurabo* – Letter XXVII, Dupèbe, *Nostradamus Lettres Inédites...*, op. cit., p.86. The words in quotation marks are ones that Nostradamus rendered in Greek

17 '*Fac, obsecro, ut si quando invisis hunc nostrum Dominum nomine nostro salvere iubeas et bene sperare, nuntiesque eius fortunam brevi felicem admodum et prosperam futuram, atque ita brevi, ut antequam sit annus ab hodierno die superveniet illi quaedam ingens et inopinata prosperitas, eaque felicissima. Quod illi spondere ausim, astris item sic indicantibus. Quare obsecro, persuade, ut quomodocunque sit ne desistat ab incoeptis, et iterum atque iterum inculcabo: NOLIT DESISTERE COEPTIS. Perveniet revera ad optatum finem non sine maxima laetitia et voluptate, idque casu non opinato; omnia inquam evenient ex animi sententia, cum morte et ruina adversantium.*' Letter XXVII, Dupèbe, *Nostradamus, Lettres Inédites...*, op. cit., p.87

18 '*cuidam iuveni Gallo qui sese nobis obtulit nuper.*' Letter XXX, Dupèbe, *Nostradamus, Lettres Inédites...*, op. cit., p.94

19 '*Scias igitur, excellentis. Domine Nostradame, me in meis fodinis ab eo*

tempore, quo meas proximas literas tibi scripsi, venam argenteam cupro mixtam invenisse quae adhuc mediocritur se ostendit, et spero hanc venam diuturnam futuram. In eodem monte, in quo mihi mea aedifica combusta sunt, in alia fodina venam etiam argenteam inveni, quae, quanquam exigua sit, tamen magnae spei est, ac diligentissime indefatigatoque labore persequetur, quemadmodum et tu mihi suades.' Letter XXXIV, Dupèbe, *Nostradamus, Lettres Inédites...*, op. cit., pp.111–12

20 *'In alio monte aliam etiam habeo fodinam, in qua spiritus terrestris apparuit fossoribus octo integris diebus singuli noctibus. Is, quando fossores ex fodinis venerunt, sevum quo utuntur loco candelarum muro ex lapillis sepit, et magnum strepitum in fodina excitavit. Haec et similia fossores magni faciunt sperantque se optimas venas ibi reperturos. Et sine dubio in eo impletur tua praedictio, quando ais appariturum aliquid in specubus quod fossores perterre faciat, sed iterum evanescet.'* Ibid., p.112

21 *'Facere autem non potui, cum ex omnibus tuis literis humanissime scriptis promptum tuum erga nos animum singularemque amorem perspexissem, quin has ad te darem literas, ex quibus nos omnes bona et prospera Deo iuvante valetudine uti intelligeres; quod idem de te saepius intelligendum nisi longinquitas loci interdieceret, mihi longe esset gratissimum. Quantum ad fodinas meas attinet, scias quasdam in felici statu, quasdam vero bonae spei esse. Ante quinquennium reperta est apud fodinam meam, quae vocatur Sanctus Sigismundus indicium metallicum, seu vena argentea angusta, quae a meis fossoribus neglecta, et ab eo tempore usque ad quinque menses proxime elapsos tota fodina deserta est, sed nunc rursus elaboratur, et venula illa diligentius quam antea investigatur, seque magis magisque dilatat, et directe in montem tendit. Spero igitur venam illam exiguam esse, cuius in literis tuis mentionem facis, cum ais venam in principio futuram exiguam, sed si diligenter et indefatigato labore perquiratur, perpetuam, et indesinentem scaturiginem orituram, et sane si ea esse valde dilataret, tunc mihi perpetua vena metallica cum maximo reditu speranda esset. Alia etiam fodina nunc elaboratur, quae ante sexennium fuit relicta, haec vocatur Sanctus Rudolphus: huius vena directe in montem versus orientem in profundum cadit, et haec quoque magnae spei est, sed apud fodinam quae vocatur Sancius Vitus, in qua spiritus terrestris auditus, cuius in meis proximis literis mentionem feci, nullum adhuc metallum repertum est: speramus tamen id brevi futurum; nam spiritus terrestris adhuc saepius exauditur, et hoc fossores re experta magni faciunt: nam sciunt mox inde metallum secuturum. Vena in fodina plumbea, de qua et proximis literis tibi scripsi, magis magisque se dilatat crescitque: quare firmiter spero, quemadmodum in proximis tuis literiis spem mihi iniecisti, quando Cancer futurus sit in ascendente, tunc meam fortunam in rebus metallicis sese amplificaturam.'* Letter XXXVII, Dupèbe, *Nostradamus, Lettres Inédites...*, op. cit., p.126

22 *'Spero me brevi visurum etiam Rosenbergium nostrum, cuius fodinas audio paulatim florescere.'* Letter XXXVIII, Dupèbe, *Nostradamus, Lettres Inédites...*, op. cit., p.129

23 This information has been derived from simple tourist information concerning Fieberbrunn's history that is readily available over the Internet

CHAPTER 13

Royal Visitors

About the time of the improvement to Rosenberger's fortunes, that is, towards the end of 1561, Nostradamus as we have seen suffered his arrest by the Count of Tende and his spell of 'imprisonment' at Marignane. This episode, just after his fifty-ninth and his youngest daughter Anne's second birthday, cannot have been prolonged. At least as early as January 20, 1562 he was back home in Salon sending the Toulouse 'Roman gold' hunters on their Spanish wild-goose chase, and a fortnight later advising the canons of Orange how to recover their sacred treasures.

Nor would he appear to have been discomfited by whatever degree of confinement he experienced at Marignane. He made no mention of it in his relatively prolific correspondence with Tubbe, Rosenberger and others preserved from around this time. On February 13 he had the confidence and the resources to invest a further hundred crowns in Adam de Craponne's canal enterprises. And as another indication of his continuing prosperity, some time during this same year of 1562 he arranged for an artist to create his portrait, for in the Bibliothèque Nationale there is preserved an engraving by Pierre Woieriot, the Latin inscription of which identifies it as being of 'M. Nostradamus in the fifty-ninth year of his age'.[1]

It is unlikely that this is the original portrait, which was probably a lost panel painting from which Woieriot made his engraving. But whatever the original, even the engraving is a considerable advance on the mere glimpses of Nostradamus' physical appearance that we have had from the 'at work in his study' woodcuts used for the title-pages of his publications. The Woieriot portrait also accords well with a sole surviving verbal description which the newly recruited secretary Chavigny years later included in his *Brief Discourse*:

He was a little shorter than moderate height, physically robust, lively and vigorous He had a wide, open forehead, a straight,

Nostradamus, age 59. From an engraving by Pierre Woieriot, dated 1562.
Bibliothèque Nationale, Paris, Ed.5.b.Rés., fol.36.

regular-shaped nose and grey eyes, their expression soft though blazing when angry. Facially he could appear both severe and smiling, of the kind that with the severity could be seen combined in him a great humanity. He was ruddy-cheeked, evident even towards old age, [and] with a long, thick beard.[2]

Another indication of the heights Nostradamus' career had reached is the fact that there had already grown up a surprisingly flourishing industry issuing fake almanacs under his name. Hans Rosenberger, in his letter of December 15, 1561, remarked that he had encountered some serious difficulties trying to obtain an authentic copy of Nostradamus' *Almanac* for 1562, as dedicated to Pope Pius IV:

> I have written to Lyons to try to obtain this. I now know of many miscreants who adulterate your almanacs (whose truthfulness is confirmed from daily experience), and who print their corrupted versions under your name. This has made it so difficult to find authentic copies that I have given up trying.[3]

The same counterfeiting would recur in the case of the 1563 Almanac that Nostradamus, following his normal practice, was working on during early 1562. One such fake, a crude French-language collage of earlier Nostradamian material, printed in Paris, is preserved in the public library at Lille.[4] Another, a translation from this French fake into English, and entitled *An Almanack for the yere MDLXIII*

Composed by M. Michael Nostradamus, is in the library of the University of Illinois.[5] As noted by the early twentieth-century English scholar Eustace Bosanquet, the England of Queen Elizabeth I actually had a remarkably prolific industry all of its own producing such Nostradamus forgeries:

> For some reason the books by Nostradamus appear to have been more pirated than any others, and several printers were fined by the Company of Stationers, the best-known case being that of the edition printed by William Powell in 1562/3. For printing this Powell himself was fined 2s. 6d. and no fewer than nineteen booksellers were fined also for selling it, some of them as much as 3s 4d., the fines being perhaps proportioned to the number of copies each had sold.[6]

Intriguingly, even Englishmen with no special interest in Nostradamus took quite a pride in their ability to distinguish the forgeries from the genuine article. Thus in November 1562 the Bilbao-based English envoy Henry Cobham wrote to his superior Sir Thomas Challoner, English ambassador in Spain, enclosing what he called 'a marvellous prognostication in Spanish' for the coming year, which he blithely described as the work of a friar who had 'put it forth in the name of Nostradamus'.[7]

While Nostradamus might have been expected to be upset by such flagrant pirating of his name and reputation, in actuality he appears to have been making too comfortable a living from the genuine article to be seriously bothered. Indeed, had he been party to the Cobham-Challoner correspondence, he would probably have been flattered that even England's highest diplomats were treating his name as a household word, bandying counterfeits of his prophecies between each other.

Nostradamus might also have been flattered to learn that people would be faking prophecies in his name five centuries into the future. But what certainly caused him great concern in the early 1560s, and with good reason, was the continuing intense religious strife between Catholics and Protestants, or, as the French version of the latter should now be labelled, the Huguenots. Towards the end of 1561 Lorenz Tubbe had gone to Antwerp, then in the Spanish Netherlands, part of King Philip II of Spain's vast and very Catholic empire. In a letter from there Tubbe reported:

> There is some relaxing by the Spanish Inquisition, which was in the habit of dealing very harshly with those whom it suspected [of Protestantism]. But now they have new methods. Those whom

they suspect they seize in their own homes and incarcerate. Without any noise or trial they tie them hand and foot and plunge them in barrels of water. In this way they avoid any public outcry, that would otherwise occur if such things were done openly. Only today I was told that during the last two weeks or thereabouts there perished three honest and pious women who overnight were taken from their homes in this way.[8]

In his response to Tubbe of May 13, 1562 Nostradamus expressed what seems to have been totally genuine outrage at such Catholic atrocities:

What you have written me from Antwerp…fills me with bile, that such cruel, inhuman and unheard-of barbarities should be perpetrated against Christians, overnight, and without any trial.[9]

After offering, characteristically, a profound quotation from a classical author – one equally typically acquired second-hand, in this instance from Erasmus' *Adatia* – Nostradamus lamented with Tubbe

Catholics persecuting Protestants in the Netherlands.
From a contemporary engraving.

about the terrible times that they were living through. For to top Tubbe's story he had his own vivid tale of some of the sectarian violence that had been happening on his own doorstep in Provence during the past year. Summarising from what he called a kind of diary that he had been keeping of the recent events, he reported:

> Last February [of 1561] the Estates-General [France's highest legislative assembly] were held here in our own Salon in Provence, convened by the royal governor and other great nobles...Amongst the many matters they discussed, that of religion predominated. The popular 'Mob Monster' did everything to prevent evangelical preaching. Nevertheless each town had its ministers of God's Word. At Aix (which is the capital of Provence and the seat of its Parlement...) the Cathedral there is especially full of ignorant priests. Fearing for their benefices, they paid gold for the services of a nobleman fallen on hard times, called Flassans. The worst kinds of violence were exerted against those of the Christian religious sect. The clergy extended the strongest support towards this man who was upholding their interests. The populace created him Consul, along with two others of the same ilk. Swords were taken up [?] and each night more and more violence was aroused against the Christians and those in authority. At length the Christians...decided to defend themselves by sending one of their own to the King and to the Queen-Mother...the Count of Crussol, accompanied by two councillors, was charged with setting up an enquiry into the troubles and given authority to restore order in Provence.[10]

By the 'Christians' Nostradamus unquestionably meant the Protestant Huguenots, apparently holding them in significantly higher regard than their 'Mob Monster' persecutors the Catholics. As for the Count of Crussol, sent from Paris to restore order, this was Antoine de Crussol who with some fellow-councillors had set out on December 10, 1561 and during the time that Nostradamus was under arrest and imprisonment by the Count of Tende had ridden rapidly southwards along much the same route Nostradamus had taken in 1555. After a brief stop at Lyons, Crussol's delegation reached Provence on January 10. At the Palace of the Popes at Avignon they were received in some style by Fabrizio Serbelloni, Pope Pius IV's cousin, who only the previous November had been sent here to help reinforce the Catholics' suppression of the Huguenots. After another brief stop, at Tarascon, Crussol's party arrived at Salon where, as Nostradamus related, 'Crussol spent around a month staying with the governor the Count of Tender'. As Nostradamus continued the story:

During this time two emissaries were sent to Aix to ask if the town would receive them, with a view to a meeting being held, but they were refused. So an army was raised against the rebels. Meanwhile Flassans fortified Aix. At the news that the Counts had raised an army, the Parlement decided to open the town's gates. Flassans then left with an armed band which ravaged the eastern part of Provence. A Franciscan whipped up the mob's fury. They took Tourves, up to that time held by those of the Christian faith... On being accepted at Aix the Counts decided to pursue Flassans. They sent to him as emissary D. de l'Estrange, a Parisian nobleman who eloquently urged him to give up his struggle and to put down his arms, but in vain. Faced with an army 4,770 strong Flassans withdrew and shut himself inside the town of Barjols. After a four-day siege, this was taken, though Flassans, with a number of others, managed to escape via a tunnel.[11]

As Nostradamus, who claimed that he had predicted this victory for the Counts,[12] continued:

During this time at Arles, Ventabren,[13] a man of courage but sworn enemy of the evangelical doctrine, raised a troop of horsemen from monks and priests to come to Flassans' aid. As this approached Salon they heard the news of Flassans' defeat, and beat a retreat. At Aix the Counts installed a garrison of 500 soldiers, under the command of Antoine called Tripoli, of Salon, to protect the town.[14]

As Nostradamus' son César would later note in his *History and Chronicle of Provence*, this 'Antoine called Tripoli' was none other than Antoine Marc, who with his brother Palamède as we have seen was a close friend and neighbour of Nostradamus and his wife. César positively confirmed Antoine Marc as a Huguenot sympathiser, and it seemed that the Huguenot moderates amongst the Provençal nobility were happy to co-operate with similarly moderate Catholics in the hope that the eventual outcome could be peace and toleration for all.

In this regard the sceptic James Randi, presenting a similar synoptic version of Nostradamus' account of these turbulent events, has laid great stress on his use of the sympathetic word 'Christians' when referring to Huguenots. For Randi, this showed that Nostradamus exhibited 'a blatant duplicity',[15] sometimes expressing sympathy towards Huguenot Protestantism, in other instances representing himself as pro-Catholic. For anyone who can see issues only in black and white, duplicity might indeed seem the only logical interpretation. However, such a stance overlooks the truth that, whenever a country is torn by deep religious or political hatreds, there is almost always a large, moderate middle ground which, whether leaning towards one or other side, deeply deplores atrocities committed by extremists on both sides. As the contemporary Huguenot François de la Noue ably expressed it: 'I found myself siding with those of the Religion, and yet I must admit that on the other side I had a dozen friends who were as dear to me as my own brothers.'[16] Arguably Nostradamus' position was something along these lines. And had Randi properly explored the historical background he would have seen that these were times in which not only Nostradamus, but everyone in France, from King Charles IX and the Queen Mother downwards, found their loyalties similarly and repeatedly compromised.

Thus, in the immediate aftermath of the Guise eclipse following King François II's death, the Queen Regent, without the slightest wavering of her Catholic orthodoxy, had sensibly introduced the Edict of January granting a wide measure of toleration towards the Huguenots. As a most deliberate and callous snub to this moderate-mindedness, in February 1562 the ultra-Catholic François, Duke of Guise, at the head of his own private army, ruthlessly slaughtered a Huguenot congregation in the village of Vassy. He and his troops then entered Paris in triumph, to rousing applause from the city's predominantly pro-Catholic populace. This immediately prompted the flight of moderate Huguenot members of Catherine's royal council, whereupon an ultra-Catholic, Guise-led Triumvirate forcefully installed itself in their place. The Queen Regent, Catherine de Medici, and her not yet twelve-year-old son King Charles IX were reduced to the status of mere puppets.

This effective *coup* led in turn to the Huguenot leaders, the Prince of Condé and Admiral Coligny, taking up arms, seizing Orléans, and calling upon all patriotic Frenchmen to resist the Guise tyranny. Predictably, the Guise faction moved menacingly against them, compelling Condé and Coligny to turn to the nearest overseas source of help, the Protestant England of Queen Elizabeth I. With classic Renaissance subtlety Elizabeth made sympathetic noises towards envoys from the Guise-controlled monarchy, yet at the same time secretly negotiating a deal with the Huguenot faction by which they would be sent 6,000 English troops. Conditional on this was that they make available the port of Le Havre as an operating base, and the return of Calais to English control in the event of a successful outcome. Such an agreement, giving away a sovereign part of France, was so treasonable that it drove Catherine far further towards the Guise side than had hitherto been her inclination. Fearful that any prevarication might allow time for the English reinforcements to arrive, she formally approved the Triumvirate's attack on the Huguenot-held city of Rouen. On October 15, 1562 the city duly fell, and amongst the seriously wounded was Antoine de Navarre, the pro-Huguenot Prince of the Blood to whom Nostradamus had dedicated his 1557 'Prognostication'. Shot in the shoulder, Antoine died a little over a month later when the wound became irreversibly infected. A further Guise v. Huguenot skirmish at Dreux on December 19 was only very narrowly won by the Guise side, but it brought about the capture of the Prince of Condé, another severe blow to the Huguenot cause.

Though Nostradamus, like many of his fellow-Frenchmen, would have grieved over the unnecessary deaths of fine individuals on both sides, there was one particular fatality which might have troubled his conscience, in view of his likely responsibility for it. According to a *History of France* written later in the sixteenth century by the nobleman Henri Lancelot-Voisin,[17] some time in the early part of 1562 a promising young Catholic army officer, Captain Pins, visited Nostradamus at Salon, anxious to find out what the future held for him.

With his characteristically authoritative air Nostradamus assured the young officer that the stars promised him a future with great honours and responsibilities. However, he advised him that it was important first to demonstrate his worthiness by exhibiting valour on the field of battle. Fired by such explicit astrological assurance, Pins appears to have interpreted this to mean that he could take risks with some confidence. Accordingly on June 6, 1562 he daringly led an assault up the walls of the Huguenot-held town of Limoux unprotected by any armour, and armed only with a sword and dagger. He presented an all too easy target for the musket shot which went straight through his body, and died very shortly after, having acted with a rashness that was, arguably, directly due to Nostradamus.

Though there is no record that he ever learned of the tragic effect of this particular piece of astrological advice, Nostradamus himself was scarcely immune from the bloody turmoil that was now gripping the entire nation. In his letter to Tubbe dated May 13, 1562 he described himself as staying gamely on with his family in Salon at the mercy of 'mob rule',[18] all the town's known Huguenot sympathisers having fled. Everywhere it was a matter of luck which particular religious faction held sway. Only three weeks beforehand Nostradamus' aristocratic neighbour Antoine Marc had been obliged to abandon Aix because the local Catholics no longer wanted his garrison there. Only two weeks before an already strongly pro-Huguenot Lyons had fallen to the Huguenot side.[19] At Orange, where the canons had had their valuables stolen in December, the militant Huguenots were continuing to make it impossible to hold a Catholic mass. And with Catherine de Medici and Charles IX still under the control of the Guises, orders were sent from Paris for the Count of Tende to be replaced in his duties by his markedly more pro-Catholic son Honorat.

With regard to the prophetic part of his 1563 Almanac, Nostradamus was clearly at work during this turbulent time, punctiliously noting that he had completed it on May 7, 1562. On July 20 he put the finishing touches to its dedicatory epistle. As in the case of his previous Almanacs, it was typical of him to choose someone of topical significance to whom he could dedicate the work. The previous year, it may be recalled, he had thus 'honoured' Pope Pius IV, seemingly in order to demonstrate his Catholic orthodoxy. And, as at the middle of 1562, he seems to have been anxious to continue this policy. Hence he dedicated the 1563 Almanac to Pope Pius IV's cousin Fabrizzio Serbelloni, the man who only the previous November had been sent to Avignon to help reinforce the Catholic cause and suppress the Huguenots.

A copy of this 1563 Almanac has survived at Aix-en-Provence,[20] from which it can be seen that Nostradamus framed his dedicatory epistle in Italian, obviously for Serbelloni's benefit:

> To the most illustrious lord, the Lord Francisco Fabrizzio de Serbelloni, [legate] to his Holiness with regard to the general war in France.[21]

Surprisingly, given his sympathetic remarks about 'Christians' to Tubbe only the same month, Nostradamus also sang a litany of praise for the way that Serbelloni had saved not only Avignon, but Provence, the Dauphiné and Languedoc from their enemies, and notably from the 'seditious madmen and tyrants of the new sect'.[22]

Here the keywords are 'madmen and tyrants', for they indicate, just as we suspected, that Nostradamus had as much antipathy towards the extremists of the Protestant variety as he had towards their 'Mob Monster' Catholic counterparts. And he was also careful to include, amongst his adulatory platitudes to Serbelloni, a particularly strident defence of his business of astrology:

> The wise man can, by contemplating nature and the state of secondary causes, foresee a good number of things which otherwise remain hidden and unknown to those who set no store by the excellent art of Astrology.[23]

Whatever else we may make of Nostradamus, it is hard to deny that even in these unpredictable times he lived up to the self-styled reputation as a wise man that he worked so hard to cultivate. By backing the Catholic Serbelloni at a time when victory might easily have gone to the other side he yet again exhibited some uncanny foresight. Despite fierce Huguenot opposition Serbelloni successfully fulfilled his mandate to re-establish Catholic control. Likewise, at Aix, the Catholic-funded mercenary Flassans succeeded in taking charge, resuming the consulship of the town on Antoine Marc's departure. And throughout Provence, in a bitterly fought struggle, the Count of Tende's son Honorat – to whom Nostradamus would also dedicate a later Almanac – forcefully and systematically went about extinguishing all pockets of Huguenot resistance.

In the north the Huguenot cause fared similarly badly, the 5,000 English troops whom Elizabeth's government had sent to Le Havre finding themselves isolated and without the large wave of local Huguenot support that they had been counting on. Things grew worse when they were stricken by a plague described as more terrible than 'all the cannon of France', which began killing them at the rate of 200 a week. By the end July 1562 their plight was so bad that they were obliged to begin to seek terms for a peaceful, honourable yet ultimately humiliating abandonment of the whole enterprise.

At the beginning of 1563, with their cause all but dead, the Huguenots committed a Parthian act of revenge. In the middle of February, when the Duke of Guise was riding home at dusk for dinner with his wife, a Huguenot assassin suddenly stepped out of the gloom and fired his pistol point-blank into the Duke's chest. Exactly as in the case of Navarre before him, Guise's wound proved mortal. Catherine de Medici found herself mourning an individual who deserved the highest admiration as one of her late husband's finest military commanders, yet who from her point of view had been a serious thorn in her side.

In the event Guise's death proved a strangely healing event, with the country at large enjoying great elation at England's humiliation over Le Havre, and with both the Huguenot and the Catholic extremists reduced to licking some deep and painful wounds. The breathing space thus created enabled the thirteen-year-old Charles IX and his mother to settle themselves a little more securely and comfortably on the French throne. As a temporary setback, in September Catherine suffered a severe fall from her horse This brought on pains in her head so intense that she was unable to move, most probably due to a blood clot on the brain. It is therefore a remarkable testimony to French surgery's rapidly improving skills that, when her surgeons drilled a small opening in her skull, she experienced immediate relief and went on to make a rapid and complete recovery.

Indeed, so positive was the turnabout in Catherine's health that within weeks of her surgery, and as a complete change from the normal royal routine of moving from one château to another around the environs of Paris, she conceived a plan for taking Charles on a full-scale tour of his entire kingdom. It was a risk, for though Charles was tall, he was still painfully thin and his health was not robust. But he positively enjoyed riding, and a winter in the warm south would be much better for him than the cold, dank mists so often enshrouding the Loire châteaux. Catherine also reasoned that it would be good for Charles to see and appreciate at first hand the great diversity of the realm he had inherited, while for the country as a whole a royal tour could only be a timely public relations exercise after all the sectarian troubles that it had recently been through.

Such a tour was no small undertaking. By a tradition well established under King François I, when any French King or Queen went on a ride around their dominions, every conceivable item or service that they might need had to accompany them, in a style that makes a modern-day American presidential entourage seem positively miserly. The royal pair had to be accompanied by their Gentlemen of the Household, by the Queen Regent's famous personal retinue of eighty maids of honour (dubbed her *Escadron Volant* or 'Flying Squad'), and by the foreign ambassadors and their envoys, together with any number of ancillary servants and messengers. To ensure that their royal personages were always seen at their best they had to have with them the royal Wardrobe with its retinue of tailors, barbers, spur-makers and expert craft-workers in gold, silver, leather, and so on. To satisfy every culinary whim the entourage had to include an army of cooks, fruiterers, salad chefs and bakery chefs, together with all their necessary cooking utensils, table linen, and silverware, all of which of course needed transport. To avoid the slightest possibility of attack, the party had to be guarded by suitably large numbers of troops, Catherine and Charles' travelling retinue including a colourfully dressed Swiss Guard contingent, a Scots Guard contingent and teams of archers. Because Charles IX enjoyed hawking and hunting, falconers with their birds and hunters with their hounds always had to be at the ready. The horses alone for this 'travelling city' have been numbered at 8,000, with the aristocrats' mounts all needing grooms and attendants. And everywhere that the royal tour went emissaries had to be sent ahead to warn the cities and towns *en route* to prepare their welcoming pageantry and to make all necessary accommodation arrangements.

Brain surgery as practised in the 16th century, from a contemporary engraving. The use of this on Catherine de Medici, after a fall from her horse, effected a remarkable cure.

Catherine's plan appears to have been to start by travelling outwards from Paris, mostly due south in the direction of Marseilles. Salon was near the end of this first leg of the journey. The first major stop-over was at Troyes, where, in the wake of England's humiliation over Le Havre, English ambassadors accompanying the tour thrashed out the final terms of the new peace treaty with France. Moving steadily onwards through Châlons-sur-Marne, Bar-le-Duc, Langres and Dijon, the travelling court then boarded boats for Mâcon. There Catherine met the fiercely Huguenot Jeanne d'Albret, widow of Antoine of Navarre, who frostily insisted on being accompanied by eight Calvinist ministers and a protective guard of several hundred cavalry. Absolutely no love was lost between these two forceful women, not least because Jeanne's fatherless young son Henri, prince of Navarre, who was accompanying the royal tour, was obliged to receive his upbringing at the court in and around Paris, rather than with his mother in her domains, specifically in order to prevent his being infected with Huguenot doctrines.

After Mâcon the royal road-show made its way steadily further south to cosmopolitan Lyons where, despite the strongly Huguenot population, they were given a suitably rousing and colourful welcome, the staff of Nostradamus' various Lyons printing establishments doubtless amongst the cheering crowds lining the streets.

Here there was bad news, however: plague was in the vicinity. And before the royal party had time to move on, it struck with its all too characteristic swiftness and severity. The newly appointed English ambassador to the court, Sir Thomas Smith – a man with a great personal interest in astrology – reported back to London on July 12 that Lyons had become 'the most miserable and inhuman town he ever saw'. When his servants went out to buy provisions they reportedly encountered:

> ...sometimes ten and twelve corpses lying in the streets dead of plague, some naked, and there they lie till night or till the deputies

for those matters, clothed in yellow, come. They almost have no place to bury them. A great number they cast into the river because they will not be at the cost to make graves...[24]

In a further, late dispatch Smith darkly stated:

...the Rhône men dare eat no fish nor fishers lay their engines and nets, because instead of fish they take up the pestiferous carcasses which are thrown in.[25]

Such inattention to basic hygiene was serious, not least for Nostradamus and his fellow-citizens 145 miles (230 km) to the south in Salon, since whatever was thrown into the river Rhône at Lyons inevitably found its way downstream to their locality, a situation that Adam de Craponne's splendid new canal system had actually exacerbated, bringing divers sources of river-water much closer to Salon than ever before. It is therefore scarcely a surprise to learn that when on October 17 the royal party clattered towards Salon's Avignon gate the plague had preceded them. As César de Nostredame, at that time only ten years old, would later record in his *History and Chronicle of Provence*:

The plague had already declared itself in this poor place [i.e. Salon], where contagiously and with extraordinary swiftness four to five hundred people were snuffed out. The town was empty of people and their representatives... inns were places of sorrow, and the houses in a pitiful state to receive a royal party.[26]

Charles IX, anxious to be received fittingly as a king, immediately sent out criers to call upon all those who had abandoned their homes to return to them, along with their furnishings. And in the event an adequate welcome was mustered. In César's words:

For the King's entry some simple arcades had been erected from branches of box-wood. These stretched from the Avignon gate almost to the doors of the castle [i.e. the Château de l'Empéri], the magnificent pontifical lodging. The roads were paved with a covering of sand, scattered with beautifully flowering rosemary, which gave off a very pleasant perfume. The king was riding an African horse with a grey coat, with trappings of black velvet trimmed with gold fringes. He himself was dressed in a mantle of Phoenician purple, popularly described as violet, embellished with silver braid, his hat and its feathers matching his costume.[27]

Salon's civic dignitaries were assembled at the Avignon gate, where a dais draped in white and violet damask had been created for them. According to César de Nostredame his father was amongst this reception party, wearing his best velvet hat and supported by a silver walking stick. Nostradamus was duly presented to King Charles, whereupon:

> ... making very humble and proper obeisance, with frankness and philosophical liberty, [he] recited the Latin poetic verse 'Great man of war, second to none in piety'.[28]

Given the fourteen-year-old King's scrawny build, together with the peacock-like finery in which he had been dressed by his royal wardrobe department, Nostradamus' choice of verse was less than appropriate, particularly coming from one whose business was that of a seer. No one seems to have worried, though, and according to César, his father, hobbling somewhat from the gout with which he had begun to suffer, duly accompanied the royal party to their overnight quarters at the Château de l'Empéri.

As already noted from the Rosenberger correspondence, in October 1561, at the behest of some unidentified member of the court, Nostradamus had drawn up Charles' horoscope 'at the price of many night vigils'. Yet none of the surviving subsequent documentation has yet given us the slightest clue to what kind of reaction, if any, this horoscope may have excited. This visit by Charles IX and Catherine de Medici was therefore Nostradamus' first known opportunity to determine just how interested these royal personages were in his predictions for them. As we are about to see, they were extremely interested. And Nostradamus, in direct anticipation of their visit, had already given their futures a great deal of thought.

NOTES

1. 'M. NOSTRADAMUS AETATIS LVIIII ANN'. – Print in the Paris Bibliothèque Nationale, ref. Ed. 5.b. Rés., fol 36
2. 'Il estoit de stature un peu moindre que la mediocre, de corps robuste, alegre & vigoureux. Il avoit le front grand & ouvert, le nez droit & esgal, les yeux gris, le regard doux & en ire comme flaboyant, le visage severe & riant, de sorte qu'avec la severité se voyoit en iceluy conjoint une grande humanité: les joues vermeilles, voire jusques à l'extreme eage, la barbe logue & espoisse ...'
3. 'Scripsissem Lugdunum ut ibi emerentur, sed cum sciam tibi plurimos infensos esse, qui tuas Ephemerides, quae tamen ex diuturna experentia verissimae sunt, corrumpunt, et aliter sub tuo nomine imprimi curant, ut vix verum exemplar inveniatur, intermisi – Dupèbe, Nostradamus, Lettres Inédites..., op. cit., p.113

The Chateau de l'Empéri, Salon-de-Provence, where Charles IX and his mother lodged the night of their consultation with Nostradamus.

4 Ref. 13984 – see Brind'Amour, *Nostradamus Astrophile...*, op. cit., p.488

5 Ibid.

6 Eustace F. Bosanquet, *English Printed Almanacks and Prognostications, A Bibliographical History to the Year 1600*, London, Bibliographic Society, 1917, p.35

7 J. Stevenson (ed.), *Calendar of State Papers for the Reign of Elizabeth, Foreign, 1562*, London, 1867, p.445

8 '*Nonnihil tamen remissum est de inquisitione Hispanica, qua accerimé etiam in suspectos animadverti solebat. Sed vide novas artes. Qui suspecti sunt, noctu comprehensi in propriis aedibus abstrahuntur in carcerem, ibique sine ullo strepitu ac forma iudicii submerguntur in dolio aquae quadrupedes constricti. Id eo consilio fit ne quid publicé oriatur turbae, si publicé sumeretur de talibus supplicium. Ita mihi hodie relatum est intra XV. dies proximos tres honestas et pias matronas ob haeresis suspicionem hoc modo clam é domibus noctu extractas periisse.*' Letter XXXIII, reproduced in Dupèbe, *Nostradamus, Lettres Inédites...*, op. cit., p.107

9 '*Quas Antverpiae scripseras...tum vero crudelitas illa inaudita immanitasque barbara, quae in Christianos exercetur et noctu et indicta causa, mihi plane bilem movit.*' Letter XXXIX, reproduced in Dupèbe, *Nostradamus, Lettres Inédites...*, op. cit., pp.131

10 Letter XXXIX reproduced in Dupèbe, *Nostradamus, Lettres Inédites...*, op. cit., pp.131–5. For brevity, this is an abbreviated version from Dupèbe's summary of the original Latin text

11 Ibid., p.134

12 *Atque hanc victoriam D. Comitibus praediximus*, ibid.

13 This was Jean de Quinqueran, called Ventabren

14 As note 10

15 James Randi, *The Mask of Nostradamus...*, op. cit., pp.52–3

16 François La Noue, *Mémoires*, Michaud et Poujoulat, eds., *Nouvelle collection des mémoires sur l'histoire de France*, series I, vol. IX, p.595, quoted in translation in Irene Mahoney, *Madame Catherine*, op. cit., p.91

17 Henri Lancelot-Voisin *L'Histoire de France Enrichie des plus notable occurrences survenues ez provinces de l'Europe & Pays voisins...Depuis lan 1550 jusques a ces temps*, Abraham H., 1581, quoted in Brind'Amour, *Nostradamus Astrophile...*, op. cit., p.441

18 'vel autoritate principum, sed plebis furore et mera insania'. Dupèbe, *Nostradamus, Lettres Inédites...*, op. cit., p.132

19 Jean Guéraud, *La Chronique lyonnaise de Jean Guéraud...*, op. cit., p.153

20 *Almanach pour l'an MDLXIII avec les presages...calculé et expliqué par M. Michel Nostradamus, docteur en médicine, astrophile de Salon-de-Craux en Provence*, Musée Paul Arbaud, Aix-en-Provence, ref. S.385. A privately-printed, limited edition facsimile reprint of a copy of this Almanac was made at Mariebourg in 1905, see Leroy, *Nostradamus, Ses Origines...*, op. cit., p.151

21 'allo illustrissimo Signore, il S. Fran. Fabrittio de Serbelloni, per sua Santita, nelle cose de la guerra in Francia, Generale'. Quoted in Leroy, *Nostradamus, Ses Origines...*, op. cit., p.150

22 'gli arrabiati seditiosi e Tirani della novella setta', quoted in Leroy, *Nostradamus, Ses Origines...*, op. cit., p.151

23 'l'huomo saggio puo, contemplando la natura e lo stato delle seconde cause, prevedere molte cose, lequali a chi non é fondato in questa eccelente arte d'Astrologia, sono ascose ed incognite.' Quoted in Brind'Amour, *Nostradamus Astrophile...*, op. cit., p.448

24 J. Stephenson (ed.), *Calendar of State Papers, Foreign 1564–65*, entry 553, p.175

25 J. Stephenson (ed.), *Calendar of State Papers, Foreign 1564–66*, entry 592

26 'Déjà était la peste déclarée en ce pauvre lieu, où elle avait contagieusement et d'une merveilleuse sudaineté estoffé de quatre à cinq cents personnes...la ville estoit vuide de gens et de membre...les logements bien tristes et le maysons en piteux estat de recevoir un train royal.' César de Nostredame, *Histoire et Chronique de Provence*, op. cit., quoted in Leroy, *Nostradamus, Ses Origines...*, op. cit., p.97

27 'A l'entree du Monarque...on avoit dressé quelques simples arcades de branches de buys, depuis la porte d'Avignon jusques aux portaux du chasteau, logis magnifique et pontifical. Le pavé des rues avoit esté couvert de sablon, semé de romarin qui rendoit une odeur trés agréable et bien fleurante. Le roi estoit assis sur un cheval african de manteau gris, harnaché de velours noir, à larges passemens et franges d'or. Sa personne estoit couverte d'un habillement cramoysi phénicien, qu'on dit vulgairement violet, enrichi de cordons d'argent, le chapeau et les pennaches respondans à son vestement.' Ibid.

28 'tout en faisant très humble et convenable révérence, d'une franche et philosophique liberté, prononça ce vers du poète: Vir magnus bello, nulli pietate secundus.' Ibid.

CHAPTER 14

Matchmaker, Matchmaker

Much like the modern-day fashion industry, in the sixteenth century Nostradamus and his fellow almanac-makers had to anticipate what would be fashionable, or topical, at least a year in advance. This was in order to allow time for the printing of their almanacs, so that they could be distributed and available just ahead of each coming year. To this end Nostradamus always gave a lot of thought to choosing to whom his next almanac should be dedicated, much in the manner that today's magazine editors agonise over which new starlet they should feature on their next cover.

With Nostradamus living at such a distance from the royal court it actually says a great deal for his prophetic insight – or for his finger being on the contemporary pulse – that it appears to be no later than mid-April 1564 that he decided upon the teenage King Charles IX as the dedicatee for his 1565 Almanac.[1] Seemingly (though not certainly), this choice was made before he learned that the King and his mother were making a nationwide tour that would bring them to his doorstep just about the time that the Almanac would be going on sale nationally.

Nor is that all. For again, in this same 1565 Almanac, amongst Nostradamus' predictions for the month of May we find that in the spring of 1564 he had apparently penned:

> A certain most great and supreme Virgin will be matrimonially conjoined with the Trojan blood when Saturn and Jupiter come together after no longer turning away.[2]

Enigmatic as this may sound, astrologically Nostradamus was referring to the planets Saturn and Jupiter returning together to their normal course after being long in retrograde. This was a neat reflection of what had been happening politically, with England and France, after centuries of 'turning away' from each other, actually signing a joint peace treaty at Troyes on April 12, 1564. And amongst

Europe's crowned heads of the early 1560s the 'great and supreme Virgin' could only mean England's Virgin Queen Elizabeth, while 'Trojan blood' equally clearly meant King Charles IX, this being the poetic way that Nostradamus liked to refer to France's reigning monarch.[3] So in the light of the unequivocal words 'matrimonially conjoined' Nostradamus was clearly prophesying that England's Queen Elizabeth and France's King Charles IX would be marrying some time during 1565.

With King Charles a spindly fourteen-year-old and Queen Elizabeth a mature woman of thirty, such an idea was extraordinarily audacious, if not downright bizarre. Yet it was far from inconceivable. After all, there had been an eleven-year age difference between Philip II of Spain and England's Mary Tudor when they had been married only a decade before. And what better than a marriage between Protestant England and Catholic France for sealing the end of their old enmities?

But even if the prophecy were feasible, how could it be translated into reality? By October 17, 1564, with his next year's Almanac on the presses, and with Charles IX and his Queen Regent mother in Salon, Nostradamus had an unprecedented opportunity to tell the royal pair directly that this was what he foresaw. And it was made all the easier as they both exhibited every appearance of being as awed by his astrological wizardry as he was by their royal status. According to César, his father was invited to stroll with the royals from Salon's Avignon or northern gate all the way to the gates of the Château del'Empéri where they were lodging. He was later formally received by them in the château's Chamber of Honour, where he apparently lingered 'a very long time with the young King and the Queen-Regent'. Indeed, if we can believe César, such was the favourable impression he made that King Charles and Queen Catherine invited him to bring his whole family to meet them, for César proudly recorded their 'human curiosity to see them all, even a daughter still breast-feeding', a clear reference to his newest sister Diane.

That some time during the royal party's first evening at Salon Nostradamus forthrightly put his prophecy to Charles and his mother is quite definite, and can be gleaned, not from César's history, but from reports by attendant foreign ambassadors. Equally definite is that the royal pair was not at all taken aback by the bold prediction. Rather, shortly after they left Salon Catherine cheerfully reported to her great confidante, the seventy-four-year-old Constable Anne de Montmorency, who had welcomed Nostradamus to Paris nine years earlier:

As we passed through Salon we saw Nostradamus, who promised everything good for the King my son. Also that he will live as long as yourself, for whom he says death will not come before your ninetieth year. I pray to God that he is speaking the truth, and that you too will have the good health you wish for.[4]

Heading south from Salon, the travelling court negotiated Marignane's watery environs and then moved east to Aix-en-Provence, the coast and Marseilles. This bustling seaport had some poignant memories for Catherine, since it was where, thirty-one years before, as a fourteen-year-old, and after a sea-voyage from Italy, she had first met and married her husband, then Prince Henri. While halted at Marseilles, Charles and Catherine took the opportunity to summon the English ambassador Sir Thomas Smith for a private audience, whereupon, much to Smith's surprise, they began quizzing him closely as to when his mistress Queen Elizabeth intended to marry. They also wanted to know whether her chosen husband would be the English nobleman Robert Dudley, as was then widely rumoured. As Smith reported directly to Elizabeth herself on November 9:

To the first [question] I said I knew not. To the second I thought rather nay than yea, for nothing letted her marrying him long ago if it had been her pleasure.[5]

With adroit diplomacy Smith refused to be drawn on the further question whether Elizabeth was minded to 'marry someone from inside or outside her own country'.

A week later the court was back at Marignane, following which its progress was temporarily halted at Arles as the Rhône river was in flood. Since Arles was a mere twenty-five miles (40 km) from Salon, this gave Charles and Catherine the opportunity to summon Nostradamus back for further consultation. As recorded by César: 'During his stay [the

'A certain most great and supreme Virgin will be matrimonially conjoined...' Queen Elizabeth I of England, whom Nostradamus foresaw as bride for Charles IX of France.

King] wanted to spend more time with my father, and he sent for him to come with speed.'6

Despite Nostradamus, now sixty-one, needing a stick for his walk with the royal party through the streets of Salon, he was apparently still fit enough to make the ride across the flat Rhône delta, for he answered this particular summons promptly enough. As César continued, when he joined the court at Arles:

> ... they [Charles IX and Nostradamus] had many discussions. And knowing how much he [Nostradamus] had been esteemed by his father, the late King Henri II of very heroic memory, and having been much graced by his journey in France he sent him away with a gift of two hundred gold crowns, and half of this given him by the Queen, together with the title of Councillor and Physician in Ordinary [to the King] with all pensions, privileges and honours pertaining to this.7

That Nostradamus was cock-a-hoop at receiving such titles is evident from the rapidity with which they appeared alongside his name in all ongoing publications. Indeed, since 'Medecin du Roy' or 'Doctor to the King' occurs on the title-page of the only surviving published copy of his Almanac for 1565,8 this arouses more than a suspicion that this particular copy was one of a batch he altered in the wake of the royal visit – even though the date it bears makes it look as if it had gone to press beforehand.

Meanwhile the signs are unmistakable that Charles and Catherine were pursuing with astonishing vigour the realisation of the matrimonial prophecy. On January 24, 1565 Catherine dispatched by secret courier a letter to Paul de Foix, her ambassador in London, apparently carrying the forthright suggestion that Elizabeth should agree to marry Charles. The courier bearing this message must have ridden like the wind all the way from the south of France, for it was as early as February 14, St Valentine's day, that the ambassador was able formally to hand the marriage proposal to Elizabeth in London.

Even before this proposal had reached England, however, an inkling of its contents had come to the ever-vigilant ears of the Spanish ambassador to the French Court, Don Francisco de Alava, only recently arrived as a replacement for a predecessor whom Catherine had found insufferably arrogant. Via two messages that Alava sent back to Philip of Spain we learn just how deeply Nostradamus was responsible for Charles' and his mother's extraordinarily impassioned wooing of Elizabeth. This was Alava's despatch of February 4, 1565:

Your Majesty should know that everything has gone mad here. I am told that the Queen [Mother], when she passed by the place where Nostradamus lives, summoned him to her and awarded him two hundred crowns. She asked him to draw a horoscope for the King and another for herself. This man is surely the most malicious in the world...The Queen said to me today, when I said that I hoped with the aid of God the talks would bring about great good for Christianity, 'Did you know...that Nostradamus has assured me that there will be a general peace throughout the world in 1566, and that the realm of France will be very tranquil?...' In speaking thus, she talks with the air of profundity [you would expect] if she were quoting from St John or St Luke.[9]

On February 20, when the travelling, court had reached Toulouse, Alava followed up with a further message back to Spain conveying what he had been able to glean of the secret goings on between France and England:

Tomorrow morning a gentleman envoy is leaving very secretly for the Queen of England, I am informed that this ambassador, in his anxiety, hid the negotiations from the ministers of the princes and was mistrustful towards them lest they create some impediment. In fifteen days certain submissions and understandings will be with the Queen of England. The first day that the King and Queen met Nostradamus, he told them that the king will marry the said queen [i.e. Elizabeth]. It may be that they have embarked upon a negotiation as an expression of their devotion to him, for already this ambassador [Sir Thomas Smith] has sent the [astrological] interpretation to his mistress.[10]

As we now know from the other surviving international correspondence, this information from ambassador Alava was both inaccurate and already quite out of date. Nonetheless Alava had good cause to try as best he could to learn what was going on between the French and English courts. In terms of the balance of power any major marriage alliance between England and France had to be bad for Spanish interests. But obviously, for the fulfilment of Nostradamus' prophecy rather more was needed than just French keeness. In Nostradamus' favour was the fact that not only was England's ambassador Smith an enthusiast for astrology, but Queen Elizabeth herself was by no means hostile to the subject. It is a matter of historical record that six years earlier, when she was new to the throne, she had consulted Nostradamus' English counterpart Dr John Dee, specifically

for his astrological advice on the most propitious date for her coronation. Given that Elizabeth would go on to reign for forty-five years,
she hardly had cause to doubt the value of that advice. Elizabeth was
certainly so impressed by Dee that throughout her reign she would
occasionally drop in on his Mortlake home – conveniently situated
between her Greenwich and Richmond palaces – whenever she felt the
need of some further astrological guidance.[11]

The drawback for Nostradamus, however, was that from the
moment Catherine's and Charles' matrimonial proposition arrived at
the English court, Elizabeth used her feminine wiles to the utmost to
play hard to get. Via her chief minister Sir William Cecil she sent back
a cordial, tentative, stalling response as early as the next day. Yet
Catherine and Charles, buoyed by Nostradamus' prophecy, and from
their perspective representing the bigger, stronger country, felt in no
mood to take 'no' as a final answer. So, with the tour still steadily
making its wide circuit around France, it was not long before ambassador Smith again found himself summoned to a private audience with
Catherine and her son.

At this meeting Charles, who it should be pointed out had never
even met Elizabeth, outrightly and ardently declared before Smith that
he was in love with the English Queen. Smith's astonishment was such
that his knee-jerk response was a shade less than diplomatic: 'At your
age, Sire, one does not yet know the meaning of love', which caused
Charles visibly to blush.

Unperturbed by this slightly tactless snub to her royal son,
Catherine insisted on patiently exploring with Smith all the possible
objections that Elizabeth might have to marrying Charles, and how
these might be overcome. Inevitably the first and the most serious difficulty was the couple's fifteen-year age difference. Of this, according
to Smith's report of the conversation, Catherine remarked, 'If she likes
the age of my son he will find no fault with hers.' To this Charles
emphatically affirmed: '*I* find no fault. I would that she could be as
well content with me as I with her age.' Another difficulty was that, if
Elizabeth were married to Charles, she would need sometimes to leave
England to be in France. To this Catherine pointed out that such a
problem cut both ways, since Charles for his part would sometimes be
required to leave France to be in England. However, with 'wise men'
deputising in both countries there should be no problem. And whereas
Elizabeth currently gave herself the empty title 'Queen of France', if
she were to marry Charles she would be able to boast that title with
absolute truthfulness.

With Catherine's encouragement Smith even sent to Elizabeth
detailed descriptions of Charles' physical appearance: 'Slender…

amiable of countenance...tractable and wise for his years and [he] understands more of his affairs...than a man would easily think.' Perhaps mindful of Charles' late brother François' sexual under-development, Catherine urged her ambassador in London to assure Elizabeth that she would find everything about Charles – 'both his body and his soul' – to her liking. But the May of 1565 passed without the England–France matrimonial conjunction that Nostradamus had prophesied. And by July, ambassador de Foix could only report back to France the Queen of England's profound regret that her principal advisers had counselled her against the marriage because of 'the great disparity of age'.

Nostradamus, inevitably not privy to the communications flying between England and a court once more hundreds of miles away from him, nonetheless continued to hope. His Almanac for 1566, which was printed by Jean Brotot's son Pierre in partnership with Anthoine Volant,[12] was completed on April 21, 1565. And in the calendar section he tried to anticipate a suitable spread of 'hit' dates for when some royal marriage, at least, might be celebrated:

For the full moon of January 1566:
Besides they will celebrate *great nuptials and marriages* of great consequence. And they will be very happy who make these in the course of the present month of January.[13]

For the first quarter of the moon of April, 1566:
Also there will arrive during this Moon several ambassadors, legates and others sent by the monarchs, and of Kings to Kings, likewise concerning some *great marriage matters.*[14]

For the new moon of June 1566:
During this orbit of the Moon there will be new negotiations of nuptials, *of marriages, of divers alliances of great Lords and monarchs* of the world, which they will accomplish with great joy, gladness and contentment on each side. And to each reign will be accorded much rejoicing and gladness, and feasts and celebrations will be held.[15]

For the last quarter of the September moon of 1566:
Also in the month of September and the rest of the year following there is threat of great commotion and division between the kings, one against the other, on account of public enemies and adversaries. And the greater part of their commotions and the hardly minor controversies at the end of which they will reach agreements one with the other, principally to make *marriages, nuptials and*

royal promises, and of supreme consequence. Towards the end of the year most of the marriages will be agreed, and the greater part of Christianity will be united together in peace, love, unity and perfect concord.[16]

Yet it was not to be. Nonetheless, just to keep everyone on tenter-hooks, the marriage prediction was by no means the only surprise that Nostradamus sprang during the time he had the ear of Charles and Catherine in Salon. Charles' elder sister Elisabeth of Valois, it may be recalled, had married Philip II of Spain at the time of her father Henri II's fatal joust. Not only was she now, at twenty, Queen of Spain,[17] she was Catherine de Medici's favourite daughter, and throughout the four years she had been at the Spanish court, she had already endured several debilitating miscarriages in the attempt to produce an heir for Philip. Accordingly, when Nostradamus, while with the royal party at Arles, announced with great confidence that Elisabeth de Valois was once again pregnant, nothing could have been more calculated to induce in Catherine a frenzy of Italianate maternal anxiety.

Just twenty days later, on November 28, 1564, the royal secretary Robertet, one of the household staff amongst the travelling court, wrote to Jean de Saint-Sulpice, France's ambassador to the Spanish court. He stated that everyone was most anxiously awaiting the return from Spain of Constable Anne de Montmorency's son Charles. According to Robertet: 'From him we are waiting to hear the truth of that which Nostradamus assures us, that the Catholic Queen is big [with child]. May God will this and give you, monsieur a good and long life.'[18]

The moment that he had made his pronouncement Catherine had sent another member of her entourage galloping off to find out whether it was true – yet another instance of the extraordinary hold that Nostradamus had attained over the minds of some of Europe's greatest personages. History does not appear to record whatever immediate news Charles de Montmorency may have brought back with him from the Spanish court. In early March 1565, however, just four months after Nostradamus' pronouncement, the Spanish court positively confirmed that Elisabeth of Valois genuinely was pregnant. For Queen Catherine the unfortunate side of this, however, was that because of Elisabeth's history of miscarriages the royal physicians had advised her against making any long journey, in order to give this par-ticular pregnancy every chance of success. This immediately dashed a plan that Catherine had been hatching, whereby she and Charles could enjoy their first reunion with Elisabeth in over four years. The plan had been for Elisabeth to ride north from Madrid to the

'The Escorial Palace, near Madrid, construction of which had commenced shortly before the supposed pregnancy which Nostradamus predicted for Elisabeth of Austria.'

border with France to coincide with Catherine's and Charles' arrival at the most southwesterly point of their itinerary, but Elisabeth and her unborn baby's health were clearly the greater priority.

Within a few days, however, there followed a rescinding of the diagnosis: apparently Elisabeth had not been pregnant after all. This at least enabled the plan for a royal rendezvous to be revived, and Catherine and Charles met up with a very Hispanicised Elisabeth at Hendaye, a short distance from the pleasant southwest French town of Bayonne. But from the point of view of Nostradamus' credibility, his professed clair-voyancy in this instance must be considered more than a little shaky. The sad irony was that it was in childbirth that Elisabeth died only three years later, in her mid-twenties, the poignant Hendaye family reunion being the last sight that Charles and Catherine would have of her.

The other prediction that Nostradamus reportedly made while the court was at Salon concerned none other than the Huguenot Jeanne d'Albret and the late Antoine de Navarre's son, the young Prince Henri of Navarre. Ten years old and next in line of succession to the French throne after Catherine's two younger sons, this was the young man whom Catherine had insisted be brought up at the royal court, away from Jeanne d'Albret's Calvinist ministers' influence. He was thus part of the travelling entourage. According to the story, while Prince Henri was at Salon he was billeted, not with Catherine and Charles at the Château de l'Empéri, but at the house of one Pierre Tronc de Coudoulet, who would later marry Nostradamus' nineteen-year-old niece Jeanne, daughter of his brother Bertrand.

It is reported that when Nostradamus' eyes alighted on Henri he became so interested in him that he drew up his horoscope. He also arranged that early the next morning he should be present at the boy's *lever*, or waking from sleep, so that he could examine him before he put on his shirt. On the strength of this examination, one particularly directed, apparently, at the moles on the boy's skin, Nostradamus solemnly pronounced that Henri would one day 'have the heritage',[19] that is, inherit the kingdom of France. This, as French history richly confirms, indeed transpired. Prince Henri of Navarre in 1589 not only succeeded to the French throne as King Henri IV, despite all the odds against it in 1564, but also, in the course of a twenty-one-year reign, became one of France's greatest kings.

Such is the uncritical nature of most Nostradamian literature that this story of Nostradamus prophesying the young Henri IV's future appears in some garbled form or other in virtually every potted biography.[20] The actuality, however, as well recognised by the conscientious Dr Edgar Leroy, is that the earliest surviving account of the story is a late seventeenth-century one by a claimed descendant of Pierre Tronc de Coudoulet, hardly a witness with a sound claim to independence. Nor is the story's credibility in any way enhanced by a painting accredited to the early twentieth-century painter-engraver Louis-Joseph Denis, or Denis-Valverane, which depicts Nostradamus examining young Henri's moles, with a bemused Catherine de Medici most improbably looking on.

The hard fact remains, therefore, that this story's historicity is highly suspect. Nor has anything ever been heard of the horoscope which Nostradamus allegedly drew up for the young prince, a horoscope which, had its predictions matched the well-recorded details of the later reign of King Henri IV, would have been a very interesting document indeed.

But as it happens there is a horoscope that Nostradamus made for another young prince at this time, which has survived. That prince too went on to have a long, eventful and well-documented reign. And the great curiosity is that this extremely interesting document has been neglected by every previous Nostradamus researcher until the present.

NOTES

1 *Almanach pour l'An M.D.LXV... Composée par M. Michel Nostredame*

2 *Quelque grandissime & supreme vierge sera avecques le sang Troyen conjoincte matrimoniallement, que puis apres ne se tournant assembler Saturne & Jupiter* – 1565 Almanac, folio E[1]4r, quoted Brind'Amour, *Nostradamus Astrophile...*, op. cit., p.52, n.137

3 See for instance Nostradamus' *Prophecies*, C.II, q.61, in which '*sang Troyen*' ('Trojan blood') appears in the unmistakably French context of the Gironde and La Rochelle

4 '*Pasant par Salons, avons veu Nostradamus, qui promest tou playn de bien au Roy mon filz, et qu'il vivera aultant que vous, qu'il dist aurés avant mourir quatre vins et dis ans. Je prie Dieu que dis vroy et qui vous dovint aussi bonne santé que la vou desire.*' MS BN fonds français no.3205, fol. 1, reproduced in M. le Cte Baguenault de Puchesse (ed.), *Lettres de Catherine de Médicis*, vol. X, Supplement, Paris, 1909, p.145. The letter is undated, but

can only have been sent shortly after the royal party's departure from Salon. The Nostradamian author Peter Lemesurier, it should be noted, says on p.41 of *The Nostradamus Encyclopaedia* that 'Nostradamus is nowhere referred to in the Queen's (i.e. Catherine de Medici's) voluminous correspondence.' Yet even the sceptic James Randi, whose book *The Mask of Nostradamus* Lemesurier reviewed, was aware of this particular letter

5 J. Stephenson (ed.), *Calendar of State Papers, Foreign Series of the Reign of Elizabeth 1564–1565*, London, 1870, pp.240–1

6 '*Pendant son sejour [le roy] fut desireux devoir plus amplement mon pere. Qu'il envoya querir expres…*'

7 '*…apres plusieurs discours, sçachant fort bien que le feu Roy Henry second de tres heroique memoire son pere, en avoit fait cas particulier, & l'avoit beaucoup honoré à son voyage de France, il fit despecher avec un present de deux cents escus d'or, & la moytié autant que la Reyne lui donna, ses patents de Conseiller & Medecin ordinaire, aux gages, prerogatives & honneurs accoustumez.*' César de Nostredame, *Histoire et Chronique de Provence…*, op. cit., p.802

8 This copy is preserved in the Biblioteca August Del Comune di Perugia. Curiously, in this edition the text of the prophetic quatrains bears some significant differences to those that Chavigny recorded in his *Compilation* as belonging to this particular Almanac. It therefore looks as if the Perugia copy could be a specially amended edition of the 1565 Almanac, which Nostradamus brought out after the royal visit, but dated to make it appear that he had composed it beforehand. In the absence of an alternative, pre-amended version of the 1565 Almanac this is difficult to prove. This is one of a number of instances of suspicious practices on Nostradamus' part, which need lengthier and more scholarly study than has been possible for the purposes of this book

9 '*Porque vea V. M^d. Aquellega la lunandad de aqui dire como esta Reyna quando passo por el lugar donde vive el Nostradamo, le envio a llamar. y le señalo d. cientos escudos de gages. Mando que echase un Juyzio à este Rey y otro à la dicha Reyna. Con sei toda la malicia del mundo…Dixo me y esta Reyna diziendo le que esperava en Dios q. de estas vistas avia de resultar granbien a la christiandad, sabed que el Nostradamo me ha dicho afirmadamente que el año de sessenta y seis hade aver paz general en el mundo y que este Reyno hade estar muy quieto y asseritadas la cosas del y esto tan enarcadas las cosas como si se lo huvieran dicho sanct Juan. o sanct Lucas.*' Spanish National Archives ref. K1503, 30, quoted in Brind'Amour, *Nostradamus Astrophile…*, op. cit., p.51

10 '*Embian mañana muy secretamente un gentilhombre a la Reyna de Inglaterra de que entiendo aue este Embax. Esta zeloso tanto que ha dicho q. es esconder sas negociaciones a lost ministros de los Principes y desconfiar dellos […] ser causa de que se los desbaratan algunas vessel [amano]. y […] despachos han [ven]ydo en quinze dias a la donha de Inglaterra. El primer dia que este Rey y Reyna vieron el Nostradamus les dixo affirmadamente que este Rey se casaria con la dicha Reyna, esto podria sehazer les mover alguna negociacion para atraer la a su devocion porque ya este Embax. Ha embiado á su ama este Juyzio.* Spanish National Archives ref. K1503, 37, quoted with translation into French in Brind'Amour, *Nostradamus Astrophile…*, op. cit., p.53

11 See Benjamin Woolley's excellent *The Queen's Conjuror, The Science and Magic of Dr Dee*, London, HarperCollins, 2001, pp.87, 198, and 225

12 *Almanach pour l'an M.D.LXVI. avec ses amples significations & explications, composé par Maistre Michel de Nostradame Docteur en medecine, Conseiller & Medecin ordinaire du Roy.* A facsimile of this was reproduced in the *Cahiers Michel Nostradamus* vols. 5–6, 1987–8, pp.69–104

13 'Au reste se celebreront de grandes noces & mariages de grande consequence: & seront tres felices ceux qui se feront durant le circuit de ce present mois de Janvier.' The text of this and the further three quotations has been drawn from Brind'Amour, *Nostradamus Astrophile...*, op. cit., pp.53–4

14 'Aussi arriveront durant cette Lune quelques ambassadeurs, legats & autres envoyez des monarques, & de Rois à Rois, mesmes concernant quelques grand cas de mariage.'

15 'Durant cete revolution de Lune nouvelle lon traitera de nopces, de mariages, de diverses conjonctions des plus grands Seigneurs & monarque du monde, qui à la parfin s'accompliront avec grande joye, alegresse & contentement d'un chacun & de chacun regne sera mandé de soy resjouir & alegrer, & demener festes & hilaritez.'

16 'Aussi dans ce mois de Septembre & le reste de l'an ensuivant menace d'une grande commotion & diversité des Rois les uns alencontre des autres pour cause d'ennemis publiques & adversaires; & la plus part de leurs commotions & non petites controverses à la parfin s'accorderont les uns avec les autres, principalement pour le fait de mariages, de nopces, de promesses royales & de supreme consequence. Devers la fin de l'an la plus part des mariages accordés & sera la plus part de la Chrestineté unie ensemble en paix, amour, union & parfaite concorde.'

17 She is, of course, immortalised as the heroine of Verdi's opera *Don Carlos*

18 'Par lui nous attendons la vérité de ce que Nostradamus nous assure que la reine cathol. est grosse. Dieu le veuille, et vous donne, mr. bonne et longue vie.' From *Ambassade en Espagne de Jean Ebrard Seigneur de Saint-Sulpice de 1562 à 1565 et mission de ce diplomate dans la même pays en 1566*, Documents classés, annotés et publiés par Edmond Cabié, Albi, 1903, p.322, quoted in Brind'Amour, *Nostradamus Astrophile...*, op. cit., p.52

19 'qu'il aurait l'heritage'

20 See for instance Laver, *Nostradamus or the Future Foretold*, op. cit., p.69 and Peter Lemesurier, *The Nostradamus Encyclopaedia*, op. cit., p.40

CHAPTER 15

A Princely Horoscope

In the same year of 1564 that Nostradamus found himself as consultant prophet to the French court during its sojourn in Salon, over eight hundred miles (1,300 km) to the east died Ferdinand I, ruler of Austria, Hungary and Bohemia. Culturally a rather limited individual, though a strong supporter of Hebrew studies, Ferdinand was the brother to whom in 1556 a tired and ailing Charles V had ceded the eastern divisions of his Habsburg Empire. It was Ferdinand who had acted as protector to Nostradamus' client Hans Rosenberger during the latter's financial troubles over his mines at Fieberbrunn, Austria. He was succeeded by his thirty-seven-year-old son Maximilian II who, though moderate and pro-Protestant by inclination, was lovelessly married to his cousin (and Charles V's daughter), the neurotic, fiercely pro-Catholic Maria of Spain. Maria had borne Maximilian two sons, Rudolf, now twelve, and Ernst, one year younger, both, as their portraits show, inheriting the massive lower jaw that was so dominant through their double ration of Habsburg genes.

Only the year previously Rudolf and Ernst had been sent for the furtherance of their education to their uncle Philip II's Catholic court in Spain. There they would remain until full adulthood in 1571. But when Maximilian succeeded to his

The Emperor Maximilian II with his wife Maria of Spain, also the Princes Rudolf and Ernst, and their sister, from a group portrait in the Kunsthistorisches Museum, Vienna.

father's dominions, Prince Rudolf automatically became next in line of succession. This was a point at which it was seemingly traditional amongst the Habsburg dynasty's northern branch to have their horoscopes cast;[1] Maximilian II's great-grandfather Frederick III (1463–1525) 'the Wise' was known as the astrologer Emperor because of his strong interest in such matters. Since Nostradamus, in the wake of the death of Luca Gaurico, had acquired the reputation as the foremost astrologer of the age, it naturally followed that he should be invited to cast the young Prince Rudolf's horoscope, with Prince Ernst's being added at the same time, for good measure.

As in the case of other horoscopes prepared by Nostradamus, we could easily know very little about the circumstances surrounding this particular commission. Fortunately, however, at the very end of the Bibliothèque Nationale's Latin manuscript of Nostradamus correspondence, just where the Rosenberger-Tubbe exchange of letters abruptly terminates, there is to be found a series of communications between the seer and a Dr Hans Lobbet[2] of Lyons. Originally from Augsburg, Lobbet acted as a French agent for Daniel Rechlinger, a former Augsburg nobleman who was closely connected with Maximilian II's eastern European court.

Amongst a total of six letters in this group the earliest is one from Lobbet to Nostradamus dated June 14, 1565. In this Lobbet enquired about the state of progress on horoscopes for the 'illustrious princes, sons of his imperial Majesty, who are now in Spain'.[3] Apparently at Maximilian II's court in Vienna the two princes' horoscopes had been anxiously awaited for some while. Promising that once Nostradamus had fulfilled this task he would be suitably rewarded, Lobbet made clear that he was asking on behalf of both Rechlinger and the Emperor. And he stressed that he needed Nostradamus' response as soon as possible, so that he could pass it on to Rechlinger and to Maximilian.

When Lobbet's letter arrived at Salon, Nostradamus had apparently been away in Aix-en-Provence, probably visiting his brother Jehan, for the opening words of his response, as sent to Lobbet on July 7, 1565, were: 'As I returned from Aix, our daughter handed me your letter.' Since Nostradamus' younger daughters Anne and Diane were still infants, this particular daughter can only have been the fourteen-year-old Madeleine, clearly now of a maturity and competence to take some interest in her father's business. Also apparent is that Nostradamus, at sixty-two, was still mobile enough to make social calls as far as Aix, about the same distance east of Salon as Arles to the west.

Nonetheless Nostradamus' tone towards Lobbet in his response was distinctly offhand and crotchety. While he insisted that he would keep his promise and complete the task that Rechlinger asked of him, he complained that no one realised the huge amount of work which such princely horoscopes demanded. He estimated that the exercise had already cost him thirty crowns, together with a further six crowns for his secretary Chavigny's time. As in the case of the horoscopes for Rosenberg, he insisted on composing these for Lobbet in French, even though he was well aware that his clients were German-speaking, and that Latin would have been the appropriate *lingua franca*.

Even so, Lobbet's forceful reminder had the effect of stirring rather more action than had been evident hitherto. In a further letter sent on August 7, Nostradamus announced that the more important horoscope, the one for Prince Rudolf, had been completed. Indeed, he included it with his letter. As he pointed out, the task had taken him fourteen months, from which we can glean that it had been commissioned around June 1564. And from his account of its comprehensiveness, it is easy to see why it had taken him so long:

> The nativity of the Prince and King Rudolf, in which is contained…first his life, health and the disposition of his body, matters of importance, travels, religion, his brothers, sisters and near relations of his father's line, of his uncle, grandparents and great-grandparents, his children, his pleasures and tastes and pursuits, his illnesses, his servants, of his marriage and which family and country his wife will be from; and at what time and how many wives; of public and other enemies, of his death and what form this will take, in what year and from what; how the dead may relinquish reigns, heredity, fear, anxiety, poison, foreign travels, religion, peregrinations; in what year there may be changes to religion, empire, legislatures; of the loyalty, hot-headedness and supreme power, of friends not of the blood, who are in great number, of the secret and hidden enemies, of prisons, and exiles, and captivity in hostile territories.[4]

Upon safe receipt of the horoscope, on August 16, 1565 Hans Lobbet responded much more warmly. From a preliminary perusal he was clearly deeply impressed by the amount of work that Nostradamus had put into it. He promised that it was being forwarded to his contact Daniel Rechlinger with all possible speed, the understanding being that Rechlinger would then arrange for translation into German, following which it would be formally presented to Rudolf's father, the Emperor Maximilian II. Frustratingly, the six letters of the Lobbet–Nostradamus correspondence fizzle out with both of them puzzling over the fact that by November 19, 1565 Lobbet had not yet received any acknowledgement from Rechlinger. So the reaction of the ultimate interested party, Rudolf's father Maximilian, has been lost to us.

Historically, however, the happy circumstance is that the horoscope must have reached Rechlinger, and was definitely translated into German. We can be sure of this because the translation is preserved to this day in the Royal Library at Stockholm,[5] as it has been since at least as early as 1734, the date that the Swedish royal collection was first catalogued. The document is unique as the only known surviving full horoscope cast by Nostradamus for a single individual's future. Its opening page reads:

Of the most serene prince and high-born lord Rudolf; archduke of Austria, first-born son of the Roman king the lord Maximilian, and his future successor, born July 18 at 6.45 p.m. in the year 1552 at Vienna in Austria with the height of the pole at 48°. A true description of his nativity and birth by the discovery of the degree of the ascendant sign, and of all that this signifies. Interpreted and calculated to the best of his abilities by Michael Nostradamus in the year 1564.[6]

There follows an astrological chart for Rudolf's birthdate details, signed off in Latin: 'Made by M. Nostradamus, Councillor in Medicine and Mathematics to the King of France, Salon of Provence, beginning in 1564.[7]

The full manuscript is divided into forty-six chapters, followed by twenty-eight sayings, and it comprises 119 numbered pages almost entirely in sixteenth-century German, written in an elegant cursive script. Exactly how and why this particular manuscript should have ended up in Stockholm has yet to be determined. Nonetheless here, unquestionably, is an authentic contemporary translation of the horoscope that in the years 1564–5 Nostradamus had prepared for Prince Rudolf in French, and had sent to Rudolf's father Maximilian II via the intermediaries Hans Lobbet and Daniel Rechlinger.

The further happy circumstance is that Prince Rudolf, whom Nostradamus specifically described as 'Prince and King' in his letter of August 7 to Lobbet, indeed went on to become a king. Some five years after Nostradamus' death Rudolf made the long journey from Spain to Vienna, where, just as Catherine de Medici had found with her daughter Elisabeth de Valois during their reunion at Hendaye, the Austrian court immediately noted how very Hispanicised he had become in dress and manners. Five years later still, on the death of his father Maximilian in 1576, Rudolf succeeded to the Habsburg throne.

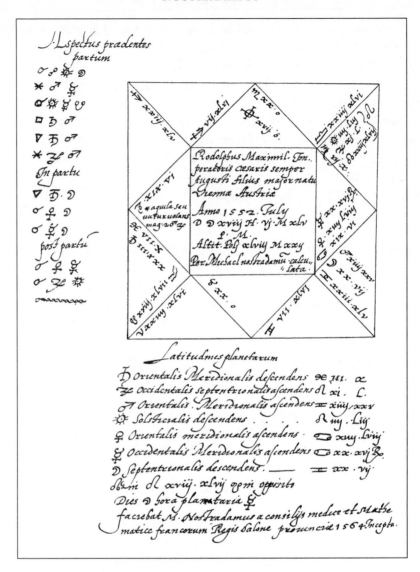

Nostradamus' birth chart for Prince Rudolf. From the horoscope manuscript D 1343 preserved in the Royal Library, Stockholm.

For historians the long reign of Rudolf II represents a most happy hunting ground for psychological profiling. Contemporary commentators were unanimous in characterising Rudolf as exceptionally stiff and dignified in his manner, melancholy, and subject to bouts of withdrawal, characteristics unlikely to have been improved by the stern religious dogmatism that would have been drilled into him at the Spanish court. As the Elizabethan courtier Sir Philip Sidney described him, he was 'sullen of disposition, very secret and resolute, nothing the manner of his father had in winning men in his behaviour'.[8]

In fact, Rudolf was by no means alone amongst his Habsburg

family in exhibiting these and other distinctly untoward psychological traits. By two lines of descent, his mother's and his father's, he was great-grandson of one of European history's most deranged royals, the so-called Joanna the Mad of Castile. Likewise, seventy years ago the German psychoanalyst H. Luxemberger identified his mother Maria as a schizoid psychopath.[9] And whatever credence we may attach to Luxemberger's prognosis, it is undeniable that along with his Habsburg jaw Rudolf inherited some of this family's less than desirable traits, as is apparent from the bizarre sexual tastes and homicidal tendencies exhibited by his illegitimate son Don Giuho.[10] Among many indications of Rudolf's own mental imbalance was his obsessive and prodigal collecting of all things mechanical, particularly clocks. A result of this is that Prague, to which he moved his capital, is to this day a city of clocks. He failed over three decades to enter into a legitimate marriage, despite any number of willing and suitably high-born potential brides. And he was notable for his dark dabblings in spiritualism, Hermeticism and alchemy, in 1584 attracting to Prague England's equivalent of Nostradamus, Dr John Dee, together with his shadowy associate Edward Kelley.

Yet on the credit side Rudolf II was well-read, fluent in German, Spanish, Italian, Latin and French, and he managed to reign for thirty-two years, the first twenty of these relatively tranquilly and successfully. His realms, like most others in Europe, were deeply riven by the disputes between Roman Catholics and Protestants. In contrast to his father's easy-going tolerance his Catholic upbringing caused him to act repressively towards the Protestants. Even so, it was only after 1598, when his mental instability became more marked, that he encountered serious opposition. Under pressure from Habsburg archdukes, in 1608 he was obliged to cede Austria, Hungary and Moravia to his more popular younger brother Matthias, and he eventually died in 1612.

From all this it should be evident that Rudolf's personality and career were historically so clear-cut, distinctive and well-documented that the question of how much they matched up to Nostradamus' predictions for him in 1564–5 has to represent one of the most significant tests for the seer's true abilities. Considering the hundreds of volumes written on Nostradamus, and

Rudolf II shortly after his accession as Holy Roman Emperor, from a contemporary medallion.

the length of time the horoscope has been available in one of the world's major libraries, the biggest surprise in the course of researching this book was to discover that not a single Nostradamian author has hitherto even begun to study the Rudolf horoscope. Although Peter Lemesurier managed to reproduce a picture of the birthchart on p.61 of his *Nostradamus Encyclopaedia*, his caption for it reveals a complete ignorance of the subject's identity. He even mistakes Rudolf's birthdate of 1552 for the date that Nostradamus had prepared the chart, despite the latter being clearly legible on the bottom line of his illustration. The only Nostradamian author hitherto to have recognised the horoscope's significance was the Canadian Professor Pierre Brind'Amour, and although he obtained a microfilm of the manuscript and noted that it needed to be properly published, he died in 1995 before being able to set to work on it.

When I contacted the Manuscripts department of the Royal Library in Stockholm to arrange for a microfilm for my own research purposes, they put me in touch with a German researcher, Dr Elmar Gruber of Munich, with whom I happened to have had some earlier acquaintance through a common interest in the Turin Shroud. Gruber very amiably told me that he was following exactly the same line of enquiry into the Rudolf horoscope as myself. Furthermore, he had apparently discovered – which I had not – the existence of two further surviving copies of the horoscope, one in Latin, the other in French. According to Gruber the French version, the location of which he understandably did not disclose, is of particular interest since it seems to be an original deriving from Nostradamus' dictation to a secretary, most probably Chavigny.

As Gruber further informed me, he too was working on a commissioned biography of Nostradamus. Because he still had much work to do deciphering the Rudolf horoscope, and making a scholarly comparison between the French and German versions, he anticipated only marginally referring to the horoscope in this. This latter would form the subject of a second, later, more specialised publication. In view of what he called the 'awful lot of time, money and energy' that he had already spent researching the horoscope, he hoped that I would not try to pre-empt him publication-wise.

While I expressed considerable sympathy towards his aspiration, my overriding responsibility was to produce the most exhaustive study of Nostradamus that was possible within the time constraints allotted to me. The Rudolf horoscope had been accessible in the public domain for centuries. So if I could gain some significant insights from my own perusal of it, then it was only right that these should be included in my book. As already noted the manuscript is very well preserved, and its

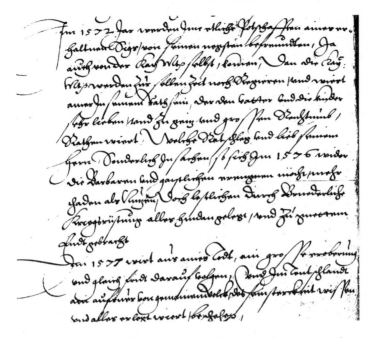

A page from the Rudolf horoscope, apparently showing prediction for the years 1572, 1576 and 1577. From the horoscope manuscript D 1343 preserved in the Royal Library, Stockholm.

handwriting looks beguilingly clear and regular. So even though my grasp of German is very limited I anticipated being able to discern at least a few key predictions that could be evaluated against the known historical facts.

To my considerable frustration, however, the handwriting proved to be so stylised that it was possible to make out little more than the occasional word or phrase, and never sufficient to read a full prediction. The Brisbane suburb of Bellbowrie, where my wife and I were living, has a number of residents for whom German is their first language. When these were consulted, they found similar difficulty with the handwriting to my own. Friends and relatives in Germany whom they in their turn consulted also drew a blank. The task clearly called for a specialist. And to have invoked such aid would not only have required even on the expert's part a lot more time than I had available to me publication-wise, it would also have contravened the essential spirit of my accord with Elmar Gruber.

In the event, therefore, all that has been determined from my personal perusal of the impressively lengthy horoscope, which is signed off as completed on 20 July 1565, with appended aphorisms added up to 7 August, is that in it Nostradamus necessarily made a number of clear, specific predictions for Prince Rudolf. Several dates can be glimpsed that were in the future when Nostradamus composed it, and from these and from the known major highlights of Rudolf's later life as Rudolf II it looks unlikely that there is any convincing match, which is almost certainly why the document has hitherto reposed in such obscurity. However prior to Elmar Gruber's eventual full and proper decipherment any such appraisal is necessarily very provisional. What is certain is that the horoscope represents an absolutely prime resource for determining for once and for all whether or not Nostradamus had genuine prophetic powers, and 'Nostradamian' authors' neglect of it thus far has been little short of inexcusable.

Returning now to the year 1565, anxious perhaps to demonstrate his continuing devotion to his own monarch, towards the end of the year Nostradamus turned his attention to some further work on King Charles IX's horoscope. In the library of the Paul Arbaud Museum at Aix-en-Provence there is preserved a printed version of a letter which, if genuine, was addressed by Nostradamus to Catherine de Medici, his 'sovereign Lady and Mistress',[11] on December 21, 1565.[12] The printer was Benoît Rigaud of Lyons, the same who in 1568 would print a new edition of the *Prophecies*.

Nostradamus explained that though all might not seem well for the kingdom at the present time, his astrological calculations allowed him to foresee a better future. By his calculations, 'I find some brief interruption of time and place and for the rest all to be in peace, love, agreement and harmony.'[13] This was not to suppose there would not be some great difficulties, 'contradictions and disputes'. But at the end each would be returned to contentment, by mouth and heart.

Nostradamus contented himself for the present with this brief discourse, which he wanted 'to venture to send to his Majesty',[14] keeping in store other details if the Queen desired: 'that which your Majesty says and does shall be promptly said, done and executed'.[15]

Nostradamus asked Catherine to 'send [him] the celestial plan for the thirteenth year of the very Christian King her son, in order to improve upon his explanations,'[16] since the astrological calculations showed:

for this year, some great and very happy fortune of prolonged peace in his realm. But that this should be exactly calculated (this celestial chart), for it to agree with mine, and I become obliged to make that which I hold, for my King, for my sovereign Lord and Majesty. After I have prayed to the Creator of the world may he give you, Madame, long life, in health and all constant prosperity, accompanied by the entire accomplishment of your Majesty's royal desires.[17]

This rather rambling document is known only from Rigaud's printed version, Rigaud of Lyons being a printer with whom Nostradamus is not known otherwise to have associated. Even if it is genuine, therefore (and this is far from certain), exactly what Nostradamus might have had in mind by such an approach to Catherine is by no means clear. Perhaps he wanted to do something to justify the titles and favours bestowed upon him a year before.

But whatever Nostradamus' concern for young King Charles IX's future, his own sands of time had but months to run.

NOTES

1 As earlier noted in the discussion of Hans Rosenberger, there is a book in the Bibliothèque Nationale, Paris, ref. BN Rés. V.1300, which contains a list of notables of the time who had had their genitures or astrological birthcharts drawn up. This list included Maximilian II, his father Ferdinand I, his grandfather Maximilan I, King Christian of Denmark and three of the electors of Saxony. Hans Rosenberger's name appears in this list. The book concerned is a 1546 copy of Albohali's book on judgements of birthcharts. See Lynn Thorndike, *History of Magic and Experimental Science...*, op. cit., vol. VI, p.105

2 This is rendered 'Lobetius' in the Latin of the correspondence manuscript

3 *'Pro illustriss. Principibus Caesareae maiestat. Filiis, qui nunc in Hispania sunt.'* Letter XLVI, reproduced in Dupèbe, *Nostradamus, Lettres Inédites...*, op. cit., p.152

4 *'la nativité de ce Prince & Roy inclite Rodolphe, dans la quelle est contenu amplement & compris beaucoup de grands articles concernant premierement sa vie, santé & disposition de son corps, des substances, voyages, religion, des freres, soeurs & proches parents du sang du pere, de l'Once, ayeuls & bisayeuls, des enfans, des plaisirs & delices & expeditions, des maladies, des serviteurs, du mariage & de quelle famille & nation sera la femme, & en quel temps, & combien de femmes, des ennemis publiques & autres, de la mort & espece d'icelle, & en quel temps & de ce, que les morts lou auront delaissé es regnes, d'hereditès, de poeur, de crainte, de poisons, de voyages, des religions, peregrinations & en quel temps il changera de religion, d'empire, de magistrat; de devotion, de exaltation & de supreme puissance, de ses amis hors de sang, qui seront en grand nombre, des ennemis secrets & occults, de prisons & exilemens & captiveté par voye hostile.'* Appendix I, Dupèbe, *Nostradamus, Lettres Inédites...*, op. cit., p.166

5 At the Royal Library it is known as manuscript D 1343

6 *'Des durchleuchtigisten und hochgebornen fursten und herrn Rudolphs Ertzherczogen Zw Osterreich, Herrn Maximilans, Romischen Königs Erstgebornen Sons und kunfftigem Successores volger dem achtzehenden Julij umbsechs uhr funfundvierzig Minuten nach Mittag Im fünftzehenhundert und zway und funftzigesten Jar Zw Wien in Ostereich under des Pole hoch achtundvierzig grad geborn Aigentliche bescheibung siner Nativität und geburt durch die erfindung, des grads des aufstigenden Zaichens und seiner gantzen bedeutung mitt allem Vleiss ausgelegt und gerechnet durch*

Michael Nostradamum im 1564 Jar.'

7 *Faciebat M. Nostradamus a consiliis medice* [sic] *et mathmatice* [sic] *francorum Regis Salone provinciae 1564 incepto.*

8 Albert Feuillerat (ed.), *The Complete Works of Philip Sidney*, Cambridge, Cambridge University Press, 1912–26, vol. 3, pp.109–14

9 H. Luxemberger, 'Psychiatrisch-erbbiologisches Gutachen über Don Julio d'Austria', *Mitteilungen des Vereins für Geschichte der Deutschen in Böhmen*, 70 (1932), pp.41–54, quoted in R.J.W. Evans, *Rudolf II and his World*, Oxford, Clarendon Press, 1973, p.49

10 ibid.

11 'souveraine Dame et Maîtresse'

12 *Lettre de maistre Michel Nostradamus de Salon-de-Craux-en-Provence. A la Royne mére du Roy.* Lyon, Benoist Rigaud, 1566. The extracts that follow derive from Leroy, *Nostradamus, Ses Origines...*, op. cit., p.101

13 'je treuve quelque briefve prorogation de temps et de lieu, et le tout estre en paix, amour, union et concorde.' *Lettre de maistre...*, op. cit.

14 's'est voulu aventurer d'envoyer á Sa Majesté'

15 'Ce que votre Majesté dira et fera, sera promptement dit, fait et exécuté'

16 [[lui) *mander la figure celeste, astronomique del'an Xiii^{me} du Roy*

17 'pour icelle année, quelque grande et trés félice fortune de paix, longue, en son royaume. Mais qu'elle soyt exactement calculée (cette figure céleste), pour la conférer avec la mienne, et je me parforcerai defaire ce que je me suis tenu, pour mon Roy, mon souverain Seigneur et Maistre: apres que j'auray prié Créateur de tout le monde, vous donner, Madame, vie longue, en santé et toute constante prosperité, accompagnée de l'entier accomplissement des royaux desirs de vostre Majesté.'

CHAPTER 16

'A Strange Migration'

Over a year before his death, Nostradamus was showing signs of a presentiment that his life was soon to end. Following his usual practice, he prepared for Almanac for 1566,[1] the year of his death, early during the previous year, that is, the spring of 1565. But this time his preamble took on a markedly more devotional tone:

> O my Lord, eternal God, Father, Son and Holy Spirit, at this night hour and at this moment on Sunday March 11, 1565, when the Sun makes its entry to the first point of Aries, with hands joined [in prayer], I come to you in trembling supplication. I implore you to have mercy on me, to pardon me, and to open my senses, my memory and my receptivity, so that I can faithfully explain the signs and portents for the present year 1566, according to the perfect judgement of the stars. Grant me a perception pure and serene, far from all earthly chatter, and a spirit purged of all filth and sinful villainy. After which, following the right way of truth, I can make manifest for the French people that which the stars portend for us during the coming year.[2]

Exactly what was ailing him during the last months of his life is by no means clear. Nostradamian authors often describe him as suffering from dropsy or fluid accumulation, which explains nothing, since this is simply a symptom of some more deep-seated problem rather than an ailment in itself. According to César, even at the time of the royal visit in November 1564 his father had needed a stick to help him walk through Salon's streets. Yet as we noted in the last chapter, in July 1565, that is, over seven months later, he was still able to ride over Aix to visit his brother, a round trip of more than forty miles (64 km). Likewise, from his 1566 Almanac he was apparently fit enough in the spring of 1565 to make a night-time climb to the top of the tower at the Château de l'Empéri, Salon's highest landmark. At the start of this

Almanac's prognostication for April he pointedly described himself as 'writing this from the tower of the castle of this town of Salon',[3] following this with a quote from a Latin poem:

> *At the moment when, from far above*
> *– a most beautiful winged omen –*
> *a bird flew to the left [i.e., in augury, to the East],*
> *At that same moment*
> *there rose the golden orb of the Sun.*[4]

It is conceivable that Nostradamus never climbed the Empéri tower's staircase at all, but simply invented this piece of lyricism – the words in any event borrowed from the second-century BC Roman epic poet Quintus Ennius – to refute those of his contemporary critics who alleged that he never studied the stars in the actual night sky. Quite definite, however, is that during the last week of November of 1565 he was becoming seriously and painfully incapacitated. In his letter to Dr Hans Lobbet of December 13, 1565 expressing his sympathy over Daniel Rechlinger's failure to acknowledge safe receipt of the Rudolf horoscope, he remarked how he had suffered considerable physical discomfort throughout the past three weeks:

> Why it should happen I do not know, but the day after Gaspar Flechamar, the civic dignitary from Augsburg, visited me, I became afflicted with such rheumatic pain in my hands that I was not able to supply him with his horoscope on the day that we had agreed. The pains grew worse and went from my hands to my right knee, then into my foot. It is now twenty-one days since I had a good night's sleep...[5]

Hardly helping improve Nostradamus' sense of well-being would have been the awareness that the following day was his sixty-second birthday, marking his entry into his sixty-third year. As he more than most would have realised, numerologically this meant the imminence of his 'climacteric'. Deriving from an ancient and arcane superstition was the belief that certain particularly numbered hours, days, months and years were 'climacterics', or danger points for mortality. Multiples of nine and seven were regarded with particular foreboding, as is evident from a letter of the Roman Emperor Augustus to his grandson Gaius:

> I hope you have celebrated my sixty-fourth birthday in health and happiness. For you see I have passed the climacteric common to all old men, the sixty-third year.[6]

Nostradamus' vantage point for star-gazing? A tower of Salon-de-Provence's Chateau de l'Empéri, which Nostradamus claimed to have climbed the year before his death.

Yet even though there can be no doubt that by the end of 1565 Nostradamus' physical health was a cause of serious concern, equally evident is that mentally he was suffering no impairment. With admirable conscientiousness, during early 1566 he even managed to compose his Almanac for 1567, of which no French version survives,[7] but of which an Italian edition is still extant in the Library of the Jagiellonski University, Krakow, Poland.[8] With an eye to this Italian readership, one section of the Almanac, completed on April 22, 1566, was dedicated to 'Principi Amanuel Philiberto', that is, to Duke Emanuel-Philibert of Savoy. With his wife, the Princess Marguerite of Valois, the Duke continued to be eternally grateful for the now four-year-old son, Charles-Emmanuel, whom Nostradamus had predicted for them.

The Almanac's main section, however, was dedicated to Michel de l'Hôpital's successor as the French Chancellor, René de Birague. An Italian born protégé of the Queen Regent, he was now the acting Lieutenant for the Lyons region, from which the Almanac was published. This dedication Nostradamus completed on June 15, 1566, just seventeen days before his death. According to the text of it as preserved in the Italian-language version:

> To the very illustrious Lord, the Lord of Birague, Councillor of the Secret Council of the King of France, Governor and Lieutenant General for His Majesty in the region of Lyons and of Beaujolais in the absence of the Lord Prince and Duke of Nemours, Michel Nostradamus sends his greetings and wishes for a good and happy life.

In this dedication Nostradamus directly addressed a criticism that theologians had frequently levelled at him, that it was not for humankind to know what the future held. He expressed his full acceptance of Jesus' dictum: 'It is not for you to know times or dates that the Father has decided by his own authority'.[9] He further acknowledged that it was 'impossible to determine anything with certainty',[10] thereby effectively admitting that even his own personal predictions carried no guarantee of accuracy. He was at pains to stress, however, that he had a genuine and unique destiny to warn people concerning whatever it was that the stars threatened for them. Equally strongly, he dismissed as malicious lies the claims of those who alleged that his prophecies derived from some kind of evil or demon summoned for the purpose.[11]

Just two days after completing that dedication, Nostradamus summoned to his house a small but select number of Salon worthies for the purpose of preparing and witnessing his last will and testament. Holding the near-universal belief in the immortality of the soul, people of Nostradamus' time set considerable store by 'dying well'. There was even a popular self-help textbook, the *Ars Moriendi*, as a guide to making the necessary preparations. A key part of those preparations was the death-bed dictation of a last will, which, thankfully, despite the loss of so much other documentary material, is today preserved in the local archives at Marseilles.[12] And ironically it provides us with a closer glimpse of Nostradamus' domestic circumstances and surroundings than anything hitherto gleaned from his earlier writings.

Leader of the group that arrived at his house that seventeenth day of June 1566 was Salon's 'royal notary' Joseph Roche, in whose handwriting the document is likely to have been drawn up. Accompanying him was Nostradamus' long-standing aristocratic friend and neighbour Palamède Marc, a former Consul of the town. Also among those present were Martin Manson, the Consul for that year, the town's treasurer Jean Allegret, councillor Joseph Raynaud, and not least, Friar Vidal de Vidal, the Superior of the local Franciscan friary.[13] Distinguished and influential though these visitors were, Nostradamus almost certainly received them in bed, for as the will specifies, he was at this time 'of great age and kept confined by a certain physical ailment'.[14] Furthermore, as the will also makes clear, at the time Roche drew it up Nostradamus' bed was conveniently situated in the hall, the very location where today's visitors to the Nostradamus Museum purchase their guidebooks and souvenir postcards.

Following the prescribed (and still standard) legal formula, Nostradamus' will established him as being in full command of his faculties.[15] The point is corroborated by the correct description of him in the way he preferred to be styled at this time, as 'Doctor in Medicine and *Astrophile* (literally 'star-lover')',[16] followed by 'Councillor and Physician-in-Ordinary to the King',[17] the royally bestowed titles of which he was so proud.

Confounding those who would see Nostradamus as having been of some unorthodox religious persuasion, the will also establishes him as 'a true and faithful Christian'. Together with the presence of Friar

Superior Vidal de Vidal, an individual who had otherwise not figured in his life story as far as is known, this profession does not seem to have been hypocritical. However, it is a surprise that he should have turned to the local Franciscan Order, given that it had been Franciscans who, nearly thirty years before, had brought charges against him while he was at Agen. In the customary demonstration of this Christian charity Nostradamus decreed that the time of his death should be marked by the distribution of alms to thirteen beggars, in the hardly over-generous sum of six sous each. He further bequeathed one crown to the local Observantines, the strictest branch of the Franciscan Order, and another to the Chapel of Our Lady of the White Penitents. The amounts are indicative that, while he might have conformed to the prevailing Roman Catholicism of the country, he was not exactly one of its most ardent enthusiasts.

In marked contrast, he bequeathed ten gold pistolets of his fortune to his niece Madeleine Besaudine, conditional on her marrying. These minor gifts aside, the entire remainder of his estate was bequeathed to his immediate family, that is, to his wife Anne Ponsarde, and to the three young sons and three young daughters that he had sired by her.

Ironically, it is via the will that we are able to gain some measure of the high regard and affection in which Nostradamus held his wife. The document specifically describes her as 'beloved' or 'well-loved',[18] a description that Shakespeare would later conspicuously fail to summon up for his wife Anne Hathaway. As we know, there is no known record of Anne Ponsarde's date of birth. However, given that she had already been widowed when Nostradamus married her in 1547, by 1566 she is unlikely to have been younger that her late thirties. She was probably not much older either, since the will actually took account of the possibility that she might be pregnant at the time it was drawn up, and might go on to bear further children.

Significantly, Nostradamus decreed that it should be Anne, rather than any of his brothers, who should have the direct management and charge[19] of his family and their inheritance in the wake of his death. He formally appointed her as legal 'guardian and testamentary administratix' of the children and their possessions, providing she kept proper accounts.

He left her suitably provided for, with an estate of 400 gold pistolets, ownership of the family furniture, bedding, cutlery and other utensils. The will affords us a unique peek at the bed which Nostradamus shared with Anne on those nights he was not burning the midnight oil; this item of furniture was fitted with 'mattress cover, mattresses, spring, bolster, tapestry cover...curtains and drapes... also six winding sheets'.[20] By contrast, we find the tableware, also itemised to have been surprisingly modest: 'a half-dozen dishes, a half-dozen plates, a half-dozen porringers, two pitchers large and small, a cup and a salt cellar, all of pewter'.[21] Nostradamus further left Anne his personal 'robes, clothes, rings and jewels',[22] together with the lifetime occupancy of a third of the family home. The one 'male chauvinistic' note was that he made the legacy conditional upon Anne's not remarrying.

To his eldest daughter Madeleine, then fifteen, Nostradamus bequeathed 600 gold crowns, payable the day of her marriage. For his two younger daughters Anne, then eight, and Diane, then five, he left 500 crowns each, again payable on marriage. In the case of his sons, to the two younger, Charles, then ten, and André, then nine, he awarded an inheritance of 100 gold crowns, payable to each on reaching the age of twenty-five. This bequest aside, Nostradamus left the entire, substantial family mansion to his eldest son César, then twelve. This was on the understanding that Anne Ponsarde should continue to have free use of it except if she should remarry, and the younger sons Charles and André would likewise be free to live in it until each of them reached the age of twenty-five.

Clearly concerned about the welfare of his large collection of books and correspondence, Nostradamus specified that these should be inherited by:

> that one of his sons who will profit most by study, and who will have inhaled the most of the smoke of the lamp. These books, together with the letters that will be found in the house of the said testator, the said testator has willed not be catalogued at all, nor placed by their description, but to be tied up in parcels and baskets, until the one who is to have them is of age to take them, and that they be placed and locked up in a room of the house of the said testator.[23]

This is an interesting clause, since here the 'prophet' Nostradamus seemed to be saying that, at this pivotal moment in his life, he could not be sure which of his sons would inherit his mantle. Yet he had made much of his living selling to his clients answers to precisely such questions of the 'what does the future hold for me and my heirs' type!

In Nostradamus' time, with no widely available banking system, people customarily kept their monetary wealth locked away in coffers in their homes. And this was certainly the case with Nostradamus. The will assesses his total fortune as 3,444 crowns, 10 sous, subject to liabilities of 1,600 crowns. This was a very considerable sum, roughly equivalent in today's values to around half a million pounds. Every variety of coin had to be itemised for the will's purposes, and this interestingly shows up a diversity of coin types, reflective of Nostradamus' international clientèle:

> 36 rose nobles, 101 simple ducats, 79 angelots, 126 double ducats, 4 old crowns, two lions d'or in the form of old crowns, a crown of King Louis, a gold metal worth two crowns, 8 German florins, 10 imperials, 17 marionettes, 8 half-crowns, 1,419 crowns, 1,200 crowns pistolets, and 3 gold pieces 'said to be Portuguese' worth 36 crowns.[24]

Amongst these items, 'the gold medal worth two crowns' was almost certainly the one that Hans Rosenberger had given him.

According to the will Nostradamus kept this 'treasure' in 'three coffers or chests' located in his house, the keys to which were held by the two executors, Palamède Marc and Jacques Suffren. Though Suffren was not present at the drawing up of the will, ten years earlier he had been godfather to the Nostredames' son Charles[25] and in the same year acted as a witness to Nostradamus' investment in the Craponne canal scheme. We will also learn later that Nostradamus had cast a horoscope for his son Antoine. So clearly Jacques Suffren too was a close and trusted family friend.

Within two weeks of the lawyer Joseph Roche drawing up this particular will, he and Allegret were back at the Nostradamus house, this time for the drawing up of a codicil. The main witnesses for this were now Antoine Paris, doctor of medicine, Guillaume Eyraud, apothecary, and Gervais Berard, surgeon. With all these being involved in some branch of medicine the strong inference is that Nostradamus' condition had markedly worsened. In these circumstances the codicil's purpose would seem principally to have been to confer upon César, as an addition to all that he had received by the will proper, '...his brass Astolabe, together with his large gold ring with the cornelian set in it'.[26]

Given that César was now notably referred to as Nostradamus' 'well loved son'[27] we may further deduce that, during the preceding thirteen days, something had persuaded him that he should make young César his astrological as well as legal heir, the bequest of the astrolabe and ring being, in effect, his handling on of his magician's crown.

But Nostradamus sprang a further surprise in this codicil – this time with regard to his eldest daughter Madeleine. Again, in addition to her earlier bequest he conferred upon her 'two walnut coffers' located in his study, explaining that in these she would find 'clothes, rings and jewels'. Rather enigmatically Nostradamus insisted that no one else aside from Madeleine should be 'permitted to see or look at that which will be [found] therein'.[28] In the absence of any further information about the contents of these coffers we can only infer that Nostradamus, the fond father, had apparently been quietly setting aside for his favourite daughter a few extra gifts that he wanted no one else to know about. Or perhaps they were heirlooms from his first marriage that he had never brought himself to show Anne Ponsarde.

Such affection and thoughtfulness for his eldest offspring makes all the more marked his omission from the will of other people theoretically close to him, whom he might have been expected to remember in some way. His young brothers and sisters, several of whom were still alive, were entirely excluded. As he seems to have stayed in friendly touch with them (certainly in the case of Jehan), this may simply have been because he deemed them not in need of any largesse from him.

Somewhat more disquieting is the omission of secretary Jean-Aimé de Chavigny, his employee for some five years, who gave legibility to Nostradamus' execrable handwriting. Chavigny figures neither as an executor nor as a witness, nor as a beneficiary of any kind, despite the fact that, according to his own account, he was working for Nostradamus right up to and including the night he died. Possibly Chavigny later exaggerated his closeness to his employer. However, another possibility is that Nostradamus eschewed any kind of 'memento' bequests to those whom he regarded as hired servants and business associates. Printer Pierre Brotot, with his father another long-term associate, was another such individual similarly overlooked. The will is likewise lacking in any token or souvenir bequests to close colleagues and friends of the kind that Shakespeare, for all his deficiencies in respect of his wife, awarded his fellow-actors. Overall the impression is that for Nostradamus, his wife and his own offspring were paramount. And in fairness to him this was an understandable enough attitude, given the extreme youth of his children and his own advanced age.

Weak as he was, Nostradamus summoned the strength to sign the codicil. From study of the original as preserved at Montpellier, the 'M' for 'Michel' can be seen still to resemble closely the way he had signed himself when he had enrolled at Montpellier. But the rest is a tired scrawl, even so clearly forming not 'de Nostredame', but an unmistakable 'Nostradamus'.

It was the seer's last known act of writing. Secretary Chavigny, who appears to have borne his master no grudges, later provided for posterity just a few meagre glimpses of his last hours. What seems to have most impressed Chavigny was Nostradamus' apparent cognisance of

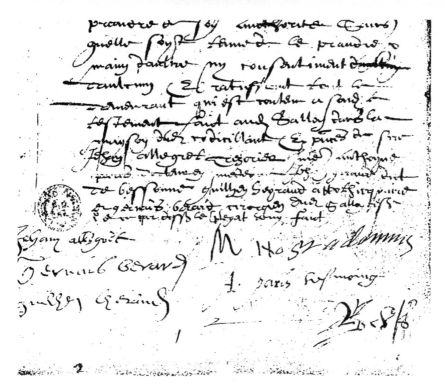

Detail of the signatures on the codicil to Nostradamus' will. From
the manuscript preserved in Marseilles.

the day, and even the time, when he would die. As he later recorded in
his *Brief Discourse*:

> That he truly knew the time of his death to the day, even to the
> hour, I can attest as a fact. I recall clearly that at the end of June of
> the said year [1566] he wrote in his own hand in the *Ephemerides
> of Jean Stadius* these Latin words *Hic prope mors est*. That is to
> say 'my death draws near'. And the day before he exchanged this
> life for the next, I having assisted him for a very considerable time,
> and very late taking leave of him until the next morning, he said
> these words to me: 'You will not see me alive at sunrise.'[29]

Nostradamus was apparently found dead at first light the next
morning, his body already cold. According to the inscription that
Anne Ponsarde later had engraved on his tomb, the day of his death
was July 2, 1566. Characteristically observant of the associations of
any day in the calendar year, César noted this to have been the 'day of
the Visitation, true day of Our Lady [i.e. Notre Dame]'. Amongst
Nostradamian authors, however, much has been made of the fact that
in Nostradamus' Almanac for 1566, prepared over a year earlier, he

had written for July 1 'a Strange Transmigration'. As they have suggested, it is more than likely that he died some time before midnight on July 1, the 'Strange Transmigration' predicted being a prophecy of his own end.

Whatever the answer, Nostradamus had decreed in his will that his burial should be in the Church of the Cordeliers, that is, the church of the local Franciscan friary. Probably he had arranged this some time beforehand with Superior Friar Vidal de Vidal. Indeed, presumably he had also arranged with Vidal the exact placing and the type of his tomb, since he specified that it should be located 'between the great door and the altar of St Martha'[30] and that it should take the form of 'a tomb' or monument constructed against the wall'.[31]

Though César was only twelve at the time, in his later monumental *History and Chronicle of Provence* he recorded the main details of Nostradamus' interment.[32] The corpse was solemnly carried to the 'ancient church of the Friars Minor [Franciscans], to the left of the entrance',[33] where it was laid to rest accompanied by Nostradamus'

> portrait from the life, and his coat of arms, which were gules [red], comprising a broken wheel with eight spokes, composed of two crosses of silver quartered with gold, together with the head of an eagle, in black.[34]

In recognition of Anne Ponsarde's role in taking charge after Nostradamus' death, the inscription on his tomb is historically recorded as having included the line that she had arranged it on behalf of her 'beloved' husband. It was, however, composed in Latin, which it is very unlikely that Anne would have known. Furthermore, it begins with the initials 'D. M.', an abbreviation for *DIS MANIBUS*, 'to the spirits of the dead'. This was a classic Roman formula which Nostradamus undoubtedly came across during his youthful wanderings amongst the Roman gravestones littering the environs of his birthplace St-Remy, since in Century VIII, q.66 of his *Prophecies* we find:

> *When the inscription 'D.M.' is found*
> *And ancient cellar with lamp discovered...*[35]

So did Nostradamus, ever mindful of how posterity would view him, write his own epitaph? As the tombstone inscription went on:

> Here lie the bones of Michel de Nostredame, unique among all humanity in being judged worthy, whose near divine pen described

the future happenings of the whole world as influenced by the stars. He expired at Salon de Crau in Provence in 1566, having lived sixty-two years, six months and ten days. May posterity not begrudge his repose. This epitaph was made by Anne Ponsarde Gemelle, to her beloved husband.[36]

While exactly who composed the Latin of this epitaph is a matter of debate, the source of its inspiration is much less conjectural. As noted by secretary Chavigny (who, for reasons best known to himself, in reproducing the same epitaph omitted the line concerning Anne Ponsarde), its wording was unmistakably in imitation of, or closely modelled upon, the inscription on the tombstone of the Roman author Titus Livy. In 1413, to much contemporary excitement, this had been unearthed at Livy's home town of Padua.[37] It cannot therefore be ruled out that Nostradamus, who probably viewed Livy's tombstone while passing through Padua *en route* to Venice, decided to 'borrow' the quote for his own epitaph, just as he had borrowed so many other quotes for literary and correspondence purposes during his lifetime.

If this were the case it would be difficult not to regard Nostradamus, who never shrank from seizing any opportunity for self-glorification, as having committed the ultimate vanity. Thankfully, however, his son César has saved his father's reputation in this case by suggesting that he himself composed the epitaph, even though he was only twelve at the time. In César's words:

If I had composed this, it would not be from any showing off, or other superfluity of vanity, but as a worthy piece of work, accompanied by a wish to spread further and wider the name of him who brought me into the world, leaving some impression of an excellent and rare honour...He well deserved this niche so small and

Nostradamus' coat of arms, as displayed
on his tomb. After Edgar Leroy.

modest amongst so many other illustrious and magnificent memorial shrines and tokens of immortality.[38]

By the use of the subtle 'if' César left in truly Nostradamian obscurity the question of whether it really was his father who had composed the epitaph for himself, or whether César genuinely did so on his father's behalf. But whatever the truth, during the ensuing decades both César and Chavigny would certainly use every means and opportunity available to them – not always truthfully, and certainly not without a significant degree of self-interest – to spread Nostradamus' memory as far and wide as they possibly could.

NOTES

1 *Almanach pour l'an 1566, avec ses amples significations & explications, composé par Maistre Michel de Nostradame, Docteur en Médicine, Conseiller et Médecin ordinaire du Roy, de Salon de Craux en Provence,* Lyons, Antoine Volant et Pierre Brotot, 1565

2 '*O mon Seigneur, Dieu eternel, Pere, Fils & saint Esprit, à cette heure nocturne & en ce moment du dimanche xi de Mars 1565 ou le Soleil fait son entrée au premier point d'Aries, à mains jointes, je te viens supplier d'une tremblante supplication par ta misericorde me vouloir pardonner & m'ouvrir le sens, la memoire & entendement, afin que je puisse fidellement expliquer les significations & presages de la presente annee 1566, jouxte le parfait jugement des astres, & me veuil les octroyer un entendement pur & serain, eslongné de toute terrienne conversation, & l'ame purgée de toute ordure & vilennie de peché, à fin que suivant le droit sentier de verité je puisse faire entendre manifestement au peuple François ce que les astres nous viennent à presager dans la présente année.*' Nostradamus Almanac for 1566, folio C^2ir, quoted in Brind'Amour, *Nostradamus Astrophile...*, op. cit., p.434

3 '*Escrivant cecil de la tour du chasteau deste ville de Salon...*'

4 '*Simul ex alto longe pulcherrima praepes, Laeva volavit avis. Simul aureus exoritur Sol*', quoted in Brind'Amour, *Nostradamus Astrophile...*, op. cit., p.72

5 '*Contigit nescio quo fato, clariss. D. Lobeti, ut postridie quam Gaspar Flechamerus civis et patritius Augustanus me invisisset, tanto dolore chyragrae detentus sim, ut quae de eius genesi calculanda atque explicanda ei pollicitus fueram, ad praescriptum diem cxcqui non potuerim... Vehementior enim ille dolor de manu insiliit in dextrum genu, deinde in pedem; quae ita affecit, ut pervigil et miserandus totos XXI dies exegerim.*' Letter LI, reproduced in Dupèbe, *Nostradamus, Lettres Inédites...*, op. cit., pp.163–4

6 Aulus Gellius, *Attic Nights*, 15.7.3

7 The abbé Rigaux is known to have possessed a copy at the end of the nineteenth century. This was subsequently reproduced by Henri Douchet in 1904, but has since disappeared

8 *Almanach per l'anno D M LXVII posto per M. Michel Nostradamo Dottor in Medicina et Consigliero del Re Christianissimo.* Mondovi, L. Torrentino, 1567

9 Acts 1: 7

10 *'non che dare certezza della minima parete'*

11 The full text of this dedication is reproduced in Brind'Amour, *Nostradamus Astrophile...*, op. cit., pp.445–6. The Italian translation from which Brind'Amour derived this text is preserved in the Library of Jagiellonski University, Krakow, ref. Matemakya 1397 (Nr inw. 7052)

12 Departmental Archives of the Bouches-du-Rhône (Marseilles), fonds 375E, sigle Salon 2-675-676

13 Also listed as present for witnessing purposes were Joseph Raynaud, described as a citizen, Guillaume Giraud, Arnaud d'Amiranes and Jaumet Viguier

14 *'son ancien eage et certaine maladie corporelle, de laquelle il est à présent destenu'*

15 *'en son bon entendement'*

16 *'Docteur en médecine et Astrophile'*

17 *'Conseiller et Médecin ordinaire du Roy'*

18 *'bien aimée'*

19 *'aucun mainiement et charge'*

20 *'sa baissaque, matelats, coultre, traversier, couverte de tapisserie, les cortines et rideaux ... et aussy six linceuls'*

21 *'demi-douzaine de plats, demi-douzaine d'assiettes, demi-douzaine d'écuelles, deux pichieres une grande et une petit, une eyguedière et une sailiére'*

22 *'ses robes, habillement, bagues et joyaux'*

23 *'...à celluy de ses fils qui profitera plus à l'étude, et qui aura plus de la fumée de la lucerne; lesquels livres, ensemble toutes les lettres missives que se trouveront dans la maison dudit testateur, led testateur n'a vollu aucunement estres inventorissées ne mis par description, ains estre serrés en paquets et banastes, jusques à ce que celluy que les doit avoir soit de l'eage de les prendre et mis et serrés dans une chambre de la maison dud' testateur'*

24 *'...trente-six nobles à la Rose; ducats simple cent et un; Angelots, septante neuf; double ducats, cent vingt et six; escus vieux, quatre; lyons d'or en forme Tescus vieux deux; un escu du Roy Louys; une médaille d'or vallant deux escus; florins d'Allemagne, huict; impérialles, dix; marionettes, dix sept; demi-écus sol, huict; escus sol, mil quatre dix neuf; escus pistollets, douze cents; trois pieces d'or dittes Portugaise, vallant trente six escus.'*

25 Leroy, *Nostredamus, Ses Origines...*, op. cit., p.127, after Baron du Roure, *Notes et documents pour servir à la généalogie des familles provençales*, Marseilles, 1899, p.117

26 *'son Astrolabe de leton, ensemble son gros anneau d'or avecques la corneline y enchâssee'*

27 *'son fils bien aimé'*

28 *'nul puisse voir ny regarder ce que sera dans yceux'*

29 *'Que le temps de son trespas luy fut notoire, mesmes le jour, voire l'heure, je le puis tesmoigner avec verité. Me souvenant tresbien que sur la fin de Juin, ladite année, il avoit escrit de sa main aux Ephemerides de Jean Stadius, ces mots Latins Hic propre mors est. C'est à dire, Icy proche est ma mort. Et le jour devant qu'il est eschange de ceste vie à l'autre, luy ayant assisté bien longuement, & sur le tard prenant congé de luy jusques au lendemain matin,*

il me dit ces parolles, Vous ne me verrez pas en vie au Soleil levant.' Jean
Aimé de Chavigny, *Bref Discours sur la Vie...*, op. cit.

30 *'entre la grande porte... et l'autel de Ste Marthe'*

31 *'faicte une tombe ou monument contre la muraille'*

32 César de Nostredame, *Histoire et Chronique de Provence*, op. cit., p.894
A.B.

33 *'au vieil et ancien temple des Frères Mineurs, à main gauche de l'entrée'*

34 *'son pourtraict au naturel et ses armes qui sont de gueulles à une roue brisée,
à huit rayons, composée de deux croix potencées d'argent écartelé d'or à une
tete d'aigle, de sable'*

35 *'Quand l'escriture D.M. trouvee
Et cave antique à lampe descouverte...'*

36 *OSSA CLARISIMI MICHAELIS NOSTRADAMI UNIUS OMNIUM
MORTALIUM IUDICIO DIGNI CUIUS PENE DIVINO CALAMO
TOTIUS ORBIS ET ASTRORUM INFLEXU FUTURI EVENTUS CON-
SCRIBERENTUR. VIXIT ANNOS LXII MENSES VI DIES X OBIIT
SALLONAE DLXIVI. QUIETEM POSTERE NE INVIDETE. ANNA
PONTIA GEMELLA CONIUGI OPTIMO. V.F.* Quoted in Leroy,
Nostradamus, Ses Origines..., op. cit., p.107, after the transcription given in
César de Nostredame's *Histoire et Chronique de Provence...*, op. cit.

37 Livy's inscription read:
*OSSA.T.LIVII.PATAVINI.UNIUS.OMNIVM.MORTALIVM.
IVDICIO.DIGNI.CVIVS.PROPE.INVICTO.CALAMO.
INVICTI.P.R.RES.GESTAE.CONSCRIBERENTVR*
(The bones of T[itus] Livius of Padua, unique among all humanity in being
judged worthy, whose near invincible pen described the deeds of the invinci-
ble [Roman] Republic.) Quoted in Brind'Amour, *Nostradamus Astrophile...*,
op. cit., p.61, after Théodore Mommsen, *Corpus Inscriptionum Latinarum,
Inscriptiones Galliae Cisalpinae Latinae*, no.2865

38 *'Si j'ai composé cette inscription, ce n'est ni par ostension, ni superflue
vanité, mais par un juste devoir, accompagné d'un désir de jeter plus loin et
plus avant le nom de celui qui m'a mis au monde, laissé quelque trace d'honneur excellent et non commun...Il a bien mérité cette niche exiguë et
modeste tant d'illustres et magnifiques trophées et marque d'immortalité.'*

CHAPTER 17

Gilding the Legend

Nine years before his death, writing the title-page subtitles for his *Great Prognostication for 1557*,[1] Nostradamus grandiosely predicted:

> *In life I am immortal, and in death even more so*
> *After my death my name will live on throughout the world.*[2]

Whatever may be our personal attitude towards Nostradamus' prophetic capabilities, it is undeniable that even with his physical passing the momentum of his self-generated 'futures' industry hardly faltered. Thanks to his diligence in working up to almost his last breath, his 1567 *Almanac* was able to appear virtually complete and on schedule. As earlier remarked, no known original copies of the French edition survive. However, from a single surviving copy of an early twentieth-century reprint[3] preserved in the late Daniel Ruzo's collection this last, posthumously-published almanac is known to have carried a succinct 'Stop Press' message. This informed the readership of Nostradamus' recent demise, offered it as the excuse for any possible deficiencies in the almanac's content, and usefully corroborated Chavigny's later assertion that Nostradamus seemed genuinely to have foreseen the very hour of his death:

> On the second day of last July [Nostradamus] exchanged this troubled and unhappy life for the other, better one, and because of this he could not bring to an end the present prophecy, which he had begun a few days beforehand, and which he pursued with great diligence, having the foresight that the hour of his death was nigh.[4]

Sixteenth-century almanacs, whether by Nostradamus or another writer, by their very nature were designed to be discarded after their year of usefulness, much like today's weekly magazines and annual calendars. Hence, as repeatedly encountered during this book, the very patchy survival down to our own time even of single copies of any one year's almanac.

With what we can perhaps now described as characteristic foresight, Nostradamus left to posterity a publication which, because it looked so far into the future – indeed, as far ahead as the year 3797 – potentially had a much more enduring value: his *Prophecies*. One enterprising Lyons printer, Benoît Rigaud, seems to have very quickly recognised this long-term potential and boldly seized his opportunity. Exactly how and when Rigaud first came on to the scene is unclear. According to Peter Lemesurier's *Nostradamus Encyclopaedia* he had printed Nostradamus' 1565 *Almanac*, but this is an error – the 1565 volume was the work of another Lyons printer with the same Christian name, Benoît Odo.

As noted in Chapter 9, it is possible, indeed more than likely, that it had been Benoît Rigaud who in 1558 had printed the first 'full' edition of the *Prophecies*, long since lost, complete with Nostradamus' rambling letter to King Henri II; also the third and final set of his 'Centuries' up to and including Century X. Because as early as 1560 foreign ambassadors were already quoting certain verses from Century X of this 'full edition', it must have already been published by that date. And as we are about to discover, the very nature of the edition of the *Prophecies* that Rigaud brought out shortly after their author's death suggests either that it was Rigaud who had printed the lost 1558 edition, or that he came to an appropriate business arrangement with someone who had.

For in 1568, that is, within two years of Nostradamus' death, Rigaud brought out a curious two-section edition of the *Prophecies*, the print-run of which must have been quite large, since a substantial number of original copies survives in public libraries and collections in France, principally at Grasse, Châteauroux and Aix-en-Provence (at the Musée Arbaud and Bibliothèque Méjanes), and in Germany at the public library in Dresden. The first section of this 1568 edition, comprising 126 pages and still including Nostradamus' now quaint-sounding original letter to the one-year-old César, falsely described itself as containing '300 prophecies never before printed, newly adjusted by their author'.[5] This statement we positively know to be false, since exactly the same prophecies, accompanied by exactly the same statement, had first been printed nine years earlier in the 1557 edition of the *Prophecies* produced by Antoine du Rosne. As may be recalled, surviving copies of this edition were found only as recently as 1983 in Budapest and Moscow (see Chapter 9, page 117).

The second section of the 1568 edition[6] comprised seventy-six pages, including Nostradamus' now out-of-date letter to the late King Henri II, also Centuries VIII, IX and X. Again the introductory page described these three last 'Centuries' as being printed for the first time. Yet, as earlier remarked, this statement again cannot have been correct, in view of the correspondence of foreign ambassadors which showed them quoting verses of *Prophecies* Century X as early as 1560.

This 1568 edition has long been the *editio princeps* for modern-day Nostradamians, since it is the earliest *Prophecies* to survive. Therefore the only sensible explanation for Rigaud's curious two-section edition is that it was produced as a kind of facsimile amalgam of the earlier 1557 and 1558 editions, the latter otherwise lost to us. Concomitant with this, even editions that were published several decades later would notably carry the same 'never before printed' wording, justifiable again only if they had 'facsimile' status. And certainly despite all Jean and Pierre Brotot's long-standing loyalty, it was Benoît Rigaud who carried the Nostradamian torch forward; in due course it was taken up by his son Pierre, who succeeded to his father's business in 1597, and went on to produce further 'facsimile' editions of his own.

Whatever we may make of printer Rigaud, at least he used Nostradamus' genuine prophetic writings. Just as, during the seer's lifetime, some had published prophecies of their own falsely using his name, so in the wake of his death there sprang up yet more opportunists who did the same. One such fraudster, calling himself Philippe de Nostredame, claimed to be the seer's nephew. He seems principally to have addressed himself to the Italians, since there survives from him an Italian almanac for the year 1566 entitled 'A True Forecast for the Year 1566...by Philip Nostradamus'[7]. This was followed by 'Discourses of the excellent astrologer Philip Nostradamus'[8] published from Bologna in 1575, followed in turn by 'First part of a discourse and forecast by Monsieur Philip Nostradamus'[9] published in 1587.

There is no known Philippe de Nostredame to be found amongst the true Nostredame family. That they themselves were aware of this impostor is apparent from a letter of January 25, 1570 which Nostradamus' brother Jéhan addressed to Scipio Cibo, a relative of the Giovanni Cibo Boerius with whom Nostradamus had been in correspondence in 1557 (see Chapter 8, p.103). In this Jéhan remarked:

As for this so-called Philippe de Nostredame, I don't know who he is and on my life and my honour he has falsely assumed the name of Nostredame, in order that his prattlings should carry more authority.[10]

'Philippe' was far from alone in his activities. Another fraudster, who called himself Antoine Crispin Nostradamus, boldly issued an Almanac for the year 1571 entitled:

> Prognostication with its predictions for the year 1571 composed and calculated for all nine of the world's zones by M. Antoine Crispin called Nostradamus, from Marseilles in Provence, doctor of mathematics, manservant to the King, and physician to the Count of Tende, Admiral of the West. Paris, at the house of Robert Colombel...[11]

The titles 'Antoine Crispin' assumed are nonsense, yet whoever he was, he seems to have had some significant success with this publication, since he quickly and unabashedly followed it up with:

> A verse epistle dedicated to the most high and Christian Charles IX king of France, by M. Antoine Crispin Nostradamus, Councillor, physician and astrologer to His Majesty. Concerning an admirable sign of a comet appearing in the sky, complete with the interpretation of the Ferrara earthquake and the flooding of Holland, Antwerp and Lyons the effects of which will continue to the year 1584.[12]

In 1577 'Antoine Crispin Nostradamus' continued the series with predictions up to 1586, then from 1586 to 1591, then again from 1587 to 1592.

Another of a seemingly endless stream of such tricksters called himself Michel Nostradamus the Younger. 'Michel' began his Almanac and similar predictive publications even before the true Nostradamus' death and then went on producing them for several further years, issuing them just as if he were the true Nostradamus' spiritual heir. In 1574 his predictions 'up to the year 1585' were even being published by Benoît Rigaud, the very printer who republished the true Nostradamus' *Prophecies*. One story told about Michel the Younger is that he predicted the burning of the town of le Pouzin in the Ardèche, only to be caught in the act of setting fire to it in order to fulfil his own prophecy. However, determining the truth of this story is difficult, not least since one 'authority' puts the date for Michel's death as 1574, another as 1629.[13]

What had happened to the Nostradamus family after his death? Amidst these blatant adulterations of her late husband's memory the now twice-widowed Anne Ponsarde quietly and stoically continued looking after her family of six young, and now fatherless, children. As she was fully entitled to by Nostradamus' will, she lived on in the Salon house for a further sixteen years, until her death on July 18, 1582,[14] in her turn being buried in the Church of the Cordeliers next to her husband. She therefore had ample time to see all six of her children safely through childhood and into adulthood, and it was quite remarkable for those plague-ridden times that she lost not a single one of them from illness or accident.

The eldest son and principal heir, César, within a few years of his father's death was noted as pursuing studies in Paris. The same letter from Nostradamus' brother Jehan to Scipio Cibo that reported the false 'Philip' Nostradamus described young César as away 'studying mathematics'.[15] In the sixteenth century 'mathematics' was often used as a synonym for astrology, which suggests that César, following the bestowal upon him of the astrolabe and magic ring, may at this stage have been minded to follow in his father's footsteps. However, precisely thanks to Nostradamus' labours, César had been left a substantial legacy which enabled him to live as a leisured gentleman, and the airs and graces of this status he enjoyed to the full, as his writings make clear. After Paris he went on to undertake further studies at Avignon and Rome, the latter perhaps to develop his talents for music and for painting, since at least one portrait of his father, albeit posthumous, is attributed to his hand.[16] In 1589, seven years after his mother's death, he was in Rome. In 1590 he was back in Salon and came near to death, but was 'miraculously' cured by an excellent physician. Two years later, in company with Salon's First Consul, Philippe de Cadenet, he showed around the town the dynamic young Duke of Savoy, Charles-Emanuel, whose birth Nostradamus had predicted more than thirty years before. César lived on into his seventies. We will return later to the late phases of his career.

Meanwhile Nostradamus' eldest daughter Madeleine, to whom he had accorded the special 'secret' extra bequest, seems amply to have lived up to her father's high expectations for her. She made a very good marriage to the nobleman Claude de Pérussis, baron of Lauris and of Oppède, of whom César wrote that he was 'one of the most accomplished gentlemen of his time, a very excellent player of the lute.'[17] The couple had a son named

Nostradamus' eldest son César, from a portrait in the Hôtel de Ville, Salon-de-Provence.

after his father, destined in adulthood to become attorney for Vitrolles.[18] From surviving documents describing Madeleine as a widow we know that she outlived her husband. Indeed, she reached her seventies, her funeral at Lauris being recorded as taking place on April 7, 1623.

Charles Nostradamus' second son, likewise seemingly made a good marriage, in 1588, at the age of thirty-two, to Louis Becq.[19] The couple moved to the small town of Alleins, near Arles, where two years later Louise produced a daughter, Anne. In 1594 Charles was described by his relative Pierre Hozier as 'Captain of the town of Salon',[20] but he seems to have inherited his father's poetic tendencies, for he was described as 'among the three leading Provençal poets of his time'.[21] Charles too lived on into his seventies, dying in 1629.

Such was the poetic muse in the Nostradamian genes that André, the youngest son, proved to be yet another with such inclinations, being rated as a good poet in Latin and French.[22] He joined the household of France's Grand Prior, Henri of Valois, as one of his gentlemen, but when he was thirty became embroiled in a dispute during which he killed an individual called Cornillon. As a result he was thrown into prison. In the sixteenth century one of the ways that a gentleman could avoid being executed in such circumstances was by taking religious vows,[23] and André, on his late father's birthday in December 1587, duly became a Capuchin friar.[24] Before going off to Avignon for his novitiate, he had one last fling, holding a great banquet for all his local aristocratic friends. As 'Brother Seraphim' he appears to have proved unsuited to monastic life, however, and unlike most other members of the Nostradame family he died relatively young, in 1601, aged only forty-four.

Anne, Nostradamus' second daughter, is known to have married one Pierre de Sève, of Seva, from a notable family resident at Beaucaire in the Languedoc. The couple gave birth to a son, Melchior, but Anne died in her late thirties, some time before 1597. Diane, the daughter who had been at her mother's breast at the time of Catherine de Medici and Charles IX's visit to Salon in 1564, never married, and, following the family tradition, appears to have lived on into her seventies. According to César she was of a somewhat disagreeable disposition, perhaps both cause and effect of her long spinsterhood.

Throughout all the years that Nostradamus' three sons and three daughters lived out their lives, there unfolded some colourful chapters of French history of the kind that their father had at least affected to predict, even if the main events were far to the north, in and around Paris. It may be recalled that Nostradamus, in his letter to Tubbe of May 1562, had confidently prophesied that France's wars of religion would worsen, as indeed they did. In August 1572 César was still in Paris, pursuing his 'mathematical' studies, when there took place one of the worst excesses of this religious strife, the Massacre of St Bartholomew.

Throughout the previous eight years there had been no less than three wars between the Catholics and the Protestant Huguenots, all of which the Huguenots had lost. Nevertheless, whilst Catherine de Medici was still acting as regent on behalf of her son, she endeavoured to maintain some toleration towards the troublesome reformist sect. Not least, she arranged for her unwilling daughter Marguerite to be married to the Calvinist Jeanne d'Albret's son, Prince Henri of Navarre, the young man in whom Nostradamus had reputedly taken such an interest during the royal visit to Salon in 1564. Likewise King Charles IX, on reaching his early twenties, showed a lot of support for the dashing Huguenot leader Admiral Coligny, who was urging France to help the Dutch Protestants in their struggle against Spain.

In August 1572, therefore, the situation was sufficiently calm for the cream of the Huguenots' nobility to feel it at least reasonably safe to come to fiercely Catholic Paris for the wedding of Prince Henri of Navarre and Princess Marguerite. What they could not know was that, behind the scenes, leading members of the ultra-Catholic Guise family had hatched a bold plan to assassinate Admiral Coligny, who rightly or wrongly they continued to blame for Duke François of Guise's shock assassination in 1563. Fearful of the growing hold that Admiral Coligny was exerting over her son, Queen Catherine had secretly acquiesced to this plan. But all began to go wrong when the Guises' hired assassin, who discharged his pistol at Coligny shortly after he left an audience with King Charles, only wounded him. Fearful that her part in the plot against him would come to light, Queen Catherine panicked. She and her predominantly Italian advisers, among them René de Birague, to whom Nostradamus had dedicated his posthumous 1567 *Almanac*, persuaded the easily malleable Charles that Coligny and his fellow-Huguenots had been planning to murder the Guise faction and overthrow the monarchy. They therefore insisted that it was time to act to deprive the Huguenots of any opportunity to carry out such intentions.

With the Paris populace already nurturing a deep hatred for the Protestants it therefore needed little more than for Charles to give the appropriate nod, accompanied by a pre-arranged sounding of the bell at the Palace of Justice, for a full-blooded Catholic slaughter of France's Huguenots to be unleashed. Coligny was first on the hit list, being ruthlessly murdered in his sickbed, his body summarily tossed out of the window. According to some estimates, all around the country tens of thousands died, with only the young bridegroom Prince Henri of Navarre and a few others being spared.

Yet, rather than resolving the situation, the St Bartholomew's Day Massacre only intensified Huguenot resistance. The effect of this was to redouble Catherine de Medici's inclination, in the absence of her revered Nostradamus, to turn to other of the numerous astrologers who lingered around her court. Her support of certain of these is now legendary. One was an Italian, Cosmo Ruggieri, and at the still magnificent royal château at Chaumont-sur-Loire Catherine is said to have built for him a special laboratory or séance room. According to the late sixteenth-century diarist Nicholas Pasquier, it was in this laboratory that there took place a spiritualist-type séance knows as the Consultation of the Magic Mirror, during which Ruggieri reputedly invoked the angel Anael to show the Queen her royal line's future.

As related by Pasquier, in Ruggieri's magical glass Queen Catherine saw the images of her sons as if they had been in a next-door room. The fact that in the British Museum is preserved a similar magic mirror that belonged to the Elizabethan equivalent of Nostradamus, Dr John Dee, adds some credence to the story. As Catherine studied the mirror image, her deceased eldest son, the ill-fated King François II, moved round the room just once, signifying the single unhappy year that he had reigned. Then she saw the present King, Charles IX, move round fourteen times, suggesting that he would reign just fourteen years. Finally she saw her third son Henri move round the room fifteen times, suggesting that he would reign fifteen years. Whatever the truth of this story, a generation later Shakespeare included a very similar scene in *Macbeth* – written for the deeply superstitious King James I of England and VI of Scots – as a prediction of the succession of the Scottish royal line.[25] Furthermore, although Ruggieri's laboratory was demolished in the eighteenth century, even today next to the Bourse du Commerce in the former Halles district there stands a tall observatory that Catherine built for him adjoining the Paris residence, the Hôtel de la Reine, which her architects Delorme and Bullant designed and built for her from around 1572.

Frustratingly, with the exception of Pasquier's reporting, Ruggieri's predictions for Queen Catherine and her sons are so poorly documented that little or no value can be placed upon them. In Nostradamus' case, however, we may recall that in 1564, following her visit to Salon, Catherine had written to the septuagenarian Constable Anne de Montmorency excitedly telling him how Nostradamus had assured her that the fourteen-year-old King Charles IX would live to be as old as he was. Furthermore, Nostradamus had apparently confidently forecast that Montmorency would live on to

The Château of Chaumont-sur-Loire, where Catherine de Medici encouraged Italian-born astrologer Cosmo Ruggieri to conjure séance-type visions of the future.

his ninetieth year. Cruelly, the very different actuality was that Montmorency died only three years later[26] aged seventy-seven. As for the young King Charles, he died in 1574, having reached only his twenty-fourth birthday, one third of the lifespan that Nostradamus had predicted for him.

Utterly dominated by his mother, Charles IX had never been an effective monarch in the manner of his father Henri II and his grandfather François I. Prone to terrible rages, he combined an over-energetic passion for hunting with unspeakable sadism towards animals. There was therefore no great grief, even from Queen Catherine, when uncontrollable haemorrhaging and fevers brought about his ultimately demise. The one problem was that his twenty-three-year-old brother Henri, Duke of Anjou, who earlier had been elected King of Poland, was little better as a successor. When told at the Polish court that the French throne was now his he rode like the wind back to Paris, whereupon as King Henri III he lost little time 'coming out' as a homosexual, dressing up in outrageous fashions and drawing to him a coterie of *mignons* or 'darlings' who dressed equally extravagantly. In 1584 his remaining brother, the Duke of Alençon, died, leaving Henri III as the last surviving member of the Valois dynasty. In view of Henri's

The tall observatory tower that Catherine de Medici had constructed for Ruggieri alongside her Paris residence. Today it stands next to the Bourse du Commerce.

sexual inclinations and the concomitant unlikelihood of producing offspring, the royal line was due to pass to the Huguenot Prince Henri of Navarre. Amongst the pro-Catholic Parisian populace a movement quickly grew to replace Henri III with yet another Henri, the current leader of the Catholic League, the Duke of Guise.

Such a move King Henri, even though he was no Huguenot, simply could not countenance. Having summoned France's Parliament, the Estates General, to the magnificent château of Blois on the Loire, he invited Henri Duke of Guise to join this assembly at a Council meeting. And there, on the morning of December 22, 1588, King Henri had the Duke coldly murdered, and shortly afterwards his Cardinal brother. At the time the seventy-year-old Queen Catherine lay ill in bed in the same château, and when she was told the news she immediately perceived her royal son's terrible political miscalculation. But by now she was too old and too infirm to make any significant protest and within two weeks she too breathed her last.

As King Henri III should have foreseen, but clearly did not, reprisal against him was inevitable. To the fiercely pro-Catholic citizens of Paris the murder of their hero, the Duke of Guise, made the King even more unpopular than before. The Pope, for his part, though he prevaricated, could hardly allow the murder of such a Catholic champion to go unpunished. He therefore formally excommunicated Henri. But it was Guise family's retribution that Henri had to fear most. On August 1, 1589 a Dominican monk was allowed into Henri's presence to deliver a secret letter, while the King was relieving his bowels on a commode. In a flash, from out of his sleeve, the monk produced not a letter but an open dagger which, before anyone could stop him, he drove deep into Henri's lower bowel. Within twenty-four hours the King was dead, whereupon the succession fell to the rightful heir, the Huguenot Prince Henri of Navarre, even though he would have a fierce struggle to establish himself. It may be remembered that, against all odds at the time, Nostradamus had reportedly predicted this succession twenty-five years before, at the time of the royal visit to Salon.

This colourful train of events, coupled with the launch by King Philip II of the Spanish Armada against Elizabeth I's England the previous year, sparked off a rash of reprints of Nostradamus' *Prophecies*. In 1588 the Paris printer Pierre Ménier brought out an edition that was virtually identical to the Rigaud one of 1568, and it proved so successful that Ménier reprinted it the next year. The Charles Roger printing establishment did likewise in Paris in 1589. A Rouen printing house, that of Raphael du Petit Val, joined in the free-for-all. This flurry of reprints continued into 1590, with an edition by Jacques Rousseau of Cahors again reproducing the 1568 Benoît Rigaud edition. Not to be outdone, the now elderly Rigaud himself followed up with reprints which he brought out in 1594 and 1596, after which he gave up his business in favour of his son Pierre.

It was inevitable, therefore, that with so many freshly printed copies of the *Prophecies* flooding the market those who read them would scour them for anything that might have predicted the action-packed times they were experiencing. And they were not disappointed. The diarist Estienne Pasquier remarked of the events surrounding the murder of the Duke of Guise:

> In the 'Centuries' of Nostradamus from the year 1553 there is a quatrain which seemed to predict the emotion which we have seen

The assassination of Henri, Duke of Guise, at Blois. From a contemporary engraving.

during the past year, between the King and the Parisians. And a few couplets after there is another, of which the two verses are these:

Paris conjures the committing of a great murder
*Blois will make the departure to full effect.*²⁷

Pasquier went on:

It reminds me that going to Blois with Monsieur des Marquets, France's Treasurer General at Dijon, one of my greatest friends, we fell on the four verses of Nostradamus:

In the year when an eye will reign in France
The court will be in serious trouble
The great one of Blois will murder his friend
*The Kingdom cast into evil and double uncertainty.*²⁸

And if people in and around Paris were reading fresh, up-to-the-minute significance into some of the forty-year-old verses, it was inevitable that those in the seer's own town of Salon and its environs would not be long in doing likewise. On September 13, 1589 Henri of Navarre's Huguenots were beaten at Mallemort, a Provençal village in the vicinity of Alleins and Vauvenargues, and again at Mount Lubéron, near the river Durance, in a battle in which the Catholic League's famous Provençal supporter Ampus was killed. Nostradamus' son César, now in his mid-forties accordingly noted that his father seemed to have predicted exactly these events in his very first edition of the *Prophecies*, as published in 1555:

On the green fields of Alleins and of Vauvenargues,
Of Mount Lubéron, near to the Durance
A camp in two parts, conflict will be so bitter
My apostasy [i.e. Huguenot movement?] will be enfeebled in
   *France.*²⁹

It was inevitable that anyone in and around Salon who possessed physical memorabilia of Nostradamus, or who retained interesting personal recollections of the seer, would begin to look these out or write them down to exploit their commercial worth. Nostradamus' secretary, Jean Aimé de Chavigny, now in his fifties, appears to have been either allowed by the de Nostradame family to put together or to have assembled for himself a collection of his dead employer's published Almanacs of a comprehensiveness that can only be dreamed of by modern-day Nostradamus aficionados. He carefully gathered and analysed key extracts from these publications in the huge but frustratingly poorly preserved *Recueil* or *Compilation* manuscript, earlier mentioned as rediscovered eleven years ago by Lyons' conservator of antique books, P. Guinard. In 1589, that is, in the immediate aftermath of the flurry of fresh interest in Nostradamus, Chavigny gave this work the title-page:

> A Compilation of Prose Predictions by M. Michel de Nostradame, when he was alive Councillor of the most Christian King Charles IX, and Physician in Ordinary to his Majesty: A work which tells the truth of our age's marvels, in which the eye can see all the history of our troubles and civil wars in France from the time these began up to their end. And not only concerning our own time, but also many other rare and singular happenings that are to come with regard to the most powerful empires, kingdoms and principalities which today hold sway over the earth. Extracted from his [Chavigny's] personal commentaries, and reduced to twelve books by Jean Aimé de Chavigny of Beaune. Grenoble of the Allobrogi ... 1589.[30]

In fact Chavigny would appear to have intended the *Compilation* not for publication, but rather as research notes for other publications that he had in mind. For in 1594 he brought out *The First Face of the French Janus*,[31] consisting of commentaries on the quatrains in the *Prophecies*, with the monthly quatrains that had appeared in the Almanacs. It was also as a preface to this particular work that he composed his *Brief Discourse* on Nostradamus' life which from time to time has been alluded to throughout this book. The fact that, despite his employment as Nostradamus' secretary, this *Discourse* was far from accurate in a number of aspects, suggests that Chavigny had never been quite as close to the seer as he tried to make out. Nevertheless, in his middle age he clearly saw an opportunity to capitalise on the fact that his recollections of Nostradamus were likely to be rather better than those of the family who were still alive (since they had all been children at the time), and he seized this. In 1596[32] and 1603[33] he brought out further publications, interpreting and commenting on Nostradamus' almanacs and *Prophecies*.

Chavigny died shortly after the appearance of the 1603 publication, which he entitled *Pléiades*, and this seems to have been the cue for Nostradamus' eldest son César suddenly to take on a new lease of life. In 1594 Henri of Navarre, after having converted to Roman

Catholicism to win over the recalcitrant Parisians ('Paris is worth a mass', as he famously and cynically put it), had at last installed himself in his capital as King Henri IV. He now set out to become the first truly effective monarch that France had seen since Henri II's untimely death. At this point, in 1604 César, having been a bachelor throughout all of his fifty years, decided upon marriage. In his characteristically flowery style he wrote:

> The god Hymen destined me for the eldest daughter of Jean de Grignan and Jeanne de Craponne – Claire, in name and in fact endowed with a singular grace and beauty.[34]

César thereby married into the same de Craponne family in whom his father had invested so heavily, and so wisely, fifty years earlier. The year after César's marriage the printer Pierre Rigaud brought out in association with Vincent de Sève of Beaucaire – who must surely have been some relation of the Pierre de Sève who had married César's sister Anne – an edition of Nostradamus' *Prophecies* incorporating a collection of poetic quatrains called the *Présages* or Portents. This publication was entitled *The Prophecies of Michel Nostradamus in 10 Centuries, with 141 portents, drawn from those made by Nostradamus from the years 1555 and after, through to 1567, with the admirable predictions for the current years of this century, collected by Vincent Sève, Lyons, Benoît Rigaud, 1568.*[35] Also published at much the same time, again in association with Vincent Sève, but with the printer unnamed, was yet another edition of the *Prophecies*,[36] this in its turn breaking new ground by having as its second section fifty-eight stanzas called Sixains, or six-line verses. This work Sève dedicated to 'the great, invincible and most merciful Prince Henri IV, the living King of France and of Navarre'. But although Sève declared in his dedicatory message that he had 'verified and checked' the sixains, these, like so much other material that surfaced subsequent to Nostradamus' death, are not entirely free of doubt as to whether they truly derive from Nostradamus' authorship.

At this period César had been working for some while on a *magnum opus*, the *History and Chronicle of Provence*, for which the Estates of Provence voted him sums of money between 1602 and 1608. This he published in 1614, a monumental tome of more than a thousand pages printed by Simon Rigaud of the Rigaud family business. Though excerpts and anecdotes which César de Nostredame slipped in to his *History and Chronicle* have provided us with many details of his father's life that would otherwise be lost to us, we have already noted that both he and Chavigny had a tendency to introduce

César de Nostredame, as depicted on the title page of his magnum opus, *History and Chronicle of Provence*.

a lot of mythology and false information.

For the year 1554, for instance, César described how a two-headed child was born in Sénas, just south of Orgon, a small town on the Durance.[37] The child was reputedly brought to Nostradamus for examination, to be followed six weeks later by a two-headed black and white kid, born in the hill village of Aurons to the east of Salon. According to César, Nostradamus presented the kid at a banquet which his friend Palamède Marc, at that time Salon's First Consul, was holding for the Governor of Provence, the Duke of Tende, and other notables. To this assembly's discomfiture Nostradamus interpreted these 'hideous monsters' as 'infallibly' presaging the Wars of Religion that were about to divide France over the next several decades.

Such anecdotes from César were all too transparently designed to gild his father's legend, and they must be taken with more than a pinch of salt. However, this does not excuse the sceptic James Randi, in his supposedly myth-busting *The Mask of Nostradamus*, from having mistakenly introduced myths entirely of his own making in relation to César. According to Randi, César's monumental tome

> was unfinished when César died, and his nephew, another César who became governor of Provence, eventually completed and published his uncles book.[38]

This is quite wrong. There was no 'nephew' called César. The *History* was entirely the work of Nostradamus' son César, who successfully saw it to completion. It was published in 1614 and César lived on for at least another sixteen years after its publication. Randi seems to have confused Nostradamus' son César, of whom there was only one of Nostradamian ilk, with the seer's brother Jehan who, it may be recalled, went to work in Aix as a notary. Jehan, who died in 1578, had written a history of the poets of Provence[39] from which César certainly later drew for his *History*, but both authors saw their respective works through to publication.

Furthermore, posterity has reason to be particularly grateful to César for one other, and arguably paramount, achievement, the preservation of the Latin manuscript of his father's correspondence with Hans Rosenberger, Lawrence Tubbe, Dr Lobbet and others. Without that particular document, innumerable details of Nostradamus' life and thought would have remained unknown to us, just as up to now they have remained unknown to many of my predecessors who have written books on Nostradamus. How that document came down to us therefore deserves its own special place in the Nostradamus story.

NOTES

1 *La Grand' Prognostication nouvelle avec portenteuse prediction pour l'An MDLVII.* Paris, Jacques Kerver, 1557

2 '*Immortalis ero vivus, moriensque, magisque, /Post mortem nomen vivet in orbe meum*'

3 This re-edition was the work of Henri Douchet

4 '[Nostradamus] *a fait eschange de cette vie peineuse et misérable à l'autre meilleure, le second jour de juillet dernier passé et pour ce, ne peut conduire à fin la présente prédiction, que peu de jours auparavant il avait commencée, et avec grand diligence pursuivie, prévoyant assez que l'heure de son passage estoit venue.*'
Quoted on Robert Benazra's Nostradamus website
perso.infonie. fr/nostredame/pronost1

5 '*Les Prophéties de M. Michel Nostradamus. Dont il y en a trois cents qui n'ont encores jamais esté imprimées. Adjoustées de nouveau par ledict autheur*'

6 '*Les Prophéties de M. Michel Nostradamus...Centuries VIII, IX & X, qui n'ont encores jamais esté imprimées*'

7 *Pronostico o vero giudicio sopra l'anno 1566...Philippo Nostradamo*

8 *Discorsi dell'eccell astrologo M. Philippo Nostradamo...*

9 *Prima parte del discorso et pronostico de Missier Filippo Nostro Adamo*

10 '*Quant à ce quidam Philippe e Nostredame, je ne sçay quel il est, et sur ma vie et sur mon honneur, il emprunte le surnom de Nostredame, afin que ses bavarderies soient plus autorisées...*', quoted in Jehan de Nostredame, *Les vies de plus célèbres et anciens poètes provençaux*, ed. C. Chabaneau & J. Anglade, Paris, 1913

11 *Prognostication avec ses présages pour l'an MDLXXI, composée et calculée pour tous les neuf climats de la terre par M. Antoine Crispin dict Nostradamus, de Marseille en Provence, docteur mathématique, vallet de chambre ordinaire du Roy et médecin ordinaire de M. le Comte de Tante, admiral du Livant.* Paris, Robert Colombel

12 *Epistre en vers, dédié au très hault et très chrétien Charles IX, roy de France, par M. Antoine Crespin Nostradamus, conseiller, médecin et astrologue ordinaire de sa Majesté; d'un signe admirable, d'une comète apparue au ciel, ensemble [sic] l'interprétation du tremblement de terre de Ferrare et du déluge de Hollande, Anvers et Lyon qui suyvront leurs effects jusqu'en l'année 1584.* Paris, Martin le Jeune, 1571

13 Leroy, *Nostradamus, Ses Origines...*, op. cit., p.132

14 Leroy, *Nostradamus Ses Origines...*, op. cit., p.130, after César de Nostredame, *Histoire et Chronique...*, op. cit.

15 'César était aux études de la mathématique'

16 This is in Bibliothèque Méjanes, Aix en Provence. It is reproduced in Leroy, *Nostradamus, Ses Origines...*, in the photographic section immediately after the family trees

17 'l'un des plus accomplis gentilhommes de son temps, joueur de luth très excellent.'. César de Nostredame, *Histoire et Chronique de Provence...*, op. cit.

18 Register in Salon, no.58, fol. 60, quoted in Leroy, *Nostradamus, Ses Origines...*, op. cit., p.112

19 Register no.9 fol. 50

20 'Capitaine de la ville de Salon'

21 P.-J. de Haitze, *Vie de Nostradamus*, p.154, quoted in Leroy, *Nostradamus, Ses Origines...*, op. cit., p.128

22 Ibid., p.116

23 In 1598 the English poet Ben Jonson, after killing the bad-tempered actor Gabriel in a duel, similarly escaped execution by claiming 'benefit of clergy'

24 Leroy, *Nostradamus, Ses Origines...*, op. cit., p.128

25 Shakespeare, *Macbeth*, Act IV, scene I, line 119, 'the eighth [king] appears who bears a glass/ Which shows me many more'

26 i.e. in 1567

27 'Paris conjure un grand meurtre commettre,
    Bloys le fera sortir en plain effet.' C.III, q.51

28 *En l'an qu'un oeil en France regnera,
    La Cour sera en un bien fascheux trouble,
    Le grand de Bloys son amy tuera
    Le Regne mis en mal & doute double.* C.3, q.55.
    Quoted from Etienne Pasquier, *Lettres Historiques pour les années 1556–1594...*

29 *Aux champs herbeux d'Allein et du Varneigue
    Du mont Lébron, proche de la Durance
    Camp de deux parts, conflit sera si aigre
    Mes [o]potasie [apostasy?] défaillir[a] en la France.* C.III, q.99.
    This is the text as given in Leroy, op. cit., p.175. Lemesurier in his *Nostradamus Encyclopaedia* gives the first word of the last line as 'Mesopotamie', i.e. Mesopotamia.

30 *Recueil des Presages Prosaiques e M. Michel de Nostradame Lors qu'il vivoit, Conseillier du Roy Treschr[est]ien Charles IX du nom, et Medecin ordinaire de sa Mag^te. Oeuvre qui se peut dire à la verité, Les merveilles de nostre temps, ou se verra à l'oeil toute l'histoire de noz troubles et guerres civiles de la france dez le temps qu'elles on commencé, jusques à leur entiere*

fin et periode non seulement, mais aussi plusieurs choses rares et singulieres advenues et à venir en l'estat des plus puissans empires, royaumes et principautez, qui aujourdhuy levent le chef sur la terre. Extrait des Commentaires d'iceluy & reduit en XII livres par Iean Aime de Chavigny Beaunois. Cularonae Allobrogum M.D.LXXXIX

As the title indicates, the manuscript is divided into twelve parts corresponding to almanacs and predictions for a variety of years – I: 1550–1555; II: 1557, III: 1558, up to XII, the final Almanac in 1567. The work consists of a series of Nostradamus quotes in prose, each in numbered order, with Chavigny's notes on which had come to pass, and which were still to happen. It seems to have been an attempt by Chavigny to record every prediction made by Nostradamus outside the *Prophecies* and to correlate them with known events. As commented by Brind'Amour, 'When restoration makes it accessible this document, with its thousands of extracts, will be one of our principal sources for the study of Nostradamus.' Brind'Amour, *Nostradamus Astrophile...*, op. cit., p.502

31 *Premiere face du Janus François, contenant sommairement les troubles, guerres civiles & autres choses memorables advenuës en la France & ailleurs dés l'an de salut MDXXXIII jusques à l'an MDLXXXIX fin de la maison Valesienne. Extraite et colligee des centuries et autres commentaires de M. Michel de Nostredame...par Jean Aimes de Chavigny Beaunois.* Lyons, Pierre Roussin, 1594

32 *Commentaires du Sr. de Chavigny Beaunois sur les centuries et proognostications de feu M. Michel de Nostradamus...*, Paris, Anthoine de Breuil, 1596

33 *Les Pleiades du S. de Chavigny Paeunois, divisees en VII Livres.* Lyons, Pierre Rigaud 1603

34 'Le dieu Hymen me destina la fille aînée de Jean de Grignan et de Jean de Craponne, Claire, de nom et d'effet, douée d'une singulière grâce et beaute.' César de Nostredame, *Histoire et Chronique de Provence*, p.345

35 *Les Prophéties de Michel Nostradamus en dix centuries, avec 141 présages, tirez de ceux faicts par Nostradamus ès-années 1555 et suivantes, jusques en 1567, avec les prédictions admirables pour les an courants en ce siècle, recueillies par Vincent Sève*, Lyons, Benoît Rigaud, 1568. Note the 'backdating' of the date

36 *Prophéties de M. Michel Nostradamus, médecin du roy Charles IX et l'un des plus excellens astronomes qui furent jamais*

37 For text, from César de Nostredame, *Histoire et Chronique de Provence...*, op. cit., p.775, see Leroy, *Nostradamus, Ses Origines...*, pp.76–7

38 James Randi, *The Mask of Nostradamus...*, op. cit.

39 *Les vies des plus célèbres et anciens Poètes provensaux, qui ont floury du temps des comtes do Provence.* Lyons, Alexandre Marsilii, 1575

CHAPTER 18

Prophecies Fulfilled?

By 1629 Nostradamus' eldest son César had reached the age of seventy-five, no mean age before the inception of modern medicine. Like his father before him, in his old age he remained in full command of his faculties, as is quite evident from some correspondence of this year which survives in the Bibliothèque Nationale.[1] In a letter of February 4, 1629, César told a correspondent called Peiresc that he was in the process of sorting out some old papers. He was contacting his nephew Melchoir de Sève, his deceased sister Anne's son, in the hope of locating a particular 'book of Latin letters'[2] that he wanted Peiresc to have.

On March 20, 1529 a clearly anxious César wrote to Sève, then in Toulon, saying that he had been 'looking in vain for the book of birthcharts' and thought that it must be with him. Invoking what he called 'the power which birthright and blood give me over you', César urged his nephew to put this document into the hands of 'Councillor Mr Peiresc' as soon as possible. De Sève appears swiftly to have complied, for in reply to a later letter from Peiresc acknowledging that the document was now safely in his possession, a very relieved César wrote:

> I have never received a letter that has pleased me more than the one which your manservant brought me yesterday...Nothing could make me happier than to hear that the manuscript of Latin letters has so fortuitously come into hands as worthy as yours. I commend it to you, then, with a solemn prayer carrying the force of an honourable vow, urging you to guard it most diligently, [and] to correct it on any points that might cause offence...[3]

The 'book of Latin letters' and the 'book of birthcharts' were, as we now know, one and the same document. They comprised the Latin manuscript of fair copies of Nostradamus' various letters to and from

Hans Rosenberger, Lorenz Tubbe and others, repeatedly quoted from in the course of this book. A number of the letters were accompanied by copies of the birthcharts that Nostradamus had prepared for these various correspondents, hence the 'book of birthcharts' description. César's intense anxiety to get this document to Peiresc appears to have been prompted by his concern that it be preserved for posterity, in the awareness that his life was rapidly drawing to its close.

For, as is evident from another cache of correspondence between César and his cousin Pierre d'Hozier dating from later in the same year,[4] César had fallen upon hard times. Long-lived though most of his brothers and sisters had been, since the recent death of his brother Charles, César and his unpleasant and unmarried youngest sister Diane were now the only remaining children of Nostradamus and Anne Ponsarde. As a result of his longevity César's once comfortable fortune had been whittled away, so that he was now in need of a pension. His marriage to Claire de Grignan had been childless. To cap it all, late in 1629 plague again began ravaging Provence, whereupon, whether or not he had actually contracted it, his health began to fail.

Accordingly, on January 23, 1630 César had his will drawn up by Salon's notary, M. Tronc, this document apparently being prepared, for unexplained reasons, 'in the refectory of the Capuchin Fathers'. César's instructions were that he should be buried 'in the church of the Friars Minor[5] of Salon...near to his father...with neither pomp nor fasting, hands and feet bound, the face uncovered, and accompanied by fifteen truly poor people each with a white candle weighing one pound'.[6] Exactly when those instructions were carried out we do not know, for this was the last that anything was heard of César in his life-time, and no record was kept of the inscription on his tombstone by which we might have learnt the date of his death.

With César's passing, the aforementioned Peiresc would have been left in charge of the manuscript of Latin letters. Yet all too few present-day Nostradamian authors have troubled to find out who Peiresc was. Peter Lemesurier, for instance, neglected to provide an entry for him in his ostensibly exhaustive Nostradamian 'Who's Who', a strange omission for, as César evidently realised, in the 1630s there were few worthier individuals to take an interest in Nostradamus' prophecies. Born in 1580, Nicolas-Claude Fabri de Peiresc was a seventeenth-century French polymath who, like Leonardo da Vinci took the deepest interest in everything from astronomy to zoology. One feat that he shared with César was his compilation of a history of Provence – in his case a rather shorter version than César's. But perhaps his greatest achievement was the writing of some 14,000 letters, said to be a record for anyone from the seventeenth century, about half of which have survived, scattered in various repositories. Though at the end of the nineteenth century the French scholar Philippe Tamizey de Larroque made a valiant attempt to edit and publish them, his editing skills were less than adequate for such an enormous task and he died long before he could complete it.

Even so we know that Peiresc died in his late fifties in 1637 – therefore within a very few years of his dealings with César – but not before coming to the attention of the theologian Pierre Gassendi, twelve years his junior and with similarly wide-ranging interests. Almost certainly, there would have been discussion of Nostradamus between Peiresc and Gassendi, and it is possible that documented evidence of this may still be buried amongst Peiresc's unedited correspondence. That Gassendi took a significant interest in the now long-dead seer is evident from his work *On the effects of the stars* in which he described what he had learned about the accuracy of a particular Nostradamus horoscope.[7] This derived from a meeting that he had had in Salon with Jean-Baptiste Suffren, son of one of the town's most prominent former judges, Antoine Suffren.

Apparently, some time around the mid-sixteenth century Nostradamus had been invited to cast Antoine's horoscope, when the latter had been but a boy. Well into the seventeenth century this document was apparently still preserved amongst the Suffren family's archives, where it was studied by Antoine's son Jean-Baptiste in the light of what he directly knew of his father's subsequent life and career. It showed the quality of Nostradamus' long-term forecasting to have been highly questionable.

According to Pierre Gassendi, Antoine Suffren had been born at Salon on January 13, 1543, at twenty-two minutes after midday. As we have seen earlier, amongst the data needed for the casting of a sixteenth-century horoscope was the latitude at which the individual was born, and Gassendi expressed some minor criticism that Nostradamus had calculated Salon's latitude as 44 degrees. This Gassendi adjudged to be an error of a third of a degree; in fact by modern-day computations he too had been inaccurate, for the town's true latitude is 43 degrees 38 minutes.

For Gassendi, altogether more serious, however, were the results of a careful comparison that Jean-Baptiste Suffren had made between his father Antoine's life as the facts were directly known to him, and what Nostradamus had predicted when Antoine was a boy. Thus Nostradamus had predicted, 'He will have a long, slightly curly beard'.[8] As Jean-Baptiste attested, Antoine had always gone clean-shaven. Nostradamus had added, 'When middle-aged, he will have brownish teeth'.[9] According to Jean-Baptiste, throughout Antoine's life, right up to his death, his teeth had stayed very white. Nostradamus had said, 'In his old age he will be very stooped'.[10] Jean-Baptiste was insistent that to the end of his life his father had kept himself very upright. Nostradamus had predicted, 'At nineteen years of age, or a little after, he will be enriched by a legacy coming from outside his family.'[11] Jean-Baptiste was totally confident that Antoine had never received any such early legacy, his only inheritance deriving from his father at a later stage. Nostradamus had said, 'He will be ambushed by his brothers',[12] and a little further on in the same horoscope, 'When he is thirty-seven he will be wounded by his half-brothers'.[13] Antoine had been an only child, with no brothers or sisters, and his father had only ever had one marriage. Nostradamus had said, 'He will take a foreign wife'.[14] In actuality, however, Antoine had married a girl from his native Salon. Not least, Nostradamus had predicted, 'At twenty-five years old, under the influence of many masters, he will throw himself into theology',[15] followed by this:

> He will busy himself with natural science more than any other, and also with the occult philosophy, and magic. He will also assiduously devote himself to geometry and arithmetic as well as public speaking, disciplines which he will pursue with extreme zeal and great diligence; likewise the liberal arts which will be his greatest love. Becoming old he will give himself greatly to navigation as well as to music and musical instruments.'[16]

In reality judge Antoine had never thrown himself into theology, nor had he ever dabbled in occult philosophy, nor did he have musical inclinations, nor did he ever become interested in navigation. The law, its theory and practice was the subject to which he had devoted virtually his entire life, an all-important fact which Nostradamus had singularly omitted even to hint at. Nor did Nostradamus suggest anything of Antoine's taking a post with the Parlement at Aix at the early age of twenty-five. Finally, whereas Nostradamus had predicted that Antoine would not live 'beyond his seventy-fifth year',[17] he did not in fact even reach the age of fifty-four, dying in 1597. Small wonder, therefore, that with commendable understatement Gassendi concluded of Nostradamus: 'It is difficult to understand the confidence that is accorded to this man's prophecies'.[18]

Gassendi's forthright, down-to-earth analysis, as derived from Jean-Baptiste's data, represents an outstanding example of an individual, even as early as the seventeenth century, adopting a thoroughly scientific approach to Nostradamus' predictions, and for very good reasons finding them seriously wanting. But this approach was all too rare, since among the populace at large there had grown sufficient momentum in favour of according him true powers of prophecy for such considerations to be brushed aside. Thus, whenever a crisis dawned, there repeatedly arose a corresponding urge to look to Nostradamus' prophecies for guidance on what might happen next. Even when the nearly one thousand of his published quatrains were found wanting, there were always some enterprising characters more than ready to invent new ones in the seer's name, to suit their own particular propaganda purposes.

While domestically France enjoyed a relatively settled period under King Henri IV, which continued even after the King's assassination in 1610, crisis loomed again in 1649. This was actually the start of what would be a long and illustrious reign for the 'Sun King', Louis XIV. At this stage, however, Louis was still a minor; all political power had passed from the wily Cardinal Richelieu to his equally loathed successor Cardinal Jules Mazarin, as a result of which the country erupted into a bitter civil war known historically as the Fronde. The Frondeurs, who opposed Mazarin, arranged for the printing in Paris of an edition of Nostradamus' *Prophecies* that was falsely dated to 1568, and was equally falsely supplied with two hitherto unknown quatrains all too transparently directed against Mazarin. One of these was particularly explicit:

> *When Innocent holds the place of Peter*
> *The Sicilian Nizaram* [anag.: Mazarin] *will see himself*
> *In great honour, but afterwards he will fall*
> *Into the welter of a civil war.*[19]

There is absolutely no doubt that these quatrains were Frondeur forgeries concocted in a convincing imitation of Nostradamus' style. The Pope directly contemporary with Mazarin's period of power was Innocent X. The anagram 'Nizaram' by which Mazarin's name is conveyed corresponds closely to Nostradamus' usage in calling Paris 'Rapis' in Century VI. Furthermore, the quatrain's 'Cicilien' or Sicilian, as a description of Mazarin's roots, had a clever subtlety to it. While Mazarin, whose original name was Giulio Raimondo Mazzarino, was actually born at Pescina, to the east of Rome, his father Pietro had been a Romanised Sicilian. And even though Mazarin soared to become holder of France's highest office next to that of the king, he spoke French with such an atrocious accent that pamphleteers of the time loved to ridicule him for it in their so-called Mazarinades.[20]

Such was the continued reputation that the name of Nostradamus

Cardinal Jules Mazarin. His 17th century political opponnts invented 'Nostradamus' prophecies in his name for propaganda purposes. From a pastel by Vaillant in the Albertina Collection, Vienna.

enjoyed that the Frondeur's invocation of it as anti-Mazarin propaganda proved highly effective. To this day, copies of the fake 1568 edition of the *Prophecies* are disproportionately common compared to other early editions, including the version that had truly been printed in 1568.

Nor was France the only country to be hanging unquestioningly on to the predictions of astrologers and fortune-tellers. A little earlier, in 1642, England had succumbed to its own Civil War against the absolutism of King Charles I, and this crisis in its turn sparked off a wave of astrological fervour. In modern-day books and encyclopaedias of the so-called paranormal, 'Mother Shipton' is usually identified as a Yorkshirewoman who lived around the time of Henry VIII and Cardinal Wolsey, therefore early in the sixteenth century.[21] In fact, however, since she is completely unheard of before 1641 she seems to have been the invention of someone from this period of the seventeenth century, arguably in order to capitalise on the national uncertainty.[22] It was specifically in 1642 that English newspapers, which had begun their very existence only two decades earlier (and not yet as dailies), began publishing the first astrological predictions[23] as predecessors of the 'stars' section that is so popular today.

For England at this period, Nostradamus' living equivalent was William Lilly who, whatever his true astrological validity, had achieved a huge popular following, and whose propaganda value for the Parliamentarian or anti-Royalist side, which he favoured, was enormous.[24] In 1644 Lilly produced his first almanac, *Merlinus Anglicus Junior, the English Merlin revived*, which publication, just like Nostradamus with his annual almanacs, Lilly then continued every year to his death, at the ripe old age of seventy-nine, in 1681. It was said that if the ill-fated King Charles I had ever been able to persuade Lilly to switch his allegiance 'he [Lilly] would have been worth more than half a dozen regiments',[25] but this was not to be. Though the Royalists actually had their own morale-boosting astrologer in the person of one John Humphrey, the hollowness of the latter's predictions became all too apparent when their army was defeated at the siege of Colchester, following which Humphrey rapidly faded into obscurity.

With no Nostradamus almanacs annually published in English, and with Nostradamus' main enduring work, the *Prophecies*, remaining as yet untranslated, knowledge of the seer and his predictions was bound to be very limited among the English general public during the Civil War period. However, a major revival of English interest in Nostradamus was not far off. This was because he became associated with the prediction of two major events in English history which occurred around the middle of the seventeenth century, the execution of King Charles I in 1649, and the Great Fire of London, some seventeen years later. In the case of the Fire, initially it was not Nostradamus but the fictional Mother Shipton who was accredited with having foreseen it. According to the famous diarist Samuel Pepys, when the news of the Fire was brought to Charles I's nephew Prince Rupert, all the Prince said was that 'now Shipton's prophecy was out'.[26]

But on October 3, 1666 a letter written from the Middle Temple, and preserved in the Bodleian Library,[27] made some percipient comments specifically linking verses from Nostradamus' *Prophecies* to recent events:

> We have now (as tis usual in all extraordinary accidents), several prophecies started up: none more remarkable than that of Nostredame a Frenchman who wrote a *Book of Prophecies* above an hundred years since & therein exactly predicted (Cent[urie] 9, st[anza] 49), the Parliament putting our King to death...[28]

Century 9, quatrain 49 of Nostradamus' *Prophecies* reads in its original French: '*Senat de Londres mettront à mort leur roy*', that is: 'The Senate [i.e. Parliament] of London will put their King to death'.

As even sceptics must acknowledge, this is a quite remarkable statement, given that in 1649, by coincidence or not the same year as the number of the quatrain, the Cromwellian Parliament or 'Senate' had staged King Charles I's public beheading in Whitehall. And Nostradamus' apparent prophecy of this had been committed to hard print almost certainly in 1558 and absolutely no later than 1568.

But this was not all. As the Middle Temple letter-writer went on:

> & in his book (Cent[urie] 2nd, Stanza 51), [Nostradamus] hath this:
> *Le Sang du Just a Londres fera haute*
> *Brusle par foudres de vignt* [sic] *trois les six*
> *La Dome Antique cherra de place haute*
> *De mesme sect plusieurs serront occis*

A reasonably accurate transcription from Century II, quatrain 51 of Nostradamus' *Prophecies*, this may equally reasonably be translated as:

> *The blood of the just will be demanded from London*
> *Burned by fireballs in thrice twenty and six*
> *The Old Cathedral shall fall from its high place*
> *And many [buildings?] of the same sect will be destroyed.*

In Nostradamus' *Prophecies*, this quatrain is the sole reference to a London fire. So the fact that it should be associated with a year ending in sixty-six is undeniably intriguing even on its own, given that throughout London's long history the only truly devastating fire was in 1666, exactly a century after Nostradamus' death. The Great Fire broke out on Sunday September 2, after what had been an unusually hot, arid summer, with London's timber houses all tinder-dry. Over the next five days it spread to destroy 13,000 houses, 87 churches, 52 company halls and much else. A huge proportion of the existing city including the Old St Paul's Cathedral, was reduced to blackened ruins. The destruction of the 'Old Cathedral' was undoubtedly the Great Fire's most spectacular casualty, being featured in all the main contemporary woodcuts depicting the disaster.

There should be a little surprise, therefore, that just two years after the Fire, in 1668, a new French-language edition of the *Prophecies* was published from Amsterdam.[29] This displayed on its title-page images of the beheading of Charles I in 1649 and the Fire of London of 1666, just as if Nostradamus had predicted these events. It also carried a portrait of him accompanied by a Latin inscription translatable thus: 'It is truth I speak, not falsehoods. It is not I who speaks, but God by gift from on high.'[30]

Four years later, J. de Jant, bookseller to Louis XIV's brother, brought out a new French interpretative edition of the *Prophecies*. The title of this may be translated as 'Predictions drawn from the Centuries of Nostradamus which truly can be applied to the present time and to the war that will break out between France and England versus the United Provinces'.[31] Up to this point Nostradamus' *Prophecies* had never been translated into English. Now, however, arguably because of the recent apparent fulfilment of two of the seer's predictions pertaining to England, an English-language edition was not slow in forthcoming.

By way of a curtain-raiser, in January 1671 there appeared a satirical poem entitled 'An Ancient Prophecy written originally in French by Nostradamus and now done into English'.[32] Wrongly ascribed to the English poet Andrew Marvell, this poem's true authorship is unknown, but it began:

The blood of the Just London's firm Doome shall fix
And cover it in flames in sixty six;
Fireballs shall flye and but few see the traine
As far from Whitehall to Pudden Lane...[33]

Hot on the heels of this, there followed in 1672 *The true Prophecies or Prognostications of Michael Nostradamus, Physician to Henry II, Francis II and Charles IX, Kings of France and one of the best Astronomers that ever were. A work full of Curiosity and Learning, translated and Commented by Theophilus Garencieres, Doctor in Physik Colleg. Lond.* For the first time this publication made available in English the entire text of the *Prophecies* plus translations of the prefaces addressed to César and Henri II. The translator was the sixty-two-year-old Theophilus Garencières, a French-born physician who had taken a degree at Oxford in 1657. In 1665, during the Great Plague of London, in true Nostradamian manner he had already published an English-language book of prescriptions for how to ward off the disease. Now Garencières made Nostradamus available to the general English public for the first time. As part of his Introduction to the *Prophecies*, he recalled how during his early seventeenth-century childhood this work was used as a basic French

Title page of the 1668 edition of Nostradamus Prophecies, printed in Amsterdam. The images of Charles I's execution in 1649 and the Great Fire of London in 1666 show that contemporaries accredited Nostradamus with having predicted both these events.

reader in schools – remarkable given the obscurity of many of Nostradamus' expressions, even to those for whom French is their first language. Garencières, also noted a number of textual errors that had crept in over the years, though being human he went on to make more than a few of his own.

His work would seem to have attracted widespread attention, for there quickly followed at least another four editions published during the next nineteen years.[34] Likewise the antiquary John Aubrey, who assembled numerous jottings on individuals of note up to his death in 1697, remarked that copies of Nostradamus' 'Centuries' had become common in his time.[35] And in 1681, when England was reverberating with the Popish Plot and Exclusion Crisis, and Charles II, despite his legendary philandering, had produced no legitimate heir (though plenty of illegitimate ones), a pamphlet was put about entitled *Great and Joyful news for England: or, the Prophecy of the renowned Michael Nostradamus that Charles II ... shall have a son of his own body*.[36] As an interpretation of a Nostradamus prophecy it proved without substance, for Charles' long-suffering Queen Catherine of Braganza, already forty-three, remained barren. However, it showed that in the late seventeenth-century England the name Nostradamus had once again become a household word, just as it had in the sixteenth century.

Not unexpectedly in the light of the troubled circumstances around 1688 – when amongst great international uncertainty the Dutch William of Orange was invited to take the English throne – there was a flurry of further publications of the *Prophecies* in continental Europe. In France alone new editions appeared in Paris in 1668 and 1669; in Rouen and Cologne in 1689, and in Lyons in 1697 and 1698. In 1693 B. Guynaud, governor of the pages attendant upon Louis XIV, brought out a *Concordance between Nostradamus' Prophecies and History*,[37] in which he analysed what he interpreted as the fulfilment of nearly 120 of the quatrains. Even Nostradamus' tomb in the Church of the Cordeliers at Salon was becoming quite a tourist attraction, an unidentified traveller from near Clermont-Ferrnad describing how in June 1688, after attending mass in the church, he had viewed:

> ... the epitaph of Michel Nostradamus, physician and very celebrated Montpellier doctor, born at Saint-Rémy and who died at Salon in the year 1566. His portrait as made by his son César Nostradamus, who was almost as talented as his father, is on his tomb. His wife and children are buried by his side in the church.[38]

Then, despite the oft-quoted claim that Nostradamus has never been out of print since his lifetime, there passed nearly a century without any significant Nostradamian publication. But it was always in times of the greatest crisis that interest in Nostradamus' prophecies intensified. Given that, it should come as no surprise that when he next surfaced it was at that great turning-point of French history, the French Revolution of 1789.

Curiously, from the viewpoint of sceptics, several astrologers who lived well before Nostradamus' birth had billed 1789 as likely to be a particularly momentous year. In the tenth century the Arab astrologer Albumasar had noted that it would feature one of the great conjunctions of Saturn, indicating that it was likely to be marked by some great social upheaval.[39] Albumasar was followed by the fifteenth-century French Cardinal Pierre d'Ailly who in his *Image of the World*,[40] the manuscript of which is preserved in the Douai library, predicted:

> ... numerous great and astonishing alterations and transformations of the world, particularly as concerns the law and religious sects, will take place in the year 1789.[41]

The early sixteenth-century astrologer Pierre Turrel of Autun, who was brought before the Parlement of Dijon on charges of sorcery, effectively repeated the Albumasar and d'Ailly predictions for 1789, remarking:

> Let us speak of ... the marvellous conjunction which astrologers say occurs about the year 1789, with ten revolutions of Saturn, and moreover twenty-five years later will be the fourth and last station of the altitudinary firmament. All these things considered and calculated, the astrologers conclude that if the world lasts until then (which is known to God), very great and remarkable changes and alterations will be in the world, especially concerning sects and laws.[42]

As noted earlier in this book, Nostradamus for the most part studiously avoided putting exact years to any of his prophecies, and no equivalent to Albumasar's, d'Ailly's or Turrel's predictions for 1789 is to be found anywhere in his surviving writings. The only 'French Revolution' year which he did single out, and in this instance quite explicitly, was 1792. In his Letter to Henri II, which originally prefaced the lost 1558 edition of his *Prophecies*, he predicted:

> great persecution of the Christian Church, more than that which has been wreaked in Africa, will last until 1792, following which there will be a new age.[43]

This is rather strange, given that in 1793 French Revolutionaries per-petrated huge destruction upon churches throughout France, including the Church of the Cordeliers, where Nostradamus and his family were buried. According to the nineteenth-century local historian Louis Gimon, a detachment of revolutionary troops billeted at Salon, in the course of wreaking general mayhem upon the historic old church, deliberately smashed open Nostradamus' tomb and scattered the seer's remains. Reputedly one trooper even dared to show off by drinking from the skull, dying an unpleasant death, it is chillingly reported, a few weeks later. The only way that the mayor of the time, citizen David, managed to restore order was by claiming that Nostradamus had predicted the 'Liberty' that they had achieved. He was thereby able to gather up whatever bones he could retrieve, and subsequently to transfer them to their present resting-place in the church of St Laurent.

But, as repeatedly insisted by Nostradamus devotees from at least as early as the time of the Revolution, a number of quatrains from the *Prophecies* seem unmistakably to be sixteenth-century predictions of events that were fulfilled during its course. Most famous of these is quatrain 20 of Century IX.

> *By night will come through the forest of Reines*
> *A married couple, by a devious route*
> *Herne, the white stone, the black monk in grey, into Varennes*
> *The elected Cap[et?]. The result will be tempest, fire, blood – and*
> *cutting off.*[44]

Book after book on Nostradamus has interpreted this quatrain, from the final section of the *Prophecies* produced in 1558, as a prediction of King Louis XVI's and Queen Marie Antoinette's ill-fated attempt to escape the revolutionary mob. The historical facts are that under cover of darkness on the night of June 20, 1791 the King and Queen, wearing hoods as disguise, slipped out of a side door of the Palace of the Tuileries, climbed into a pre-arranged royal coach, and headed north-east by a cross-country route in the hope of reaching a loyal gar-rison of troops at the French border. To their misfortune they were recognised at the tiny town of Varennes, detained, and thereupon forcibly returned to Paris. There, nineteen months later, Louis was famously decapitated under the blade of the guillotine, followed a little later by his wife.

The undeniably spooky aspect to this quatrain is that in all France's rich history, and amongst all the tens of thousands of French place-names, Varennes' sole claim to fame is as the stopping-place of the

The ill-fated King Louis XVI and his Queen Marie Antoinette,
from their tomb sculpture in the basilica of St Denis, Paris.
According to Nostradamians, Nostradamus predicted their execution.

fleeing royal couple that ill-fated night. As a descendant of the original
Merovingian king Hugh Capet (AD 987–96) it was legitimate for King
Louis XVI to be poetically described as a Capet. By dint of the special
circumstances of the Revolution, he was the only French king to have
been elected as such by the National Assembly. And the quatrain's
final word *'tranche'* – 'cut off' – could hardly have more appositely
described the tragic fate of Louis and his Queen.

Amongst those living during the period who saw this and a number
of other Nostradamus quatrains as predictions of the Revolutionary
events was Théodore Bouys. A mathematics professor from Nevers, in
1806 he brought out a work that he grandiloquently entitled *New
Considerations Drawn concerning Mankind's Instinctive Clairvoyance, on Oracles, Sibyls and Prophecies, and particularly on Nostradamus*.[45] Buoys explained how the significance of the 'Varennes'
quatrain had first been pointed out to him by another Nevers
resident, M. de Vaudeuil. The son of a former president of Toulouses's
Parlement, Vaudeuil had convinced him that it was indeed the
events of the French Revolution that Nostradamus had so eerily
foreseen.

In this light, therefore, we should not be surprised that the year
1792 saw a rush of fresh editions of the *Prophecies*, thereby fuelling a
new round of Nostradamian fervour. Nor should we be surprised that
much the same pattern would be repeated with the next major episode

of French history, following hot on the heels of the French Revolution, the meteoric rise of Napoleon Bonaparte.

NOTES

1 Bibliothèque Nationale BN ms. Fr. 9538, fol. 180 r to 102 v. See Philippe Tamizey de Larroque (ed.), *Les correspondants de Peiresc II: César de Nostredame, Lettres Inédites, écrites de Salon à Peiresc en 1628–9*, Marseilles, 1880

2 '*tome des Epistres latines*'

3 '*Je nay jamais receu lettre qui m'ayt plus contenté que celle que vostre laquay me rendit hier… ny de vray nouvelle plus heureuse qu d'avoir appris que le manuscrit des Epistres latines soyt tumbé par une si bonne fortune en si dignes mains que les vostres. Je vous renvoye donc aveq une solennelle priere qui aye force d'une honnorable conjuration de le garder, inviolablement, le traitter et corriger sur les points qui pourroynt continir en eux quelque aigreur …*' Quoted in Dupèbe, *Nostradamus, Lettres Inédites…*, op. cit., p.11, after Philippe Tamizey de Larroque (ed.), *Les correspondants…*, op. cit.

4 Quoted in Leroy, *Nostradamus, Ses Origines…*, op. cit., p.123, after Mouan, in *Mémoires de l'Académie d'Aix*, t.X, 1873, p.470

5 i.e. Franciscans

6 '*dans l'église des Frères Mineur de Salon… près de son père… sans pompe ni faste, les mains et les pieds liés, en criminel, le visage descouvert… accompagné de quinze vrays pauvres avec chachun un cierge blanc d'une livre.*' Quoted in Leroy, *Nostradamus, Ses Origines…*, op. cit., p.124, n.1 after Bibliothèque Nationale, f.fr. 4332, fol. 89–93

7 Petrus Gassendi, *De effectibus siderum*, in the six volumes of collected works of the same author, *Opera omnia*, published in Lyons, 1658, V, pp.745–6. The relevant extract appears in Pierre Brind'Amour's *Nostradamus Astrophile…*, op. cit., pp.467–70

8 '*Il aura la barbe longue e un peu frisée*'

9 '*Sur le midi de son âge, il aura les dents brunâtres*'

10 '*Dans sa vieillesse il sera si courbe*'

11 '*À 19 ans ou à peu près, il s'enrichera d'un héritage venu d'ailleurs*'

12 '*Il souffrira des embûches de ses frères*'

13 '*à 37 ans il sera blessé par ses frèrs utérins*'

14 '*il prendra femme à l'étranger*'

15 '*À 25 ans, sous l'influence de plusieurs maîtres, il se lancera dans la théologie*'

16 '*il s'occupera des sciences naturelles plus qu'aucan autre, et aussi de la philosophie occulte, par la magie; il se consacrera aussi assidúment à la géometrie et l'arithmétique qu'à l'art oratoire, disciplines qu'il poursuivra avec un zèle extreme, et une prompte diligence: arts libéraux (qu'il poursuivra) avec le plus grand amour*'

17 '*il ne passera pas la 75ᵉ année de son âge*'

18 '*on peut comprendre par là quelle confiance accorder aux vaticinations de cet homme*'

19 '*Quant Innocent tiendre le lieu de Pierre*

Le Nizaram cicilien se verra
En grands honneurs mais apr`es il cherra
Dans le bourbier d'une civille guerre'

20 For example: '*C'est merveille comme il dégoise*
Quand il veut en langue Françoise
Il sait fort bien dire 'Buon jour
Comme vous portez-vous, Moussour?'
– one of the 'Mazarinades' preserved in a twenty-volume collection in the Taylorian, Oxford

21 See for example Justine Glass, *The Story of Unfulfilled Prophecy*, London, Cassell, 1969, pp.132–9

22 W.H. Harrison, *Mother Shipton, The Yorkshire Sibyl Investigated, The Results of a Critical Examination of the Extant Literature Relating to the Yorkshire Sibyl*, Reissue by Holmes Publishing Group, 2001

23 J. Frank, *The Beginnings of the English Newspaper, 1620–60*, Cambridge, Massachusetts, 1961, pp.177, 212, 215, etc

24 H. Rusche, '*Merlini Anglici*, astrology and propaganda from 1644 to 1651', *English Historical Review*, LXXX, 1965

25 Keith Thomas, *Religion and the Decline of Magic*, Oxford, Oxford University Press, 1997, p.343, after *The Late Storie of Mr. William Lilly*, p.7

26 Samuel Pepys, *Diary*, October 20, 1666. See also W.G. Bell, *The Great Fire of London*, Westport, Connecticut, Greenwood Press, 1971, reissue of edition of 1923, p.316

27 Gough MS London 14

28 Quoted in H.M. Margoliouth (ed.), *The Poems and Letters of Andrew Marvell*, 2 vols., Oxford, Clarendon Press, 1927, pp.292–3

29 *Les Vrayes Centuries et Prophéties de Maistre Michel Nostradamus*, printed by Jean Jansson

30 *Vera loquor, nec falsa loquor, sed munere coeli*
Qui loquitur Deus est, non ego Nostradamus.
In Leroy, *Nostradamus, Ses Origines...*, op. cit., p.159

31 *Prédictions tirées des Centuries de Nostradamus qui vraysemblement se peuvent appliquer au temps présent et à la guerre qui va commencer entre la France et l'Angleterre contre les Provinces Unies*, 1672

32 'An Ancient Prophecy written originally in French by Nosterdam [*sic*] & now done into English', January 6, 1671

33 H.M. Margoliouth (ed.), *The Poems and Letters of Andrew Marvell*, op. cit., p.170

34 According to Keith Thomas in *Religion and the Decline of Magic*, 'Wing lists five publications of Nostradamus' prophecies between 1672 and 1691' – citing H.M. Margoliouth (ed.), *The Poems and Letters of Andrew Marvell*, op. cit., pp.292–3

35 John Aubrey's jottings became the famous *Brief Lives* as edited by Anthony à Wood. Aubrey's reference to Nostradamus is noted, regrettably without source details, in Laver, *Nostradamus or the Future Foretold*, op. cit., p.242

36 Keith Thomas, *Religion and the Decline of Magic*, op. cit., p.415

37 *Concordance des Prophéties de Nostradamus avec l'Histoire*, Paris, Jacques Morel, 1693

38 A Marignan, 'Quelques notes sur le midi de la France par un voyageur de Vice-le-Comte en 1688', *Mém. Acadèm. de Nîmes*, 1902, p.41

39 Albumaser, *De Magnis Conjunctionibus*, Tract ii, Diff. 8, quoted in Charles Ward, *Oracles of Nostradamus*, London, Leadenhall Press, 1891

40 *Imago Mundi*

41 Quoted in Baron de Novaye, *Aujourd'hui et Demain*, Paris, P. Lethielleux, 1934

42 'Or laissons à parler des chouses faictes, et que ont fact, que quasi tous hommes sçavent, s'ilz ne sont ignorants, et parlongs de la huictiéme maxime, et merveilleuse coniunction que les astrologues disent estre faicte environ lers ans de Notre Seigneur mil sept cens octante et neuf, avec dix revolutions saturnelles; et oultre vinct-cinq ans après sera la quatrième et dernière station de l'altitudinaire si le monde iusques-là dure (qu'est à Dieu tant congneu) de tres-grandes et admirables mutations et alterations seront au monde: mesmes des sectes et des loix.' From Turrel's *La Période, c'est-a'dire la fin du monde, contenant la disposition des chouses terrestres par la vertu et influence des corps celestes*, quoted in Laver, op. cit., p.139

43 *...plus grande persecution à l'Eglise Chrestienne, que n'a esté faicte en Afrique...durera...jusques à l'an mil sept cens nonante deux que l'on cuidera estre une renovation du siecle*

44 *De nuict viendra par la forest de Reines
Deux pars vaultorté Herne la pierre blanche
Le moine noir en gris dedans Varennes
Esleu cap, cause tempeste feu, sang tranché*

45 *Nouvelles Considérations puisées dans la Clairvoyance Instinctive de l'Homme, sur les Oracles, les Sibylles et les Prophéties, et particulièrement sur Nostradamus*, by Théodore Bouys, Paris, 1806

CHAPTER 19

Plaything of Propagandists

When a country is riven with crisis and uncertainty, times can be very rewarding for its astrologers, a point richly borne out by the fortunes of English astrological journals of the late eighteenth and early nineteenth century. At the very turn of the eighteenth century, an enterprising Londoner called Francis Moore had founded an astrological almanac entitled *Vox Stellarum* – 'Voice of the Stars'. A quack physician cum pills-and-potions pedlar, much along the same lines as Nostradamus, Moore had started the almanac principally to help sell his pharmaceutical wares. Quickly, however, the publication became a successful commodity in its own right, and under its now far more familiar title *Old Moore's Almanac*, has continued right into modern times.

The earliest annual sales for *Old Moore's* are unrecorded, but by 1768 it was already selling an impressive 107,00 copies. Then came the nerve-tingling 1790s when England saw its closest neighbour France rocked to its roots by the French Revolution's 'Reign of Terror'. When Austria's and Prussia's monarchs attempted to intervene on their French counterpart's behalf, France's revolutionaries mobilised a huge army. No longer led by amateurish aristocrats but instead by professionals risen through the ranks, this quickly became the most formidable in Europe, used to great effect by the dynamic young general Napoleon to crush France's continental neighbours. Within a truly astonishing ten years of France's becoming a republic Napoleon had amassed for it a European empire on a scale not seen in a thousand years. Small wonder, therefore, that a fearful British populace, relying for protection almost entirely upon the English Channel and Nelson's navy, turned to whatever comfort they might glean from *Old Moore's Almanac*. By 1803, merely months before Napoleon had formally proclaimed himself Emperor, *Old Moore's* sales reached 393,750 copies, a near quadrupling of its 1768 circulation. In readership terms this meant that at least one in every five of Britain's entire literate population had become hooked in some way on astrological forecasting.[1]

Meanwhile the French populace of the Napoleonic era, enjoying a huge upsurge in national pride as a result of their meteoric new leader's astonishing military success, looked to their homegrown *Prophecies*, already over two hundred years old, for whatever these might contain concerning their unexpected new Emperor and Empire. Earlier we noted how Théodore Bouys, the professor from Nevers, had interpreted several of Nostradamus' quatrains as predicting the French Revolution. In this same work, published in 1806 (therefore just after the French navy's defeat at Trafalgar, but with Napoleon's land armies still enjoying great successes), Bouys confidently noted that Nostradamus had foretold for Europe:

> …the brilliant destinies of Napoleon the great, which are to enjoy a long and happy reign, to bring lasting peace to the Continent, to be one day as redoubtable on the sea as he is on land, and to conquer England in order to give all nations the Freedom of the Seas.[2]

Whichever of Nostradamus' quatrains Bouys might have seized upon as prophecies of Napoleon, the eventual brutal facts of history were of course very different. Hunger, desertion and the Russian winter decimated Napoleon's 600,000-strong French army in the course of its long, humiliating retreat from a burnt-out Moscow, and despite a dramatic hundred-day comeback he was fully and finally defeated at Waterloo in 1815. Napoleon never subjugated Britain and never ultimately ruled over an enduring European empire, so Bouys was completely wrong in his interpretation of the prophecies.

This would not, of course, prevent more modern-day Nostradamians from looking to other quatrains which could be interpreted as foretelling the true, non-victorious version of Napoleon's story, and promulgating these as indicative of Nostradamus' prophetic powers. Amongst their most favoured has been Century I, quatrain 60:

> *An Emperor will be born near Italy*
> *Who will cost the Empire dear*
> *When those with whom he allies are spoken of*
> *He will be found to be less a prince than a butcher.*[3]

As book after book on Nostradamus has repeatedly argued, Napoleon's birthplace in Corsica can readily be described as 'near Italy'. And Napoleon certainly cost the Empire that he had created a lot of unnecessary bloodshed, all ultimately to no avail.

Even those living in the immediate aftermath of Napoleon's defeat, however, saw this as in no way any kind of setback for Nostradamus' prophetic reputation. Indeed, there lingered amongst the French of the post-Napoleonic era such a nostalgia for their unrealised dream that unknown spin-doctors of the early nineteenth century actually went to the lengths of inventing fresh Nostradamian-type prophecies for their propagandist purposes.

Thus in 1839 the French Nostradamian historian Eugène Bareste brought to public attention what was claimed to be the recent discovery of an enigmatic manuscript, purportedly dated to 1542, i.e. within Nostradamus' lifetime, entitled *The Prophecies of Master Noël Olivarius*.[4] This was mysteriously lost again shortly after coming to light, but not before it had been transcribed. It apparently prophesied the coming of a great leader who, although not born on the French mainland, would adopt France as his country and with the aid of a vast army would establish himself as an emperor over many lands. During a far-flung campaign he would then come to a great city which his enemies would have burnt before his arrival. As a result he and his men would:

> Depart…over ashes and ruins; and…having no more bread and water, by great cold which will be so unfortunate for them, two-thirds of his army will perish, and half the rest will be no more under his domination.[5]

Even Bareste admitted that he had never seen the original of this manuscript, only a copy allegedly made in 1793. In the belief that there really had been an original manuscript dating back to 1542, a number of Nostradamian authors have supposed this to have been a genuine prophetic work, and by Nostradamus. However, the 'transcribed' text's sixteenth-century French is thoroughly unconvincing, its uncannily correct prophecy of Napoleon's Russian campaign has a 'far-too-good-to-be-true' air about it, while the document's further prophecy that another, later leader would ultimately realise the French Imperial dream smacks of the purest Napoleonic Messianism. There can be little doubt, therefore, that this was a none too clever forgery by some Frenchman smarting under the temporary restoration of France's monarchy after 1814, in a push for a return to the days of Imperial glory.

As we have already seen from the two 'Mazarin' quatrains forged in Nostradamus' name during the seventeenth-century Fronde, this was far from the first faking of Nostradamus' and Nostradamus-type prophecies for propaganda purposes, and it would certainly not be the last. But in the interim the industry surrounding the authentic Nostradamus was entering another of its most productive phases.

As we saw in the last chapter, Nostradamus' tomb in Salon-de-Provence's old Church of the Cordeliers had been smashed open during the worst excesses of the French Revolution. The rest of this church, including the family's tombs, appears to have been so ravaged that all became obliterated without trace. However, Nostradamus' remains, or what purported to be them, were solemnly re-interred in their present location, the imposing, spire-topped church of St Laurent, a little to the north of the town centre. Here in July 1813, on the wall of what had been the Chapel of St Roche, now appropriately renamed the Chapel of Our Lady, a stonemason carved a new Latin epitaph prefaced with the explanatory notice: 'The remains of Michel Nostradamus were transferred to this chapel after 1789. His epitaph was remade in the month of July 1813.'[6]

Almost simultaneously with this restoration, a further French-language edition of the *Prophecies* was issued in Paris. Then in 1840 Bareste brought out his *Nostradamus*,[7] virtually the first modern semi-scholarly approach to the seer, and still valuable for its information on certain historic Nostradamus publications that were then still extant, but have subsequently been lost to us. This book attracted so much popular attention that it went through two reprints in its first year of publication.

Then in the second half of the nineteenth century there emerged on to the scene the redoubtable figure of the Abbé H. Torné, curé of the tiny hamlet of La Clotte in the Charente-Maritime district of western France. Claiming to be a descendant of Nostradamus' secretary Chavigny, the Abbé liked to style himself Torné-Chavigny. During Torné-Chavigny's formative years, France had witnessed some momentous events. In 1830 there had been a fresh Revolution, which had thrown out the Bourbon King Charles X and replaced him with

Nostradamus' restored tomb inscription, as set on the wall of the
Church of St Laurent, Salon-de-Provence, after the rescue of his remains from
the Church of the Cordeliers, destroyed during the French Revolution.

Louis Philippe d'Orléans. Then in 1848 Louis-Philippe in his turn had been overthrown and a Second Republic proclaimed. As if in fulfilment of the faked 'Olivarius' prophecies, Napoleon Bonaparte's nephew Napoleon III had then instituted a Second Empire, coinciding with the period when Torné-Chavigny was flourishing.

In the light of these happenings, Torné-Chavigny, firmly believing that he was witnessing the fulfilment of Nostradamus' prophecies of three centuries earlier, between 1860 and 1862 brought out a three-volume *magnum opus* entitled *History Predicted and Judged by Nostradamus*.[8] Two of the volumes were described as 'commentaries and translations of the edition of the *Prophecies* of 1566 [sic], at Lyons, by Pierre Rigaud, with proofs drawn from the best-known authors'.[9] These volumes added to Nostradamian folklore a substantial number of stories with little foundation except from Torné's over-fertile imagination. The third volume was devoted to how Nostradamus had predicted the eras of Louis-Philippe, the Republic of 1848 and the advent of Emperor Napoleon III.

An ardent monarchist, Torné-Chavigny was convinced by his studies of Nostradamus that Emperor Napoleon III would be succeeded by a legitimate king, a King Henri V in the person of the Comte de Chambord, France's most blue-blooded surviving aristocrat. For this reason Napoleon III's government regarded Torné-Chavigny's writings as highly seditious, to the extent of occasionally seizing them, though this served only to accentuate public interest both in Torné-Chavigny and in Nostradamus. Unabashed, Torné-Chavigny added to this repertoire *The Apocalypse Interpreted by Nostradamus*, a concordance representing the early Christian evangelist St John of Patmos as supporting Nostradamus' apparent predictions of the restoration of France's monarchy. And such were the highly political implications behind Torné-Chavigny's interpretations that even the popular, liberal-minded pontiff Pope Pius IX became drawn into the discussion; Torné duly visited Rome for consultations with some of the Pope's aides.

In 1872, Napoleon III had been succeeded by a Third Republic that would last until the Second World War, and not by Torné-Chavigny's anticipated Count de Chambord. The Abbé's energies now turned to republication of the faked *Prophecies of Olivarius*, together with a similar forgery, the *Prophecy of Orval*.[10] This latter, its credentials as suspicious as those of *Olivarius*, purported to derive from a sixteenth-century book, similarly no longer extant, that aristocrats fleeing the Revolution had found at the Abbey of Orval in the Ardennes region of France. This seemingly predicted the demise of King Louis-Philippe. Torné-Chavigny not only insisted that both works were genuine, he argued that Nostradamus had been their true author, and in 1874 began turning out a Nostradamus-type annual almanac, 'Ce qui sera!' or 'What will be!', which he continued publishing almost up to his death in 1880.

Whilst in La Clotte Torné-Chavigny was using dubious methods to promote Nostradamus' memory, to the south-east the civic leaders at Nostradamus' birthplace of St-Rémy-de-Provence and at his adopted town of Salon-de-Provence both instituted projects to promote greater public awareness of their Nostradamian connections. In the late 1850s St-Rémy commissioned the sculptor Ambroise Liotard (1810–1876) to create a bust of Nostradamus atop a fountain on the corner of the Rue Carnot and Rue Nostradamus, the latter specially renamed in the seer's honour. This fountain soon began figuring in St-Rémy's souvenir postcards, featuring long-skirted local mothers relaxing beneath Nostradamus' gaze, cooling their children's feet in its basin. Not to be outdone, Salon-de-Provence commissioned from the sculptor Joseph Ré a life-size stone statue of Nostradamus in commemoration of the third centenary of his death. In 1866 this was erected at the junction of the Rue des Cordeliers and Rue d'Hozier, where it stands to this day, marking the site of Nostradamus' original resting place, the Church of the Cordeliers.

Both before and after the Abbé Torné's death in 1880 there was no shortage of other Nostradamian authors keen to make ever more ingenious links between Prophecies, quatrains and real-life contemporary events, in the process adding to the ever-burgeoning Nostradamian folklore. One prolific late nineteenth-century French Nostradamian author was Anatole Le Pelletier, who The Oracles of Michel de Nostredame,[11] a complete new edition of the Prophecies, was published in 1867. England had Charles A. Ward, whose highly fanciful Oracles of Nostradamus[12] was first published in 1891. Another Frenchman was the Abbé Charles Nicoullaud, whose Nostradamus, his Prophecies[13] was published in 1914 at the start of the First World War.

In part Nicoullaud looked back on the fact that the Emperor Napoleon III, after rashly going to war against Prussia in 1870, had quickly been forced into a humiliating surrender at the French town of Sedan. Struck by an otherwise all-too-typically obscure phrase from Nostradamus' Century VIII, quatrain 43, 'Dedans Lectoyre' ('Within Lectoyre'), Nicoullaud ingeniously interpreted this as an anagram of 'Sedan le decroyt', or 'Sedan overthrows him', a 'clear' prophecy of Napoleon III's defeat.

But Nicoullaud also looked forward to Nostradamus' predictions that were yet to be fulfilled. One verse that particularly fascinated him

Fountain in honour of Nostradamus, created for St-Rémy-de-Provence in the mid-19th century by the sculptor Ambroise Liotard.

Below: Statue in honour of Nostradamus, sculpted by Joseph Ré in 1866 for Salon-de-Provence to commemorate the third centenary of the seer's death.

was Century III, quatrain 57, a necessarily very loose and provisional translation of which is as follows:

> Seven times you will see the British
>   people change,
> Tinged with blood, in 290 years
> France not by supporting Germany
> Aries doubts its Bastarnian Pole.[14]

To Nicoullaud, this quatrain's main trust seemed to be that over a period of 290 years Britain would change her ruling dynasty seven times. The difficulty, however, was determining when the 290-year period might begin. If taken from 1603, i.e. from the end of the reign of Elizabeth I and the beginning of the Stuart dynasty, the period ended in 1893, a year when nothing special happened, since the long-lived Queen Victoria still had another eight years of her reign to run. Altogether more interesting, however, was if the 290 years were started from the date of Charles I's execution, 1649, thus ending in 1939, twenty-five years after the publication of Nicoullaud's book in 1914. So was there something 'tinged

with blood' that was going to happen to British, German and French history in 1939?

In 1921 and obscure ex-painter named Adolf Hitler was languishing in a Munich jail. That same year Nicoullaud's interest in this quatrain was taken up by a Berlin-based German postal worker, C. Loog, in a brief book entitled *The Prophecies of Nostradamus*.[15] Agreeing with

Nicoullaud that 1649 was the right starting date, Loog combined this with a valuable elucidation that Le Pelletier had provided concerning Nostradamus' reference to 'Bastarnan'. Since Nostradamus was characteristically fond of referring to countries by the names of the tribes that had held those territories in Roman times, Loog adjudged that this reference to the Bastarnae tribe, whose territory lay east of the river Vistula, had to mean Poland. So did this mean that Poland was going to be implicated in whatever bloody event was going to happen in 1939?

Loog's book, the product of a very minor publisher, attracted hardly a ripple of interest. However, one writer who had taken early note of it was a Dr H.H. Kritzinger, who duly mentioned Loog's Poland interpretation in his *Mysteries of the Sun and the Soul*,[16] a work that was published as early as 1922, but which was continuing to enjoy a lively readership nearly two decades later.

It is, of course, a matter of historic record that on September 1, 1939 Adolf Hitler, after a career rise to Chancellor of breathtakingly swift Germany's Third Reich, ordered his panzer divisions and warplanes to sweep into Poland, fully anticipating that this action would precipitate war with Britain and France. It is equally well documented that only a few weeks later Magda Goebbels, wife of Hitler's Propaganda Minister Dr Josef Goebbels, happened to be in bed late at night reading the relevant section of Kritzinger's book when she recognised that Loog's interpretation of Nostradamus' quatrain had been most dramatically fulfilled by her country's recent invasion of Poland. Although her husband – easily the most intellectual of the Nazi top brass – was already asleep she felt impelled to wake him specially to tell him.

From late October through to December of 1939 the minutes of ministerial meetings at Goebbels' Propaganda Ministry show that

matters both Nostradamian and generally astrological had become unusually hot topics. As early as November 22, the decision was taken to produce a Nostradamus leaflet in French, inevitably for propaganda purposes. A few days later a very apprehensive Kritzinger found himself summoned to the Ministry for some keen questioning

The book by German postal worker C. Loog which convinced Frau Magda Goebbels that Nostradamus had predicted the outbreak of the Second World War.

concerning all that he knew about Nostradamus and his powers of prophecy. The date was December 4, 1939, and as Kritzinger subsequently recalled the experience:

> He [Goebbels] began by talking about Loog's now famous interpretation of quatrain III, 57, the one that begins *Sept fois changer verrez gent Britannique*.[17] It was the manner in which this prophecy had apparently been fulfilled that impressed Dr Goebbels and others at the Propaganda Ministry. They could see a host of psychological warfare possibilities and obviously supposed that any Nostradamus expert would be able to provide other surprising instances for use for propaganda purposes outside Germany.
>
> 'Have you got anything else on the same lines?' he kept on asking, as if I could shake one interesting prediction after another about Great Britain and the war out of my sleeve. 'What's going to happen next?' was another question he asked. I said that I had no idea. But Dr Goebbels was insistent. 'But surely since you understand the basis of the thing [i.e. Nostradamus] you must at least have an inkling.'[18]

Not without difficulty, Kritzinger managed to persuade Goebbels that he personally possessed absolutely no powers of predicting the future. He also succeeded in persuading Goebbels that he was quite the wrong person to be asked to comb Nostradamus' writings for anything and everything that might serve the interests of Third Reich propaganda. As he pointed out, his work as director of a scientific research institute attached to the German Army's Ordnance department kept him more than fully occupied, and he therefore simply had no spare time for the task that Goebbels had in mind.

Nonetheless, Goebbels and his Ministry were determined that the opportunity to use Nostradamus for propaganda purposes should not be missed. Under intense pressure Kritzinger eventually provided them with the name of one Nostradamus expert who might be able to help. This was Karl Ernst Krafft, a thirty-nine-year-old astrologer and researcher into the paranormal, living quietly with his wife at Urberg in the Black Forest. Krafft, in his innocence at that time, proved initially delighted to be asked to work on such a project. The minutes of Goebbels' ministerial conference of March 27, 1940 recorded a decision to go ahead with producing a 'Nostradamus brochure'; this appears to be the propagandist booklet Krafft had provided quoting Nostradamus as predicting Germany's victorious conquest of all Europe. According to authoritative sources, by the middle of 1940 83,000 copies of this brochure had been printed – 20,000 in French,

5,000 in Dutch, 10,000 in Italian, 10,000 in Serbian, 25,000 in Croatian, 5,000 in Rumanian, 5,000 in Swedish, together with 3,000 in English for dissemination in the USA.[19] As a more specialist exercise Krafft also began, in partnership with one George Lucht, the preparation of a limited edition of the *Prophecies*, again with a view to furthering the idea that they favoured a German victory.

Meanwhile, in blitz-ravaged London, Louis de Wohl, a seriously overweight Hungarian-born refugee novelist with a special interest in astrology, had learned from a neutral diplomat friend of the Nazi High Command's appointment of Krafft. The information with which de Wohl had been provided was, however, sketchy, leading him to supplement it with some improbably founded guesses. From his astrological knowledge de Wohl found himself highly impressed by how Hitler had launched the daring *Blitzkrieg* that rapidly engulfed Holland, then Belgium, shortly followed by France. The launch date, May 10, 1940, was astrologically just about the most propitious that anyone could have chosen for such a risky venture. De Wohl's confident deduction was that a personal astrologer was advising Hitler on his military decisions and that this astrologer was Karl Krafft. De Wohl reasoned, therefore, that getting to know how Krafft's mind operated could be of great strategic importance. He also suspected that the Germans were operating a deliberate propaganda campaign to infiltrate the United States with articles and letters in mass-circulation journals making it appear that Nostradamus predicted certain defeat for Britain. The United States would hence be foolhardy even to contemplate joining any war against the certain might of Germany.

From all that has subsequently come to light amongst the Third Reich's surviving documentation, de Wohl was actually quite wrong in presuming that Krafft was acting as Hitler's personal Nostradamus. As is evident from some of his recorded conversations, Hitler actually had a healthy scepticism towards astrologers, and there is absolutely no evidence that he and Krafft ever met. Instead, Krafft's main employers were the German News Office,[20] for whom he certainly produced a 200-page French-language book, *How Nostradamus foresaw Europe's Future*,[21] which was duly published in 1941 as a morale-destroyer for the French. In this Krafft discussed some forty Nostradamus quatrains, some of which he specially highlighted as showing that Britain would be bound to lose the war. As but one of these, Krafft focused on Century II, quatrain 100, translatable as:

> *Within the Isles such horrible tumult*
> *Well may it be that only all-out war will be heard*

So great will be the injuries from the predators
That the great League will range itself against them.[22]

According to Krafft's interpretation, 'the Isles' meant the British Isles. The 'predators' were the British, a people whom he regarded as particularly prone to robbery and pillage. Reputedly the 'tumult' or chaos within Britain would become so great that the whole country would succumb to all-out war (Nostradamus' *'bellique brigue'*). At this point the might of Hitlerian Europe ('the great League') would then combine to crush them.

De Wohl therefore had an inflated idea of Krafft's status under the Third Reich. Under this misapprehension, and while working for Britain's Special Operations Executive (SOE), run by the now legendary Sefton Delmer, he set about creating appropriate counter-propaganda. For if Krafft was so convincingly making Nostradamus appear to have predicted Britain's defeat, then the British response had to be to circulate material indicating that in actuality the prediction was for Germany's defeat.

Something of this kind had already been devised in all sincerity by a Nostradamian Frenchman, Dr Max de Fontbrune, even before the Second World War had begun. De Fontbrune's *The Prophecies of Master Michel Nostradamus Explained and Commented upon*[23] had been published in 1938, and this impressively predicted, on the basis of Nostradamus' *Prophecies*, both that World War II was inevitable and that its eventual outcome would be Germany's defeat. Indeed, the book proved such an embarrassment for the collaborationist Vichy government that in 1940 it was formally banned throughout France.[24]

De Wohl's plan was therefore to supplement the De Fontbrune argument by forging a number of booklets saying much the same, creating some that appeared to have been produced within Germany by German Nostradamus experts. One such production was *Nostradamus Predicts the Course of the War*,[25] ostensibly a genuine German publication written by a *bonafide* German authority on Nostradamus, Bruno Winckler.[26] In the book's Introduction de Wohl, the actual author, made 'Winckler' thank Dr Heinrich Lesse, curator of the manuscript collection at Regensburg for the loan of a unique (but in actuality non-existent) Nostradamus manuscript. The book took the form of fifty Nostradamus quatrains, reproduced in their 'original' French, with below each quatrain a German translation; some of the quatrains were cleverly doctored to make them appear to refer to Hitler.

In this context, in support of the faking of references to Hitler was the fact that a number of authentic quatrains quite genuinely

contained references to a 'Hister' associated with Germany. The point
had already caused a number of Nostradamians to assume that
'Hister' must have been how the seer referred to Adolf Hitler. The fact
is that 'Hister' was Nostradamus' way of referring to the river
Danube, after the old Roman name for it. However, the confusion had
already been created, as a result of which (as but one example) de
Wohl blithely changed Century III, quatrain 30 from '*Celuy qu'en
luitte & fer au faict bellique...*' to '*Hister qu'en luitte...*' This thereby
altered its meaning in German translation from 'he who' to 'Hitler
who':

> Hister [i.e. Hitler] who carried off more victories (prizes) in his
> warlike fight than was good for him: six [men] will murder him
> in the night. Naked, taken unawares without his armour, he
> succumbs.[27]

De Wohl had thereby quite unashamedly falsified a Nostradamus
verse to make it appear to prophesy a treacherous and shameful end
for Hitler.

And there was a further piece of mischief, which de Wohl directed
against Krafft personally. Totally fluent in German (hence his value to
the British war effort), de Wohl skilfully forged a private letter purportedly written by Krafft disclosing that he believed that Germany
would lose the war and that Hitler would come to a very unpleasant
end. Via the various undercover avenues open to him, de Wohl
arranged for this letter to fall into the hands of the Gestapo, the idea
being that Krafft would thereby be arrested and would have his standing with Hitler destroyed. Unknown to de Wohl, however, Krafft had
been arrested some months earlier for quite different reasons, and was
already languishing in jail. So in the event the Gestapo, on reading the
letter, would readily have recognised it as a hoax.

Overall, however, the fascinating aspect of both British and German
usage of Nostradamus' quatrains during World War II was the total
absence of scruple, on both sides, as to whether the quotations might
or might not be the seer's genuine utterances. In the heat of war, truth
was readily expendable in the interests of expediency.[28]

Nor were the Americans, geographically immune though they were
from the terror of Hitler's devastating *Luftwaffe*, reluctant to adulter-
ate Nostradamus' verses in much the same manner when they became
committed to joining the war. Soon after President Roosevelt had
made the necessary military commitment, the famous Metro-
Goldwyn-Mayer studios quickly went into production with a series of
short films aimed at swaying American public opinion. The very first

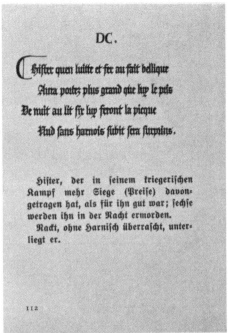

Example of Louis de Wohl's handiwork, a genuine Nostradamus prophecy carefully 'doctored' to make it appear that Adolf Hitler would meet a shameful end.

of these, entitled *Nostradamus Says So*, was specifically aimed at showing that Nostradamus had predicted victory for the Allies. Lighting upon the word *flambeau* in Sixain 15,[29] a word usually translated into English as 'torch' MGM's producers unashamedly twisted the passage to make it sound as if Nostradamus had been referring to the Statue of Liberty:

> *The chosen protector of the great country*
> *For endless years will hold the famed torch*
> *It will serve to guide this great people*
> *And in its name they will struggle and triumph.*

A rather more literal translation of exactly these same lines reads very differently:

> *The newly elected patron of the great vessel*
> *Will see the clear flame shine for a long time*
> *Which will serve as a lamp to this great territory*
> *At which time the armies under his name*
> *Will join with those happily of Bourbon*
> *From east to west resting his memory.*

Topical and high-profile as Nostradamus had been for both sides' propaganda purposes throughout World War II, hardly had the Allied victory been won before the dust was being blown off his verses yet again. In 1947 the New York bookseller Henry C. Roberts, having purchased 'at an almost prohibitive price'[30] a copy of Theophilus de Garencières' 1672 English-language translation of the *Prophecies*, was struck by the fact that 'not since 1672' had there been 'an English edition of his [Nostradamus'] complete quatrains'. Roberts was right. Previous English-language books such as Charles A. Ward's *Oracles of Nostradamus* had merely quoted only from certain selected verses, as had James Laver's *Nostradamus or the Future Foretold*. Accordingly, regarding his expensively acquired Garencières text as the 'most authoritative' available, Roberts duly brought out his own ostensibly pioneering new translation and set of interpretations, even forming his own publishing company for the enterprise. And he was highly successful, his translation in the USA alone (without counting UK editions) being successively reprinted in 1949, 1962, 1964, 1966, 1968 and 1969, after which from 1982 onwards his son Lee Roberts Amsterdam continued with a similarly successful 're-edited' version.

The irony is that both as a translation and as a historical interpretation the Roberts publication can only be accounted as naïve and inept in the extreme. To analyse everything critically would be wearisome, but I will cite one example. The Lee Roberts Amsterdam 're-edited' edition included a blunder which Lee inherited from his father, who had in turn inherited it from Garencières, who had in turn inherited it from the Fronde propagandists. For the edition of the *Prophecies* from which Garencières had worked for his 1672 translation was the falsely dated '1568' edition which the Frondeurs had put out in 1649, containing as propaganda their two faked 'Mazarin' verses as Centuries VII, q.42 and 43. Because Garencières had not recognised that these verses were fake, neither did Roberts, as a result of which the latter duly described Century VII, q.42 as 'remarkable for its clarity of wording and exactness of its fulfilment' in the person of the historical Cardinal Mazarin. Indeed, it might have been had it been genuinely written by Nostradamus, rather than during Mazarin's own lifetime.

This lack of any true critical sense has all too sadly continued to typify almost the entire output of English-language Nostradamiana as perpetuated to this day. Noting the lucrative business that the Robertses, father and son, had created for themselves, others have subsequently produced their own alternative English-language 'translations', these rarely revealing anything like appropriate linguistic skills, let alone demonstrating any historical grasp.

Thus in the 1970s Erika Cheetham produced first *The Prophecies of*

Nostradamus, then *The Further Prophecies of Nostradamus*, then in 1989 *the Final Prophecies of Nostradamus*. As Nostradamus sceptic James Randi has noted of Cheetham's historical interpretations:

> [She] has French king Louis XV as the *son* of the 'Sun King', she appoints Philippe Egalité, the Duke of Orléans, as the *brother* of Louis XVI (he was not related) and she startles us with the assertion that Henri IV was a member of the Valois line (hardly!). She mixes up astrological signs and characteristics as well as history in any fashion that serves to prove her points.[31]

The linguist and pro-Nostradamian Peter Lemesurier has castigated Cheetham's translations as 'full of quite basic errors'.[32]

Nor have Nostradamian studies exactly been edified by John Hogue, author of *Nostradamus and the Millennium* (1987), *The Nostradamus Date Book* (1989), and *Nostradamus: The New Revelations* (1993). Again neither sceptic Randi nor Nostradamian Lemesurier have any time for Hogue. In the words of Randi's tongue-in-cheek accolade: 'His power of distorting words and twisting anagrams out of shape in highly imaginative ways has seldom been surpassed.'[33]

To add to an almost irretrievably confused and myth-filled field, in the 1980s Michael Baignet, Richard Leigh and Henry Lincoln introduced Nostradamus into their best-selling but highly fanciful *The Holy Blood and the Holy Grail*. Here, affecting a knowledge of Nostradamus' life that is lacking in any authoritative historical source, the trio represented him as having learnt all his prophetic knowledge at 'the mysterious Abbey of Orval' – thereby yet again uncritically resurrecting the *Prophecy of Orval* forgery.[34] The actuality, as earlier noted, is that any linking of Nostradamus with the Abbey of Orval may be dismissed as a piece of pure fiction that was coined in the early nineteenth century. But the temptation not to pass over such a myth when it can help give credence to another one is almost irresistible.

Inevitably Nostradamus' prophecies have been combed for any reference to Princess Diana's tragic death in 1997 – and not found wanting. Two quatrains refer to 'Diane', or Diana. In the second (Century IX, quatrain 12) the name occurs in association with Mercury, so it must refer to the Roman goddess. But the first (Century II, quatrain 28) speaks of 'the penultimate with the surname of prophet who will take Diane to her day of rest.' Dodi al-Fayed's father, Harrods department store owner Mohammed al-Fayed, was of course named after the Islamic religion's prophet Mohammed. So, with a bit of manipulation, the first two lines of this particular quatrain have been made to read:

The last son of the man with the Prophet's name
Will bring Diana to her day of rest.

Topical as Nostradamus' prophecies have seemed for every fresh crisis
that has occurred during the last five hundred years, they reached a
fresh level of topicality only as recently as 1999. As earlier noted, all
too rarely did Nostradamus ever quote any exact year for the fulfilment of his quatrains. However, one exception was his Century X,
quatrain 72, in which, according to most available translations, he
prophesied with unusual clarity:

> *The year 1999, seven months,*
> *From the sky will come a great king of Terror*
> *To bring back to life the great King of the Mongols,*
> *Before and after Mars to reign by good luck.*[35]

America's Erika Cheetham was one of those who, prior to 1999 (also,
of course, prior to September 11, 2001), confidently assumed this
verse to be one of Nostradamus' more straightforward predictions.
Mars being the Roman god of war, Cheetham supposed the verse to
mean the arising of a great Mongol warlord, nothing less than the
coming of a third Antichrist. John Hogue conservatively anticipated
that it predicted the destruction of the civilised world. The Frenchman
Fontbrune opted for an airborne invasion of France. Britain's Peter
Lemesurier fancied a Muslim invasion of the Middle East. However, it
is only in later texts of the *Prophecies* that the second line reads: '*Du
ciel viendra un grand Roy d'effrayeur*', legitimately translatable as:
'From the sky will come a great King of Terror'. In the original
Bonhomme-printed edition of 1555 this same line reads: '*Du ciel
viendra un grand Roy deffraieur*', which broadly means: 'From the sky
will come a great appeaser King', inevitably putting a rather different
complexion on the prediction.

Furthermore, in all early versions the third lines reads: '*Resusciter le
grand Roy d'Angolmois*'. Amongst all leading English-language
Nostradamian authors the consensus has been that 'Angolmois' must
be a typically Nostradamian anagram for 'Mongols'. This has given
them free rein to represent Nostradamus as predicting the rise from
the East of some fearsome twenty-first-century Genghis Khan. The
reality, however, is that 'Angoumois', alternatively styled 'Angolmois'
or 'Angoulmois' before spellings became standardised, was in
Nostradamus' lifetime one of the territories belonging to the Queen of
Navarre, and was broadly equivalent to the present-day French
département of the Charente. The territory was formerly owned by

the counts of Angoulême, whose main seat was the present-day town of Angoulême north-east of Bordeaux.

In blissful ignorance of such an altogether more localised and less sensationalist interpretation of this particular quatrain, in 1947 Henry Roberts took Nostradamus to be warning of:

> ...a tremendous world revolution...to take place in the year 1999 with a complete upheaval of existing social orders, preceded by world-wide wars.[36]

With Erika Cheetham, John Hogue and Peter Lemesurier following up in later decades with much the same line it is scarcely surprising, therefore, that Nostradamus fever should have reached quite a pitch leading up to July 1999, that is, the 'seventh month' to which the prediction seemed to refer.

By this time the Nostradamus Society of America had been formed, fronted by 'author/researcher and Nostradamus expert' Victor Baines, with its own lively Internet website. In Japan a poll taken specifically at that time showed that some 20 per cent of the Japanese actually believed that the purported 'King of Terror' prediction would be fulfilled during this year, a credible enough percentage in view of the 185 different books on Nostradamus then available in print in Tokyo. In England the TV Channel 4 devoted virtually its entire output for the night of Saturday July 4, 1999 to a 'Nostradamus night', featuring non-stop focus on the subject including documentaries and a film, from 8.30 pm to 3.20 am.

As everyone now knows, nothing particularly extraordinary happened in July 1999. By all normal standards of logic this might have rendered any ordinary, living, prophetic guru totally and utterly discredited – but not, of course Nostradamus.

NOTES

1 This is necessarily an approximation, based on the readership of a publication such as *Old Moore's* being calculable as three to four readers per copy. Though at the start of the nineteenth century England's total population was around ten million, something less than 50% of all adults were literate

2 Quoted in translation in Laver, *Nostradamus or the Future Foretold...*, op. cit., p.174

3 *Un Empereur naistra pres d'Italie,*
   Qui a l'Empire sera vendu bien cher
   Diront avecques quels gens il se ralie
   Qu'on trouvera moins prince que boucher

4 Bareste told this story in an article in a contemporary magazine *Le Capitole* dated October 21, 1839

5 Quoted in Laver, *Nostradamus or the Future Foretold*, op. cit., p.254

6 '*RELIQUAE MICHAELIS NOSTRADAMI IN HOC SACELLUM TRANSLATAE FUERUNT POST ANNUM MDCCLXXXIX. EPITAPHIUM RESTITUTUM MENSE JULII MDCCCXIII*'

7 Eugène Bareste, *Nostradamus*, Paris, 1840

8 H. Torné-Chavigny, *L'Histoire prédite et jugée par Nostradamus*, 3 vols., Bordeaux, 1860–2

9 '*Commentaires et traductions de l'édition des Prophéties de 1566* [? – the Rigaud edition was in 1568], *à Lyon, par Pierre Rigaud, avec les preuves tirées des auteurs les plus connus*,' quoted in Leroy, *Nostradamus, Ses Origines...*, op. cit., p.181

10 *Prophétie d'Orval*

11 Anatole Le Pelletier, *Les Oracles de Michel de Nostredame*, 2 vols., Paris, 1867

12 Charles A. Ward, *The Oracles of Nostradamus*, London, 1891

13 *Nostradamus, ses prophéties*, Paris, 1914

14 '*Sept foys changer verrés gent Britannique
Taintz en sang en deux cent nonante an:
Franche non point par apui Germanique
Aries doute son pole Bastarnan*

15 C. Loog, *Die Weissagungen des Nostradamus*, Pfullingen, Johannes Baum, 1921

16 H.H. Kritzinger, *Mysterien von Sonne und Seele, Psychische Studien zur Klaerung der Okkulten*, Berlin, Verlag, Universitas Buch, 1922

17 This was the line as quoted by Howe, after Kritzinger, and is not exact to the first edition of Nostradamus' *Prophecies*, as quoted earlier

18 Quoted from a tape-recorded interview with Dr Kritzinger in Ellic Howe, *Urania's Children: The Strange World of the Astrologers*, London, William Kimber, 1967, p.164

19 W.A. Boelcke, *Kriegspropaganda 1939–41*, 1966, p.304, quoted in Howe, *Urania's Children*, op. cit., p.185, footnote 2

20 *Deutsche Nachrichtenbüro*

21 *Comment Nostradamus a-t-il entrevu l'Avenir l'Europe*

22 '*Dedans les isles si horrible tumulte
Bien on n'orra qu'une bellique brigue
Tant grand sera des predateurs l'insulte
Qu'on se viendra ranger à la grand ligue.*

23 De Fontbrune, *Les prophéties de Maistre Michel Nostradamus expliquées et commentées...*, 1938

24 Ibid., eleventh edition, 1958, p.6

25 *Nostradamus prophezeit den Kriegsverlauf*

26 In 1940 Winckler had in actual fact written *Englands Aufstieg und Niedergang nach den Prophezeiungen des grossen französischen Sehers der Jahre 1555 und 1558*, Leipzig, 1940

27 Ellic Howe, *Urania's Children*, op. cit., p.217, note 2

28 Equally a matter of curiosity is that despite the scarcity of paper in Britain during World War II, making the publication of any book extremely difficult, somehow or other the Englishman Laver's *Nostradamus or the Future Foretold* managed to achieve publication in 1942, that is, at the height of the

war. Laver, in his introduction, actually singled out Louis de Wohl for special thanks – ostensibly for explaining to him how a horoscope is cast – without any further elucidation

29 *Nouveau esleu patron du grand vaisseau*
Verra long temps briller le clere flambeau
Qui sert de lampe à ce grand territoire
Et auquel temps [les] armez sous son nom
Joinctes à celles de l'heureux de Bourbon
Levant, Ponant & Couchant sa memoire

30 This and the subsequent quotes derive from Henry C. Roberts' Introduction to *The Complete Prophecies of Nostradamus*, translated, edited and interpreted by Henry C. Roberts, New York, Nostradamus Co., 1947

31 Randi, *The Mask of Nostradamus*, op. cit., p.143

32 Peter Lemesurier, *The Essential Nostradamus*, London, Piatkus, 1999, p.69

33 Randi, *The Mask of Nostradamus*, op. cit., p.148

34 According to the trio, basing their information on no reliable source for Nostradamus' life, much of the seer's prophetic expertise derived from a considerable part of his career purportedly spent in the Duchy of Lorraine in north-eastern France:

> ... this would appear to have been some sort of novitiate, or period of probation, after which he was supposedly 'initiated' into some portentous secret. More specifically, he is said to have been shown an ancient and arcane book, *on which he based all his own subsequent work* [italics mine]. And this book was reportedly divulged to him at a very significant place – the mysterious Abbey of Orval ... where ... the Prieuré de Sion may have had its inception.

In *The Holy Blood and the Holy Grail* Baigent, Leigh and Lincoln's thesis was that Jesus did not die on the Jerusalem cross, but instead escaped to sire children by Mary Magdalen, their progeny subsequently becoming France's Merovingian dynasty. The secret of this blood-line had reputedly been preserved from generation to generation by 'grand masters' of a brotherhood known as the Prior of Sion. It therefore suited Baigent, Leigh and Lincoln's story that Nostradamus should be explained as deriving all his knowledge from their Priory brotherhood, the Nostradamus link, however tenuous, with the Abbey of Orval providing rich fuel for their argument

35 *L'an mil neuf cens nonante neuf sept mois*
Du ciel viendra un grand Roy deffraieur
Resusciter le grand Roy d'Angolmois
Avant apres Mars regner par bon heur

36 Henry C. Roberts (ed.), *The Complete Prophecies of Nostradamus...*, op. cit., p.336

CHAPTER 20

His First 500 Years

It is now all but 500 years since Nostradamus took his first gulp of Provençal air, and well over 400 since he breathed his last. Yet it is impossible to visit Salon-de-Provence without still bumping into him.

Walk just a few hundred yards around central Salon and you can find yourself in a Boulevard Nostradamus, a Rue Nostradamus or a Place Nostradamus, not to mention Rues Ponsard, d'Hozier and Suffren, a Place des Centuries and Allées de Craponne. You can eat in Café Nostradamus, drink in Bar Nostradamus. Step out of the Nostradamus sound-and-light show in the Maison Nostradamus museum and within a few paces you will confront a very avant-garde (and enigmatically eyeless) metal statue of the seer that the sculptor François Bouché created in 1966 to mark the 400th anniversary of his death. Look to the end of the same pedestrianised street, and you cannot miss a giant sepia-coloured Nostradamus portrait, enlarged from a rather over-romanticised nineteenth-century engraving, that has been painted three storeys high on an end wall.

Whatever your personal assessment of Nostradamus, not only is his memory still very much to the fore in Salon, but also copies of his *Prophecies*, however execrable their translation, are to be found in virtually every major bookshop throughout Europe, America and Australia. His very name has long become synonymous with future-gazing throughout virtually the entire world. However incongruous it might seem to the sceptic, from the moment that this planet's 'civilised' populations began quaking in the wake of the terrible events of September 11, 2001, it was the words of Nostradamus that they looked to in their millions, and not those of Jesus, of Muhammad, or of Buddha. All this raises the question: can this four-hundred-years-dead Provençal physician truly deserve such fame, such veneration – and not least, such credence?

Positively not, according to one group who might be expected to be

Left Giant portrait of Nostradamus that commands one of Salon-de-Provence's historic streets. This is based on a 19th centry print emphasizing Nostradamus' Jewishness. *Right* The present-day Nostradamus tourist industry. Souvenir doll made in the likeness of Nostradamus, offered for sale in a Salon gift shop.

amongst his staunchest supporters, the ranks of today's professional astrologers. These are the words of Jim Tester, author of the authoritative *A History of Western Astrology* published in 1989, explaining in a footnote his reasons why his 'definitive' main text carries absolutely no mention of Nostradamus:

> It may be worth a note, since some readers may look for his name in a book such as this, to say that Nostradamus (1503–1566) is irrelevant to any history of astrology. He did practise astrology, it is true, but only as a quack and among other forms of occultism.[1]

By any standards, this is a breathtaking piece of elitist arrogance. As pointed out earlier, I make no pretence of understanding the many convoluted intricacies of astrological practice. Nonetheless I do know sufficient to be able to state with confidence that astrology is *all* quackery, whether it be practised by a twenty-first century Tester or by a sixteenth-century Nostradamus. However purist the methodology may be – and Nostradamus was probably deservedly castigated by his own astrologer contemporaries for being sloppy in his methods – astrology remains based on planetary positions that were calculated more than 2,000 years ago. And because of slight cosmic variables which those calculations did not take into account, it has long since lost any relation to astronomical truth. This is quite aside from the vexed issue of whether planetary positions can influence our personalities and destinies, for which so far there exists not a shred of serious scientific evidence. At least Nostradamus, living before the invention of the telescope, remained honestly unaware of the astronomical discrepancies. The same cannot be said for Tester.

But in any event, if Nostradamus really was such a bad astrologer, in the eyes of his own contemporary fellow-practitioners as well as today's gurus of the craft, this only makes it all the more astonishing that he should have gained such a powerful and widespread level of credence in his own lifetime – and then, even in the impotence of death, managed to hold on to it so successfully, right up to and including our own time.

For he was, after all, from a racial stock, the Jews, whom the generality of sixteenth-century Europeans had absolutely no qualms about wanting exterminated from the face of the earth. He was of less than average height, with nothing specially appealing or impressive reported about his physical appearance. As a physician, though he had attended the highly respected Montpellier Medical School, there are grounds for doubts that he stayed the course, his medical credentials thereby being more than a little shaky. We have just noted how low his rating was, and continues to be, as a practising astrologer. As a writer, he lived in a far-flung and then primitive corner of France where the nearest printing press lay 140 miles (224 km) away in Lyons. And the Royal court, the one place of real importance where he might hope to get himself noticed, lay 250 miles (400 km) further on.

Yet it is a straight fact of history, one that not even a James Randi can deny, that somehow in his own lifetime Nostradamus managed to get not only France's royal court (which he visited just once), but a number of other major European royal courts (which he visited not at all), hanging on to his every prophetic word. Those monarchs whom he thus hooked were not gullible simpletons. Mostly they were astute, pragmatic, highly autocratic individuals who had the political clout and caprice to hurl armies of thousands at each other whenever they felt so disposed. Yet in a world in which their own in-house court astrologers were two-a-penny, Nostradamus from his distant Salon somehow managed to ordain it that it was *his* predictions that they took seriously, it was *his* horoscopes that they needed to take account of whenever they were contemplating their next diplomatic marital alliance.

Nor was such deference towards Nostradamus confined just to the crowned heads. The French army chief Blaise de Monluc was as practical and hard-headed as any general of his time, yet he went on record as speaking of Nostradamus with an almost reverential awe. Monluc's admiral counterpart the Baron Paulin de Garde was likewise so impressed by Nostradamus that he gave him a valuable astrolabe. The Spanish king Philip II's sea-captains and their mariners regarded Nostradamus with such awe that they deferred the sailing of their entire fleet on the strength of the storm warnings in his Almanac. Hans Rosenberger, the German mining magnate, even when he was most sorely pressed financially, sent his messengers hundreds of miles across Europe for Nostradamus' advice on where he should sink his next mineshaft. England's Archbishop of Canterbury, Matthew Parker, while no fan, had such a healthy respect for Nostradamus' Rasputin-like hold over his contemporaries that he found himself obliged positively to deny that Nostradamus had had any effect upon his own personal decision-making.

As we have seen, during Nostradamus' lifetime his reputation was mostly based on his annually published almanacs, and on his individually-cast horoscopes for those wealthy enough to afford them. After his death in 1566 interest and credence in his predictions might therefore have been expected to decline rapidly. It is a matter of yet more surprise, therefore, that, as we have seen, it actually increased, the focus smoothly switching to the *Prophecies*. Almost instinctively each new generation turned to these verses in their every major crisis, and saw in them Nostradamus' powers of foresight, whether this was concerning France's religious wars, England's Civil War, London's Great Fire, France's Revolution of 1789, the rise of Napoleon or twentieth-century Europe's traumatic brush with the tyrant Hitler.

Small wonder, therefore, that no one was unduly troubled when it appeared that Nostradamus' 'appeaser king'/King of Terror' prophecy had not been fulfilled on the predicted date of July 1999. After all, they had not long to wait for a suitable mega-event as a substitute. As all the world knows, on the other side of the turn of the millennium, and at the high-profile target of New York's greatest financial institution's skyscrapers, 'Terror' indeed struck from the sky. And it struck so devastatingly and so unexpectedly that it triggered precisely the kind of public alarm which sent the stargazers, and the world of Nostradamiana in particular, into a feeding frenzy.

Some undeniably strange 'coincidences' amongst the numbers involved heightened the sense of some Armageddon-like destiny unfolding. Given the fact that the World Trade Center's Twin Towers resembled a huge '11' on New York's waterfront, was it not strange that the clearly pre-planned date of the attack was September 11? That the first plane to hit the towers was Flight 11? That this had 92 passengers on board, 9 plus 2 equalling 11? That the second plane to hit had 65 passengers on board, 6 plus 5 equalling 11? That New York was the eleventh state to have joined the American Union, that 'New York City' comprises eleven letters, as does 'Afghanistan', as does (though no one, to my knowledge, mentioned it at the time) 'Nostradamus'...

Fuelling the September 11 frenzy, which was intensified by the mostly uncritical media attention, was of course an outright lie, in the form of the undoubtedly deliberate adulterations of verses of the *Prophecies* by persons unknown that we noted in the Introduction to this book. What was not apparent then, but which we certainly know now, is that such adulterations were nothing new. We have already seen how Nostradamus' verses were being tampered with for propaganda and psychological warfare purposes, and new ones invented in his name, from at least as early as the seventeenth century. Though beyond the scope of this book, it would be truly interesting to know who was behind the hoax verses put out in the immediate aftermath of the September 11 tragedy, that they should have become so swiftly disseminated through the media. Could this actually have been a cell of Al-Qaeda operating very much like Louis de Wohl within Britain's Special Operations Executive counter-propaganda unit during World War II?

Such propagandist warfare would never, of course, even have been thought of, let alone been likely to achieve its desired effect, but for the high level of credence which Nostradamus had already attained in the minds of the public at large, which returns us again to the question why this should be so? After all, in the course of this book we have seen some well-documented, unambiguous prophecies that Nostradamus made in very exposed circumstances in which his predictions turned out to be plain wrong.

For instance, the civil war troubles that he predicted for England during the first year of Queen Elizabeth I's reign did not materialise, any more than did the storms and shipwrecks that he forecast for the English Channel in the August of 1559. He was proved quite wrong in his prophecy to Queen Regent Catherine de Medici that her son King Charles IX would live to his seventies and in his estimation of Constable Anne de Montmorency's longevity. In the horoscope that he prepared for Judge Antoine Suffren of Salon he did not make just one or two minor errors, from all that can be determined, he was well off the mark throughout the whole document. As for the elaborately produced horoscope for Prince Rudolf, who went on to be King

Rudolf II of Bohemia and Hungary, my prediction is that this will be found to be riddled with similar mistakes. If Nostradamus' reputation were adjudged to rest solely on these clear, unequivocal and simply erroneous forecasts of the future, then that reputation would deservedly lie in tatters.

But of course his reputation does not rest solely on these; indeed, chiefly because of neglect by the present-day Nostradamus industry, the public at large has mostly been kept in blissful ignorance of such glitches. Instead his enormous continuing credence has rested almost entirely on the altogether vaguer and more obscure predictions that he enshrined in his *Prophecies*, on which Nostradamian authors have expended huge efforts arguing for this or that verse's 'prediction' of some particular real-life historical event. With Nostradamus shown to have seriously erred in prophecies in which he was at his clearest and most explicit, why should anyone have even the slightest time for those prophecies in which he was at his vaguest, however ingeniously these may have been interpreted?

This is a very good and serious question. The redoubtable English Jesuit scholar Father Herbert Thurston, who became interested in Nostradamus' verses when they were being widely identified with events of the First World War, noted at that time how their vagueness seemed to lie at the very heart of the way he achieved his reputation. In Thurston's words:

> Undoubtedly the unrivalled success of Nostradamus' oracles is due to the fact that, avoiding all orderly arrangement, either chronological or topographical, and refraining almost entirely from categorical statements, it is impossible ever to say that a particular prognostic has missed its mark…Nostradamus provided an ingenious system of divination in which the misses can never be recorded and only the hits come to the surface. For the reputation of the would-be prophet, such conditions are naturally ideal.[2]

The serious possibility, in the light of Thurston's remarks, is that this was all there ever was to Nostradamus, that he was just a clever confidence trickster. Arguably, just as in his younger, wandering pedlar days he had enjoyed concocting recipes for pills and potions, so later in his life he dreamed up the recipe for making the perfect, fail-safe and therefore foolproof prediction.

It is far from clear that Nostradamus can be retrieved from such an assessment. However, if he is to be – and that is a very big 'if' – one thing is certain: substantially better standards are needed from the present-day Nostradamus industry, particularly from those currently catering for an English-speaking readership. In the course of my researches for this book, a source of immense frustration was the highly unsatisfactory quality of essentially all current published translations of the *Prophecies* into English. They almost invariably exhibited poor linguistic skills and a complete lack of the requisite interpretative balance. Peter Lemesurier, a professional linguist, has rightly castigated his fellow Nostradamians for their poor efforts, yet despite his remarks, the task of providing a definitive English-language *Prophecies* to anything like satisfactory scholarly standards has yet to be fulfilled.

Perhaps even more pertinent, is the need to make Nostradamus' entire oeuvre available in some kind of Compendium equivalent to the *Complete Works of Shakespeare*. For another source of great frustration in the course of researching this book was the sheer inaccessibility of the texts of several of the *Almanacs*, even when single copies of these for certain key years are known to exist. It is understandable that private collectors who have paid thousands of dollars for these may be disinclined to have their assets thumbed by a succession of researchers. The very least they could do, however, would be to allow the making of facsimiles from which the all-important texts could be transcribed for publication purposes. The special value of the *Almanacs* is that they were the publications by which Nostradamus largely achieved his reputation during his own time. So in fairness to him, a proper quantitative analysis of these against the known historical facts would be a far better check on him than any arbitrary castigation of him for making some isolated slip.

Equally needed is a full translation into English, together with scholarly annotations, of the Latin manuscript of the fifty-one letters of his correspondence with Hans Rosenberger, Lorenz Tubbe and others. Likewise needed is the full text of the Horoscope of Prince Rudolf, which has yet to be fully transcribed even from its original handwritten manuscript. Dr Elmar Gruber, as already remarked, is working on producing a definitive scholarly edition of it, but this in its turn will need to be translated from German into other languages. Also not to be forgotten is a translation into English of Nostradamus' *Treatise of Cosmetics and Jams*, which contains yet further insights into the seer's mind, yet to be properly evaluated. If the present-day Nostradamus industry has anything worthwhile in it therefore – and Lemesurier is at least, as we have seen, a professional linguist – then the compilation of a properly authoritative *Complete Works of Nostradamus*, with suitable scholarly apparatus, should be its number one task.

Overall, the position is that while this book has raised some serious questions concerning Nostradamus' credibility, it would be quite unfair, certainly in the current state of our knowledge, to rule out the possibility that he had some genuine prophetic powers. The huge impression that he made on his contemporaries, which for the reasons given above we do not fully understand, cannot simply be dismissed out of hand. However vain, garrulous and insufferably fond of parading his erudition Nostradamus may have been (and he was all of those), nothing in his writings suggests that he lacked sincerity. As we have seen, he had made more than enough money to have retired long before his death, even allowing for the fact that he wanted to make sure that his young family was well provided for. Yet he worked right up to his last breath, arguably in the firm belief that he was doing something good and worthwhile by his future-gazing. We therefore have absolutely no reason to believe that he did not honestly compose the quatrains of his *Prophecies* exactly as he said he did, alone in his study, late at night, allowing his mind to go into a visionary state. So who can say that during this state at least some of the images that came into his mind might not have been glimpses of the real future?

For unlike the James Randis of this world, I am not one to dismiss out of hand the possibility that some of us, in certain circumstances, can and do have some prophetic insights. It is a firm yet still unexplained fact that the method by which Nostradamus claimed he gazed into the future was near-identical to that practised by the Tibetans during the centuries before their culture was so barbarously overrun by Communist China. These are the words of the very scholarly Lama Chime Rada, Rinpoche, head of the British Library's Tibetan section during the 1980s:

> The [Tibetan] diviner or *tra-pa* focuses his attention, free from particular thoughts and images, by gazing into a small mirror made of polished stone or metal, or into the still waters of a lake, or into the clear sky. Having addressed himself to the question or problem to which he seeks the answer, he empties and concentrates his mind, usually by reciting *mantras*, or sacred formulae associated with particular divinities or spiritual principles...As the *tra-pa's* concentration and absorption deepen, a certain current of consciousness begins to flow, and a vision appears before him.[3]

By such methods Tibetans over many centuries 'saw' visions of who would be their future Dalai Lama, and even the present Dalai Lama was foreseen by this means. And does not this method forcefully remind us of that which Nostradamus said he used? That the ancient Aztecs of Mexico, again for similarly unexplained reasons, used strikingly similar methods has been noted by the great expert on the Aztec civilisation George Vaillant.[4] Vaillant has pointed to contemporary reports describing how the last Aztec emperor Montezuma saw in a 'magic' mirror a vision of men in armour, a glimpse of the Spanish Conquistadors who would shortly invade and conquer his country.

Such mirror-gazing aside, the phenomenon of gaining glimpses of the future has been reported so repeatedly in so many cultures across the world that I for one simply cannot dismiss it *all* as rubbish. This is not least because, without professing the slightest prophetic gift, I can cite my own kindred personal experience of more than thirty years ago. One day in 1965, skimming a sheaf of applications just received for a job in the department of which I was manager, my gaze fell on one particular handwritten letter. It was from a young graduate psychologist named Judith. Absurdly, since I had never even met the sender of the letter, I instinctively found myself 'knowing' that this person would become my wife. She did, and Judith and I have now been married for more than thirty-four years. To this day I can offer absolutely no explanation for how or why I was vouchsafed this glimpse into the future. Yet I can no more deny that it happened than I can deny you my own identity.

Likewise, therefore, I cannot dismiss – as yet, at least – the possibility that Nostradamus, despite all the obscurities with which he clouded his verses, had *some* similar perfectly genuine glimpses of the future. And there is one bold prophecy of his that he quite definitely

The universality of Nostradamus' prophetic 'technique'.
The Aztec emperor Montezuma depicted using a magic mirror to foresee the coming of the Spanish conquistadors who conquered his kingdom. From the Codex Florentino.

got right. In the letter to King Henri II that he wrote in 1557 to accompany his completion of the final verses of the *Prophecies*, he solemnly predicted: 'As time elapses after my death, my writings will have more weight than during my lifetime.'

No one, whatever their views on Nostradamus, can deny that he was right on that one...

NOTES

1 James Tester, *A History of Western Astrology*, Woodbridge, Boydell press, 1987, p.215, n.14
2 Quoted in Randi, *The Mask of Nostradamus*, op. cit., p.165
3 Michael Lowe & Carmen Blacker (eds.), *Divination and Oracles*, London, Allen & Unwin, 1981, pp.8 & 9
4 George C. Vaillant, *The Aztecs of Mexico*, London, Penguin, 1950, pp.231-2

INDEX